A SPECTACLE FOR A SPANISH PRINCESS

BURGUNDICA

VOLUME 35

Publié sous la direction de
Jean-Marie Cauchies, *Centre européen d'études bourguignonnes (XIVe-XVIes.)*

Collection
BURGUNDICA

Peu de périodes, de tranches d'histoire ont suscité et continuent à susciter auprès d'un large public autant d'intérêt voire d'engouement que le « siècle de Bourgogne ». Il est vrai qu'à la charnière de ce que l'on dénomme aussi vaguement que commodément « bas moyen âge » et « Renaissance », les douze décennies qui séparent l'avènement de Phillipe le Hardi en Flandre (1384) de la mort de Philippe le Beau (1506) forment un réceptacle d'idées et de pratiques contrastées. Et ce constat s'applique à toutes les facettes de la société. La collection Burgundica se donne pour objectif de présenter toutes ces facettes, de les reconstruire – nous n'oserions écrire, ce serait utopique, de les ressusciter – à travers un choix d'études de haut niveau scientifique mais dont tout « honnête homme » pourra faire son miel. Elle mettra mieux ainsi en lumière les jaons que le temps des ducs Valois de Bourgogne et de leurs successeurs immédiats, Maximilien et Philippe de Habsbourg, fournit à l'historien dans la découverte d'une Europe moderne alors en pleine croissance.

A Spectacle for a Spanish Princess

The Festive Entry of Joanna of Castile into Brussels (1496)

edited by
DAGMAR H. EICHBERGER

BREPOLS

Published with the support of the Centro de Estudios Europa Hispánica (Madrid).

Cover illustration: *Last Judgement Triptych of Zierikzee*, right wing painting of a lost altarpiece, photo © MRBAB, Brussels

© 2023, Brepols Publishers n.v., Turnhout, Belgium.

All rights reserved. No part of this publication may be reproduced, stored in a retrieval system, or transmitted, in any form or by any means, electronic, mechanical, photocopying, recording, or otherwise without the prior permission of the publisher.

D/2023/0095/213
ISBN 978-2-503-59443-9
eISBN 978-2-503-60089-5
DOI 10.1484/M.BURG-EB.5.130171
ISSN 1780-3209
eISSN 2295-0354

Printed in the EU on acid-free paper.

Contents

List of Illustrations — 7

List of Contributors — 13

Acknowledgements — 19

The Festive Entry of Joanna of Castile into Brussels. An Introduction
Dagmar EICHBERGER — 21

Joanna of Castile's first residence in the Low Countries (1496-1501). The Transformation of a Trastámara Princess
Raymond FAGEL — 39

Joanna, Infanta of Castile and Habsburg Archduchess. Recreating a lost Wardrobe and Trousseau in 1496
Annemarie JORDAN GSCHWEND — 53

The Self-representation of Brussels in Times of Uncertainty
Claire BILLEN and Chloé DELIGNE — 77

***In unam pacis accordantiam*. The Role of City Poet Jan Smeken and Other Rhetoricians in Organizing the Brussels Entry**
Remco SLEIDERINK and Amber SOULEYMANE — 107

Role Models for a Queen's Daughter
Wim BLOCKMANS — 123

Arguing with the Old Testament. Moral and Political Lessons for Princess Joanna of Castile
Dagmar EICHBERGER — 143

To move the hearts and spirits of men towards joy and recreation. The Entry of Joanna of Castile as Entertainment
Laura WEIGERT — 165

The Brussels Town Hall. A Worthy Emblem for a Capital City
Sascha KÖHL — 181

Illustrating Contemporary Events in Watercolour on Paper. A New Genre of Memorial Books
Anne-Marie Legaré   207

Manuscript 78 D5. A Codicological Description
Dagmar Eichberger   227

Manuscript 78 D5. Short Descriptions of the Miniatures
Helga Kaiser-Minn   237

Manuscript 78 D5. The Latin Text: Transcription and Translation
Verena Demoed   255

Manuscript 78 D5. Reproduction of Text and Images   279

Bibliography   413

Index   439

List of Illustrations

0.1	Southern Netherlandish, *Choir Book of Joanna of Castile and Philip the Fair*, fols 1^v-2^r: *Double portrait of Philip the Fair with St Philip the Apostle and Joanna of Castile with St John the Baptist*, 1504-1506, parchment, 38,1 × 27,4 cm, Brussels, Royal Library of Belgium, Cabinet des Manuscrits, 9126	16
0.2	Spanish (Granada), piece of black velvet from the prayer stool of Joanna of Castile, decorated with the combined coats of arms of Joanna of Castile and Philip the Fair, topped by a crown, surrounded by the chain of the order of the Golden Fleece, accompanied by the emblem of bundles of arrows	18

Dagmar Eichberger

1.1	Southern Netherlandish, *The Festive Entry of Joanna of Castile into Brussels*, fol. 1^v: *Saint Michael defeats the Devil*, 1496, Berlin, SMPK, Kupferstichkabinett, ms. 78 D5.	23
1.2	Saint Michael, *Weather vane from the tower of the Brussels town hall*, H: 5,70 m, bronze with gilding, 1455, Brussels, Musée de la Ville de Bruxelles, photo: Stephanek	24
1.3a/b	Southern Netherlandish, *Book of Hours of Joanna of Castile*, a) fol. 25^v: *Saint Michael fighting the Dragon*, b) fol. 26^r: *Joanna of Castile in prayer with St John the Baptist and her guardian Angel*, parchment, 110 × 80 mm, 1496, London, British Library, ms Add 18852	25
1.4	Master of the David scenes in the Grimani Breviary, *Book of Hours*, fol. 25^r: *Saint Matthew*, parchment, 20,5 × 14 cm, 1515-1520, Oxford, Bodleian Libraries, ms Douce 112.	26
1.5	Master of the David scenes in the Grimani Breviary, *Book of Hours*, fol. 157^r: *Saint George*, parchment, 20,5 × 14 cm, 1515-1520, Oxford, Bodleian Libraries, ms Douce 112.	26
1.6	Anonymous, *The Virgin of Onze-Lieve-Vrouw ten Zavel (Notre-Dame du Sablon) with Beatrix Soetkens and a Ferryman*, painted wood, 17th century, Brussels, Our-Blessed-Lady of the Sablon, southern transept	29
1.7a/b	Master of the Joseph sequence, a) *Philip the Fair and Joanna of Castile*, two wings from the Zierikzee Triptych, 125 × 48 cm, oil on oak, c. 1505-06, Brussels, Royal Museums of Fine Arts of Belgium (Brussels), inv. 2405. Photo: F. Maes	36
1.8	Southern Netherlandish, *Book of Hours of Joanna of Castile*, fol. 287v: *Virgin and Child*, fol. 288r: *Joanna kneeling at her prie-dieu with St John the Evangelist*, 110 × 80 mm, 1496, London, British Library, ms Add 18852	38

Raymond Fagel

2.1	Pedro Marcuello, *Rimado de la Conquista de Granada*, fols 30ᵛ and 31ʳ: *The Catholic Kings and Infanta Joanna*, tempera on parchment, 21,5 × 14,5 cm, c. 1482-1502, Chantilly, Bibliothèque, Musée Condé, ms 604 (1339)	41
2.2	Master of the Magdalene legend, *Philip the Fair*, oil on wood, 24,5 × 15,5 cm, c. 1493, 's-Heerenberg, Collection Huis Bergh, inv. No. 740	44
Table I.	Itinerary of Joanna of Castile, 10 September 1496 – 16 November 1501, based on Aram, *Reina*, p. 331-37.	45
2.3	Master of the Joseph Sequence, *Joanna of Castile*, oil on wood, 34,7 × 22,4 cm, 1501-1510, Valladolid, Museo Nacional de Escultura, CE 2684. Photo: Javier Muñoz y Paz Pastor	46
2.4	Master of the Saint George Legend, *Charles as a two-year-old Child with his two Sisters, Eleonor (1498-1558) and Isabel (1501-1525)*, oil on wood, each panel: 31,5 × 14 cm, Vienna, Kunsthistorisches Museum, inv. no. 4452	48

Annemarie Jordan Gschwend

3.1	Workshop of the Master of the Legend of Mary Magdalene, *Philip the Fair*, oil on wood, 42 × 27 cm, c. 1495, Paris, Musée du Louvre, photo	54
3.2	Leonard Beck, *Philip the Fair and his Courtiers come to meet Joanna when arriving in Zeeland*, woodcut, 22.1 × 20 cm, c. 1514-1516, London, British Museum, Prints and Drawings, inv. no. 1837,0616.301	56
3.3	Adrien Baltyn, *Traicté de l'antiquité et preeminence des maisons d'Habsbourg et d'Austrice: (detail) Philip the Fair and Joanna of Castile with their coats of arms*, gouache, ink and gold on parchment, c. 1616, London, V&A Museum, National Art Library, NAL Pressmark: KRP.C.61	58
3.4	Spanish, *Marriage Chest with the Coat of Arms and Portraits of Philip the Fair and Joanna I of Castile*, wood, L: 116 cm, H: 71.5 cm, Lima, Peru, Pedro de Osma Museum. Courtesy of BALaT	61
3.5	*Silk Fragment with Lions and Pomegranates*, Granada, silk, lampas weave, 23.3 × 25.7 cm, late 15th century, New York, The Cloister Collection, acc. no. 2011.480	64
3.6	Spanish, *Pair of chopines*, wood, leather, covered with green silk damask, H: 12.5 cm, London, c. 1580-1620, V&A Museum, acc. no. T.419&A-1913	65
3.7	German (Augsburg or Nuremberg), *Trachtenbuch (Códice de Trajes)*, fols 1ʳ-2ʳ: *Costumes of aristocratic Spanish Ladies*, black ink and watercolour on paper, 21 × 20 cm, c. 1530-1560, Madrid, Biblioteca Nacional de España, Res/285	66
3.8	Spanish, *Portrait of Queen Isabella I of Spain, Queen of Castile*, oil on wood, 37.5 × 26.9 cm, c. 1470-1504, London, Royal Collection Trust, inv. no. RCIN 403445. Royal Collection Trust	68
3.9	Northern European, *Diamond Pendant*, gold, engraved with black *champlevé* enamel, mounted with table-cut diamonds, H. 4.2 cm, W: 2.9 cm, c. 1560, London, V&A Museum, acc. no. M.76-1975	70

3.10 Southern Netherlandish, *The Festive Entry of Joanna of Castile into Brussels*, fol. 31ʳ: *Joanna entering the Grand-Place with members of the Crossbowman's Guild*, 1496, Berlin, SMPK, Kupferstichkabinett, ms 78 D5   72

3.11 Southern Netherlandish, *Stain glass panel depicting Joanna of Castile at prayer*, window, H: 112 cm, W: 51 cm, *c.* 1500-1505, London, V&A Museum, acc. no. 293:1, 2-1874   74

Claire Billen and Chloé Deligne

4.1 Antoine de Succa, *Les Mémoriaux*, fol. 74ʳ: *The tomb of Jeanne, Duchess of Brabant, and William of Burgundy in the Carmelite church of Brussels*, drawing on paper, between 1601 and 1615, KBR, ms 1862/1   85

4.2 Southern Netherlandish, *The Festive Entry of Joanna of Castile into Brussels*, fol. 10ʳ (detail): *A Representative of the Guild of Saint Luke*, 1496, Berlin, SMPK, Kupferstichkabinett, ms 78 D5   89

4.3 Aert van den Bossche, *Triptych of the Martyrdom of Saint Crispin and Saint Crispinian for the Cobblers and Shoemakers of Brussels*, Brussels, oil on wood, 1490, Musée de la Ville de Bruxelles, K1977 1 et 2   99

4.4a/b Southern Netherlandish, *The Festive Entry of Joanna of Castile into Brussels*, a) fol. 29ʳ (detail): *A Crossbowman wearing a hat badge with a grill*, b) fol. 31ʳ (detail): *A Crossbowman wearing a hat badge with Notre Dame du Sablon and two additional Figures standing on a Boat*, 1496, Berlin, SMPK, Kupferstichkabinett, ms 78 D5   102

4.5 Brussels, collection of the Great Guild of the Crossbow: *Ornament for a processional stick representing the miraculous Statue of Onze-Lieve-Vrouw ten Zavel (Notre-Dame du Sablon) on a boat*, silver, composite object with three crossbows attached   103

4.6 Denijs van Alsloot and workshop, *The Ommegang of 1615. Parade of craftsmen on the Brussels Grand-Place* (detail): *The Fountain on the Fish Market*, Brussels, Musées Royaux des Beaux-Arts de Belgique, inv. 170. Photo: J. Geleyns   103

Remco Sleiderink and Amber Souleymane

5.1 Membership list of rhetoricians chamber *De Lelie* (The Lily) from early 1499, starting with Jan Smeken and Johannes Pertcheval, *Liber authenticus of the Seven Sorrows Confraternity of Brussels*, Brussels, Stadsarchief, hs. 3413, fol. 161ʳ   109

5.2 Heraldic representation of the rhetoricians chamber *De Lelie* (The Lily) with its motto *Liefde groeit* (Love grows). Illustration made by Johannes Pertcheval in the *Liber authenticus of the Seven Sorrows Confraternity of Brussels*. Brussels, Stadsarchief, hs. 3413, fol. 1ʳ   114

5.3 The *Liber authenticus* honors the four founding fathers of the Seven Sorrows Confraternity of Brussels. The second blazon – an anvil with three hammers – represents city poet Jan Smeken. Brussels, Stadsarchief, hs. 3413, fol. 159ᵛ-160ʳ   119

Wim Blockmans

6.1 Ambrogio de Predis, *Maximilian as King of the Romans*, oil on wood, 44 × 30.3 cm, 1502, Vienna, Kunsthistorisches Museum, GG 4431   126

6.2   Ambrogio de Predis, *Bianca Maria Sforza*, oil on poplar, 51 × 32.5 cm, *c.* 1493, Washington, National Gallery of Art, Widener Collection, 1942.9.53   127

Dagmar Eichberger

7.1   Southern Netherlandish, *Duchess Mary of Burgundy*, stained-glass window from the Holy Blood Chapel in Bruges, 182.9 × 77.5 cm (framed), *c.* 1496-1500, London, Victoria & Albert Museum   146

7.2   Jan van Battel, *Heraldic Triptych with Archduke Charles as Spanish King*, oil on wood, 88 × 57 cm (central panel); 90 × 25 cm (wings) *c.* 1517-18   148

7.3   Anonymous, after Jan van Battel, *Heraldic Triptych with Emperor Charles V*, oil on wood, *c.* 1540-50, Berlin, Deutsches Historisches Museum, Gm 2003/71   149

7.4   Salomon Kleiner, *Heraldic tower in Innsbruck (1496-99)*, engraving, 36,5 × 22,4 cm, *c.* 1496-1500, in *Monumenta Augustae Domus Austriacae*, ed. by Herrgott Marquart (Vienna: L. J. Kaliwoda, 1760) vol. 1, Pl. XV.   150

7.5   Southern Netherlandish, *Archduke Maximilian, King of the Romans*, Stained glass window from the Holy Blood Chapel in Bruges, 182.9 × 77.5 cm (framed), London, Victoria and Albert Museum   152

7.6a/b   *Maximilian I as King of the Romans*, Real d'Or, coin, gold, diameter: 38,9 mm, 1487, recto: ˚MAXIMILIAИVS*DEI*GRA*ROMAИORV*REX*SEP'*AVG' – verso: TEИE*MEИSVRAM*ET*RESPICE*FIИEM*MCCCCLXXXVII Vienna, KHM, MK 23bα   153

7.7   Spanish, *Queen Isabella of Castile and King Ferdinand II of Aragon*, oil on wood, a) 37.5 × 26.9 cm, b) 37.35 × 27 cm, London, Royal Collection Trust, RCIN 403445 and 403448. Royal Collection Trust   160

7.8   Erhard Schön, *Six of twelve Famous Women from the Old Testament*, two woodcuts, 19,8 × 38,2 cm, *c.* 1530, woodcut no. 2: Ruth, Michal, Abigail, Judith, Esther und Susanna   161

Laura Weigert

8.1   Southern Netherlandish, *The Festive Entry of Joanna of Castile into Brussels*, fol. 30ʳ (detail): Crossbow Bearers, 1496, Berlin, SMPK, Kupferstichkabinett, ms. 78 D5   166

8.2   Southern Netherlandish, *The Festive Entry of Joanna of Castile into Brussels*, fol. 29ʳ (detail): *Members of the Archers Guild of Saint Sebastian with silver ornaments on their sleeves*, 1496, Berlin, SMPK Kupferstichkabinett, ms. 78 D5   167

8.3   Southern Nether-landish, *The Festive Entry of Joanna of Castile into Brussels*, fol. 11ʳ (detail): *A Fool whose sleeve is decorated with three red flowers and crossbows*, 1496, Berlin, SMPK, Kupferstichkabinett, ms. 78 D5   168

8.4   Southern Netherlandish, *The Festive Entry of Joanna of Castile into Brussels*, fol. 11ʳ (detail): *A fool in striped garments*, Berlin, 1496, SPKB, Kupferstich-kabinett, ms. 78 D5   171

8.5   Southern Netherlandish, *The Festive Entry of Joanna of Castile into Brussels*, fol. 13ʳ (detail): *An Ethiopian Princess on a mule, accompanied by wild women*, 1496, Berlin, SMPK, Kupferstichkabinett, ms. 78 D5   172

Sascha Köhl

9.1	Brussels, *town hall*, built in two stages between 1401 and 1455	183
9.2	Southern Netherlandish (circle of Dieric Bouts), *Crucifixion* (detail): *several towers of Brussels*, oil on wood, 88 × 71cm, *c.* 1470/80, Berlin, SPKB, Gemäldegalerie	184
9.3	Melchisedech van Hooren, *The town hall of Brussels*, engraving, 1565	186
9.4	Frans Hogenberg and Joris Bruin, *Bruxella*, coloured woodcut, 1572	188
9.5	Southern Netherlandish (after Rogier van der Weyden), *The justice of Trajan and Herkinbald* (detail): *The Justice of Herkinbald*, tapestry, *c.* 1440/50, Bern, Historisches Museum	192
9.6	Abraham van Santvoort, *town hall of Brussels, bird's eye view of the building complex depicting the Boterpot on the right*, engraving, *c.* 1650	195
9.7	David Noveliers, *Parade of Giants and of the Horse Bayard* (detail), panel painting, 1616, Spain, private collection	196
9.8	Bruges, *Chapel of St Basil and the Holy Blood*, 12th and 15th centuries	198
9.9	Heverlee, *Arenberg castle*, 15th and 16th centuries	199
9.10	Hans Memling, *St John Altarpiece*, central panel, (detail): *St Barbara sitting next to her tower*, oil on wood, 1479, Bruges, Sint-Janshospitaal / Memlingmuseum, photo: Alexey Yakovlev	200
9.11	*The town hall of Brussels* (detail): *The right corner of the town hall with figures of rulers*, engraving, in Puteanus, *Bruxella* (1646)	204
9.12	*Façade of the Bruges town hall with the counts' statues*, engraving, in Danckaert, *Stadhuys* (1711)	205

Anne-Marie Legaré

10.1	Southern Netherlandish, *The Festive Entry of Joanna of Castile into Brussels*, fol. 31^r: *Joanna of Castile and the members of the Great Crossbow guild reach the Grand-Place in Brussels*, coloured pen drawings, 1496, Berlin, SMPK, Kupferstichkabinett, ms. 78 D5	209
10.2	Southern Netherlandish, *De Excellente Cronike van Vlaenderen* fol. 361^v: *Mary of Burgundy on horseback*, coloured drawing on paper, *c.* 1480, Bruges, Openbare Bibliotheek, ms 437	212
10.3	Southern Netherlandish, *De Excellente Cronike van Vlaenderen*, fol. 352^v: *Charles the Bold at the Battlefield of Nancy*, drawing, watercolour and lead point on paper, Bruges, *c.* 1484, 28 × 21 cm, New York, Morgan Library, ms M.435.	213
10.4a/b	German, *Bamberg Heiltumsbuch*: doublespread, a) fol. 35^v: *A Man in full Armour, holding a Banner with Saint George*, b) fol. 36^r: *A Reliquary Procession for Relics of Henry II before Bamberg Cathedral*, paper, pen drawings with watercolour, 48 × 32 cm, 1508-1509, London, British Library, Add ms 15689	215
10.5	German, *Bamberg Heiltumsbuch*, fol. 2^r: *Banners of St George and the Holy Roman Emperor Henry II*, paper, pen drawings with watercolour, 48 × 32 cm, 1508-1509, London, British Library, Add ms 15689	216
10.6	French, *Pas de Saumur* (The Book of Tournaments for René d'Anjou) fol. 24^v: *The Fight between King René and the Duke of Alençon*, pen drawings with washes,	218

36 × 27 cm, c. 1470, Saint Petersburg, National Library of Russia, Saltykov-Chtchedrine, ms Fr. F. p. XIV, 4

10.7 Provencal, Barthélemy d'Eyck, *Livre des Tournois* (King René's Tournament book), fol. 103^v: *The award ceremony*, coloured pen drawings on paper, 36 × 25,9 cm, c. 1460, Paris, Bibliothèque nationale de France, ms Français 2695   220

10.8 Southern German, *Freydal, the Book of Tournaments of Emperor Maximilian I*, fol. 17^r: *Freydal fighting Count Wolfgang von Fürstenberg*, paper, coloured pen drawings, 1512-1515, Vienna, Kunsthistorisches Museum, inv. no. Kunstkammer 5073   222

10.9 Lorraine, Jean du Prier, *Le songe du Pastourel*, fol. 8^v: *The author in his bedroom, in the foreground an illustration of his dream of a sick man with two doctors*, coloured drawings on parchment, 38 × 29,5cm, c. 1515, Vienna, Österreichische Nationalbibliothek, ms 2556   224

Dagmar Eichberger

11.1 Berlin, Kupferstichkabinett, ms 78 D5, 19th century binding, photo: Dietmar Katz   228

11.2 Berlin, Kupferstichkabinett, ms 78 D5, fol. 1^r: stamp of the 'Königliches Kupferstichkabinett' with the inscription '148-1884', photo: Dietmar Katz   229

11.3 Berlin, Kupferstichkabinett, ms 78 D5, fol. 1^v: indentations seen in raking light, photo: Dagmar Eichberger   230

11.4 Berlin, Kupferstichkabinett, ms 78 D5, fol. 62^r: indentations seen in raking light, photo: Dagmar Eichberger   231

11.5 Berlin, Kupferstichkabinett, ms 78 D5, watermark 'P' on fol. 5^r, photo: Luise Maul   232

11.6 Berlin, Kupferstichkabinett, ms 78 D5, fol. 31^r: *Joanna's dress with highlights in gold pigment*, photo: Dagmar Eichberger   234

11.7 Berlin, Kupferstichkabinett, ms 78 D5, fol. 2^r: *rubrications*, photo: Dietmar Katz   235

List of Contributors

Claire Billen is Honorary Professor at the *Université Libre de Bruxelles* where she taught social and economic history of the Middle Ages, comparative urban and ecological history. She is a member of the research group sociAMM. claire.billen@ulb.be

Wim Blockmans is Professor emeritus of Medieval History at Leiden University and former Rector of the *Netherlands Institute for Advanced Study*. wimblockmans7@gmail.com

Chloé Deligne is Research Associate of the FRS-FNRS at the *Université Libre de Bruxelles*, Department of History, Arts & Archaeology. Chloe.Deligne@ulb.be

Verena Demoed completed her doctoral dissertation on sixteenth century Latin Theatre at the *Huizinga Institute* (Dutch National Research School for Cultural History) in Utrecht and at the University of Amsterdam, Netherlands. verena@demoedvertalingen.nl

Dagmar Eichberger is Professor emerita of Art History in the Department of Fine Arts at the *University of Heidelberg*, Germany. d.eichberger@zegk.uni-heidelberg.de

Raymond Fagel is Lecturer in Early Modern History at the *History Institute of Leiden University*, Netherlands. r.p.fagel@hum.leidenuniv.nl

Annemarie Jordan Gschwend is Senior Research Scholar and Curator at the *Centro de Humanidades* (CHAM), Zurich, Switzerland and Lisbon, Portugal. jordan.gschwend@bluewin.ch

Helga Kaiser-Minn retired as Senior Lecturer in the Department of Fine Arts at the *University of Heidelberg*. helga.kaiser-minn@web.de

Sascha Köhl is Lecturer in Art History at the *Heinrich Heine University Düsseldorf*, Department of Art History, Germany. sascha.koehl@hhu.de

Anne-Marie Legaré is Professor emerita of Medieval Art History at the *University of Lille*, France. annemarie.legare@gmail.com

Remco Sleiderink is Professor of Medieval Dutch Literature at the *University of Antwerp*, Belgium. remco.sleiderink@uantwerpen.be

Amber Souleymane graduated with a Research Master in History at the *University of Groningen*, Netherlands, specializing in historical Dutch literature. ambersouleymane@gmail.com

Laura Weigert is Professor of Art History at *Rutgers University*, New Brunswick, USA. weigert@arthist.rutgers.edu

0.1 Southern Netherlandish, *Choir Book of Joanna of Castile and Philip the Fair*, fols 1ᵛ-2ʳ: *Double portrait of Philip the Fair with St Philip the Apostle and Joanna of Castile with St John the Baptist*, 1504-1506, parchment, 38,1 × 27,4 cm, Brussels, Royal Library of Belgium, Cabinet des Manuscrits, 9126

0.2 Spanish (Granada), piece of black velvet from the prayer stool of Joanna of Castile, decorated with the combined coats of arms of Joanna of Castile and Philip the Fair, topped by a crown, surrounded by the chain of the order of the Golden Fleece, accompanied by the emblem of bundles of arrows © Museo Lázaro Galdiano, Madrid. Inv. 1710

Acknowledgements*

Every publication has its own history, and so has *A Spectacle for a Spanish Princess. The Entry of Joanna of Castile into Brussels.* The first idea to prepare a book-length study on the Brussels entry of Princess Joanna, Infanta of Castile, emerged when the Berlin manuscript 78 D5 was displayed in Mechelen, during the exhibition *Women of Distinction. Margaret of York and Margaret of Austria.*[1] In 2019, Stefan Krause, a colleague from Vienna, reinvigorated my plan to finally give the festival booklet the attention it deserves. He himself had only recently published two books on Emperor Maximilian's I unfinished *Freydal* manuscript, as a facsimile and as a collection of essays.[2] A year later, an agreement was reached with Brepols to publish a book with ten scholarly essays, plus the original texts in Latin and in English translation. At the beginning of the Joanna project, the neo-Latinist Verena Demoed transcribed the Latin texts and translated them into English.

The Berlin *Kupferstichkabinett* generously gave permission to reproduce the entire manuscript at the end of the book, both texts and images. I am most grateful to the director, Dagmar Korbacher, and her curatorial staff, Michael Roth and Christien Melzer for their enthusiasm and support. My thanks also go to the conservator, Luise Maul, and to Dietmar Katz, the photographer.

But what would be the value of an abstract idea if one couldn't find a team of experts to successfully complete such a challenging project? In this case, a group of authors from different disciplines came together under difficult circumstances – we were at the height of the Covid epidemic – and grew into a highly collaborative team that complemented each other in the best possible way. It gives me great pleasure to thank the following colleagues for their brilliant contributions, their constant support and everlasting patience: Claire Billen, Wim Blockmans, Chloé Deligne, Raymond Fagel, Annemarie Jordan Gschwend, Helga Kaiser-Minn, Sascha Köhl, Anne-Marie Legaré, Remco Sleiderink, Amber Souleymane and Laura Weigert.

---

* The open choir book depicted on the previous page (Fig. 0.1) shows the ducal couple kneeling in front of an image of Virgin and Child; they are sitting on an elaborate throne inscribed SALVE REGINA, see: Sandrine Thieffrey and Michiel Verwij, 'No. 36 Livre de chœur de Philippe le Beau et Jeanne de Castille', in *Philippe le Beau (1478-1506). Les trésors du dernier duc de Bourgogne*, ed. by Bernard Bousemanne and others, Brussels, KBR, 2006), pp. 151-53.

1 Eichberger, Dagmar, ed., *Women of Distinction. Margaret of York and Margaret of Austria* (Leuven: Davidsfonds, 2005).

2 Krause, Stefan, *Freydal. Medieval Games. The Book of Tournaments of Emperor Maximilian I* (Cologne: Taschen, 2019); Krause, Stefan, *Freydal: zu einem unvollendeten Gedächtniswerk Kaiser Maximilians I.*, ed. by Stefan Krause (*Jahrbuch des Kunsthistorischen Museums Wien*, Band 21 (2019), (Vienna: Böhlau, 2020).

In the wider orbit of the project many colleagues offered help and advice. While it will not be possible to list everybody by name and thank all institutions individually, I wish to name just a few: Lisa Beaven, Veronique Bücken, Jane Davidson, Verena Demoed, Estelle Doudet, Carmen Espinosa Martín, Johann Michael Fritz, Marc-Edouard Gauthier, Holger Kaiser, Laveant Katell, Ann Kelders, Alison Kettering, Isabelle Lecoq, Tino Licht, Scot McKendrick, Samuel Mareel, Nadine Orenstein, Walter Prevenier, Carlos Sánchez Díez, Graeme P. Small, Susie Speckman Sutch, Björn Tammen, Anne-Laure Van Bruaene, Sabine Van Sprang and Ashley West.

A project of such complexity requires searching for sponsors and donors who would recognize the value of such an undertaking. Again, the book project was under a lucky star. Philippe Close, Mayor of the city of Brussels, generously supported the project, as did the Publication Fund of the *Historians of Netherlandish Art*. The *Renaissance Society of America* awarded a *Samuel H. Kress Publication Subvention for Art Historians*. Two individuals kindly contributed financially to support this costly production, Claire Billen, Brussels, and James Marrow, Princeton. Last but not least, I would like to mention José Luis Colomer, Director of the *Centro de Estudios Europa Hispánica* in Madrid, who not only became a major sponsor but in addition agreed to distribute the book in the Spanish-speaking world (https://www.ceeh.es/).

Being accepted into the Brepols *Burgundica* series is an honour, and I am grateful to the General Editor, Jean-Marie Cauchies, for having agreed to publish this book. Working with Chris VandenBorre, the Publishing Manager, is always a pleasure, which explains why this is already my fourth book under his leadership. The collaboration with his right-hand woman, Eva Anagnostaki, was easy, efficient and supportive.

Several guardian angels have been at my side while sailing through the longwinded production process. There are a few special colleagues who became friends over time and assisted me in various way, e.g. by discussing matters relevant to the book, by solving editorial problems or giving me feedback on first drafts of texts, etc. – thank you Claire, Wim, Annemarie, Helga and Holger. My husband, Jürgen Eichberger, listened to my situation report every day and occasionally got involved in research when something particularly interested him. It is invaluable to have someone at your side who listens to you on a daily basis and gives you advice when you need it most, *mille grazie*.

Dagmar Eichberger, Heidelberg, 24 April 2023

DAGMAR EICHBERGER

The Festive Entry of Joanna of Castile into Brussels

An Introduction[*]

On 30 July, 1517 Antonio de' Beatis visited the city of Brussels in the company of Cardinal Luigi d'Aragona. He noted down his first impressions as follows:

> Brusseles è terra assai grande et bella; parte d'essa sta in piano et parte in monte; et è il capo di Brabantia. Vi habbiamo visto uno palazzo de la communità con una alta et grossa torre; inante a una piazza ben spatiosa, silicata di certe pietre piccole, come se usa per tucte quelle parte, et veramente che sono assai belle. Per tucto decto palazzo che è ben grande se può andare ad cavallo commodamente, dove dentro sono XXXVI fontane de quali alcune ne ascendeno in fine al mezzo de dicta torre. In la piazza è una fontana bellissima; et per tutta la terra, secundo ne referì il burgomastro, che è il principale officio de tucte la terre tanto de la Magna Alta come defols la Bassa et se muta ogni anno, sono Fontane CCCL.
>
>> Brussels is a very large and beautiful city, situated partly on the plain and partly on a hill; it is the capital of Brabant. We saw here a town hall with a large and solid tower; in front of it is a very spacious square with a beautiful pavement made of certain small stones, such as are used everywhere for paving in these parts. In the entire town hall, which is very large, one can comfortably ride around. Inside there are thirty-six fountains, some of which rise to half the height of the tower. There is a very beautiful fountain in the square, and there are 350 in the whole town, as the mayor told us, who holds the most important office in the entire city, both in the upper city and in the lower city, and it [the position] changes every year.[1]

This colourful account was written only twenty-one years after the Spanish princess Joanna of Castile (1479-1555), daughter of Queen Isabella of Castile and King Ferdinand of Aragon and wife of Philip the Fair (1478-1506), came to Brussels for

---

[*] I am grateful to Claire Billen and Wim Blockmans for their insightful comments that helped me to improve my first draft; thanks to Lisa Beaven and Annemarie Jordan Gschwend for checking my English.
[1] de Beatis, Antonio, *Die Reise des Kardinals Luigi d'Aragona durch Deutschland, die Niederlande, Frankreich und Oberitalien, 1517-1518*, ed. by Ludwig von Pastor (Freiburg i.Br.: Herder, 1905), p. 116.

the first time in her life (fol. 31ʳ).² On this occasion, when she was sixteen, the city prepared a festive entry for the young Archduchess, and she was welcomed in regal style.³

Jean Molinet, the great chronicler of the Burgundian court, informs his readership in detail about Joanna's arrival in Zeeland and the reception she received from the city of Antwerp on 19 September 1496. Surprisingly, he does not mention a word about the spectacular entry into Brussels, which took place three months later, on 9 December 1496.⁴ Instead, Molinet concentrates on Margaret of Austria's (1480-1530) journey to Spain, where she was to marry Juan of Castile (1478-1497), Joanna's older brother.⁵ He also dedicates a lot of space to the meeting of Joanna with Margaret in Antwerp. At the time, all the court's hopes were pinned on Philip the Fair's sister Margaret, as she was seen as the future queen of Spain.⁶ As it turned out, her life took a different turn, but in 1496 her destiny was perceived to be that of a Spanish monarch.

It is a great stroke of luck that a detailed account of the Brussels entry with sixty full-page miniatures has survived. This manuscript offers an excellent insight into the city's elaborate welcoming ceremonial, entitled *Joyeuse Entrée* or festive entry. Since Joanna arrived in the city of Brussels without her husband, the festival booklet is an invaluable testimony to her role as the female head of the ruling family of the country.⁷ The manuscript 78 D5, preserved in the Berlin *Kupferstichkabinett*, is, therefore, the focus of this in-depth study.

The manuscript consists of two parts. Part I (fols 1ᵛ-31ʳ) concentrates on the long parade of officials from church, craft associations, chambers of rhetoric, shooters' guilds and civic government that went to the outskirts of Brussels to greet the young princess and escort her to the centre of the city. Part II (fols 31ᵛ-59ʳ) showcases the elaborate stages that were erected along the inner-city itinerary. This section is followed by two folios with coats of arms (fols 60ʳ and 61ʳ). The manuscript concludes with a detailed description of the Brussels town hall with all its splendid features (fols 63ʳ-63ᵛ).⁸

---

2 On Joanna's first visit to the Netherlands see the essay by Fagel, Raymond, 'Joanna of Castile's first residence in the Low Countries (1496-1501): the transformation of a Trastámara Princess'.

3 It would be worthwhile to compare the efforts made in the cities in the Burgundian Netherlands with the festivities organized in places like Burgos after Joanna's return to Spain; see: Porras Gil, María Concepción, 'Magnificentia y política. El banquete celebrado en Burgos (1502) en honor de los archiduqes de Austria', *Potestas* 22 (2023), 47-66; Porras Gil, María Concepción, *De Bruselas a Toledo. El Viaje de Los Archiduques Felipe y Juana* (Madrid: Doce Calles/ Valladolid: Ediciones Universidad de Valladolid/ Fundación Carlos de Amberes, 2016).

4 Molinet, Jean, *Chroniques*, ed. by Georges Doutrepont, and Omer Jodogne (Brussels: Palais des Académies, 1935), II (1488-1506), chapt. CCLXXI, pp. 428-32; see also Herrmann, Max, 'Lebende Bilder', in *Forschungen zur Deutschen Theatergeschichte des Mittelalters und der Renaissance* (Berlin: Weidmann, 1914), 366.

5 Molinet, *Chroniques*, II, chapt. CCLXXII, p. 432-34.

6 Molinet, *Chroniques*, II, pp. 429-30. He describes how Margaret travelled from Namur, via Brussels and Mechelen, and, in the company of Margaret of York (1446-1503), further on to Antwerp to welcome her sister-in-law.

7 No documentary sources of this civic event have survived in Brussels, as the archive lost all records from this particular period. See the essay by Remco Sleiderink and Amber Souleymane in this volume.

8 See the essay by Sascha Köhl on this aspect of the manuscript: 'The Brussels Town Hall. A Worthy Emblem for a Capital City'.

The text of this booklet was written in Latin rather than in Dutch or French as was more common on such occasions.⁹ Joanna spoke Spanish and Latin fluently, which were probably her preferred languages of communication at the time.¹⁰ For the first time, all pages of the manuscript, that is, both the text pages and the full-page miniatures, are made available to the reader in a slightly reduced format (chapter 14).¹¹ For the first time, the Latin texts have been transcribed and translated into English (chapter 13).¹² This allows for a much deeper understanding of the concept than was previously possible. Matters of physical appearance, such as size, medium, script, foliation, binding, are described in chapter 11.¹³

1.1 Southern Netherlandish, *The Festive Entry of Joanna of Castile into Brussels*, fol. 1ᵛ: *Saint Michael defeats the Devil*, 1496, Berlin, SMPK, Kupferstichkabinett, ms. 78 D5. © SMPK

The image of Archangel Michael on fol. 1ᵛ that appears in an aureole of clouds and light, precedes the main corpus of text and images (Fig. 1.1). He wears silver-coloured armour and stands with his sword raised on the dragon, which he holds at bay with his shield. Because St Michael is the patron saint of the city of Brussels, he appears in a very similar pose on the tower of the city hall (Fig. 1.2).¹⁴ It is no coincidence that the Berlin manuscript opens with this image, as it was the city of Brussels that had organised and paid for this entry. The municipality decided on the design of the procession and the structure of this book that was to document the festive entry. As can be seen from the concluding paragraph (fol. 63ʳ) it was the intention of Brussels' elite to win over the princess and persuade her to make Brussels and the *Coudenberg Palace* her preferred residence within the Burgundian-Habsburg lands. The fact that Margaret of Austria, Joanna's sister-in-law, was born in Brussels is used as an additional argument by the authorities:

---

9 See for instance the entry of Archduke Charles into Bruges on the occasion of his coming of age in 1515.
10 See the essay by Raymond Fagel.
11 Chapter 14: 'Ms 78 D5. Fols 1r – 63v. Reproduction of the entire Manuscript with Text Pages and Illuminations'.
12 Chapter 13: 'Ms 78 D5. The Latin Text: Transcription and Translation' by Verena Demoed.
13 Chapter 11: 'Ms 78 D5. A Codicological Description', by Dagmar Eichberger.
14 The sculpture was made in 1455 and has recently been restored. The original statue can now be seen in *Het Broodhuis* or the *Musée de la Ville de Bruxelles, Maison du Roi*; see: Anagnostopoulos, Pierre, 'L'archange Michel et le démon de la flèche de l'Hôtel de Ville. Une girouette médiévale exceptionnelle', *Studia Bruxellae* XII, 2018, pp. 206-34; Anagnostopoulos, Pierre, 'Le saint Michel de la flèche de l'Hôtel de Ville (Grand-Place)', *Société royale d'archéologie de Bruxelles, Bulletin d'information*, n°80, 2018, 7-12.

1.2 Saint Michael, *Weather vane from the tower of the Brussels town hall*, H: 5,70 m, bronze with gilding, 1455, Brussels, Musée de la Ville de Bruxelles, photo: Stephanek © Creative Commons Attribution-Share Alike 4.0 International license

Quibus omnibus sed et civibus hiisque que eorum sunt sicsic illustrissima hera nostra Johanna archiducissa sese oblectet fruatur uberi herede ac pro voto de hiis iubeat ut et gratissimus locus (Isque inclitissime margarete Garnapolitanorum regine nativus) affectuosissimusque populus magnificentissime dominationi sue recommendati semper habeantur.

> May all this, and the citizens and what is theirs, please our most illustrious heroine Joanna, Archduchess, in such a way; may she enjoy many heirs and may she rule over them as is her wish, so that her most magnificent rulership always favours this very pleasant place (the birthplace of the glorious Margaret, Queen consort of Granada) and its affectionate people.

In one of Joanna's books of hours, yet another portrayal of the Archangel Michael appears at the beginning of the manuscript, combined with an image of Princess Joanna kneeling in prayer on the opposite page (Fig. 1.3). The text on fol. 26^r indicates the beginning of the *Office to the Guardian Angel*. In contrast to other manuscripts, such as the *Rothschild Hours* or the *Hours of Anne de Bretagne*, the traditional image of the guardian angel has been replaced by a depiction of Saint Michael fighting the

1.3a/b Southern Netherlandish, *Book of Hours of Joanna of Castile*, a) fol. 25ᵛ: *Saint Michael fighting the Dragon*, b) fol. 26ʳ: *Joanna of Castile in prayer with St John the Baptist and her guardian Angel*, parchment, 110 × 80 mm, 1496, London, British Library, ms Add 18852 © The British Library Board

Dragon.¹⁵ This iconography is reminiscent of the iconic images used in the city of Brussels (Figs 1.1, 1.2). It can be assumed that the Oxford book of hours was given to Joanna as a wedding gift by her husband. On the margins their mottos – *Qui vouldra* and *Je le veus* – their armorial shields and the letters P & I entwined by love knots refer to the matrimonial union of Joanna of Castile and Philip the Fair.¹⁶

The Berlin manuscript has been the subject of several individual studies with particular emphasis on the *tableaux vivants* depicted in Part II (fols 32ʳ-59ʳ). This section of the book is predominantly showing scenes from the Old Testament and from ancient history, with two stages that have a more contemporary reference (fols 58ʳ, 59ʳ).¹⁷ The first to recognize the significance of these stages were theatre historians

---

15 For more information of the guardian angel in private prayer books, see: Eichberger, Dagmar, '*Oratio ad Proprium Angelum*: The Guardian Angel in the Rothschild Hours', in *The Primacy of the Image in Northern European Art, 1400-1700: Essays in Honor of Larry Silver*, ed. by Debra Cashion, Ashley West, and Henry Luttikhuizen (Leiden: Brill, 2017), pp. 150-63.

16 Twomey, Lesley K., 'Juana of Castile's Book of Hours: An Archduchess at Prayer', *Religions* (2020), 11, 201.

17 See the following articles in this volume: Remco Sleiderink and Amber Souleymane: '*In unam pacis accordantiam*. The Role of City Poet Jan Smeken and other Rhetoricians in organizing the Brussels Entry', Wim Blockmans:

1.4 Master of the David scenes in the Grimani Breviary, *Book of Hours*, fol. 25ʳ: *Saint Matthew*, parchment, 20,5 × 14 cm, 1515-1520, Oxford, Bodleian Libraries, ms Douce 112. Creative Commons licence CC-BY-NC 4.0 Photo: © Bodleian Libraries, University of Oxford

1.5 Master of the David scenes in the Grimani Breviary, *Book of Hours*, fol. 157ʳ: *Saint George*, parchment, 20,5 × 14 cm, 1515-1520, Oxford, Bodleian Libraries, ms Douce 112. Creative Commons licence CC-BY-NC 4.0 Photo: © Bodleian Libraries, University of Oxford

such as Max Hermann (1914) and Gordon Kipling (1970, 2001), followed by Laura Weigert (2015).[18] All of these authors stress the fact that the Berlin manuscript offers the earliest illustrated account of a festive entry, and the first dedicated exclusively to a woman.[19] The structure of these stages is vividly portrayed in the individual images,

---

'Role Models for a Queen's Daughter', Laura Weigert: '"To move the hearts and spirits of men towards joy and recreation." The Entry of Joanna of Castille as Entertainment', and Dagmar Eichberger: 'Arguing with the Old Testament. Moral and Political Lessons for Princess Joanna of Castile'.

18   Herrmann, 'Lebende Bilder', 364-411; Kipling, Gordon R., *From Art to Theatre. Form and Convention in the Renaissance* (Chicago: The University of Chicago Press, 1970), esp. chapter II: 'Showpiece and show-architecture. The *Tableaux vivants*', pp. 52-110; Kipling, Gordon R., 'Brussels, Juana of Castile and the Art of Theatrical Illustration (1496)', *Leeds Studies in English*, n.s., 32 (2001), 229-53; Laura Weigert, '"Vocamus Personagias": The Enlivened Figures of Ephemeral Stagings', in *French Visual Culture and the Making of Medieval Theatre* (New York: Cambridge University Press, 2015), pp. 27-73.

19   There is a great deal of specialist literature on fifteenth century festive entries with *tableaux vivants* which are only documented in writing. The essay by Mario Damen and Kim Overlaet, for instance, reconstructs the entry of Maximilian I into Antwerp (13 January 1477); Damen, Mario, and Kim Overlaet, 'Weg van de staat. Blijde

which show them to consist of a wooden scaffold with a platform, two curtains and textile decorations at the top and the bottom of the structure. This is most clearly seen in folio 56^r, a scene described as 'Three virgins' (*Tres Virgines*). In most cases, the stage is framed by red, blue and beige textiles, adorned by fringes with the same colours. The stage set on fol. 57^r, depicting *The Judgement of Paris*, stands out in its use of a more luxurious fabric to frame the stage.

While it has been observed that painters such as Hugo van der Goes took advantage of the stage set as a theatrical device,[20] the use of curtains and canopies in illuminated manuscripts has thus far been overlooked. The Book of Hours Oxford, ms Douce 112, is a good case in point (Figs 1.4, 1.5).[21] In these two miniatures showing Saint Matthew (fol. 25^r) and Saint George (fol. 157^r), the curtains appear to be more than an artful device. Instead they create a barrier between the beholder and the story, seen through a window-like opening, thus underscoring the difference between reality and illusion.[22]

After Herrmann and Kipling introduced the Berlin festival booklet to a wider public, many historians,[23] musicologists,[24] literary scholars and art historians[25] have dealt

---

Intredes in de laatmiddeleeuwse nederlanden op het snijvlak van sociale, culturele en politieke geschiedenis', *Low Countries Historical Review*, 134 (2019), 3-44; see also: Soly, Hugo, 'Plechtige intochten in de steden van de Zuidelijke Nederlanden tijdens de overgang van Middeleeuwen naar Nieuwe Tijd: communicatie, propaganda, spektakel', *Tijdschrift voor Geschiedenis* 97 (1984), 341-62; Cauchies, Jean-Marie, 'La signification politique des entrées princières dans les Pays-Bas : Maximilien d'Autriche et Philippe le Beau', in *À la Cour de Bourgogne. Le duc, son entourage, son train*, ed. by Jean-Marie Cauchies, Burgundica 1 (Turnhout: Brepols, 1998), pp. 137-52; Murphy, Neil, 'Between Court and Town: Ceremonial Entries in the *Chroniques* of Jean Molinet', in *Jean Molinet et son temps. Actes des rencontres internationales de Dunkerque, Lille et Gand*, ed. by Jean Devaux, Estelle Doudet, and Élodie Lecuppre-Desjardin (Turnhout: Brepols, 2013), pp. 155-61.

20 Hugo van der Goes, *Adoration of the Shepherds*, 99,2 × 249 cm, oil on oak, c. 1480, Berlin, Gemäldegalerie; see *Hugo van der Goes. Zwischen Schmerz und Seligkeit*, exh. cat. Berlin, Gemäldegalerie, ed. by Stephan Kemperdick, Eric Eising, and Till-Holger Borchert (Munich: Hirmer, 2023), cat. no. 27, pp. 216-25 (Stephan Kemperdick):

21 I wish to thank Karin Farkas-Kleisinger who alerted me to this book illumination (unpublished Master thesis, University of Vienna 2021): 'Architekturrahmen in französischen und flämischen Stundenbüchern des 15./16. Jahrhunderts'; ms Douce 112 dates from c. 1515-20.

22 Stoichiţă, Victor I., *L'instauration du tableau. Métapeinture à l'aube des temps modernes* (Paris: Méridiens Klincksieck, 1993).

23 Blockmans, Wim P., 'La Joyeuse Entrée de Jeanne de Castille à Bruxelles en 1496', in *España y Holanda*, ed. by Jan Lechner, and Harm den Boer (Amsterdam: Rodopi, 1995), pp. 27-42; Blockmans, Wim P., 'Le dialogue imaginaire entre princes et sujets: les joyeuses entrées en Brabant entre 1494 et en 1496', in *À la Cour de Bourgogne. Le duc, son entourage, son train*, ed. by Jean-Marie Cauchies, Burgundica, 1 (Turnhout: Brepols, 1998), pp. 155-70; Cauchies, Jean-Marie, and Marie van Eeckenrode, '"Recevoir madame l'archiduchesse pour faire incontinent ses nopces…". Gouvernants et gouvernés autour du mariage de Philippe le Beau et de Jeanne de Castille dans les Pays-Bas (1496-1501)', in *L'héritière, le prince étranger et le pays. Le mariage de Jean l'Aveugle et d'Élisabeth*, ed. by Michel Pauly (Luxembourg: CLUDEM, 2013), pp. 263-77; Bussels, Stijn, 'Powerful Performances. *Tableaux vivants* in early Modern Joyous Entries in the Netherlands', in *Le tableau vivant ou l'image performée*, ed. by Julie Ramos (Paris: Mare & Martin, 2014), pp. 71-92.

24 Tammen, Björn, 'A Feast of the Arts: Joanna of Castile in Brussels, 1496', *Early Music History*, 30 (2011), 213-48.

25 Franke, Birgit, *Assuerus und Esther am Burgunderhof. Zur Rezeption des Buches Esther in den Niederlanden (1450 bis 1530)* (Berlin: Mann, 1998), pp. 110-12; Legaré, Anne-Marie, 'L'entrée de Jeanne de Castille à Bruxelles: un programme iconographique au féminin', in *Women at the Burgundian Court: Presence and Influence*, ed. by Dagmar Eichberger, Anne-Marie Legaré, and Wim Hüsken, Burgundica 17 (Turnhout: Brepols, 2010), pp. 43-55; Legaré, Anne-Marie, 'Joanna of Castile's Entry into Brussels: Viragos, Wise and Virtuous Women', in *Virtue Ethics for Women*, 1250-1500, ed. by Karen Green, and Constant J. Mews (Dordrecht: Springer, 2011), pp. 177-86.

with individual aspects of the manuscript.[26] Wim Blockmans and Paul Vandenbroeck deserve special mention here, as they are among the few authors who attempted to understand the manuscript in its entirety and therefore interpret its overall structure.[27]

The first half of the manuscript shows representatives of Brussels: the religious communities, the patricians, the city government, and the guilds, all of whom participate in a well-organized procession progressing towards the young princess. At first sight, this repetitive line-up of dignitaries appearing in their professional garbs, on horseback or by foot, seems somewhat monotonous. But as soon as the Latin texts are taken into account, a rich kaleidoscope of socio-political ideas emerges. The important essay written by Claire Billen and Chloé Deligne, two specialists in urban history, provides a new approach to the representation of the city and its various social groups, as presented to the reader in Part I of the manuscript (fols 3^r-31^r). As it turns out, the Berlin manuscript is as much an instrument for civic self-representation as it is an attempt to communicate with Princess Joanna about her future role as Philip's consort and 'mother of the country'[28].

This leads to four important questions: Who devised the program for this entry? Which audience did the author of the Latin texts have in mind? What can we say about the relationship between text and image? Which artist produced the illuminations with the help of his workshop?

Due to a lack of archival sources from the year of Joanna's festive entry, it is necessary to answer these questions by comparing this entry with similar events or by evaluating the information in the Berlin manuscript itself. The essay by Remco Sleiderink and Amber Souleymane weaves together the abundant information that exists on earlier and later entries in the southern Netherlands. They argue that Jan Smeken (c. 1450-1517), the official city poet of Brussels and some of the rhetoricians close to him, took the lead in the organization, together with members of the Greater Crossbowmen's Guild. The oldest and most prestigious shooters' guild occupies a place of honour in the procession in so far as they are responsible for the safety of the princess and walk closest to her (fol. 31^r).[29] These men were also in charge of the so-called *Brusselse Ommegang*, an annual procession that still takes place in honour of the miraculous statue of the Virgin Mary venerated in the church of *Onze-Lieve-Vrouw*

---

26 It would lead too far to list all the publications in which one or two miniatures from the Berlin manuscript are discussed; the bibliography will list additional publications that are relevant.

27 For Blockmans see fn. 24; Vandenbroeck concentrated predominantly on Part II of the manuscript, but underlines the significance of Part I, see: Paul Vandenbroeck, 'Una novia entre heroínas, bufones y salvajes. La Solemne Entrada de Juana de Castilla en Bruselas, 1496', in *El legado de Borgoña. Fiesta y ceremonia cortesana en la Europa de los Austrias (1454-1648)*, ed. by Krista De Jonge, Bernardo José García García, and Alicia Esteban Estríngana (Madrid: Marcial Pons and Fundación Carlos de Amberes, 2010), pp. 145-78, on the municipal authorities, see pp. 162-63; Paul Vandenbroeck, 'A Bride amidst Heroines, Fools and Savages. The Joyous Entry into Brussels by Joanna of Castile, 1496 (Berlin Kupferstichkabinett, ms 78 D5)', *Jaarboek. Koninklijk Museum voor Schone Kunst Antwerpen* (2012), 153-94.

28 This terms is less common in English as it is in Dutch (*Moeder des Vaderlands*) or German (*Landesmutter*).

29 See also the essay by Claire Billen and Chloé Deligne in this volume: 'The Self-representation of Brussels in Times of Uncertainty'.

1.6 Anonymous, *The Virgin of Onze-Lieve-Vrouw ten Zavel (Notre-Dame du Sablon) with Beatrix Soetkens and a Ferryman*, painted wood, 17th century, Brussels, Our-Blessed-Lady of the Sablon, southern transept

ten Zavel (*Notre-Dame du Sablon*). This is where the shooters guild has its chapel. A seventeenth-century sculpture in the southern transept of the church depicts the story of how in 1348, the Marian sculpture reached Brussels by boat (Fig. 1.6).

The text of the Brussels festival book makes it abundantly clear that the manuscript was not intended as a presentation copy for Joanna of Castile or a member of her family. In fact, the corresponding introductory tributes, which one would expect in a presentation copy, are missing. Only at the very end of the text is the young princess addressed in person (fol. 63[v]). The city expresses its desire to make Joanna feel at home in Brussels and their hope that the princess will adopt the ducal palace on Coudenberg as her favourite residence.

At the beginning of the manuscript (fol. 2[r]), the Latin text underlines that the city hoped to have a positive effect on Joanna of Castile by organizing this extraordinary entry and by providing multisensory entertainment: 'So the most benevolent mistress can think well of the citizens, seeing how devoted they are to her excellence'.

As a target audience, the intellectual elite and the urban ruling class are just as important as the princess. The introduction spells out that the booklet was prepared as a memento of the festive event and singles out the 'excellent minds who are keen on novelties' as well as the 'approving, sympathetic spectator'. It is stated that the booklet allows the citizens to get a complete picture of what 'he failed to notice in his over enthusiasm'.

hoc in libello summis quasi labris (folliate depictas effigies intuenti) videndum erit ubi et pro subscriptis titulis seu argumentis qui ordine quo cuiusque officii dignitatisve prosilierint denique figuris (quas personagias vocamus) quid scenis operam dantes tropologes praetenderint

> for anyone looking at the depicted images page by page, where it will be readily accessible, especially with the help of the written captions or summaries, who, in which order and from which official duty or high office they came forward; and also, what the tropologists, putting a lot of effort in the scenes, intended to depict through the figures (which we refer to as characters).

From these detailed comments, one can gauge that both the texts and the images were seen as appropriate tools to explain the city's intentions to the reader. The so-called 'tropologists' are named as artistic directors who put together the scenes (*scenis*) with the help of living figures (*personagias*). Molinet's French descriptions of Joanna's entry into Antwerp, taking place on 19 September 1496, uses a very similar terminology: *Plusieurs histoires par personages furent faits par ceulx de la ville, qui longz seroyent à les reciter.* (Several historical scenes with figures were produced by people from the city, who recited them in great detail).[30] This is not the only incidence in which French terms are translated literally into Latin, an approach that Paul Vandenbroeck describes as 'French barbarisms'[31].

The expression 'tropologists' leaves open the question of who was responsible for the program – a member of the local chamber of rhetoric, a representative from the Greater Crossbow Guild or a theologian from one of the institutions listed in the procession are possibilities. Perhaps the urban leadership did not want to favour one social group over another and therefore opted for this rather abstract term.[32] The Latin expression *tropologie* or *tropolgy* relates to the multi-layered interpretation of literature, by focusing either on the ethical lesson or moral of a story. Tropology can also stand for a figurative mode of speech or writing, and it is often used as an equivalent for allegory.[33] This application is particularly relevant to any of the illustrations in which the Latin text establishes a direct link between a historical or biblical scene and Joanna of Castile and her family.[34] Such an analogy could either contain a didactic lesson to the young princess or refer to specific circumstances that involve her relatives or even high-ranking courtiers.[35] Isabella of Castile (fols 41^v-42^r), Ferdinand of Aragon (fols 53^v-54^r), Maximilian I (fols 33^v-34) and Philip the Fair

---

30 Molinet, *Chroniques*, II, p. 429.
31 Vandenbroeck, 'A Bride amidst Heroines', p. 160.
32 These issues are discussed in the contributions by Remco Sleiderink and Amber Souleymane, as well as by Claire Billen and Chloé Deligne. I am very grateful to the following colleagues for their valuable insights and comments: Estelle Doudet, Katell Lavéant, Samuel Mareel, Graeme P. Small and Anne-Laure van Bruaene.
33 In an email (25.3.2021), Katell Lavéant, a specialist on French literature writes: "The closest situation I can think of, apart from the religious texts […] that use *tropologie* as an equivalent for *allegory*, is the use of the term in a French Farce (*La Farce des Théologastres*). It is used by an allegorical character, the [sacred] text, to complain about the way it has been used by the 'Bad Theologians' who have made it weak and boring by an abuse of tropology and allegory (most likely here used as synonyms)."
34 See the essays by Wim Blockmans and Dagmar Eichberger on this point.
35 One example for the latter is the mention of Admiral Don Fadrique Enríquez of fol. 37^v, who is equaled with Abner, the commander of King David, see: Vandenbroeck, 'A Bride amidst Heroines', 174.

(fols 36ᵛ-37ʳ, 39ᵛ-40ʳ) are mentioned explicitly in the text. While they were not present on 9 December 1496, they nevertheless play a prominent role in the Brussels entry as they underline the princely origin of the young couple.

The Latin term *tropologie* is used a second time at the beginning of Part II when the author explains the appearance of the *tableaux vivants* that were put up along the processional route. This text emphasizes that the stories displayed on the stages will please everybody, particularly the *literati*, that is, educated readers. The text on folio 31ᵛ reads as follows:

> Sequuntur effigies seu scemata figurarum (quas personagias vocamus) in scenis seu elevatis et clausis esschaufaudis in conis vicorum locatarum que pretereuntium cum oportunitate tum requesta cortinis ad hoc aptatis nunc velabantur nunc patebant obtutibus que nedum gestorum congrua fictione ac mirabili pomposoque apparatu quam optime condecentis tropologie (ut patebit) applicatione cunctorum (litteratorumque precipue) animos oblectavere.
>
>> What follows are the images or depictions of figures (which we refer to as characters) placed on stages or raised and closed-off platforms on the corners of streets, that were opened and closed at the convenience and request of the passers-by with curtains made for this purpose, which – with the appropriate simulation of gestures and wonderful and sensational props, applying the most fitting tropology (as will be clear) – pleased the hearts of all (but especially of the literati).

It is worth mentioning that both Paul Vandenbroeck and Björn Tammen go one step further by equating this pattern of interpretation with the medieval concept of typology.[36] Both authors refer to the notion of 'historical symbolism'. As has been shown by Alexander Linke and others, the juxtaposition of contemporary figures with scenes from the past had long been in place and was not limited to the Old Testament.[37] The transfer of this system of thought to the Brussels entry significantly contributes to our understanding of its internal structure. One example (fols 35ᵛ-36ʳ) shall suffice to illustrate this point:

> Hoc scemate Representatur Qui uti mulier Thecuites desuper fragmento mole abimelech excerebrans vita privavit Sic illustrissima domina nostra Johanna arxi austrie, Burgundie Brabancie [etc] innixa letales inimicos conterere habebit.
>
>> This depiction displays how a woman, Thecuites, took the life of Abimelech by crushing his skull with a stone from the city wall. So our most illustrious Lady Joanna, leaning on the bulwark of Austria, Burgundy, Brabant, etc. shall crush our deadly enemies.

---

36 Vandenbroeck, 'A Bride amidst Heroines', pp. 164-69; Tammen, 'A Feast for the Arts', pp. 225, 230.

37 Alexander Linke, 'What is "Typology"?', in *Visual Typology in Early Modern Europe. Continuity and Expansion*, ed. by Dagmar Eichberger, and Shelley Perlove (Turnhout: Brepols, 2018), pp. 23-59; see also Alexander Linke, *Typologie in der Frühen Neuzeit. Genese und Semantik heilsgeschichtlicher Bildprogramme von der Cappella Sistina (1480) bis San Giovanni in Laterano (1650)* (Berlin: Reimer, 2014).

While the identity of those who were responsible for the program has not been revealed, some have argued that Jan Smeken was one of the most promising candidates.[38] The situation is similar for the identification of the illuminators who executed the full-page illustrations. Scholars thus far have yet to identify a particular artist or the workshop who produced this manuscript shortly after the entry took place. As Anne-Marie Legaré has been able to demonstrate in her essay, this manuscript on paper is part of a specific genre of books that were executed in this technique, using pen drawings and watercolour on paper. No research has been undertaken to date on the artistic production of such memorial books in Brabant. The watermark 'P' suggests that the paper was produced in the larger Brussels region (see chapter 11). The internal knowledge revealed in depicting certain landmarks, such as the fountain at the Fish Market (fol. 12^r), and specific guild emblems on the clothes of the shooters' guilds, points to a local artist with a close acquaintance of the city.

Among the authors working on this publication, the question was raised whether the Berlin manuscript might have been designed as an *exemplar* to be used as model for preparing a printed book with woodcuts. Similar practices are known from the entry of Prince Charles (the future Emperor Charles V) into Bruges on 18 April 1515. In Vienna, one luxury edition on parchment still exists in the Österreichische Nationalbibliothek, originating in the Habsburg family collection.[39] Several copies of a printed version with black and white woodcuts have survived.[40] To our knowledge however, the Brussels entry only exists in one copy, the Berlin manuscript.

One of the most fascinating aspects of this manuscript is how the program has been tailored to suit a female guest of honour. On one hand, female figures from the Old Testament are introduced as models for exemplary behaviour, such as Judith, Esther, Jael and Deborah. It is explained how these women defended their people with courage, wisdom and strength. Other female models were chosen because they entered a marital union with an Old Testament hero: Sarah with Tobias, Michal with David and Rebecca with Isaac.[41]

Alternatively, heroines from ancient history are showcased to underline women's political potential. The following individuals are characterized as fierce women who did not shy away from fighting with weapons: Deiphilis, Queen Sinopis, the amazones Hippolyta and Menelopa, Empress Semiramis, Queen Lampeto, Queen Tamaris,

---

38 See the essay by Remco Sleiderink and Amber Souleymane in this volume.

39 Du Puys, Remy, *La tryumphante et solemnelle entree faicte sur le Joyeuse aduenement de Treshault et trespuissant prince Monsigneur Charles Prince des espagnes Archiduc daustrice etc en sa ville de Bruges Lan quinze centz et quinze le dixhuictiesme Jour dapuril*, Vienna, Österreichische Nationalbibliothek, Cod. 2591, http://data.onb.ac.at/rec/baa4971036.

40 Du Puys, Remy, *La tryumphante et solemnelle entree faicte sur le nouuel et ioyeux aduenement de treshault trespuissant et tresexcellent prince monsieur Charles prince des Hespaignes archiduc daustrice duc de Bourgongne conte de Flandres. [etc] En sa ville de Bruges* (Paris: Gilles de Gourmont, 1515), see: London, British Library, C.44.g.11 https://www.bl.uk/treasures/festivalbooks/BookDetails.aspx?strFest=0074; see also Du Puys, Remy, *La tryumphante entrée de Charles Prince des Espagnes en Bruges 1515*. A facsimile with an introduction by Sydney Anglo (Amsterdam: Theatrum Orbis Terrarum, [circa 1973]).

41 See the essay by Dagmar Eichberger in this volume.

Queen Teuca and Queen Penthesilia.[42] As Wim Blockmans shows, Queen Isabella of Castile is held up as the *exemplar*, the woman who outshines even the most famous viragos, with the aim of flattering Princess Joanna by praising her mother.[43] The Latin text on fol. 41ᵛ:

> Hoc scemate Representatur Invictissima Castillie hyspanie [etc.] omni laude predicanda Elizabeth Regina Johanne nostre mater Inclitissima que (ut scema prefert) garnapolitanum regem pro genibus supplicem habens famosissima illa victoria quam non tam suorum armis quam suo animo cui par numquam extitit et obsidionis diuturnitate eventuum belli diversitate ac rei magnitudine novem subsequentium ac omnium illustrium feminarum quas unquam vel muse vel hystorie celebres cecinere gloriam famamque obliterans immortales reportavit triumphos quos cum verbis musisve minime vel silentio predicare indultum est.
>
>> This image shows the invincible Queen of Castile, Spain, etc., Isabella, worthy of every praise, the renowned mother of our Joanna, who – having the King of Granada begging on his knees (as the depiction shows), belittling the glory and fame of all nine following illustrious women who have been praised in poems and famous stories with this well-known victory, not only because of the weapons of her army, but also because of her spirit, of which the like has never been found, and the length of the siege, the changes in successes during the war end the magnitude of the case – gained eternal triumphs that one may praise with words or poems, or in silence.

Overall, it can be said that womanhood is not portrayed as a delicate or weak sex for whom humility, obedience, and piety are paramount. Since the princess is expected to support Brabant and the other territories in all political matters, these more traditional feminine ideals are downplayed. The language that was chosen to describe Joanna's future actions borders on bellicose. On fols 54ᵛ-55ʳ, for instance, Jael resorts to cruel methods, and blood flows abundantly:

> Hoc scemate Representatur Qui uti Jahel mulier egregia Sizare Tempora clavo perforavit. Sic Johanna hyspanie capita inimicorum nostrorum clavo discretissime auctoritatis sue dolabit.
>
>> This depiction displays how Jael, an outstanding woman, pierced Sisera's temple with a nail. So Joanna of Spain shall batter the heads of our enemies with the nail of her exquisite power.

Despite this somewhat disconcerting view of the role of the Spanish princess as the future matriarch, the expectation of the princess and Infanta of Spain as a rich

---

42 See the essay by Wim Blockmans in this volume.
43 Blockmans, ‚Le dialogue imaginaire', 1998 and his essay in this volume. As to Isabella and her daughters see: Pérez García, Noelia, ed., *Isabel la Católica y sus hijas. El patronazgo artístico de las últimas Trastámara* (Murcia: Universidad de Murcia, 2020); Moratón, Melania Soler, 'Retratos de piedad, retratos de poder: las representaciones devocionales de Isabel I de Castilla y de su heredera, Juana I, y su simbología pública', *Potestas* 20 (2022), 25-49; https://www.e-revistes.uji.es/index.php/potestas/article/view/5828/6864.

and sumptuously dressed lady is also presented. As Annemarie Jordan Gschwend has described so aptly in this volume,[44] Joanna came from the wealthy Trastamára dynasty, and her mother Isabella spent a considerable amount of money to furnish her daughter in the richest way possible. Her trousseau was filled with jewels and precious textiles, tapestries and artefacts. The portrait of Princess Joanna on fol. 31^r of the Berlin manuscript does not really do justice to the sartorial splendour of the Spanish court, although the artist has made an effort to enhance the image of the princess by using gold paint. Jean Molinet describes her public appearance in Antwerp as follows:

> Icelle très illustre et vertueuse dame, [...], de beau port et gracieux maintieng, la plus ricemment aornée que jamais fut paravent veue és pays de monseigneur l'archiduc, estoit montée sur une mule à la mode d'Espaigne, ayent le chief descouvert, estoient accompaignie de XVI nobles jeunes dames et une matrone qui, vestues de drap d'or, montée de pareille sorte, et avoyent pages accoutréz de ric[h]es parures [...]
>
>> This very illustrious and virtuous lady, of beautiful carriage and graceful bearing, most richly adorned as has never been seen before in the country of our lord, the Archduchess, was mounted on a mule in the Spanish style, having her head uncovered, being accompanied by sixteen young noble ladies and one matron, who, dressed in gold brocade, mounted in a similar way, having pages adorned with rich finery [...][45]

In the 1496 entry, the city made every effort to create a theatrical effect that would outshine all other cities on Joanna's itinerary. The entry was held at night time, and the plentiful use of torches can be studied in many of the images that appear in the Berlin manuscript. In some cases, their effect was enhanced through the use of mirrors, as the text accompanying the wedding of Rebecca and Isaac explains (fol. 38^v).

Towards the end of the manuscript, the ingenuity of the organizers is praised by the author of the festival booklet (fol. 62^r). He even compares the effects achieved through these pyrotechnic displays with the fires of Troy and Carthage, evidently an attempt to show off his classical education.

> Notandum quod Ignium Immensitas diversarum materiarum luminumque eciam supra tecta mirabili ingenio instructorum qui ipsum opidum adinstar carbonis vivi accenderant (pro eo quod nichil deliciarum eorum effigies visui afferunt) nulla scemata ponuntur eorum tamen eam fuisse copiam aspectumque credatis que et si non troye carthaginisque incendia excessere nil tamen eis vicinius similiusve (eo dumtaxat quod non tam diu arsere) unquam visum fuerit.
>
>> It should be noted that the brightness of the fires and the torches of diverse materials, which were even placed on rooftops with great ingenuity and made

---

44 See the essay Annemarie Jordan Gschwend in this volume: 'Joanna, Infanta of Castile and Habsburg Archduchess. Recreating a lost Wardrobe and Trousseau in 1496'.
45 Molinet, *Chroniques*, II, p. 429.

the city glow like on fire, cannot be captured in the depictions (because images cannot convey their splendour to our eyes). You must believe, however, that these fires were so great in number and their effect so spectacular that, while the fires of Troy and Carthage may have been greater, nothing has ever resembled them more closely and similarly (even though they burned much shorter.

Without question, the entry of Joanna of Castile into the city of Brussels was a very ambitious undertaking, sparing neither expense nor effort. The Berlin manuscript provides a lasting account of this spectacular event by painting a portrait of the city of Brussels as the acting magistracy wanted it to be perceived in the year of her visit. As can be seen from the quote by Antonio de' Beatis cited at the beginning of this introduction, there was a fair share of 'public relations' or even 'propaganda' involved. De' Beatis second-hand stories about the city align with those told in this manuscript.

In the Berlin manuscript, the Burgundian ducal palace – commonly called *Coudenberg Palace* – is not mentioned as part of the processional route. The account stops with an extensive description of the famous town hall. The Latin text on fol. 26^v mentions in passing that a group of city employees responsible for safety and cleanliness accompanied Joanna all the way to the ducal residence, striving to light up the dark streets with their torches.

By analysing Joanna's itinerary between September 1496 and November 1501, Bethany Aram and Raymond Fagel were able to confirm that the city's strategy worked. In approximately five years, Joanna of Castile spent 1050 days in Brussels (55%), compared to 202 in Ghent and 190 in Bruges, and even less in places like Antwerp, Lier and Mechelen.[46] During her first sojourn in the Burgundian Netherlands, Joanna of Castile indeed chose Brussels as her preferred place of residence, thus contributing to the growing significance of the city as the capital of the territories that her spouse had inherited from his mother, Mary of Burgundy.

Joanna's full-length portrait on the right wing of the Zierikzee altarpiece (Fig. 1.7a/b), dating from circa 1505, presents her as Archduchess of Austria, albeit wearing an elaborate crown.[47] She is portrayed as a self-confident young woman who is aware of her political responsibility. Her mantle combines the coats of arms of the Spanish Kingdoms with the coats of arms of the Habsburg-Burgundian territories, reminiscent of fols 60^r and 61^r in the Berlin manuscript.[48] It seems as if the artist pre-

---

46 See Raymond Fagel's essay in this volume; Aram, Bethany, *La reina Juana. Gobierno, piedad y dinastía* (Madrid: Marcial Pons, 2016), pp. 331-37.

47 On this painting, both Philip the Fair and Joana wear a crown, see: Dubois, Anne, and Bart Fransen, 'Master of the Joseph Sequence, Zierikzee Triptych', in *The Flemish Primitives IV: Masters with Provisional Names*, ed. by Pascale Syfer-d'Olne, Roel Slachmuylders, Anne Dubois, Bart Fransen, and Famke Peters (Turnhout: Brepols, 2006), pp. 68-97.

48 In this context a piece of black velvet (Fig. 02), now in the collection of the Museo Lázaro Galdiano, is of great interest. It shows the combined coats of arms of the young couple; see López Redondo, Amparo, 'Tejidos de la época de los Reyes Católicos en la Colección Lázaro Galdiano', in *Isabel I. Reina de Castilla*, edited by Miguel Angel Ladero Quesado (Madrid: Dykinson, 2004), pp. 332-34.

1.7a/b Master of the Joseph sequence, a) *Philip the Fair and Joanna of Castile*, two wings from the Zierikzee Triptych, 125 × 48 cm, oil on oak, *c.* 1505-06, Brussels, Royal Museums of Fine Arts of Belgium (Brussels), inv. 2405. Photo: F. Maes © RMFAB

maturely portrayed the couple as King and Queen of Spain, even if the controversial succession to the throne had not been decided yet.

At the outset of her political career, it appears Joanna had every intention of following in her mother's footsteps. The fact that these ideas could not be realised after the death of Queen Isabella of Castile on 26 November 1504, was tragic for the young princess and reflects the difficulties an infanta could face when competing with her father and husband for access to power.[49]

This volume of essays endeavours to emphasise that the life story of Joanna of Castile – as is known above all from the tragic time following the death of her husband on 25 September 1506 – did not only have its dark sides.[50] The general expectation of a fruitful union of this young couple – as expressed on fols 40^r-41^v of the Berlin manuscript – was to be fulfilled. Joanna gave birth to six healthy children who were destined to shape the political landscape of Europe: Leonor[51] (b. 1498), Charles (b. 1500), Isabella[52] (b. 1501), Ferdinand[53] (b. 1503), Mary[54] (b. 1505) and Catharine[55] (b. 1507). The first double spread in Joanna's *Book of Hours* (Fig. 1.1/1.2) emphasizes the dynastic aspects of her life as consort of Archduke Philip the Fair. The second double spread in the same manuscript (fols 287^v-288^r) is dominated by a portrait of Joanna praying by herself in front of a popular devotional image (Fig. 1.8a/b).[56] This more intimate portrait of the young princess is inserted in between *The Office of the Virgin* (fols 194^v-286^v) and *The Penitential Psalms* (fols 293^v-318^v) and marks the beginning of the Marian prayer *Dignare me laudare te virgo sacrata* (I deserve to praise you, Holy Virgin). Deeply immersed in prayer,

---

49 This problem is dealt with in more detail in Raymond Fagel's essay. Duchess Mary of Burgundy faced a similar problem when her father, Charles the Bold (1433-77), died in Nancy; see Dumont, Jonathan, and Élodie Lecuppre-Desjardin, 'Construire la légitimité d'un pouvoir féminin', in *Marie de Bourgogne. Figure, principat et postérité d'une duchesse tardo-médiévale / 'Persona', Reign, and Legacy of a Late Medieval Duchess*, ed. by Michael Depreter, Jonathan Dumont, Elizabeth L'Estrange, and Samuel Mareel (Turnhout: Brepols, 2021), pp. 41-60.
50 Fernández Álvarez, Manuel, *Juana la Loca, la cautiva de Tordesillas* (Madrid: Espasa Calpe, 2003); Aram, Bethany, *Juana the mad: sovereignty and dynasty in Renaissance Europe* (Baltimore: Johns Hopkins University Press, 2005); Gómez, María A., Santiago Juan-Navarro, and Phyllis Zatlin (eds), *Juana of Castile: history and myth of the mad queen* (Lewisburg: Bucknell University Press, 2008).
51 Jordan Gschwend, Annemarie, 'Ma Meilleur Soeur: Leonor de Austria, Reina de Portugal y de Francia/ Leonor of Austria, Queen of Portugal and France', in *The Inventories of Charles V and the Imperial Family/ Los inventarios de Carlos V y la familia imperial*, ed. by Fernando Checa Cremades (Madrid: Fernando Villaverde: 2010), vol. III, pp. 2545-92.
52 Hein, Jorgen, 'Isabella of Austria/ Isabel de Austria', in *The Inventories of Charles V and the Imperial Family/ Los inventarios de Carlos V y la familia imperial*, ed. by Fernando Checa Cremades (Madrid: Fernando Villaverde: 2010), vol. III, pp. 2601-23.
53 Seipel, Wilfried, ed., *Kaiser Ferdinand I, 1503-1564. Das Werden der Habsburgermonarchie* (Wien: KHM, 2003).
54 Jordan Gschwend, Annemarie, and Dagmar Eichberger, 'A Discerning Agent with a Vision. Queen Mary of Hungary (1505-1558)', in *Women. The Art of Power. Three Women from the House of Habsburg*, ed. by Sabine Haag, Dagmar Eichberger and Annemarie Jordan Gschwend (Wien: KHM, 2018), pp. 37-49.
55 Jordan Gschwend, Annemarie, 'A Forgotten Infanta. Catherine of Austria, Queen of Portugal (1507-1578)', in *Women. The Art of Power. Three Women from the House of Habsburg*, ed. by Sabine Haag, Dagmar Eichberger and Annemarie Jordan Gschwend (Wien: KHM, 2018), pp. 51-63; see also Jordan Gschwend, Annemarie, Fernando Pereira, and Maria Gamito, eds, *On Portraiture. Theory, practice and fiction. From Francisco de Holanda to Susan Sontag/ O Retrato. Teoria, prática e ficção. De Francisco de Holanda a Susan Sonntag* (Lisbon: Universidade de Lisboa, 2022), online publication http://hdl.handle.net/10451/54999
56 Twomey, 'Juana of Castile's Book of Hours'; https://www.mdpi.com/2077-1444/11/4/201.

1.8 Southern Netherlandish, *Book of Hours of Joanna of Castile*, fol. 287v: *Virgin and Child*, fol. 288r: *Joanna kneeling at her prie-dieu with St John the Evangelist*, 110 × 80 mm, 1496, London, British Library, ms Add 18852

Joanna meditates on the image of Mary depicted as a mother nursing her new-born child. The model for this illumination was a prototype developed by the Brussels city painter Rogier van der Weyden that was copied many times by his workshop.[57] This cult image might well have had a special meaning for the young princess.

Joanna's first stay in the Netherlands (1496-1501) was marked by a time of cultural exploration and gave her the opportunity to familiarize herself with the Burgundian lifestyle that was entirely different to her upbringing at the Spanish court. The Berlin festival booklet allows us to accompany Joanna part of the way on this exciting journey.

---

57 The iconography of the miniature (fol. 287ᵛ) comes closest to the version in Tournai, which is unfortunately very damaged: Musée des Beaux-Arts, Rogier van der Weyden, *Virgin and Child*, oil on oak, 36 × 27 cm, *c.* 1450-60; better preserved is a version in the Chicago Art Institute: Rogier van der Weyden (workshop), *Virgin and Child*, oil on wood, 38.4 × 28.3 cm, *c.* 1460, https://www.artic.edu/artworks/16303/virgin-and-child.

RAYMOND FAGEL

Joanna of Castile's first residence in the Low Countries (1496-1501)

The Transformation of a Trastámara Princess

▼ **ABSTRACT** Between 1496 and 1501, the young Trastámara princess Joanna of Castile, engaged to the Burgundian Duke Philip the Fair, would transform into the future heir of the Spanish realms and also became a mother of three children. This first residence of Joanna in the Low Countries has so far remained in the shadow of her famous later years, including the tragic death of Philip on 25 September 1506 in Burgos and her long confinement in Tordesillas until her death on 12 April 1555. During this first period in the Low Countries there were enough acute problems for the princess to cope with in her new environment: her specific upbringing and existing cultural differences, her position within the marriage, the difficulties regarding her household, her role as a young mother, and above all the political intrigues surrounding her, especially when it became clear that she would be the next heir to the Spanish crowns.

▼ **KEYWORDS** Marriage, Philip the Fair, Royal entries, Joanna of Castile, Court, Queenship, Brussels

Introduction

Between 1496 and 1501, the young Trastámara princess Joanna of Castile, engaged to the Burgundian Duke Philip the Fair, would transform into the future heir of the Spanish realms and a mother of three children as well. As from the early age of sixteen, she was to reside in a hitherto unknown country, in which she was most likely to live for the remainder of her life. Though history would prove this assumption wrong in her particular case, married princesses generally never returned home, like it happened with her sister Catalina (Catherine of Aragon), betrothed to successively the Princes Arthur and Henry VIII of England. Joanna's prospects in life in 1496 do not resemble at all the turbulent future that awaited her.

The first residence of Joanna in the Low Countries has remained in the shadow of her famous later years, including the tragic death of Philip on 25 September 1506 in Burgos and her long confinement in Tordesillas until her death on 12 April 1555. This focus on the later phase of her life also includes the debate on her mental health, as there is no real proof of any serious mental problems related to Joanna during this first residence in the Low Countries.[1] There were enough actual problems to cope with for the princess in her new environment: her specific upbringing and existing cultural differences, her position within the marriage, the difficulties regarding her household, her role as a young mother, and above all the political intrigues surrounding her, especially when it became clear that she would become the next heir to the Spanish crowns. Though her mother Queen Isabella of Castile had set the example, early modern ruling queenships were very rare and considered to be highly problematic.[2]

The Arrival in Zeeland of a Spanish Princess

Joanna travelled to the Low Countries on an impressive armada of some twenty ships that, combined with a large number of merchant vessels, would reach up to a fleet of more than a hundred larger and smaller ships (Fig. 2.1). They left the port of Laredo on the Cantabrian coast on 22 August 1496. After storms had forced the fleet to look for protection in an English port, another disaster occurred when one of the two Genoese carracks – by far the largest ships in the fleet – stranded on the famous Flemish sandbanks. Though part of the cargo could be saved, a great deal of Joanna's personal belongings was lost at sea, along with the goods of many members of her court.[3]

Joanna disembarked in the important port of Arnemuiden on the island of Walcheren in the County of Zeeland on 10 September. Both the ships' crew and the soldiers on board of the armada would suffer severe losses during the following winter residence on the island of Walcheren, when cold weather and disease struck them mercilessly. Following the chronicles, the number of casualties rose as high as 10,000. For example, a mass grave of some 200 men was made at the Franciscan monastery in Middelburg and the clerics in Zeeland even refused to bury the unfortunate Spaniards in sacred earth if they were not paid for it accordingly.[4]

---

1   Zalama, Miguel Ángel, *Vida cotidiana y arte en el palacio de la reina Juana I en Tordesillas* (Valladolid: Universidad de Valladolid, 2003) pp. 30-35.
2   Duindam, Jeroen, *Dynasties. A Global History of Power, 1300-1800* (Cambridge: Cambridge University Press, 2016), p. 90.
3   Ladero Quesada, Miguel Ángel, *La Armada de Flandes. Un episodio en la política naval de los Reyes Católicos (1496-1497)* (Madrid: Real Academia de la Historia, 2003); Ladero Quesada, Miguel Ángel, 'Doña Juana, infanta e princesa', in *Doña Juana, reina de Castilla* (Madrid: Real Academia de la Historia, 2006), pp. 27-28; Padilla, Lorenzo de, *Crónica de Felipe I, llamado el Hermoso*, Colección de Documentos inéditos para la Historia de España, VIII (Madrid: La Viuda de Calero) p. 38.
4   Ladero Quesada, *Armada*; Unger, Willem Sybrand, *Bronnen tot de geschiedenis van Middelburg in den landsheerlijken tijd*, 3 vols (The Hague: Unger, 1923-1931), I, n. 772; Molinet, Jean, *Chroniques* (1474-1506),

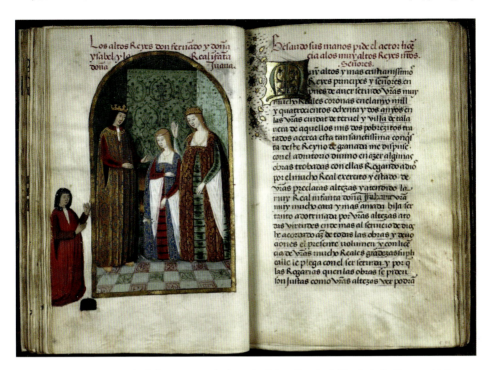

2.1 Pedro Marcuello, *Rimado de la Conquista de Granada*, fols 30ᵛ and 31ʳ: *The Catholic Kings and Infanta Joanna*, tempera on parchment, 21,5 × 14,5 cm, *c.* 1482-1502, Chantilly, Bibliothèque, Musée Condé, ms 604 (1339) © Musée Condé

A third setback was the fact that her future husband, eighteen-year-old Philip the Fair, was not in Zeeland to receive Joanna, as he was delayed from his journey to the Holy Roman Empire. It remains to be seen whether this *faux pas* of the duke was intentional or not, but at least some of his close advisors were not happy with Emperor Maximilian's choice of bride.[5] Only doña Marina Manuel, married to Burgundian nobleman Balduin of Burgundy, had travelled to Zeeland in order to welcome the princess.[6] They continued their journey to the nearby city of Bergen op Zoom in the Duchy of Brabant, where she was received by nobleman John of Bergen, first chamberlain to Philip the Fair, but somebody who favoured the Spanish match. Joanna took his recent born daughter to the font.[7] Maybe already at that point the young

---

ed. by Georges Doutrepont, and Omer Jodogne, 3 vols (Académie royale de Belgique) II (1488-1506) 1935, p. 431.

5 Aram, Bethany, *La reina Juana. Gobierno, piedad y dinastía* (Madrid: Marcial Pons, 2016), p. 34; Fleming, Gillian B., *Juana I and the Struggle for Power in an Age of Transition, 1504-1521* (online published doctoral thesis, London, School of Economics 2011) http://etheses.lse.ac.uk/234/, p. 64.

6 Cauchies, Jean-Marie, 'Baudouin de Bourgogne (v. 1446-1508), bâtard, militaire et diplomate. Une carrière exemplaire?', *Revue du Nord* 77 (1995), 257-81.

7 Aram, *Juana*, pp. 36-37.

princess started to understand that she and her followers were considered by some as an unwelcome rival court.[8]

The question is whether her upbringing and education had prepared her for a life amidst such political turmoil. Her mother, Queen Isabella of Castile, had victoriously survived a civil war, gaining a throne that almost certainly was not lawfully hers. Her father King Ferdinand of Aragon was another example of a prince well-versed in all arts necessary for the treacherous political arena of the time. All biographies on Joanna highlight her great knowledge of Latin, praised by the famous humanist Juan Luis Vives, and she was educated in the fine arts of music and literature, excelling in both dancing and playing the harpsichord. German humanist Hieronymus Münzer met her at court when she was fourteen years old and stated she was very learned for her age and sex. No wonder, as she had been taught Latin since the age of five. She also knew how to present herself, and dress to the occasion, being in possession of an impressive wardrobe.[9]

Information on her political training is much scarcer, but research on Isabella of Castile highlights the importance of the *Jardín de nobles doncellas* by Augustine friar Martín de Córdoba, written in 1468 for Isabella, but finally printed in November 1500, just a few months after Joanna had become the new heir to Castile. The author defends it is possible to have a queen regnant, if avoiding some specific female flaws, and working in close collaboration with her husband.[10] In any case, Joanna had not been educated to become a ruler in her own right, as both her brother Juan and her elder sister Isabel had better rights to inherit the thrones occupied by their parents.

The Wedding at Lier to a Burgundian Duke

When Joanna was presented to the people of Antwerp on 19 September, she had still not met any members of her new family. Burgundian chronicler Jean Molinet describes how this beautiful young lady *de beau port et gracieux maintieng*, was more richly dressed than anybody ever seen in the Burgundian lands. Accompanied by her richly dressed ladies, Joanna rode through the streets of this merchant capital on her mule *à la mode d'Espaigne*. All international merchant communities of the city participated in the event, including those of the Spanish nation, so she may have noticed the presence of her compatriots in this city. Her future sister-in-law,

---

8 Duindam, *Dynasties*, p. 101; Aram, Bethany, 'Voyages from Burgundy to Castile: Cultural Conflict and Dynastic Transitions', in *Early Modern Dynastic Marriages and Cultural Transfer*, ed. by Joan-Lluís Palos, and Magdalena S. Sánchez (Farnham: Ashgate, 2016), pp. 91-114 (95).

9 Münzer, Jerónimo, *Viaje por España y Portugal* (Madrid: Polifemo, 1991) p. 273; Fleming, *Juana*, p. 62; Aram, *Juana*, pp. 22-25; Zalama, *Vida*, p. 25; De Hemptinne, Thérèse, 'Jeanne de Castille, une reine entre folie et pouvoir, 1479-1555', in *Charles V in Context: the Making of a European Identity*, ed. by Marc Boone, and Marysa Demoor (Ghent: Ghent University, 2003), pp. 235-48, pp. 243-44; Tammen, 'Feast', p. 246.

10 Guardiola-Griffiths, Cristina, *Legitimizing the Queen: Propaganda and Ideology in the Reign of Isabel I of Castile* (Lewisburg: Bucknell University Press, 2011) p. 25; Lehfeldt, Elizabeth A., 'Ruling Sexuality: The Political Legitimacy of Isabel of Castile', *Renaissance Quarterly* 53 (2000), 31-56 (35-36); Weissberger, Barbara F., *Isabel Rules: Constructing Queenship, Wielding Power* (Minneapolis: University of Minnesota Press, 2004).

Margaret of Austria, arrived from Brussels, joined in Mechelen by Margaret of York, widow to Duke Charles the Bold, and in company of a large number of courtiers and other followers. When they arrived, Joanna was lying sick in bed in a very richly decorated room, but again the chronicler sees a cultural difference as she was lying in a low bed without bolster (*quevechure*), again *à la mode d'Espaigne*. These cultural differences also paid out when winter came in and many Spaniards from among her company died: *quand ilz avoyent une journée doulce, ilz demandoyent se l'yver estoit passé*. Contrary to the princess and her ladies, most Spaniards in her retinue were meagerly dressed. Molinet also reflects on a much more commonly acknowledged difference between Spaniards and Burgundians: the Spanish were seen as much more sober in their eating and drinking habits.[11]

Joanna would finally meet Philip (Fig. 2.2) in the Brabantine town of Lier on 17 October, with the official marriage taking place on 18 and 20 October. Molinet probably was not present at these events as he merely mentions the event taking place without offering more details than the name of Henry of Bergen as the bishop performing the religious ceremony. However, Molinet failed to mention that Joanna's first chaplain, Diego Ramírez de Villaescusa, had already blessed the marriage on 18 October, to be directly afterwards consummated by the young princely couple. After the marriage, many courtiers and followers from Spain left court to join Princess Margaret who was to travel to Spain in order to marry Don Juan. Joanna was subsequently taken to participate in several festive entries in the larger cities of Brabant, such as Mechelen and Brussels, the last entry on 9 December led to the very rich manuscript that is the centrepiece of this volume.[12]

Philip did not take part in these last events, as he escorted Margaret to the port of Flushing in Zeeland.[13] Together, the couple would participate in the official entry into the Flemish city of Ghent on 10 March 1497, followed by entries in Bruges and other cities. During this period Joanna also visited Franciscan convents in Brussels and Bruges, and participated in the Easter procession in Bruges.[14] The most important cities of Philip's states became thus acquainted with the new archduchess. However, the Coudenberg palace in Brussels would become Joanna's central residence in the following years. During 1497, Philip and Joanna remained together for most of the year, except when on 6 June the duke left Antwerp for a journey to the County of Holland. Joanna immediately departed for Brussels, where she would be reunited by

---

11 Fleming, *Juana*, pp. 64-66; Molinet, *Chroniques*, II, p. 429-31; Zalama, *Vida*, p. 30; Calderón Acedo, Mónica, 'La construcción de la imagen de la reina Juana I de Castilla a través de su guardarropa', in *Las mujeres y el universo de las artes*, ed. by Concha Lomba Serrano, Carmen Morte García, and Mónica Vázquez Astorga (Zaragoza: Institución Fernando el católico, 2020), pp. 225-35 (229); Mártir, Pedro [Pietro Martire d'Anghiera], *Epistolario*, ed. by José López de Toro, 4 vols (Madrid: Góngora, 1953-1957), Colección de Documentos Inéditos para la Historia de España, IX-XII, I, p. 331.
12 D'Hulst, Henri, *Le mariage de Philippe le Beau avec Jeanne de Castille, à Lierre le 20 octobre, 1496* (Antwerp: Lloyd, 1958); Molinet, *Chroniques*, II, p. 431; Aram, *Juana*, pp. 38-39; Cauchies, *Philippe*, pp. 50-51; Alcalá Ángel and Jacobo Sanz, *Vida y muerte del príncipe Don Juan. Historia y literatura* (Valladolid: Junta de Castilla y León. Consejería de Cultura y Turismo 1998) p. 159.
13 De Boom, Ghislaine, *Marguérite d'Autriche* (Brussels: Renaissance du Livre, 1946) p. 18.
14 Aram, *Juana*, p. 40-41; Molinet, *Chroniques*, II, p. 437.

2.2 Master of the Magdalene legend, *Philip the Fair*, oil on wood, 24,5 × 15,5 cm, *c.* 1493, 's-Heerenberg, Collection Huis Bergh, inv. No. 740 © Huis Bergh

her husband around the beginning of August.[15] In years that followed, Philip must have been away from home often, leaving Joanna behind at the Brussels palace. In Molinet's chronicle, Joanna is only mentioned once when she accompanied Margaret of Austria – who was leaving for her marriage to Philibert of Savoy – until half a mile outside of Brussels. Especially painful must have been the fact that she was not allowed to accompany her husband when he was meeting with the English King and Queen in 1500, refusing her a chance to meet her sister Catalina.[16]

Besides the apparent physical attraction between Joanna and Philip, there are hardly any direct sources on their personal relationship and much of what has been written on the subject is influenced by the debate on the mental state of the princess.

---

15 Aram, *Reina*, pp. 331-37; Fagel, Raymond, 'Juana de Castilla y los Países Bajos. La historiografía neerlandesa sobre la reina', in *Juana I de Castilla, 1504-1555. De su reclusión en Tordesillas al olvido de la historia*, ed. by Miguel Ángel Zalama (Valladolid: Ayuntamiento de Tordesillas, 2006), pp. 87-106 (95); Gachard, Louis Prosper, *Collection des voyages des souverains des Pays-Bas*, I, (Brussels: Hayez, 1876), pp. 115-20.

16 Molinet, *Chroniques*, II, pp. 462, 472-76, 489; Cauchies, *Philippe*, p. 109. According to Padilla, 'Crónica', p. 58, Juana was present at the meeting.

Table 1. Itinerary of Joanna of Castile, 10 September 1496 – 16 November 1501, based on ARAM, *Reina*, p. 331-37.

LOCALITIES	DAYS	PERCENTAGE
Brussels	1.050	55.1
Ghent	202	10.6
Bruges	190	10.0
Zeeland	35	1.8
Antwerp	25	1.3
Lier	14	0.7
Mechelen	6	0.3
Bergen op Zoom	6	0.3
Others	11	0.5
Unknown	366	19.2
Total	1.905	100.0

However, we can reconstruct the way Joanna was treated by her husband and his councillors and courtiers, without deciding on the personal role played by the young duke. Most authors emphasize the fact that Philip was heavily influenced by his advisors, earning him the nickname of *croit-conseil* by the Burgundian courtier and former preceptor of Philip, Olivier de la Marche, freely translated by Geoffrey Parker as 'Philip-believe-what-you're-told'.[17]

Court Life in Brussels

Joanna had arrived in the Low Countries with a large number of courtiers and followers. Bethany Aram counted ninety-eight Spanish men and eleven Spanish women as members of her household at her arrival (Fig. 2.3).[18] Many of them would return to Spain with the fleet of Princess Margaret, in February, and others went home because they considered life in the Low Countries too expensive. To this, her tutor Andrés de Miranda added 'the court's perilous moral atmosphere'. By March 1497, eighty Spanish men had already left Joanna's service. Furthermore, Joanna did not receive the money promised in the marriage contract to retain her own household.[19] She was excluded from all financial affairs, which was another reason for Spanish courtiers not to remain in the Low Countries.

---

17 Parker, Geoffrey, *Emperor. A New Life of Charles V* (New Haven: Yale University Press, 2019), p. 8.
18 Ladero Quesada, 'Doña Juana', p. 30; Padilla, 'Crónica', p. 35-37; Aram, 'Casa', p. 101; Aram, *Juana*, p. 41.
19 It had been stipulated that the Catholic Kings would provide Margaret annually with 20,000 escudos in Spain, while Philip would hand over the same amount to Juana; Aram, *Juana*, p. 47.

2.3 Master of the Joseph Sequence, *Joanna of Castile*, oil on wood, 34,7 × 22,4 cm, 1501-1510, Valladolid, Museo Nacional de Escultura, CE 2684. Photo: Javier Muñoz y Paz Pastor © Museo Nacional de Escultura

Telling is the story of lady Beatriz de Bobadilla, whose family found her a husband in Spain so she could return home. Philip was furious about this move, as it seemed that there were no good noblemen in the Low Countries to marry her Spanish ladies-in-waiting and that he had no money to pay for their weddings, shaming in this way his honour.[20]

The return of the Spanish courtiers opened the way for new Burgundian members of her court and it seems clear this was an intentional policy of the duke and his councillors. Isabella of Castile was aware of it and sent Pedro Ruiz de la Mota to prevent it from taking place and procure the payment of the promised 20,000 escudos a year for Joanna's household expenses. However, as Philip kept controlling all payments, some of the Spanish courtiers started to work directly for him, like treasurer Martín de Moxica and herald Miguel Franco ('Granada'). Even after official complaints had been filed, Philip would never give Joanna more than pocket money and personal gifts of jewellery and other works of art. This policy of incapacitating Joanna cannot simply be related to a kind of masculine Burgundian culture, as previous duchesses had effectively possessed control over their own income.[21]

When in August 1500 the newly arrived ambassador Fuensalida asked her why she could not have a larger part in the governance of her own 'estate and household', she responded it was because of the influence of councillor François de Busleyden on the duke. She told him Philip listened to her when they were alone, 'because she knows he loves her', but then afterwards he informed everybody, including Busleyden. For this reason she preferred not to talk about the matter anymore.[22] Another pro-French councillor, Philibert de Veyré, even forbade the Spaniards at court to speak to Joanna in Spanish, 'and if they would do so, they could consider themselves fired'.[23] In 1501, a completely new court ordinance was issued in which of 144 members only 29 may have been of Spanish origin, and all the important functions were firmly in the hands of Burgundian noblemen.[24]

A royal Birth in Ghent

Joanna would give birth to three children during her first residence in the Low Countries: Leonor was born in Brussels on 15 November 1498, Charles on 24 February 1500 in Ghent, and Isabella again in Brussels on 27 July 1501 (Fig. 2.4). This implies

---

20 Aram, *Juana*, pp. 42-45; Gómez de Fuensalida, *Correspondencia*, pp. 143-44.
21 Schnerb, Bertrand, 'Présence et influence des femmes à la cour de Bourgogne: Quelques réflexions historiographiques', in *Women at the Burgundian Court: Presence and Influence*, ed. by Dagmar Eichberger, Anne-Marie Legaré, and Wim Hüsken (Turnhout: Brepols, 2010), p. 6-7; Blockmans, Wim, 'Diplomatie van vrouwen', in *Dames met klasse. Margareta van York, Margareta van Oostenrijk*, ed. by Dagmar Eichberger (Leuven: Davidsfonds, 2005), pp. 97-101; Aram, *Juana*, p. 47.
22 'Porque conoce que la ama'. Aram, *Juana*, pp. 41-50; Gómez de Fuensalida, *Correspondencia*, p. 139; Suárez Fernández, *Política*, V, 352.
23 'y que sy la hablase, que se tuviese por despedydo'. Cauchies, 'Dans les allées'; Gómez de Fuensalida, *Correspondencia*, p. 153.
24 Aram, *Juana*, p. 45; Reynebeau. 'Hofordonnantie'.

2.4 Master of the Saint George Legend, *Charles as a two-year-old Child with his two Sisters, Eleonor (1498-1558) and Isabel (1501-1525)*, oil on wood, each panel: 31,5 × 14 cm, Vienna, Kunsthistorisches Museum, inv. no. 4452 © Wikimedia Commons – public domain

that between mid-February 1498 and her departure in November 1501, Joanna was pregnant for sixty percent of this entire period. As such, she performed perfectly well regarding the continuation of the dynasty. There exists a well-known saying that though she never actually ruled herself, she became the mother of two emperors and four queens.

Molinet reports that Leonor was born at two o'clock in the morning and he dedicates a large paragraph to the event. Emperor Maximilian had even arrived in the vicinity of Brussels, and *couroit la voix*, that he would baptise the child. He told the Spanish ambassadors that he was very happy about his daughter-in-law.[25] Molinet offers an extensive description of all festivities that were taking place in Brussels and for visitors a wonderfully decorated room was prepared, where Joanna may have been present. She was certainly present at a tournament in which Philip himself participated. A Spanish letter informs on the event, describing that after Philip had broken two lances, Joanna sent him a letter begging to stop participating in the tournament. At the baptism, the child was carried by Margaret of York. However, Maximilian did not appear at the religious ceremony and sent his representative, the

---

25 Gómez de Fuensalida, Gutierre, *Correspondencia, embajador en Alemania, Flandes e Inglaterra (1496-1509)*, ed. by Duque de Berwick y Alba (Madrid: Legare, 1907), p. 107. Mártir, *Epistolario*, I, p. 339.

Marquis of Baden. According to Bethany Aram, the Emperor was disappointed the first-born child was not a son but merely a daughter.[26]

Joanna's pregnancy with Charles may have been quite complicated, as in September 1499 a specific midwife from Lille had to come to court, and later a ring that supposedly brought 'solace to women in labour' was brought in from a convent in the vicinity of Lille.[27] Joanna had to travel to Ghent for the birth of her child, as it was considered politically important that the child was born in the Flemish city of Ghent. Two new carriages were made especially for the trip from Brussels. The celebrations over the birth of a son were much more impressive than those related to Leonor. However, it is difficult to know how much of this Joanna was able to witness, as Molinet's detailed description does not mention her. Especially since after returning to Brussels, Joanna fell seriously ill and was treated 'for forty-nine days continuously' by Philip's court physician and other doctors.[28]

The birth of Isabella on 27 July 1501 has left much less impression, and is mostly remembered for the fact that Joanna's pregnancy postponed the journey to Spain. Ambassador Fuensalida described how the princess had to hurry to reach Brussels before entering in labour, as the city had paid for the new child to be born within their walls.[29] Though as at most royal courts, taking care of small children was mainly an affair of the servants, it seems that Joanna could often be found in their vicinity: 'accounts for her hôtel between 1497-1501 show her with her children constantly'. Nevertheless, Joanna did again not succeed in influencing the choice of courtiers and servants that were to take care of her children. In October 1501 she would have to leave them behind in order to travel to Spain.[30]

Prospects of a Journey to Castile

The Catholic Kings never intended Joanna to inherit their realms. At first, after the unfortunate death of Don Juan on 4 October 1497, her sister Isabella, married to Portuguese King Manuel I, became the new heir to Castile. When she died during childbirth on 23 August 1498, there was only the new-born prince by the name of Miguel left, heir to all the Iberian realms, with the exception of Navarre. Chronicler Jerónimo Zurita writes that already after Don Juan's death, Philip had started to see himself as the new heir to Castile, but further documentary proof of these clearly

---

26 Molinet, *Chroniques*, II, pp. 450-52; Aram, *Juana*, p. 52; Domínguez Casas, Rafael, *Arte y etiqueta de los Reyes Católicos. Artistas, residencias, jardines y bosques* (Madrid: Alpuerto, 1993), pp. 628-29; De Boom, Ghislaine, *Eléonore, reine de France* (Brussels: Charles Dessart, 1943), pp. 12-15.
27 Parker, *Emperor*, p. 4.
28 Parker, *Emperor*, p. 8; Molinet, *Chroniques*, II, p. 468-71; Aram, *Juana*, p. 53.
29 Isabella's birthday is uncertain. I follow here Lobo Cabrera, Manuel, *Isabel de Austria, una reina sin ventura* (Madrid: Catédra, 2019), p. 22; Aram, *Juana*, pp. 55-56; Gómez de Fuensalida, *Correspondencia*, p. 187-88.
30 Fleming, *Juana*, p. 71, based on: Archives Départementales du Nord, B 3457 (1499-1500) – B. 3459 (1501); Aram, *Juana*, pp. 56-57; Fagel, Raymond, 'Charles Quint comme "Roi Catholique": les nominations d'évêques originaires des Pays-Bas en Espagne, 1516-1555' 38 (1998), *Publication du centre européen d'études bourguignonnes (XIVe-XVIe s.)* 38 (1998), 207-27, 8-9.

overhasty pretentions is lacking.³¹ After Miguel's death on 20 July 1500, Joanna effectively became the new heir to all Castilian realms. In his letter of condolence to the Catholic Kings, Philip directly undersigned with 'I the prince' (*Yo el Príncipe*), demonstrating his position as heir to Castile. Joanna would do the same, changing from signing as the archduchess, to signing as *Yo la Princesa*.³² All eyes in Spain were now directed towards the Burgundian court.

As from the start of his rule in 1494, Philip and his councillors tried to follow an independent policy, balancing Habsburg family interest with a peaceful diplomacy regarding France. The dynastic connection with the Catholic Kings created a further obstacle to the pro-French councillors and advisors around the duke.³³ Clearly the most important figure at court was the already mentioned, François de Busleyden, a nobleman from the Duchy of Luxembourg, preceptor of Philip and Archbishop of Besançon as from 1498. When ambassador Fuensalida arrived in Brussels in August 1500, Joanna immediately informed him on Busleyden's influence over the duke: 'It is he who governs this ship, and nothing is done that he has not ordered'. According to Joanna he could not be trusted, as 'he gave her many words... but he did not do anything... Everything he said was false'. The ambassador and the princess decided to try and buy Busleyden's loyalty. Some five months later, in February 1501, they were still following the same policy. Joanna now described Busleyden as 'a man who is never satisfied and always wants more'.³⁴

In March, Philip's pro-French policy led to the sending of an embassy to arrange a marriage between young Charles and the French princess Claude. Joanna refused to sign the requested document, and the Spanish ambassador agreed that nobody should do anything before informing the Catholic Kings, as the young prince would become King in Castile and Aragon. Philip was very angry at his wife and told her that he did not really need her signature.³⁵

In June, Fuensalida had an extensive conversation with Busleyden after he returned from Spain: 'He says wonders, showing himself as a true Castilian and as a servant of your highnesses [the Catholic Kings], that he gives envy to those who hear him'. Their plan seemed to have worked, as Busleyden now told Fuensalida he wanted to serve Joanna: 'and not in the governance of her household, or in that of her estate, nor in anything else, will there be done anything she does not order and everything

---

31 Alcalá, Ángel, and Jacobo Sanz, *Vida y muerte del príncipe Don Juan. Historia y literatura* (Valladolid: Junta de Castilla y León. Consejería de Cultura y Turismo 1998), pp. 189-90; Zurita, Jerónimo, *Historia del Rey don Fernando el Católico. De las empresas y liga de Italia*, ed. by José Javier Iso, 4 vols (Zaragoza: Fundación Fernando el Católico, 2005) book III, chapter 20.

32 Cauchies, *Philippe*, p. 131; Aram, 'Juana "the Mad's" signature', p. 334.

33 Fagel, Raymond, 'De wereld van Filips de Schone. De Europese politiek rond 1500', in *Filips de Schone, De schoonheid en de waanzin*, ed. by Paul Vandenbroeck and Miguel Ángel Zalama (Bruges: Stad Brugge, 2006), pp. 51-68 (57).

34 'es el que goviverna esta nao, y no se haze otra cosa syno lo quel hordena'; 'le dava muchas palabras, mas que no avia en el obras... todo lo que le dezia hera con falsedad'; 'un onbre que nunca se contenta y syenpre quiere mas'. Cools, Hans, *Mannen met macht. Edellieden en de moderne staat in de Bourgondisch-Habsburgse landen, 1475-1530* (Zutphen: Walburg, 2001), pp. 182-83; Gómez de Fuensalida, *Correspondencia*, pp. 138-40, 175-76; Aram, *Juana*, p. 47.

35 Gómez de Fuensalida, *Correspondencia*, p. 176.

will be done according to her wishes'.³⁶ It seemed too good to be true, and indeed he does not seem to have been entirely honest. The Catholic Kings not only paid him a pension during these years, but on 26 November 1501 they also nominated him to the episcopal see of Coria.³⁷

Fuensalida informed his sovereigns in September 1501 that the French king offered the duke to travel to Spain through France, instead of by sea with the ships the Catholic Kings had sent to the Low Countries. This was yet another insult to the Spanish sovereigns, refusing their ships and travelling through the lands of their enemy. In this last letter from the ambassador before departure, he still was unsure about the intentions of the Burgundians. Some say they were leaving by the end of October, others by the end of November. He had his doubts if they would ever take 'the road to Spain, as they have less desire to go there than to go to hell'.³⁸

Finally, Philip and Joanna would leave Brussels on 4 November in the direction of the French border, with among the court train François de Busleyden and John of Bergen. The first residence of Princess Joanna in the Low Countries was coming to an end. Two days later, they were received in Mons in Hainault, and those from the city gave her *deux pots d'argent dorés et une coupe plaine de florins d'or*.³⁹ Did they know she had turned twenty-two that same day? Unexpectedly, Joanna now returned home to her parents in Spain, as the new heir to the throne, with an enlarged household and court, and as a mother of three. It had been hard and difficult years in the Low Countries, maybe not like an inferno, but certainly nothing like paradise.

---

36 'Dize maravillas; muestrase tan castellano y tan servidor de vuestras altezas, que nos pone enbidia a los que lo oymos'; 'y que ni en governación de la casa, ni del estado, ni de otra ninguna cosa no se haria mas de lo que mandase y como lo mandase'. Gómez de Fuensalida, *Correspondencia*, p. 188; Mártir, *Epistolario*, I, p. 425, 428.
37 Fagel, 'Charles Quint', p. 219; Aram, 'Voyages', pp. 103-04. Rumours involve also the Bishopric of Segovia. Porras Gil, *De Bruselas*, p. 446. Busleyden died in Toledo on 23 August, 1502.
38 'el camino para yr a España, ni lo an mas gana quel yr al ynfierno'. Gómez de Fuensalida, *Correspondencia*, pp. 181, 192; Cauchies, Jean-Marie, '¡No tyenen más voluntad de yr a España que de yr al infierno! Los consejeros flamencos de Felipe el Hermoso y del joven Carlos V frente a la herencia española', in *La monarquía de las naciones. Patria, nación y naturaleza en la monarquía de España*, ed. by Antonio Álvarez-Ossorio Alvariño & Bernardo J. García García (Madrid: Fundación Carlos de Amberes, 2004), pp. 121-30 (121); Fagel, Raymond, 'De Spaanse zomerkoning. Filips de schone als koning van Castilië', in *Filips de Schone, een vergeten vorst? 1478-1506*, ed. by Raymond Fagel, Jac Geurts, and Michael Limberger (Maastricht: Shaker, 2008), pp. 101-33 (103-04); Lalaing, Antoine de, 'Relation du premier voyage de Philippe le Beau en Espagne, en 1501', in *Collection des voyages des souverains des Pays-Bas*, ed. Louis Prosper Gachard (Brussels: Hayez, 1876), pp. 121-385; Lalaing, 'Voyage', p. 125.
39 Molinet, *Chroniques*, vol. II, pp. 498-99; Lalaing, 'Voyage', p. 129.

ANNEMARIE JORDAN GSCHWEND

Joanna, Infanta of Castile and Habsburg Archduchess

Recreating a lost Wardrobe and Trousseau in 1496

▼ **ABSTRACT** In less than six months, Queen Isabella I of Castile curated and organised a magnificent trousseau for her daughter, Joanna, the bride of the Habsburg Archduke Philip the Fair, which cost the Spanish crown over 50,000 ducats. Joanna departed for the Netherlands in August 1496 with a cargo laden with expensive clothes cut from Italian and Spanish textiles, furs, representative jewellery and silver-gilt plate for her chapel and table. Queen Isabella intended Joanna's bridal wardrobe to impress the Habsburg-Burgundian court with the brilliance and splendour of the court of the Catholic Kings. The carrack with the bulk of the princess's belongings sank off Zeeland's coast just before she landed with her entourage. Published documents in the Archivo General de Simancas help reconstruct Joanna's lost-at-sea trousseau. Despite her losses, Joanna deployed sartorial strategies to fashion herself as a striking Spanish princess and Duchess of Brabant for her royal entries (*joyeuses entrées*) into Antwerp and Brussels in 1496.

▼ **KEYWORDS** Catholic Kings, Isabella I of Castile, Joanna I of Castile, Philip the Fair, Burgundy, Habsburg, marriage, jewels, textiles, dowry, trousseau, royal entries, *joyeuse entrée*.

Ground Zero: Laredo-Middelburg

'At midnight on 22 August 1496, a fleet of some 130 ships set sail from Laredo (Cantabria) under the command of Fadrique Enríquez, admiral of Castile. Bound for the Low Countries, the fleet had at its core an armada of two huge carracks from Genoa, fifteen *naos*, five caravels and twenty swift pinnaces. In its protective shadow, a number of merchant vessels, linked to the wool trade, were expected to offer auxiliary

3.1 Workshop of the Master of the Legend of Mary Magdalene, *Philip the Fair*, oil on wood, 42 × 27 cm, c. 1495, Paris, Musée du Louvre, photo © RMN-Grand Palais (Musée du Louvre) / Gérard Blot

firepower if needed'.[1] The journey was expected to be dangerous due to this fleet's late departure. In addition to the danger of French pirates, Atlantic currents and storms threatened the safe travel of Joanna, Infanta of Castile and Archduchess of Austria, bound for the Burgundian-Habsburg court. Since childhood, Joanna had been betrothed to Archduke Philip, son of Mary of Burgundy and Maximilian I, King of the Romans and later Holy Roman Emperor, who is depicted in a little-known panel portrait from the workshop of the Master of the Legend of Mary Magdalene, around the time they were wed (Fig. 3.1).[2] Their marriage was finally celebrated by proxy in Malines/Mechelen on 5 November 1495.

The marriage contract was then ratified by Infanta Joanna on 3 January 1496.[3] Her mother, Queen Isabella I of Castile, set her excellent operational skills into motion from this date until Joanna's departure in mid-August. With able members of her household to assist her, such as her trusted treasurer Gonzalo de Baeza, they assembled the Infanta's trousseau in the record time of six months.[4] The expected storms did assail the Spanish fleet on 31 August and forced

---

1 Translations below by the author. Quoted from Fleming, Gillian, *Juana I. Legitimacy and Conflict in Sixteenth-Century Castile* (Cham, Switzerland: Palgrave, 2018), p. 15. I have consulted the Spanish edition of Aram, Bethany, *La Reina Juana. Gobierno, piedad y dinastía* (Madrid: Marcial Pons, 2016); Aram, Bethany, 'Voyages from Burgundy to Castile: Cultural Conflict and Dynastic Transitions, 1502-06', in *Early Modern Dynastic Marriages and Cultural Transfer*, ed. by Joan-Lluís Palos, and Magdalena S. Sánchez (Farnham: Ashgate, 2016), pp. 91-114. Aram was unaware that the correspondence sent by Ambassador Juan Alonso Gámiz from the Spanish court at Valladolid to the Habsburg court in Vienna, today in the Haus-, Hof- und Staatsarchiv in Vienna, had previously been published by Hans Voltelini in 'Urkunden und Regesten aus dem K. u. K. Haus-, Hof- und Staats-Archiv in Wien', *Jahrbuch der Kunsthistorischen Sammlungen des Allerhöchsten Kaiserhauses*, 11 (1890), pp. I-LXXXIII.
2 *Duke Philip the Fair of Burgundy (1478-1506)*, c. 1495, Paris, Musée du Louvre, inv. no. 2085; C 324. Available for online consultation: https://collections.louvre.fr/en/ark:/53355/cl010061597 (accessed 30 November 2022). I am grateful to Dagmar Eichberger for bringing this portrait and its updated attribution to my attention.
3 For the marriage contracts and capitulations, see Valladolid, Archivo General de Simancas, Patronato Real 56-1. For the marriage negotiations, consult the classic study by Rodríguez Villa, Antonio, *Doña Juana la Loca. Estudio histórico* (Madrid: Librería de M. Murillo, 1892), pp. 7-19.
4 Torre, Antonio de la and Francisco de la Torre, *Cuentas de Gonzalo de Baeza, tesorero de Isabel la Católica* (Madrid: CSIC, vol. 1, 1955), pp. 346-58.

the 130 ships to take refuge in Portland, England, for five days. Bad luck kept dogging Infanta Joanna and her impressive escort of 15,000 men. Shortly before her landing at Middelburg, one of the Genoese carracks carrying the bulk of her trousseau, wardrobe, plate, and the belongings and jewels of her court ladies sunk before the coast of Zeeland.

Joanna's magnificent trousseau, so carefully curated, acquired and gifted by her mother, targeted to impress the brilliant Burgundian-Habsburg court, vanished. Research on European court systems and women as consorts, regents and rulers in the last decade has shown that 'women marrying into foreign dynasties brought with them a dynastic capital made of status, wealth and material culture', which impacted the courts they married into.[5] Foreign princesses as brides enriched and transformed court cultures with their dowries and wardrobe. Isabella's dream to showcase Joanna as the wealthy, resplendent daughter of the Catholic Kings sank with that carrack.

First impressions count. Infanta Joanna sadly disembarked in Zeeland with few personal belongings, almost literally the clothes on her back. This fantastical woodcut by Leonhard Beck is supposed to depict Philip receiving his Spanish bride as she came ashore with her ship filled with her Spanish ladies.[6] Emperor Maximilian I commissioned this fictive meeting for his idealised autobiography, *Weisskunig*, a decade after his son died. It is an *apologia* as Philip never met Joanna on the beach, as shown here since he was far away from the Low Countries with his father in the Tyrol (Fig. 3.2).[7] For Joanna, the absent husband and the loss of her 'painstakingly gathered trousseau',[8] proved advantageous as she prepared for official encounters and princely celebrations along her bridal procession. Without her entire wardrobe, Joanna was forced to reinvent herself with the clothes and textiles she could salvage before making her entries (*joyeuse entrées*) into Antwerp and Brussels.

If an inventory of Infanta Joanna's belongings had been redacted before departing Queen Isabella's court, this document was also lost at sea. Despite the lack of official checklists or a proper inventory, surviving expense accounts in the *Archivo General de Simancas* in Valladolid can shed light on Joanna's lost-at-sea trousseau. I will therefore revisit documents published in 2003 to present an overview of the strategies deployed to organise Joanna's dowry and in which manner Queen Isabella hoped to market her daughter through her clothes, textiles, plate and jewellery. How did she intend

---

5 Calvi, Giulia, 'Introduction', *Moving Elites: Women and Cultural Transfers in the European Court System. Proceedings of an International Workshop (Florence, 12-13 December 2008)*, ed. by Giulia Calvi, and Isabelle Chabot (Florence: European University Institute, 2010), pp. 9-12.
6 See the contemporary account written by Lorenzo de Padilla for Emperor Charles V, entitled 'Crónica de Felipe I llamado El Hermoso, escrita por Don Lorenzo de Padilla y dirigida al Emperador Carlos V', in *Colección de documentos inéditos para la historia de España*, ed. by Miguel Salvá, and Pedro Sainz de Baranda (Madrid: Imprenta de la Viuda de Calero, vol. VII and VIII, 1846).
7 London, British Museum, Prints and Drawings, *Philip and his courtiers have come to meet Joanna, who has just stepped ashore from a boat filled with her female entourage*, c. 1514-1516, woodcut, 22.1 × 20 cm, inv. no. 1837,0616.301.
8 Fleming, *Juana I*, p. 21.

3.2 Leonard Beck, *Philip the Fair and his Courtiers come to meet Joanna when arriving in Zeeland*, woodcut, 22.1 × 20 cm, c. 1514-1516, London, British Museum, Prints and Drawings, inv. no. 1837,0616.301 © Trustees of the British Museum

Joanna to project power and magnificence at the court of Philp the Fair?[9] Being the most beautiful and the best dressed was one primary objective. Infanta Joanna's lavish but lost wardrobe was closely tied to her future political and public roles at the Netherlandish court.

---

9 The expenses incurred for Infanta Joanna's trousseau published by Ladero Quesada, Miguel Ángel, *La armada de Flandes. Un episodio en la política naval de los Reyes Católicos (1496-1497)* (Madrid: Real Academia de la Historia, 2003).

Infanta Joanna's marriage with Archduke Philip was considered 'the' wedding of the late fifteenth century. It united the ambitious Habsburg house with the crowns of Castile and Aragon in Spain and their overseas empire in the New World. Not long after Joanna's ill-fated journey and inauspicious arrival, beginning in 1498 with the birth of her first child, the offspring of Joanna and Philip – two sons and four daughters – were destined to become future kings, emperors, queens and regents. Each of them would rule kingdoms that stretched from Portugal and Spain as far north as Denmark and east as Buda (Hungary and Bohemia). Queen Isabella could not foresee that her second daughter, Joanna, would become the *mater familias* of a dynasty on the rise, which made its impact and mark upon early modern Europe.

This illuminated folio dating *c*. 1616, from the little-known *Traicté de l'antiquité et preeminence des maisons d'Habsbourg et d'Austrice*, spotlights Joanna and Philip as the power couple of the Habsburg house (Fig. 3.3).[10] They are portrayed, side by side, in the central medallion surmounted by their crowned coat of arms held by two cherubs above them – Habsburg to the left and Castile and Leon to the right. Philip and Joanna are further framed by a Renaissance architectural niche displaying the multiple coats of arms of their vast kingdoms, territories and cities under their rule, possessions representing the fortuitous union of their two houses in 1496. Although this folio dates just over a century after their wedding, this double portrait anchors Philip and Joanna as illustrious ancestors of the Habsburg family.[11] This treatise was executed for their successors; another archducal couple, Albert VII of Austria and Isabella Clara Eugenia, appointed governors of the Netherlands after 1598. Adrien Baltyn, the author and illuminator, wanted to drive home to his patrons their distinguished heritage and lineage but, more significantly, their immense dynastic inheritance. The same armorials and escutcheons referencing Joanna, Philip and their patrimony appear respectively in folios 60ʳ (Spain: Castile and Leon) and 61ʳ (Habsburg: Austria and Burgundy) of the 1496 *Festive Entry of Joanna of Castile into Brussels* (Berlin, ms 78 D5).

---

10 London, V&A Museum, National Art Library, *c*. 1616, manuscript, pigments, ink and gold on parchment, NAL Pressmark: KRP.C.61. Inscribed: *Philippus 1er. Roy D'Espagne, et Iohanne L'Infante Sa Femme*.

11 In this miniature, Joanna is imaged not as a Spanish princess but as a Duchess of Brabant, wearing a steeple headdress (the Burgundian *hennin*), as in a later portrait of Philip's mother, Mary of Burgundy, attributed to the Tyrolean Master H. A. in New York, The Metropolitan Museum of Art, 1528, oil on fir panel, 43.9 × 30.5 cm, Robert Lehman Collection, 1975, inv. no. 1975.1.137. Consult online: https://www.metmuseum.org/art/collection/search/459079 (accessed 30 November 2022).

3.3 Adrien Baltyn, *Traicté de l'antiquité et preeminence des maisons d'Habsbourg et d'Austrice: (detail) Philip the Fair and Joanna of Castile with their coats of arms*, gouache, ink and gold on parchment, c. 1616, London, V&A Museum, National Art Library, NAL Pressmark: KRP.C.61 © V&A Museum, National Art Library

Extravagance at All Costs. Fashioning Infanta Joanna

The accounts Ladero Quesada published confirm that Queen Isabella of Castile spent the incredible sum of 50,000 ducats for Joanna's trousseau.[12] 44.5 kilos of gold (22 carats) and 121 kilos of silver were deployed to fashion jewellery for Joanna's person, the necessary utensils for her table, and ornaments for private devotion in her chapel and oratory.[13] Few, if any, items from Queen Isabella's treasury appear to have been recycled. Eleven silversmiths based in Valladolid were ordered to create the required gilt-silver plate. Objects ranged from a cross, nef, lectern, incense burner, candlesticks, and salvers, among other liturgical items, to a sceptre, maces and a seal for letters; most of these were appointed with Joanna's archducal coat of arms (*las armas del archiduquesa*). The silversmith Gabriel fabricated seven gilt-silver

---

12 Due to inflation in the sixteenth century, one gold ducat had an approximate weight of 3.56 grams.
13 Tremlett, Giles, *Isabella of Castile: Europe's First Great Queen* (London: Bloomsbury, 2017), pp. 652-53, for his conversions: 95 pounds of gold and 256 pounds of silver.

shields (*escudos*) enamelled with the archducal arms to decorate Joanna's private and public spaces in the palaces she would reside in. The chapel silver alone filled two large leather coffers secured for transportation.

Gold coifs, collars, chains, necklaces, belts and bracelets were executed by Valladolid silversmiths active in Queen Isabella's service, among them Pedro de Oñate, the Portuguese Diego Fernández (Fernandes) and Pedro de Salamanca. The latter jewellery was executed in a late medieval, Gothic style, some pieces enamelled and decorated with tiny gold crowns, others with botanical motifs such as branches (*troncos*) or leaves (*follajes*).[14] Other jewellery referenced Joanna's husband Philip the Fair and the Burgundian-Valois court. Diego de Carmona fashioned a sizeable gold collar (carcanet), counting 236 pieces and tiny *fleurs-de-lys* pendants. Hernando de Ballesteros was paid 41,180 *maravedís* for a 23-carat gold belt of thirty-three links surmounted with the letter 'P' (for Philip). Ballesteros also devised large, medium and small gold plaquettes or ornaments decorated with 'P's, which could be applied and sewn onto Joanna's coifs, garments and headdresses.[15]

Before and after the *Reconquista*, Joanna's world intersected artistically with the pervasive Islamic arts and culture of *Al-Andalus*, the Muslim-ruled area of Iberia. Five centuries of Moorish rule impacted the interior and exterior appointment of royal palaces decorated with *mudéjar* woodwork, masonry, lattice stuccowork, and colourful ceramic tiles. At the same time, patios were ornamented with multiple fountains and planted with fragrant orange trees. Islamic culture penetrated many aspects of daily life and consumption at Isabella's court, which was transfixed by the foreign and the exotic. Joanna's favourite *mudéjar*-style bracelets (*axorcas*) were devised by a talented Muslim craftsman with compartments that could be secretly scented. Another exceptional gold *axorca* had light, movable units enclosing the mysteries of the Passion, tangible evidence of the cross-cultural transfers between Muslims and Christians, which exchanges permeated Joanna's ambience. 3,221,461 *maravedís* had been spent on the princess's gold and silver items.[16]

Linens, lingerie (*ropa blanca*), chemises and headgear (cauls, caps and veils), and other textiles for Joanna's person and her private chambers (*recamara*), such as twenty-six wall hangings (*reposteros*) embroidered with her coat of arms, leather hangings (*guadamecís*), bed covers (*colchas*), silk curtains and cushions were purchased for 2,133,584 *maravedís*. A staggering 3,635,920 *maravedís* was spent on 7,595 *varas* or 6,400 metres of luxury fabrics (velvets, brocades, silks and damask) for the Infanta, her ladies and the liveries of her large household.[17] Ninety-six mules were required to take Joanna's clothes and sundries to Laredo, the port of departure.

---

14 See the ground-breaking study of Isabelline jewellery in Muller, Priscilla, *Jewels in Spain, 1500-1800* (New York: The Hispanic Society of America, 1972), pp. 7-26.
15 Ladero Quesada, *La armada*, pp. 154-56.
16 Walsh, William Thomas, *Isabella of Spain* (London: Sheed & Ward, 1935), p. 475, calculated one *maravedí* to equal in 1929 twenty American cents. In the sixteenth century, one Spanish silver *real* equalled 34 *maravedís*.
17 Ladero Quesada, *La armada*, pp. 85-192, with names and complete lists; Zalama, Miguel Ángel, 'Las hijas de los Reyes Católicos. Magnificencia y patronazgo de cuatro reinas', *Las mujeres y el universo de las artes*, ed. by Concha Lomba Serrano, Carmen Morte García, and Mónica Vázquez Astorga (Saragossa: Diputación de Zaragoza |

Since childhood, Joanna had been taught domestic skills, such as embroidery, lace-making, needlepoint, sewing, spinning, and weaving. It is not surprising that Queen Isabella's lengthy shopping list also counted practical items necessary for running an elite female household: 200 thimbles, 10,000 sewing needles, 40,000 hairpins, and dozens of different varieties of combs made from wood and ivory. The olfactory component equally had not been forgotten, adding an exotic touch to Joanna's private *recamara*. Perfumes from Valencia encompassed amber, civet musk and benzoin, and aromatic waters (ginger, rose and orange blossom) needed to scent chests and caskets. Hundreds of cloth, leather or wooden crates, coffers and boxes were made to order for storing the Infanta's costly cargo.

Joanna's portable furniture encompassed dossels, folding chairs, wooden tables, side saddles, riding equipment (bridles, headstalls and stirrups) and *tablas de cabalgar* (mounting steps), made of wood with silver fittings and gilded hinges to help the Infanta and her ladies mount their steads.[18] Kitchen and chamber utensils, primarily made from copper, were manufactured by the Muslim Ali, a resident of Torrelaguna near Madrid.

The Infanta was an accomplished musician, music playing an all-encompassing role within her household and court. Her favourite instruments, lutes, a clavichord (a late medieval keyboard instrument) and a harpsichord, were placed in the care of her three lutists (*tañedores de vihuela*) and her harpsichordist (*clavizinbamo*) by the name of Barrionuevo. Before her departure, Joanna ensured her harpsichord and clavichord were repaired, finetuned and protected for travel by the Muslim Mohammed Moferrex ('a great Moorish master from Zaragoza').[19]

Presentation chests (*arcas de aparato*) covered in crimson cloth were gilded and painted with Joanna's coat of arms by a painter named Juan de Ávila together with his team.[20] A rare, impressive chest manufactured in Spain by an anonymous master between 1501 and 1514, has a front panel deeply carved with the coat of arms of Joanna and Philip. Castile is to the left, and the double-headed Habsburg eagle and rampant lion of Burgundy are to the right, revealing that marriage chests, such as this one, were elaborately conceived of for princesses and aristocratic ladies in late medieval Spain (Fig. 3.4).[21] The inside lid displays two portrait medallions of Philip and Joanna as King and Queen of Spain, replicating well-known portrayals of the

---

Institución 'Fernando el Católico', 2020), pp. 31-54 (with previous bibliography); Lomba Serrano, 'En torno a la formación del gusto artístico de la reina Juana I', Atalaya, 20 (2020) (online): https://doi.org/10.4000/atalaya.5136 (accessed 30 November 2022).

18 Anderson, Ruth, *Hispanic Costume, 1480-1530* (New York: The Hispanic Society of America, 1979), p. 134.
19 Tremlett, *Isabella*, p. 653.
20 Ladero Quesada, *La armada*, p. 148, no. 34.
21 Lima, Peru, Pedro de Osma Museum, wood, L: 116 cm, H: 71.5 cm. Inscribed: *DONA JOANNA ESPOSA DE 1514. FELIPE EL HERMOZO. REINA D'ESPANA 151*[5] and *DON FELIPE EL HERMOZO REY DE ESPANA*. Available for consultation online: http://balat.kikirpa.be/photo.php?path=B190853&objnr=40004462&lang=en-GB&nr=27#relatedphoto (accessed 30 November 2022).

3.4 Spanish, *Marriage Chest with the Coat of Arms and Portraits of Philip the Fair and Joanna I of Castile*, wood, L: 116 cm, H: 71. 5 cm, Lima, Peru, Pedro de Osma Museum. Courtesy of BALaT

archducal couple by the Isabelline court painter Michel Sittow or the Master of the Legend of Mary Magdalene.[22]

Lastly, Isabella ensured Joanna arrived at her new court with an essential part of her wedding bed, which she would use to procreate and give birth to Philip's heirs, a sumptuous silver-plated headboard lined with crimson velvet.

---

22 For a comparable portrait, see Valladolid, *Museo Nacional de Escultura*, oil on panel, 34,7 × 22, 4 cm, inv. CE 2684. Please see Fig. 2.3 in this volume.

Showing Off

Queen Isabella tapped into the international, widespread networks of the foreign mercantile community established in Spain to outfit Joanna according to her station, relying upon Florentine and Genoese factors and agents to procure splendid textiles required for her daughter's trousseau. Florentine gold and silk thread were purchased at the renowned trade fair in Medina del Campo. Isabella spent a fortune on premium brocades, silks, damasks and crimson velvets made in Florence and Genoa. To cite several of many expenditures: 100 *varas* (92 metres) of satin brocade purchased in Florence amounted to 1,614 ducats, later shipped to Spain via Genoa. Twenty-eight thousand *maravedís* were spent on two ladies' shirts embroidered with gold thread bought in Valladolid. 1,486,986 *maravedís* was paid out for Florentine double black velvet earmarked for the elegant liveries of Joanna's servants, especially her beloved musicians (*ministriles*), harpsichordist, and six trumpet players, whose horns were adorned with white and purple damask banners (Joanna's colours?), painted with the archducal coat of arms. In the accounts of the Queen's treasurer, Gonzalo de Baeza, notable entries for fur linings for Joanna's clothes and mantles appear in 1496: sable, squirrel, marten, rabbit and cat.[23]

For these Italian merchants closely allied with Isabella's court, preparing Joanna's trousseau was an investment on many fronts. They further banked on the Infanta's wedding in the Netherlands to account for additional gain and profit, explaining why two Genoese carracks sailed with her convoy from Laredo in August 1496. As seen above, one sunk with her belongings and trousseau before the coast of Zeeland.

Infanta Joanna was a highly educated, prized bride. Queen Isabella did not question the tremendous costs of outfitting her, the princess referenced in the published documents as her beloved daughter (*la archiduquesa mi muy cara y muy amada hija*). As Queen of Spain with a global overseas empire, Isabella wanted to ensure Joanna left Iberia with an impressive wardrobe worthy of her rank and superior status.[24] At the time of her marriage, the Catholic Kings regarded her not only as a Habsburg Archduchess but also expected her to become the future Holy Roman Empress. Therefore, Isabella kept a sharp, focused eye on her daughter's imminent political roles in the Netherlands. Isabella underscored her own rule with her sumptuous attire and jewels, the latter visual markers of her 'authority and power as reigning monarch in Castile'.[25]

---

23 Anderson, *Hispanic Costume*, p. 140. For furs, clothes and sumptuous textiles at Isabella's court see the classic study by Bernis, Carmen, *Trajes y Modas en la España de los Reyes Católicos I. Las Mujeres* (Madrid: CSIC, 1978), and Fernández de Pinedo, Nadia, and María Paz Moral, 'The Royal House of Isabel I of Castile (1492-1504): use of silk, wool and linen according to the accounts of Gonzalo de Baeza', *Conservar Patrimonio*, 31 (2019), pp. 53-44.

24 Belozerskaya, Marina, *Luxury arts of the Renaissance* (Los Angeles: J. Paul Getty Museum, 2005), p. 85: 'In the Renaissance, fabrics and cuts of dress, colours and embellishments proclaimed far more emphatically the wearer's social standing and corresponding privileges and rights'.

25 Marino, Nancy, 'La indumentaria de Isabel la Católica y la retórica visual del siglo XV', *Atalaya*, 13 (2013), online: https://doi.org/10.4000/atalaya.907 (accessed 30 November 2022).

Joanna's dazzling dress should spotlight her Spanish identity and heritage.[26] As Giles Tremlett aptly observed, 'Joanna was joining one of the most flamboyant courts in Europe and one that set fashions and standards of display for the rest of the continent'.[27] A lavish wardrobe would guarantee Joanna's place at the Burgundian court, allowing her to define herself through her clothes and representative jewels (see below).[28] For the consumer culture of the early modern period, clothing was a loaded signifier of status, carrying particular weight for monarchs, especially for queens.[29] In 1489, Henry VII's ambassador, the Anglo-Portuguese Roger Machado, reported back to the Tudor court with his impressions of Queen Isabella:

> The Queen arrived on a handsome mule, its harness studded with pearls and precious stones. Over her cloth-of-gold she had a velvet cape [*mantellyne*] worked all in lozenges, black or crimson, each one carrying a large pearl [*margaritte*] and with every *margaritte* a balas [spinel or ruby] of beechnut size. Her necklace was laden with gems. On her coif was a jewel estimated at 12,000 *ecus* – two balases the size of pigeon's eggs with a large pearl at the end of each.[30]

As the envoy stressed to the English monarch, the value of the Queen's clothes and ornaments worn that day could not be accurately judged. The courtly world, as Jane Burns noted, 'depended on material extravagance and opulence, reflecting a culture obsessed with self-display and ostentation as a form of self-definition among members of the ruling elite'.[31]

Since childhood, power dressing, that is, appearance and fashion, mattered to Joanna.[32] As a young girl, contemporaries noted the Infanta's extravagant tastes and expenditures. By 1488, her possessions (primarily clothes) required ten mules to carry her luggage from one royal palace to another. At the tender age of ten, royal accounts tallied up by Gonzalo Baeza document that the Infanta received a mule, complete with reins, stirrups, and saddle covered in silk and brocade and that these trimmings cost nearly as much as her dress.[33]

Joanna's favourite colours were crimson and scarlet, red dyes that were particularly expensive. The silks deployed for her dress accessories, such as hats and

---

26 Carney, Jo Eldridge, *Fairy Tale Queens. Representations of Early Modern Queenship* (New York: Palgrave Macmillan, 2012), pp. 117-45, at p. 145.
27 Tremlett, *Isabella of Castile*, p. 656.
28 For luxury dressing at the Burgundian court, Belozerskaya, *Luxury arts*, p. 85: 'The Burgundian dukes appeared at important diplomatic gatherings in clothes so thickly covered with gold embroidery and gems that observers could not discern the color of the cloth underneath and walked away all the more awed by the power of these rulers'. For fashion at Isabella's court, Gómez-Chacón, Diana, 'Vestir a una Reina. Moda y lujo en la corte castellana del siglo XV', *Coleccionismo, mecenazgo y mercado artístico: orbis terrarum*, ed. by Antonio Holguera Cabrera, Ester Prieto Ustio, and María Uriondo Lozano (Seville: Universidad de Sevilla, 2020), pp. 178-96.
29 Carney, *Fairy Tale Queens*, p. 118.
30 Anderson, *Hispanic Costume*, p. 136.
31 Burn, Jane, *Courtly Love Undressed: Reading through Clothes in Medieval French Culture* (Philadelphia, Pa., 2002), p. 26.
32 Zalama, Miguel Ángel, 'Oro, Perlas, Brocados… La Ostentación en el vestir en la Corte de los Reyes Católicos', *Revista de Estudios Colombinos*, 8 (June 2012), pp. 13-22.
33 Anderson, *Hispanic Costume*, p. 134.

3.5 *Silk Fragment with Lions and Pomegranates*, Granada, silk, lampas weave, 23.3 × 25.7 cm, late 15th century, New York, The Cloister Collection, acc. no. 2011.480 © The Metropolitan Museum of Art

body garments, were most likely coloured by the newly discovered cochineal, a dye obtained from an insect living on the prickly pear cactus (*Opuntia*) which abounded in the Spanish territories in Mexico and Central America. Joanna grew up exposed to the splendour and hybrid culture of her mother's court, where textiles and goods manufactured in Christian and Muslim Spain, Flemish tapestries and religious paintings imported from the Netherlands, and novel rarities from the Americas formed part of her daily life. As the ambassador Roger Machado observed, Queen Isabella was accustomed to displaying wealth and power and bent on Joanna making an impression on the European stage.[34]

Striking and unusual Moorish garments, such as *camisas moriscas* (shirts) and *sayos moriscos* (skirts), counted among the Infanta's belongings, added to impress because of their exotic decoration, embroidered Arabic letters, and strange cut.[35] This

---

34 Tremlett, *Isabella of Castile*, p. 653.
35 Ladero Quesada, *La armada*, p. 150.

3.6 Spanish, *Pair of chopines*, wood, leather, covered with green silk damask, H: 12.5 cm, London, c. 1580-1620, V&A Museum, acc. no. T.419&A-1913 © V&A Museum

silk fragment with lions and pomegranates dating to the late 15th century was woven in Granada, a Nasrid stronghold and centre of silk production in Andalusia, where Islam intersected with Europe (Fig. 3.5).[36] Before and after the conquest of Granada, these fabrics symbolised wealth and status. The crowned lions imply the defeat of the Nasrids by the Catholic Kings in 1492, reflecting the type of hybrid, precious textiles Isabella sought for her daughter.

The Queen permitted Joanna's four female slaves to join her daughter's retinue travelling to the Low Countries as a political statement and display of her power in Spain and in her overseas territories in the New World. These ladies had flamboyant apparel cut from dark green and purple cloth from Barcelona.[37] Black slaves were considered luxury servants. The Infanta's Muslim, West African, and Canary Island Guanche slaves certainly astounded even the surfeited Burgundian-Habsburg court with the global reach and trade empire of the Catholic Kings.

Joanna's trousseau included sixty-two pairs of clog-like shoes, covered in silk and decorated with gold bugles, purchased in Valencia. Chopines or *chapines*, platform shoes, mostly made of cork, were popularly worn in the fifteenth and sixteenth centuries to protect women's dresses from muddy streets. The height of the chopine

---

36 New York, The Cloisters Collection, The Metropolitan Museum of Art, late 15th century, Granada, Spain, silk, lampas weave, 23.3 × 25.7 cm, accession number: 2011.480.
37 In June 1492, 8,400 *maravedís* were spent on clothes for three female slaves in Infanta Joanna's household. Cf. Torre and Torre, *Cuentas*, II, p. 20; Ladero Quesada, *La armada*, p. 179.

3.7 German (Augsburg or Nuremberg), *Trachtenbuch (Códice de Trajes)*, fols 1ʳ-2ʳ: *Costumes of aristocratic Spanish Ladies*, black ink and watercolour on paper, 21 × 20 cm, c. 1530-1560, Madrid, Biblioteca Nacional de España, Res/285, © Biblioteca Nacional de España

came to reference the cultural and social standing of the wearer; the higher the chopine, the higher the status of the wearer. This pair of wood, cork and leather chopines made in Spain are covered in green damask (Fig. 3.6).[38] These were luxury shoes worn by Muslim and Christian women, signalling privilege and forcing ladies to walk at a slow, considered pace. The platform was a bonus, adding height and grandeur. At Philip the Fair's court, Joanna and her Spanish ladies must have towered over some of his courtiers.

These two folios, watercolours from a little-known *Trachtenbuch* (Costume Book) compiled by an anonymous German author from Augsburg or Nuremberg, provide a window into the past, giving modern viewers an idea of how aristocratic and patrician women in Spain, in the first half of the sixteenth century, dressed. They are clothed in hoop skirts or *verdugados* (made from pliable twigs) and long capes wearing chopines, similar to the Spanish attire Joanna and her ladies wore at the Burgundian-Habsburg court (Fig. 3.7).[39] The lady in the middle of fol. 2ʳ wears a red velvet dress (*saya*) on top of a turquoise *verdugado*, which flaunts skilful embroidery on the hem. Hairstyles had not changed much since 1496, with long tresses braided and covered with fabric, either a coif, gold nets (with or without precious stones and pearls) or cloth caps

---

38 London, V&A Museum, *Pair of Chopines*, Spain, c. 1580-1620, wood, leather, covered with green silk damask, H: 12.5 cm, accession number: T.419&A-1913. Also, Anderson, *Hispanic Costume*, pp. 229-35, at p. 231.

39 Madrid, Biblioteca Nacional de España, 21 × 20 cm, call number: Res/285. Inscribed in German: *In Spania die Edlen Iunckfrawen* / 'In Spain the Aristocratic Maidens' (left, fol. 1ᵛ) and *In Spania die Burgerin* / 'And in Spain the Burghers' (right, fol. 2ʳ). For more regarding this manuscript, consult Mezquita Mesa, Teresa, 'El Códice de Trajes de la Biblioteca Nacional de España', *Goya: Revista de Arte*, 346 (2014), pp. 16-41.

and hoods (braid-casings), known as *cofias de tranzado*.⁴⁰ The well-dressed lady on fol. 1ᵛ, to the left, is mounted on her mule with an elegant harness and trappings. She sits sidewise on a scissors chair (*angarillas*) secured over a packsaddle, like Infanta Joanna, who sat likewise on her mule equipped with gold tack and draped with cloth-of-gold for her 1496 Brussels entry (Fig. 3.10).⁴¹

Infanta Joanna's Jewels: State of the Question

What kind of representational jewellery did Joanna possess on the eve of her departure from Laredo in August 1496? From the published documents, it is challenging to ascertain which gems or jewels of exceptional worth Queen Isabella gifted her daughter. The nuptial agreements between the Catholic Kings and Maximilian I, King of the Romans in 1495 had settled upon Joanna not being endowed with a dowry, which would also have included valuable jewels.⁴² Before she departed from Spain, no inventory of pearls and precious gemstones was drawn up or has survived. What jewellery of value she did have is said to have sunk with one of the Genoese carracks. As seen below, the jewels 'so precious and valuable' the chronicler Jean Molinet observed Joanna wearing for her entry into Antwerp may well have been pieces which I posit were salvaged from the shipwreck.

To understand what jewels formed part of Joanna's trousseau, it is necessary to consult a later published inventory of her treasury redacted in 1509, after she permanently moved to Spain. That year she relocated to her last royal residence in Tordesillas with a chest full of jewels. These magnificent pieces reflect gifts from her mother, Queen Isabella, her husband, Philip the Fair, and her sister-in-law, Margaret of Austria. At the same time, others were acquired during her ten-year residency in the Netherlands.

This inventory documents one significant heirloom from Queen Isabella's treasury.⁴³ The grandiose *Collar de los Balajes* is the ruby necklace Isabella received as a wedding gift from her mother-in-law, Joanna Enríquez, when she married Ferdinand of Aragon in 1469.⁴⁴ Treasures such as these, when not pawned or sold, connected female members of illustrious royal families, passing down as cherished, venerated heirlooms from one generation to the next. Isabella's necklace comprised seven

---

40 Anderson, *Hispanic Costume*, pp. 163-67.
41 See the essay by Laura Weigert in this volume.
42 Anderson, *Hispanic Costume*, p. 140.
43 Arbeteta Mira, Leticia, 'Joyería española en tiempos de Carlos V', *El arte de la plata y de las joyas en la España de Carlos V* (Madrid: Sociedad Estatal para la Conmemoración de los Centenarios de Felipe V y Carlos V, 2000), pp. 117-27; Arbeteta Mira, 'La *Corona Rica* y otras Joyas de Estado de la Reina Isabel I', *Isabel la Católica. La Magnificencia de un reinado* (Valladolid: Sociedad Estatal de Conmemoraciones Culturales, 2004), pp. 169-86.
44 Muller, *Jewels*, pp. 7-8. This *Balajes* necklace later inherited by Joanna's youngest daughter, Catarina, Queen of Portugal (r. 1525-1578). Cf. Jordan Gschwend, Annemarie, 'Juana de Castilla y Catalina de Austria: La formación de la colección de la reina en Tordesillas y Lisboa', *Juana I de Castilla, 1504-1555. De su reclusión en Tordesillas al olvido de la Historia. I Symposio Internacional sobre la Reina Juana de Castilla. Tordesillas (Valladolid), 23 y 24 de Noviembre 2005*, ed. by Miguel Ángel Zalama (Valladolid: Ayuntamiento de Tordesillas, 2006), pp. 143-71.

table-cut balas rubies, mounted into individual settings shaped like roses, alternating with eight pear-shaped pearls. From the middle hung a detachable, massive cabochon ruby with a pear-shaped pendant pearl, given the name *Codol Magno* and, according to legend, thought to have once belonged to King Solomon. Isabella's jeweller, Garçía Vegil, added more pearls in 1484, and before Joanna departed from Spain, the *Balajes* necklace had been valued in 1487 by a Valencian goldsmith at 40,000 ducats.[45] By 1509, when it was documented in Joanna's chest in Tordesillas, three other rubies had been added.[46] Queen Isabella's superlative necklace (without the *Codol Magno*) may very well be the jewel of 'incalculable value' that astounded Jean Molinet while observing Infanta Joanna during her Antwerp entry.

3.8 Spanish, *Portrait of Queen Isabella I of Spain, Queen of Castile*, oil on wood, 37.5 × 26.9 cm, c. 1470-1504, London, Royal Collection Trust, inv. no. RCIN 403445. Royal Collection Trust / © His Majesty King Charles III 2023

The nature and quality of Queen Isabella's jewellery can be ascertained from one of her portraits painted when Infanta Joanna left Spain by an anonymous Spanish Master.[47] Isabella wears an expensive lavish dress cut from cloth of gold with crowns and ornate foliage motifs. Around her neck is a weighty gold necklace with an enormous ruby pendant shaped like a lozenge with four pearls (Fig. 3.8). It is a gem Isabella had inherited from her father, Juan II and which was recorded in a 1453 inventory the year before he died: 'a gold jewel mounted with a large ruby and four large pearls'.[48] Royal provenances and heirloom jewellery mattered greatly to Queen Isabella, who passed on her passion for exquisite gems and jewellery to her daughter. Like her mother, Joanna prized her jewels not only as markers of wealth and power but also as objects of memory and association.

---

45 Angulo Íñiguez, Diego, *Isabel la Católica: sus retratos y sus joyas* (Santander: UIMP), 1951, pp. 27-31.
46 Ferrandis, José, *Datos documentales inéditos para la historia del arte español. 3. Inventarios reales (Juan II a Juana la Loca)* (Madrid: CSIC, 1953), p. 180; Arbeteta Mira, *La Corona*, p. 171.
47 London, Royal Collection Trust, Spanish Master, *Portrait of Queen Isabella I of Spain, Queen of Castile*, c. 1470-1504, oil on panel. 37.5 × 26.9 cm, inv. no. RCIN 403445.
48 Ferrandis, *Inventarios*, p. 20: 'vn joyel de oro [...] e en el engastonado vn rubi balax grande e quatro perlas en el puestas grandes'.

During her tenure as Archduchess in the Netherlands, Joanna was gifted or acquired outstanding gems given names: *El Emperador* (the 'Emperor' named after Maximilian I) had a large square, table-cut ruby topped by a square emerald and an oversized almond-shaped pendant pearl; the *Joyel del Penacho* ('Jewel of the Feather') comprised thirteen gold plumes set with diamonds. The *Estrella* ('Star') was mounted with a balas ruby, octagonal diamonds and three large pearls with an enamelled star on the reverse. The 'Ostrich' (*Joyel del Avestruz*) was in the shape of an ostrich with a large table-cut balas ruby in its breast. The *Corazon* ('Heart') had a table-cut emerald and pendant pearl attached to a gold chain with enamelled representations of the five wounds of Christ on the reverse. The *Joyel de las Flores* ('Jewel of the Flowers') was in the shape of enamelled green flowers with an elongated baroque ruby and three large pearls.

Finally, the *Joyel de oro de unas hojicas* ('Gold jewel with small branches'), with a large balas ruby surrounded by seven pearls, can be identified with the gem Philip the Fair gave his wife to honour the birth of their second son, Ferdinand (later Emperor Ferdinand I), who was born in Spain in 1503.[49] In celebration of this child, the Infanta's confessor, Diego Ramírez de Villaescusa, held an oration honouring Joanna's Christianity and deep devotion to the Virgin Mary, extolling Joanna's fertility and many children. He compared her fecundity to Mary's, both women directly blessed by God. For some Burgundian courtiers, when Joanna returned to her husband's court, leaving her son behind to be raised by her parents, the Catholic Kings, Philip's jewel would assume Marian connotations related to Joanna's sacrifice and the cult of the Virgin's Seven Sorrows (and Seven Joys) popular across the Netherlands at this date.[50]

A pendant to the Infanta's Marian brooch was her sumptuous 'Jesus', the *Joyel del Jesus*, composed of an interlocking letter 'S', charged with 40 diamonds, 13 rubies and pendant pearls.[51] This slightly later pendant recalls Joanna's jewel, set with twenty-six table-cut diamonds arranged with overlapping letters forming the monogram 'IHS' (Fig. 3.9).[52] Biblical legend says these three Greek letters appeared on a scroll pinned

---

49 Cf. Ferrandis, *Inventarios reales*, p. 176, 'otro Joyel de oro de unas hojicas que tiene un balax grande tunbado e alrrededor del dicho balax seys perlas grandes e otra pinjante mas gruesa que las otras e tiene en las espaldas el dicho Joyel unas hojicas esmaltados de negro' / 'another gold Jewel with some leaves that has a large table balax, and around the said balax six large pearls and another pendant [pearl] bigger than the others and on the back of the said Joyel some leaves enameled in black'.

50 Aram, *La reina Juana*, p. 127, n. 26: 'una joya con siete grandes perlas que recordaban no solo los siete grandes dolores de la Virgen sino también sus siete gozos' / 'a jewel with seven large pearls that recalled not only the seven great sorrows of the Virgin but also her seven joys'. This jewel was possibly created by a craftsman associated with The Seven Sorrows Confraternity in Brussels. See Eichberger, Dagmar, 'Visualizing the Seven Sorrows of the Virgin: Early Woodcuts and Engravings in the Context of Netherlandish Confraternities', *The Seven Sorrows Confraternity of Brussels: Drama, Ceremony, and Art Patronage (16th-17th Centuries)*, ed. by Emily Thelen (Turnhout: Brepols, 2015), pp. 113-43.

51 Muller, *Jewels*, p. 50: 'Joanna's large *Ihus* suspended from pearls and vermilion-and-white enameled gold beads strung on white ribbons, was a transversed 'S' exhibiting forty diamonds, twelve small rubies and three pendant pearls; on its reverse was the Crucifixion with nielloed images above'.

52 London, V&A Museum, *Diamond Pendant*, North Europe, c. 1560, gold, engraved with black *champlevé* enamel, mounted with table-cut diamonds, H. 4.2 cm, W: 2.9 cm, accession number: M.76-1975.

3.9 Northern European, *Diamond Pendant*, gold, engraved with black *champlevé* enamel, mounted with table-cut diamonds, H. 4.2 cm, W: 2.9 cm, c. 1560, London, V&A Museum, acc. no. M.76-1975 © V&A Museum

at the top of Christ's cross, a monogram referencing Jesus's name. This devotional jewel and Joanna's were believed to be endowed with magical properties and thaumaturgical powers thought to protect the owner.

Joanna possessed other jewellery, which constructed and reinforced her image as a Habsburg-Burgundian bride. Among them, her necklace with thirty-four gold links in the shape of the letter 'A', signifying Austria.[53] Another jewel shaped like the letter 'P' (for Philip) had six diamonds and a pearl. Yet, another, a Saint Andrew's cross comprising five large table diamonds hung from a delicate chain, which once belonged to Philip's beloved dead mother, Mary of Burgundy, a present he gave Joanna on New Year's Day in 1497.[54] St. Andrew was the patron saint of the Burgundian dukes and the Order of the Golden Fleece. This jewel is a sentimental souvenir of the mother-in-law Joanna never knew. Margaret of Austria gifted Joanna with a solitary point diamond named 'Margarita' after her.[55]

In February 1500, Philip the Fair presented Joanna in Ghent, after the birth of their first son and heir, Charles (later Emperor Charles V), a superb jewel with an enormous emerald set into a white enamelled rose, with a large pearl worth 400 *livres*.[56] He honoured her again with a second jewel, now mounted with a large baroque ruby also set into a white enamelled rose, the same gem Joanna wears in a portrait painted by an anonymous Flemish painter that same year.[57]

Joanna's most emblematic jewel was the *Tuson* (*Toison*), with a white enamelled lamb standing on green grass, below which was a rectangular ruby and an octagonal

---

53 Ferrandis, *Inventarios*, p. 182; Muller, *Jewels*, p. 56; Mármol Marín, D. M. del Mar, *Joyas en las Colecciones Reales de Isabel la Católica a Felipe II* (Madrid: Fundación Universitaria Española, 2001) p. 98.
54 Ferrandis, *Inventarios*, p. 177.
55 Ferrandis, *Inventarios*, p. 179: '[…] mas otro joyel de oro y engaste que sola tener vn diamante punta […] el qual se llamaba margarita porque lo dio madama margarita'.
56 Joanna later removed this emerald and had it set into a ring. Cf. Ferrandis, *Inventarios*, p. 179; Aram, *La reina Juana*, p. 100. Also, Matthews, Paul, 'Apparel, Status, Fashion. Woman's Clothing and Jewellery', in *Women of Distinction. Margaret of York/ Margaret of Austria*, ed. by Dagmar Eichberger (Louvain: Davidsfonds, 2005), pp. 147-53, and cat. 59, pp. 184-85 for a comparable gem set with a ruby.
57 See the portrait by the Master of the Legend of Mary Magdalene in Vienna, Kunsthistorisches Museum, Gemäldegalerie, 1495/1496, oil on panel, 36 × 24.5 cm, inv. no. GG 4450. Consult online: https://www.khm.at/objektdb/detail/2442/?offset=1&lv=list (accessed 30 November 2022). Cf. Ferrandis, *Inventarios*, p. 176: 'un rubi grande prolongado berrueco engastado sobre una rrosa de oro esmaltada de blanco'.

diamond with two large pendant pearls. The *Toison* celebrated the chivalric and Christian Order of the Golden Fleece, of which Joanna's husband Philip was Chief and Sovereign since 1491. In his portrait by the Master of the Legend of Mary Magdalene, Philip wears the Order's gold collar shaped like steel strikers, abstractly alluding to a double B for Burgundy, from which a lamb (a sheep's skin) is suspended (Fig. 3.1). As Philip's wife, Joanna would have worn her jewel for the magnificent fêtes, dances, jousts and tournaments which took place after the convening of a Chapter. Joanna presided at the celebrations held in Brussels on 17 January 1501 for the 16th Chapter.

At Renaissance courts, jewels, such as Joanna's, which were conferred unique names, were seen as insignias of power, emblems of visual magnificence and objects of devotion. Her documented gems had strong dynastic associations with tremendous symbolic value, reinforcing her status at Philip the Fair's court.[58]

The Triumphant *Joyeuses Entrées* of a Spanish Princess

Despite the setbacks Infanta Joanna suffered with the shipwreck and the loss of a significant part of her trousseau, she managed on her progress as she made her way to Antwerp, to salvage clothes and jewels that had not sunk with the Genoese carrack. Forced to reinvent herself with fewer belongings and despite her absent husband, Infanta Joanna introduced herself to her new subjects as a dignified Spanish princess. She followed Queen Isabella's instructions regarding ceremonial and etiquette, making an excellent impression upon the crowds lining her bridal route as they shouted, *Vive la princesse d'Espagne! Vive la princesse Jeanne!*[59]

The chronicler Jean Molinet admired her grace and beauty as she entered Antwerp on the evening of 19 September, bareheaded, dressed *à la mode d'Espaigne*. He was, like other spectators, awed by her magnificent apparel and jewels. It is tempting to think that Joanna may have worn Queen Isabella's ruby necklace, the *Collar de los Balajes*. Her ladies were dressed just as splendidly as she was, their brilliance shining brightly in the torchlight. The incomparable harness of Joanna's mule even dumbfounded Molinet; the value of its ornaments, in his opinion, was worth an entire county in Flanders. The Infanta's trumpeters dressed in their Florentine black velvet liveries, with the white and purple damask pennants bearing her arms, added to this spectacle. Their fanfare and soundscapes made her entry all the more resounding.

---

58 Smuts, R. Malcolm with Melinda Gough, 'Queens and the International Transmission of Political Culture', *The Court Historian. Queens and the Transmission of Political Culture: The Case of Early Modern France*, ed. by Melinda Gough and R. Malcolm Smuts, 10, 1 (October 2005), pp. 1-13, especially p. 9, in which the cultural artefacts of a dynastic family not only represented enlightened patronage but were physical objects saturated with family history. For Habsburg dynastic jewels, Eichberger, Dagmar, 'Car il me semble que vous aimez bien les carboncles. Die Schätze Margaretes von Österreich und Maximilians I', *Vom Umgang mit Schätzen: Internationaler Kongress, Krems an der Donau, 28. bis 30. Oktober 2004*, ed. by Elisabeth Vavra, Kornelia Holzner-Tobisch, and Thomas Kühtreiber (Vienna: Österreichischen Akademie der Wissenschaften, 2007), pp. 139-52.

59 Fleming, *Juana I*, p. 22.

3.10 Southern Netherlandish, *The Festive Entry of Joanna of Castile into Brussels*, fol. 31ʳ: *Joanna entering the Grand-Place with members of the Crossbowman's Guild*, 1496, Berlin, SMPK, Kupferstichkabinett, ms 78 D5 © SMPK

This very illustrious and virtuous lady, aged [sixteen], of beautiful carriage and gracious manner, the most richly adorned that ever was seen in the Archduke's country, was mounted on a mule after the manner of Spain, her head uncovered. Sixteen noble ladies and a matron followed her, all dressed in cloth of gold and mounted in the same way. There were pages dressed in luxurious liveries with twenty-eight or thirty trumpeters who did their best in this entry to raise the spirits of those present [...] This very excellent lady [Infanta Joanna] was habited in cloth of gold encrusted with jewels so precious and rich that one could not estimate their value. Even how the mule she rode was adorned was worth the value of one county.[60]

Joanna took note of the success of her Antwerp entry. She calculated to deploy similar sartorial strategies to showcase herself a few months later, when on 9 December, she made her entry into Brussels in winter. On fol. 31ʳ of the *Festive Entry of Joanna of Castile into Brussels* (Berlin, ms 78 D5), the anonymous illustrator depicts the princess entering the city after nightfall accompanied by the Crossbowman's Guild, members of which preceded her, carrying large torches with schematic escutcheons, decorated presumably with her arms and their emblems (Fig. 3.10).

Proudly on display, Joanna rides sidesaddle with expertise and poise, her mule outfitted with gold trappings and draped with gold cloth. Dressed *à la mode d'Espaigne*, Joanna wears a luxuriant cloth-of-gold dress of the same superior quality, cut in the same manner, as seen in Queen Isabella's portrait, with an identical sheer *gorguera* or *chemisette* filling the lower decolletage (Fig. 3.8). She sports long dress sleeves (*mangas*), through which the light white holland cloth is visible through the slashes, hanging down to her waist, and over the mule's back. Despite cold temperatures, Joanna purposely removed her gold-trimmed crimson velvet mantle, tucking it around her waist, so the people of Brussels and her subjects could see her shimmering gold attire. Her hair is loose but kept in check with a gold coif and a crimson velvet cap or hood

---

60 Molinet, Jean, *Chroniques de Jean Molinet*, ed. by Jean-Alexandre Bouchon (Paris: Libraire Verdière, 1828), Ch. CCLXXXVIII, pp. 61-66, at p. 62; Anderson, *Hispanic Costume*, p. 140.

to which a gold hat badge or *enseigne* has been pinned.⁶¹ Regrettably, the illustrator had opted not to depict Joanna's incomparable jewels, which Jean Molinet marvelled at in Antwerp. Only a gold necklace around her neck is visible.

As Laura Weigert demonstrates, the text accompanying this illuminated folio of Joanna's *Joyeuse entrée* centres on the brilliance of her clothes and the festive spectacle of this event (fol. 30ᵛ). Her theatrical entrance into the city's heart, the *Grote Markt* (*Grand Place*) and the site of the City Hall, where more celebrations were held, is enhanced by the bright torches in the square and those held by the opulently attired Guild members in attendance. Weigert interprets this entry as a multidimensional experience for the Infanta, the multiple guilds involved and the citizens themselves, a sensory event heightened by light, sound and a brilliant sartorial repertoire (fol. 30ᵛ).

> quorum singuli suis vestiu[m] intersigniis ge[m]mata[rum] phaleratha[rum]que manica[rum] fulgure choruscantes cum ardentibus facib[us] tumultuose populariu[m] multitudini tale silentium incusseru[n]t ut et vicissim visendi notandiq[ue] p[rese]ntibus adminiculo hiisq[ue] ac posteris miraculo fuisse potuerit.

> All of them (with their coats of arms on their clothing, glittering with bright jewels and shining ornaments that adorn the long sleeves of their tunics, with burning torches) caused such a silence among the mass of people, so that they in turn, notable and remarkable, could be an encouragement for the people present, and a source of amazement for them and posterity.⁶²

Joanna triumphed with Queen Isabella's lessons in representation and self-fashioning, well learned, together with dress choices carefully selected for her debut at this highly political venue in Brussels, where the Infanta was celebrated as 'our illustrious lady' of Brabant (*illustrissima domina nostra Johanna*).⁶³

On the Cusp of Queenship

A stain-glass panel in the Victoria & Albert Museum in London depicting Joanna of Castile at prayer can perhaps be linked – iconographically – with the series known as 'The Burgundian Windows', commissioned around 1500 for the Chapel of Holy Blood in Bruges, which contextualises, in glass, the Burgundian dynasty and its prestigious lineage and genealogy. By February 1500, Joanna had given birth to Philip the Fair's heir, Archduke Charles, thus securing the future of the Habsburg house and

---

61 Joanna owned in 1504, a late medieval gold hat medallion depicting a woman on a mule, going to the hunt with a falcon on her hand and a gentleman, falcons and dogs in attendance, all set against a green enamel background. Cf. Ferrandis, *Inventarios*, p. 196.
62 Again, consult Weigert in this volume.
63 See the translation of fol. 35ʳ ('Judges') of *The festive entry of Joanna of Castile into Brussels*, 1496, ms 78 D 5 in this volume.

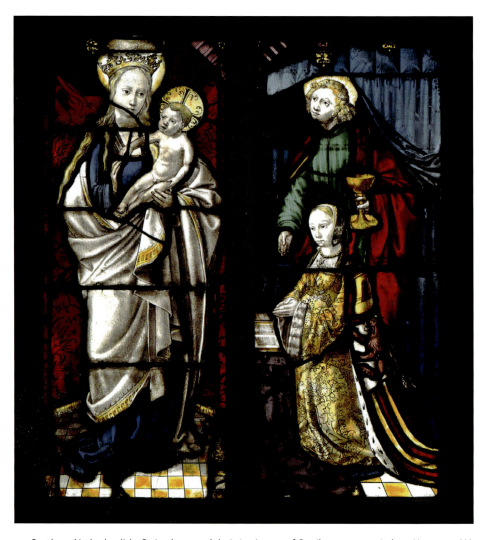

3.11 Southern Netherlandish, *Stain glass panel depicting Joanna of Castile at prayer*, window, H: 112 cm, W: 51 cm, *c*. 1500-1505, London, V&A Museum, acc. no. 293:1, 2-1874 © V&A Museum

anchoring her place in this former brilliant and translucent pantheon. The Infanta's window pane depicts her full-length as a richly appointed bride and Archduchess.[64]

In these two windows dating slight later, *c*. 1505, Joanna is portrayed as a young teenage Spanish Infanta, as she arrived in the Netherlands in 1496, but with her status now altered. She kneels at her prie-dieu covered in purple cloth (an imperial colour for rulers), protected by her patron saint, St. John the Evangelist (Fig. 3.11),

---

64 London, V&A Museum, *Stained glass panel depicting Joanna of Castile as a bride*, *c*. 1496-1500, H: 192.3 cm, W: 87 cm, accession number: C.442:1-1918. Consult online: https://collections.vam.ac.uk/item/O8716/joanna-of-castile-panel-unknown/.

praying to the Virgin Mary whom Joanna was known to have revered.[65] She is regally dressed like a queen (a prefiguration of her future role as monarch of Spain), wearing a long gold mantle lined with ermine, emblazoned with the Spanish coat of arms, that of Castile and Leon (a castle and rampant lion). Her dress, cut from gold brocade (cloth-of-gold), is woven with artichoke motifs (a symbol of her fertility) embellished with elaborate foliage, with sleeves trimmed with fur.[66] She wears a gold chain; above, a jewel hangs from a thick gold carcanet. Her French hood confirms that after her arrival, Joanna adopted Burgundian-Valois fashions to bridge both courts.

This stain-glass image underscores the importance of the resplendent clothes and textiles Queen Isabella carefully prepared for her daughter's trousseau in 1496, with the vested dreams the queen hoped Joanna would achieve as Spanish Infanta and Habsburg Archduchess in the Netherlands. She never imagined, however, that after 1502, Joanna would become heiress of Castile's throne and that she would undeniably establish herself as *mater familias* of her family, as she was configured in Adrien Baltyn's 1616 treatise. Joanna unexpectedly metamorphosed after 1496 into the matriarch of a flourishing dynasty. Her son Emperor Charles V and grandson Philip II, King of Spain, attained power and rule over a global empire through her legacy and patrimony. Her six children would fulfil Queen Isabella's wildest dreams – two sons became emperors, and four daughters became queens.

---

65 London, V&A Museum, *Stained glass panel depicting Joanna of Castile at prayer*, c. 1500-1505, window, H: 112 cm, W: 51 cm, accession number: 293:1, 2-1874. I should like to thank Adriana Concin for her assistance with this object. The provenance and former location of these two windows made in Brabant has not yet been determined. The author does not agree with the present identification of the sitter as Joanna's eldest daughter, Leonor (Eleonore) of Austria (1498-558). For Joanna's cult of the Virgin see Twomey, Leslie, 'Juana of Castile's Book of Hours: An Archduchess at Prayer', *Religions*, 11, 4 (April 2020), pp. 1-13, at, pp. 9-10.

66 Ladero Quesada, *La armada*, p. 150 for a mantle cut from tawny cloth embellished with foliage and two falcons, and p. 172, for a piece of crimson cloth with three artichokes embroidered with gold and silver thread.

CLAIRE BILLEN AND CHLOÉ DELIGNE

The Self-representation of Brussels in Times of Uncertainty*

> **▼ ABSTRACT** The first part of the Berlin manuscript devoted to the Entry of Joanna of Castile is a unique rendition of such a public event. It shows the procession of the religious authorities and the various civic bodies of the city as imagined by its organizers. Although we do not know whether or how this entry really took place, it mirrors in any case the image that the promoters of the ceremony wanted to give of Brussels, a city that had just emerged from several decades of political turmoil. Probably recruited from the chambers of rhetoric and military guilds, these organizers sought above all to show the princess that the city was peaceful, well-guarded and well-ordered. For the discerning observer, additional, more subtle messages can be detected.

> **▼ KEYWORDS** Brussels government, civic bodies, social troubles, religious institutions, patrician families, craft guilds, Brussels butchers, military guilds, civic buildings, urban space.

At the time when Brussels was preparing to welcome the new princess of the Low Countries, it was an impoverished city with a deeply fractured society and a declining population, in contrast to other cities in the Brabant like Antwerp and Mechelen.[1] Just over seven years had passed since Brussels had taken an active part in the latest revolt

---

* We wish to thank Sylvie Planel and Marc Boone for their support in editing the English version of our text.
1 Cuvelier, Joseph, *Les dénombrements de foyers en Brabant (XIVe-XVIe siècle)*, Commission royale d'Histoire, 2 vols (Brussels: Kiesseling, and Imbreghts, 1912-1913), I, pp. CCXXVII-CCXLVI; Dickstein-Bernard, Claire, 'Bruxelles résidence princière (1375-1500)', in *Histoire de Bruxelles*, ed. by Mina Martens (Toulouse: Privat, 1976), pp. 138-58; Van Uytven, Raymond, 'Le cœur des Pays-Bas bourguignons et habsbourgeois (1430-1531)', in *Histoire du Brabant du duché à nos jours*, ed. by Raymond van Uytven, Claude Bruneel, and others (Zwolle: Waanders, 2004), pp. 213-52 (219-20).

A Spectacle for a Spanish Princess, ed. by Dagmar H. Eichberger, Burgundica, 35 (Turnhout: Brepols, 2023), pp. 77–106

led by Philip of Cleves (1459-1528) against Maximilian, and political instability and bitterness were still fresh in people's memories.[2]

For the city government, the court's visit could serve as a precious instrument to rebuild the economy and restore the prestige of the city, in opposition to the preferred place of residence established by the faithful Mechelen.[3] Winning over the young archduchess was therefore a crucial project, and giving the impression of order and social and political peace was an essential condition to bring it about.

Philip the Fair's distrust of those who had revolted against his father had probably not been completely dispelled, and citizens of Brussels had played an important role among the rebels between 1488 and 1489.[4] He had delayed his Joyous Entry into the largest city of the Brabant until July 1495, almost a year after being installed as Duke of Brabant in Leuven (in September 1494) – also a rebel city – and as Marquis of Antwerp (in October 1494).[5]

In fact, the uprising against Maximilian had left its mark at the very heart of Brussels society. It had grafted itself onto and revived old conflicts between patrician families, and the redistribution of influence among the craft guilds had led to numerous divisions.[6] It is very unlikely that these could have been resolved by taking back control of the rebel city, where animosity was passed down from generation to generation.

From 1489, we see the faction formed around the de Mol family lineage reappearing in the affairs of the city. This family was all-powerful in Brussels between 1450 and 1461, and was deeply embroiled in a series of major conflicts until 1477, a period of turmoil during which the rebels of the craft guilds tried to remove the family from the scene.[7] By 1489, several of its members were once again representatives in the city government, at the cost of the rival family briefly favoured by Philip of Cleves in 1488 who had gone into exile.[8] As for the stonemasons' guild, it was very powerful during the insurrectional events following the death of Charles the Bold and was heavily repressed. Some of its members were still being prosecuted in 1495. In this way, Guillaume van Ruysbroeck, the son of the city hall architect Jan Van Ruysbroeck,

---

2 Haemers, Jelle, 'Philippe de Clèves et la Flandre. La position d'un aristocrate au cœur d'une revolte urbaine (1477-1492)', in *Entre la ville, la noblesse et l'État: Philippe de Clèves (1456-1528), homme politique et bibliophile*, ed. by Jelle Haemers, Céline Van Hoorebeeck & Hanno Wijsman, Burgundica 13, (Turnhout: Brepols, 2007), pp. 21-99; Vrancken, Valérie, *Een papier strijd in Laatmiddeleeuws Brabant. De Brusselse opstand tegen Maximiliaan van Oostenrijk (1488-1489)*, (unpublished master thesis, Katholieke Universiteit Leuven, 2012), pp. 18-21.
3 Haemers, 'Philippe de Clèves', p. 62.
4 Cauchies, Jean-Marie, 'La signification politique des entrées princières dans les Pays-Bas : Maximilien d'Autriche et Philippe le Beau', in *À la Cour de Bourgogne. Le duc, son entourage, son train*, ed. by Jean-Marie Cauchies, Burgundica 1 (Turnhout: Brepols, 1998), pp. 137-52 (143-44).
5 Smolar-Meynart, Arlette, 'Bruxelles: l'élaboration de son image de capitale en politique et en droit au moyen-âge', *Bijdragen tot de Geschiedenis*, 68 (1985), pp. 25-45.
6 Vrancken, *Een papier strijd*, pp. 33-35.
7 Favresse, Félicien, 'Documents relatifs à l'histoire politique intérieure de Bruxelles de 1477 à 1480', *Bulletin de la Commission royale d'Histoire*, 98 (1934), 29-125 (95); John Bartier, 'Un document sur les rivalités et les prévarications du patriciat bruxellois au XVe siècle', *Bulletin de la Commission royale d'Histoire*, 107 (1942), 337-79 (337-63).
8 Vrancken, *Een papier strijd*, p. 34.

was exiled for being one of the leaders of the 1477 troubles and decapitated in 1495 or 1496. It is likely that he had returned to the city hoping to be pardoned by Philip the Fair during the latter's Joyous Entry – a hope which was cruelly crushed![9] Thus, at this juncture, pacification had yet to be achieved.

What arrangements did the organisers of the ceremony in honour of Joanna of Castile deploy to represent this turbulent society in a more harmonious light and glorify its virtues, as well as its unity and order?

Until now, historiography has not considered in depth the period around the last decade of the 15th century in Brussels. Analysis of the depiction of the city corporations' procession has certainly suffered as a result. Furthermore, its contextualisation is largely absent. Authors who have studied the Berlin manuscript have focused on the *tableaux* and the entertaining or satirical episodes of the *esbattements*.[10] Wim Blockmans and Jean-Marie Cauchies are the only writers who have addressed the political and symbolic aspects of the procession of ecclesiastics, magistrates and guilds.[11] It behoves us to return to these matters more fully.

We must first emphasise the exceptional precision of the manuscript. Although the narration of the Joyous Entries often lists the various authorities coming to meet the prince, the subject is not usually treated in any depth and the chronicles make no claim to be exhaustive.[12] Our manuscript, on the other hand, describes scrupulously

---

9 Wauters, Alphonse, *À propos de l'exposition nationale d'architecture: études et anecdotes relatives à nos anciens architectes* (Brussels: Alliance typographique, 1885), pp. 12-28.

10 Blockmans, Wim P., 'La Joyeuse Entrée de Jeanne de Castille à Bruxelles en 1496', in *España y Holanda*, ed. by Jan Lechner, and Harm den Boer (Amsterdam: Rodopi, 1995), pp. 27-42; Kipling, Gordon, 'Brussels, Juana of Castile and the Art of Theatrical Illustration (1496)', *Leeds Studies in English*, n.s., 32 (2001), 229-53; Eichberger, Dagmar, 'Illustrierte Festzüge für das Haus Habsburg-Burgund: Idee und Wirklichkeit', in *Hofkultur in Frankreich und Europa im Spätmittelalter. La culture de cour en France et en Europe à la fin du Moyen Âge*, ed. by Christian Freigang, and Jean-Claude Schmitt (Berlin: Akademie-Verlag, 2005), pp. 73-98; Legaré, Anne-Marie, 'L'entrée de Jeanne de Castille à Bruxelles: un programme iconographique au féminin', in *Women at the Burgundian court. Presence and Influence*, ed. by Dagmar Eichberger, Anne-Marie Legaré, and Wim Hüsken (Turnhout: Brepols, 2010), pp. 43-56; Tammen, Björn, 'A Feast of the Arts: Joanna of Castile in Brussels, 1496', *Early Music History*, 30 (2011), 213-48; Vandenbroeck, Paul, 'A Bride Amidst Heroines, Fools and Savages. The Joyous Entry into Brussels by Joanna of Castile, 1496 (Berlin Kupferstichkabinett, ms 78 D5)', *Jaarboek Koninklijk Museum voor Schone Kunst Antwerpen* (2012), 153-94; Weigert, Laura, *French Visual Culture and the Making of Medieval Theater* (Cambridge: Cambridge University Press, 2015), pp. 26-73.

11 Blockmans, Wim P., 'Le dialogue imaginaire entre princes et sujets: les joyeuses Entrées en Brabant entre 1494 et en 1496', in *À la Cour de Bourgogne. Le duc, son entourage, son train*, ed. by Jean-Marie Cauchies, Burgundica 1 (Turnhout: Brepols, 1998), pp. 155-70; Cauchies, Jean-Marie, 'La signification politique des entrées princières dans les Pays-Bas : Maximilien d'Autriche et Philippe le Beau' in *À la Cour de Bourgogne. Le duc, son entourage, son train*, ed. by Jean-Marie Cauchies, Burgundica 1 (Turnhout: Brepols, 1998), pp. 137-52.

12 This is even the case with Molinet, despite the fact he paid particular attention to reporting princely entries, as Neil Murphy shows in 'Between Court and Town. Ceremonial Entries in the *Chroniques* of Jean Molinet', in *Jean Molinet et son temps. Actes des rencontres internationales de Dunkerque, Lille et Gand, 8-10 novembre 2007*, ed. by Jean Devaux, Estelle Doudet et Élodie Lecuppre-Desjardin (Turnhout: Brepols, 2013), pp. 155-61. For example, in the 1486 Entry of the Emperor in Brussels, he writes: *Les seigneurs de la Loy, nobles bourgois marchans et manans de la ville habituez de la parure du roy yssirent par la porte auprez de Sainte Goule et allèrent les aucuns une bonne demye lieue pour le reverender. Messeigneurs de l'église seculers et regulers, religieux possessans et mendians, soeurettes et beghinettes, a solennelle procession* [...], Georges Doutrepont et Omer Jodogne, *Chroniques de Jean Molinet*, volume 1 (1474-1488), (Brussels: Académie royale de Belgique, classe des Lettres et des Sciences morales et politiques, 1935), p. 626.

every element of the ceremony. It demonstrates a sustained preoccupation with the hierarchical ranking of the city bodies and draws attention to the ideal structure of the ceremony, supposedly respecting the sacred and learned logic of a numeration based on the number three and its multiples.[13] It is likely that this was a retrospective addition, intended to give the account more importance. There is no evidence that the Entry actually took place in the manner described. This potential departure from reality may explain some of the iconographic details that appear in the foremost part of the procession, in particular the landscapes in the background which do not bear much resemblance to the topographical reality of Brussels and its surroundings.

For the sake of clarity, let us briefly describe this section of the manuscript. Introduced by a depiction of Saint Michael and a statement of the motivations behind the creation of the work (fols 1^v and 2^r), it is followed by a depiction of the religious congregations and the city administration and government. Every image is accompanied by a text which details the composition of each group, describing their costumes, appearance and virtues. This series has often been described as 'interrupted' by six scenes depicting jesters, but we will see that these may not constitute an interruption, but rather a logical sequence.

Fols	Actors mentioned in the Latin text	Translation	Nr in the text	Nr on the image	Elements of the landscape
2-3	Opidi scolaris indoles… sub suis didascolis	Students and their schoolmasters	300	10	Buildings
3-4	Opidi venerabilis de monte carmeli emulatio	Carmelites		10	
4-5	Opidi spectabile fratrum minorum contubernium	Minorites		8	Buildings
5-6	Capellanorum numerus	Secular clergymen		9	Church
6-7	Canonicorum regularium venerabilis ecclesia	Regular canons of the Sonian forest		9	Buildings and woodland
7-8	Opidi ipsiusque patrone sancte Gudile canonicorum collegium	Canons of Saint-Gudula		9	Towers in the distance

---

13 Blockmans Wim P., and Esther Donckers, 'Self-Representation of Court and City in Flanders and Brabant in the Fifteenth and Early Sixteenth Centuries', in *Showing Status: Representations of Social Positions in the Late Middle Ages*, ed. by Wim Blockmans, and Antheun Janse (Turnhout: Brepols, 1999), pp. 81-111 (96-107).

THE SELF-REPRESENTATION OF BRUSSELS IN TIMES OF UNCERTAINTY 81

Fols	Actors mentioned in the Latin text	Translation	Nr in the text	Nr on the image	Elements of the landscape
8-9	Centenarii… sub se quilibet decem decenarios viros habens	Hundredmen and Tenthmen	44 + 44 X 10	9	
9-10	Iurati vel decani	Deans and sworn men	4	10	Bridge
10-11	Diversorum genus mimorum	Jesters		4	Inn
11-12	Hystrio	Hystrio		1	Urban background (fountain of the fish market)
12-13	Silvestres… ac ethiopissam equo insidentem	Wild men and Ethiopian princess		7+1	
13-14	Quidam… equo vectus sede vice selle usus	Fool sat on a stool on horseback		1	Noble estate
14-15	Silvestres	Wild men		4	
15-16	Quidam qui traha vecti faciesque tecti diversis musis artis sue … compegerunt	Musicians with masks		6	Towers (walls or church(es))
16-17	Carnificum opidi agilis iuventus	Young butchers	36	6	Walls in the distance
17-18	Clientes	Sergeants	27	6	Church
18-19	Famuli dominorum opidi	Messengers		8	Fenced-in woodland
19-20	Pacificatores	Peacemakers		8	
20-21	Octo qui sub nomine ghilde	Eight of the Guild		8	Watermill
21-22	Sex secretarii opidi	City secretaries		6	
22-23	Sex qui sub nomine consulum annue ex plebeia electi	Guild advisors		6	Castle/tower and walls
23-24	Receptores	Receivers		6	Town in the distance

Fols	Actors mentioned in the Latin text	Translation	Nr in the text	Nr on the image	Elements of the landscape
24-25	Consules sive legislatores quorum septem scabini … vero duo burgis seu civium magistri	7 Swornmen, 2 Burgomasters and the amman	7+2+1	10	Church
25-26	Civium seu opidanorum tam senum tam iuvenum mixta congeries	Burghers accompanying the Burgomasters		6	
26-27	Spectabilis multitudo stipendariorum opidi	Specialised officials and artists appointed by the city		8	
27-28	Colvurianorum seu bombardelliorum	Culverin Bearers [*guild of Saint Christopher*]		9	
28-29	Altera ghilda puta arcuum manualium tractores	Archers [*guild of Saint Sebastian*]		9	
29-30	Tercia ghilda que junior arbalista seu sancti Georgii dicitur	Crossbow Bearers [*guild of Saint George*] (9)		9	Watermill
30-31	Ghilda quae arbalistis utens	The Crossbow Bearers of the Great Guild (8) + the Princess and a lady of the court		8 + 2	Urban background: the *Grand-Place* and the city hall

In the following commentary, we will attempt to discern aspects of the logic underlying the representation of the official figures greeting the new princess.

The Ecclesiastics greeting Joanna (fols 2ᵛ-8ʳ)

It was customary for the members of the church to be the first officials presented to a prince. Were they not after all the natural intercessors between the rulers and their subjects? Surely the spiritual and intellectual role they provided, both to the rulers and to society as a whole, was one of the attractions of the city.

Six religious groups were presented to the archduchess, in increasing hierarchical status, as was the norm for ceremonies of this type. The manuscript first describes the impressive number of clerics, followed by school masters and their dignified and orderly pupils. Next came two groups of mendicants, the Carmelites and the Franciscan, succeeded by the officiants of the parishes and chapels, all referred to as chaplains. Then came the canons regular of the three monasteries of the Sonian Forest and, finally, the canons of the ducal college of Saint-Michael and Saint-Gudula.

We can understand the place of honour given to the canons of Saint-Gudula who brought up the rear of the procession (fols 7ᵛ-8ʳ). This longstanding institution of princely origin was a rich and powerful college, who fiercely claimed its church as the mother church of Brussels, reducing all other churches of the city to the rank of chapels.[14] Endorsing this position of dominance, the manuscript presents the parish priests as chaplains (fols 5ᵛ-6ʳ). The chapter had absolute control over the educational activities in the city, which allowed its religious to appear at the beginning and end of the procession. The proud place they held in the procession mirrors the important political position the canons had re-established following the humiliation they suffered in 1488 under Philip of Cleves' rule.[15] The manuscript's emphasis on the large number of pupils is an implied statement of the importance the city placed on education.

Should we be surprised by the absence of the Carthusians of Scheut, the Dominicans or the Beguines, when a place was allocated to the Carmelites in the procession (fols 3ᵛ-4ʳ)? These congregations were present in Brussels and had participated in other entries. The Carmelites were a mendicant order established in Brussels in 1249 on land granted by the Duke. Despite being severely restricted in their activities by the chapter, the Carmelites of Brussels had succeeded in winning the favours of

---

14 The text in the manuscript follows the tradition of assigning the establishment of the college to Lambert Balderic, also known as Lambert II Count of Leuven, in 1047. Lambert's descendants bore the title of Duke of Brabant. The charter testifying to its foundation is false but most historians believe that the first college was indeed founded in the course of the 11ᵗʰ century. See most recently: De Ridder, Paul, 'Une ville et sa cathédrale', in *La cathédrale des saints-Michel-et-Gudule*, ed. by Guido Jan Bral (Brussels: Racines, 2000), pp. 14-20. For the contents of the foundation charter see: Lefèvre, Placide, Philippe Godding, and Françoise Godding-Ganshof, *Chartes du chapitre de Sainte-Gudule à Bruxelles*, Université de Louvain, Recueil de travaux d'Histoire et de Philologie, 6ᵉ série, 45 (Louvain-la-Neuve/ Brussels: Nauwelaerts, 1993), LIV+375p., pp. 1-3.

15 Vrancken, *Een papier strijd*, pp. 19, 51.

the court.[16] The Duchess Joanna of Brabant (1322-1406) had a Carmelite confessor and asked to be buried in their church. The decision of Antoine de Bourgogne (1384-1415), Joanna's successor, to bury his son Guillaume who died aged one at the foot of the monument dedicated to the old duchess (Fig. 4.1) reinforced the role of this sanctuary as a dynastic *memoria*.[17] The chapter of the *Toison d'Or* in 1501 was given to the Carmelites by Philip the Fair, and his son Charles was received into the order when he was one year of age.[18] As well as their connection to the princes, the Carmelites also maintained close relations with the city corporations. It was often within their walls or those of the Franciscans that peacemakers convened opposing parties, as we will discuss later.[19] It was also there that the city authorities held their ceremonial dinner on the day of *Ommegang*, the famous Brussels procession which had been taking place since the second half of the 14th century to celebrate the unity of its citizens and their devotion to the prince.[20] In addition, the Nation of Saint-Laurent, to which fullers, weavers and launderers belonged, met at the Carmelites.[21] From time to time, it was also the place where the drapers' guild published their statutory decisions.[22] In this way, the Carmelites appeared as a unifying order who had gained the trust of the prince, the city and its various bodies.

The Franciscan friars held a similarly important place in the ecclesiastical landscape of Brussels (fols 4ᵛ-5ʳ). Their convent was located in the centre of the city, close to the *Grote Markt* (*Grand-Place*) and the traders' church dedicated to Saint Nicholas. It housed the tomb of Duke Jean I (1253-1294), the most prestigious of the early Brabant princes, who was buried with his second wife Marguerite de Dampierre, and also housed the tomb of Marie d'Evreux, the wife of Duke Jean III (1300-1355).[23] The shoemakers' guild gathered there to talk about their affairs.[24] The text accompanying the illustration emphasises the place the brothers held in the hearts of the citizens of Brussels.

---

16 Vrancken, *Een papier strijd*, pp. 101-02.

17 Guilardian, David, 'Les sépultures des comtes de Louvain et des ducs de Brabant (XIᵉ-1430)', in *Sépulture, mort et représentation du pouvoir au Moyen Âge*, ed. by Michel Margue, 11ᵉ Journées lotharingiennes, Publications de la section historique de l'Institut Grand-Ducal de Luxembourg, 118, pp. 491-539 (521).

18 Fagel, Raymond, 'Charles of Luxembourg. The Future Emperor as a Young Burgundian Prince (1500-1516)', in *Carolus V imperator*, ed. by Fernando Chueca Goitia, Raymond Fagel, and others (Barcelona: Lunwerg, 2007), pp. 8-16 (9).

19 Smolar-Meynart, Arlette, 'Les guerres privées et la cour des apaiseurs à Bruxelles au Moyen Âge', in *Mélanges Mina Martens*, Annales de la Société royale d'Archéologie de Bruxelles, 58 (1981), 237-54 (244).

20 Demeter, Stéphane, and Cecilia Paredes, 'Le parcours de l'Ommegang', in *Ommegang!*, ed. by Jean-Paul Heerbrant (Brussels: Centre Albert Marinus, 2013), pp. 67-80 (69).

21 Des Marez, Guillaume, *L'organisation du travail à Bruxelles au XVᵉ siècle*, Mémoires couronnés et autres mémoires publiés par l'Académie royale des Sciences, des Lettres et des Beaux-Arts de Belgique, 65, fasc. 1 (Brussels: Hayez, 1904), p. 412.

22 Henne, Alexandre, and Alphonse Wauters, *Histoire de la ville de Bruxelles*, new ed. by Mina Martens, 4 vols (Brussels: Culture et civilisation, 1975), III, p. 202.

23 Bonenfant, Pierre, and Madeleine Le Bon, *Bruxella 1238: Sous les pavés l'histoire* (Brussels: LAP assurances, 1993); Guilardian, David, 'Les sépultures', pp. 516-17; Piet Avonds, *Brabant tijdens de regering van hertog Jan III (1312-1356). Land en instellingen*, Verhandelingen van de Koninklijke Academie voor Wetenschappen, Letteren en Schone Kunsten van België, Klasse der Letteren, 53, 136 (Brussels: Palais des Académies, 1991), p. 181.

24 Des Marez, *L'organisation du travail*, p. 412.

4.1 Antoine de Succa, *Les Mémoriaux*, fol. 74ʳ: *The tomb of Jeanne, Duchess of Brabant, and William of Burgundy in the Carmelite church of Brussels*, drawing on paper, between 1601 and 1615, KBR, ms 1862/1 © KBR

The authors of the manuscript, and possibly the organisers of Joanna of Castile's Entry, therefore made a deliberate choice. They appear to have favoured religious communities that had close connections with the city administration, but also those explicitly linked to the ducal dynasty and the expression of its continuity, a concern which is also clear in the representation of the canons of Saint-Gudula.

The same preoccupation can also be seen, although harder to illustrate, in the case of the canons of the monasteries of the Sonian Forest (fols 6ᵛ-7ʳ). The latter occupied a prominent position in the procession, appearing in penultimate place, just before the religious of the powerful city chapter. These priories were relatively recent, their foundation dating to the 14th century. They grew out of the success of the movements of inner piety inspired by the *Devotio Moderna*, spread in Brussels by the influential writings of Jan van Ruusbroec (1293-1381), former chaplain of the chapter of Saint-Michael and Saint-Gudula who retired in 1343 to the community of Groenendael.[25] It was along similar lines that the hermitages of *Rouge-Cloître* and *Sept-Fontaines* were founded in forest clearings, in 1366 and 1389 respectively. All three monasteries adopted the Augustinian rule, formed a joint congregation in 1403 and were affiliated in 1412 to the Windesheim congregation.[26] Cosseted by the patrician families and the elite of the Brussels guilds as well as by the court, they became important spiritual institutions in the city. Duke Jean III (1300-1355) and the Duchess Joanna (1322-1406) had undoubtedly favoured their establishment in the vast ducal forest which bordered the city to the east and south. However, what is striking in the section devoted to them within the manuscript is the surprising portrayal of their considerable antiquity.[27] This appears to justify the forest convents' prominent positions in the procession. The author of the manuscript at this point employs an interesting device: their ancient origins are explained by the transposition on their community of a site older than Brussels itself! Rather than referring to it as the Sonian Forest, the text – with a certain literary flair – locates the monasteries in the ancient charcoal-burning forest *Sylva carbonaria,* a forest often cited in the hagiography of the early Medieval ages.[28] This ancient site, ceded to a Sonian priory, not specified in the manuscript by name, is believed to be sited close to a ducal *aula*. This suggests the centre of influence to be Tervuren, a ducal residence also situated in the heart of the Sonian Forest where Henri I (c. 1165-1235) had built a government hall (*aula*) in the first half of the 13th century.[29] Tervuren was thought to be a place of great antiquity, revered for having been the scene of the death of Hubert († 727), the bishop-saint of Tongeren-Maastricht and direct successor of Saint Lambert (c. 636-c. 705).[30] Saint Hubert was

---

25 Warnar, Geert, *Ruusbroec. Literature and Mysticism in the Fourteenth Century* (Leiden: Brill, 2011), pp. 173, 181-85.

26 Van Engen, John, *Sisters and Brothers of the Common Life. The Devotio Moderna and the World of the Later Middle Ages* (Philadelphia: University of Pennsylvania Press, 2008), pp. 32-37. *Monasticon Windesheimense*, ed. by Wilhelm Kohl, Ernest Persoons, and Anton G. Weiler, vol.1: Belgiën (Archives et Bibliothèques de Belgique), 16, 1976, pp. 45-66; 108-30; 188-200.

27 We want to thank Walter Simons who brought to our attention the importance of the founding age of an ecclesiastical institution for its order of precedence.

28 Renard, Etienne, 'La situation et l'étendue de la Forêt Charbonnière au premier millénaire: bilan historiographique et retour aux sources', in *La forêt en Lotharingie médiévale. Der Wald im mittelalterlichen Lotharingien, Actes des 18e Journées lotharingiennes, 30-31 octobre 2014,* ed. by Michel Pauly, and Hérold Pettiau, Publications de la Section Historique de l'Institut Grand-Ducal de Luxembourg, 127, Publications du CLUDEM, 43 (2014), pp. 51-75.

29 Uyttebrouck, André, 'Les résidences des ducs de Brabant, 1355-1430', in *Fürstliche Residenzen im spätmittelalterlichen Europa*, ed by Hans Patze, and Werner Paravicini, Vorträge und Forschungen, 36 (Sigmaringen: Thorbecke, 1991), pp. 189-205 (197).

30 Kupper, Jean-Louis, 'Qui était saint Hubert?', in *Le culte de saint Hubert au Pays de Liège*, ed. by. Alain Dierkens, and Jean-Marie Duvosquel, Saint-Hubert en Ardenne. Art-Histoire-Folklore, 1, 1990 (Brussels: Crédit communal de Belgique, 1991), pp. 13-17.

particularly revered by the Burgundians and the Habsburgs.[31] His supposed family ties with the Pépin family and his presence in the Brabant made him an illustrious predecessor to the Dukes of Brabant (he is thought to have owned the estate of *Fura*, which is traditionally understood as being Tervuren), linked through him to Charlemagne's line. Jean Gielemans (1427-1487), a famous Brabant hagiographer and a religious at *Rouge-Cloître* wrote extensively about these genealogical theories in his works.[32] We find them again here, almost in subliminal form, in the scholarly and somewhat convoluted writing of the narrator (and organiser?) of the Joyous Entry.

If we had to draw a conclusion from the very detailed description given in the manuscript of the secular and regular religious groups presented to the archduchess, one might think that the author wanted to demonstrate two points: firstly, to show the prosperity and good governance of the clerical order in Brussels where great numbers of new and promising recruits were mixing with experienced mentors in an environment of decency, understanding and scholarship, and secondly to demonstrate the deep dynastic roots of the Brabant princes, of which Joanna was now a member, and which each Brussels community selected in the procession served as witness, all the while enjoyed popularity with the population at large.

The lesser Bodies are presented to the Princess (fols 8^v-10^r)

The structure of the procession of the civil authorities of Brussels who followed the religious contingent also presents a series of traits, the deliberate intention of which cannot be ignored. Once again, we see this desire for hierarchical ranking. In this part of the procession, the groups thought to be the most popular within the urban polity, namely the hundredmen and the swornmen, are clearly separated from the magistrates by the interposition of six burlesque contingents.

In the Latin text, the hundredmen opening the civic procession are explicitly described as a multitude kneeling before the princess (fol. 8^v). They consisted of a group of 44 individuals, responsible for policing the 41 districts of Brussels in which they led their daily life.[33] In charge of a squadron of ten men, they were responsible for the prevention of fires and revolts. The creation of a 'captain' for each district was introduced in 1421, following a revolt against the governing lineage of the city favoured by Duke Jean IV (1403-1427).[34] Between 1422 and 1423, craftsmen and shopkeepers who populated its ranks were allowed for a very short time to play an

---

31 Van Sprang, Sabine, 'Van Loon et les tableaux de la chapelle ducale Saint-Hubert à Tervueren', in *Theodoor Van Loon, 'pictor ingenius' et contemporain de Rubens*, ed by Sabine van Sprang, Cahiers des Musées royaux des Beaux-Arts de Belgique, 10 (Brussels: Snoeck, 2011), pp. 43-59 (45-51).

32 Hazebrouck-Souche, Véronique, *Spiritualité, sainteté et patriotisme. Glorification du Brabant dans l'œuvre hagiographique de Jean Gielemans (1427-1487)*, Hagiologia 6 (Turnhout: Brepols, 2007), p. 132.

33 Cuvelier, *Les dénombrements*, I, pp. 220-84. At this stage we cannot explain why the number of the hundredmen is 44 and not 41.

34 Favresse, Félicien, *L'avènement du régime démocratique à Bruxelles pendant le moyen âge (1306-1423)*, Mémoires de l'Académie royale de Belgique, classe des Lettres et des Sciences morales et politiques, 30 (Brussels: Hayez, 1932), pp. 204-22, p. 233.

important political role alongside the swornmen.[35] Their corps long maintained the memory of their ability to intervene in city affairs. The role of certain hundredmen of the Brussels insurgency following the death of Charles the Bold in 1477 was decisive and explains the ruling class' longstanding distrust of them.[36]

For the period of the Entry, we have records mentioning the names of the hundredmen and their exact social status. The listing of the houses in Brussels from May 1496 was carried out on the basis of each district a hundredman was responsible for. They were skilled and undoubtedly wealthy craftsmen. Among them were upholsterers, cobblers, brewers, tanners, a carpenter, a belt maker, a painter and well-known rhetorician: Hubert Steemaer, aka Pertcheval![37] The hundredmen were closely administered by the city council, to whom they swore absolute loyalty.[38] The swornmen were their leaders.

The latter are represented in the following pages (fol. 9^v-10^r) as the leaders of the 'masses' (*quasi plebeiorum capita*) who would have been occasionally consulted by the city government. They were without doubt the elites of the craft guilds. However, in reality, the swornmen were a key part of the city government, along with the hundredmen. As a unit they formed the 'Third member' of government, and in this capacity one of their roles consisted of making fiscal and financial decisions.[39]

The author of the manuscript enumerates four swornmen for each corporation. This was the maximum number for each corporation, and in reality, it varied among the professions.[40] The figures we see displaying the emblems of their corporation were cobblers, armourers, brewers, locksmiths, tailors, blacksmiths, ragmen, haberdashers and painters. By placing the haberdashers and painters at the front of the illustration (Fig. 4.2), the manuscript draws attention to these craft guilds, who are certainly involved in the organisation of the procession.[41] The swornmen and deans of the guilds were co-opted within the guilds and appointed by the aldermen.[42]

---

35 Favresse, Félicien, 'Esquisse de l'évolution constitutionnelle de Bruxelles depuis le XIIIe siècle jusqu'en 1477', in *Etudes sur les métiers bruxellois au Moyen Âge*, Centre d'Histoire économique et sociale (Brussels: Université libre de Bruxelles, Institut de sociologie, 1961), pp. 218-52, p. 235, pp. 265-68.

36 Van Uytven, Raymond, '1477 in Brabant', in *Le privilège général et les privilèges régionaux de Marie de Bourgogne pour les Pays-Bas 1477*, ed. by Wim P. Blockmans, (Kortrijk: UGA, 1985), Anciens pays et assemblées d'états LXXX, 253-85 (256).

37 Cuvelier, *Les dénombrements*, p. 236. Hubert was the father of Jan Pertcheval, see Remco Sleiderink, 'Johannes Steemaer alias Pertcheval. De naam en faam ven een Brusselse rederijker', in *Want hi verkende dien name wale. Opstellen voor Willem Kuiper*, ed. by Marjolein Hogenbirk, and Roel Zemel (Amsterdam: Stichting Neerlandistiek VU, Munster: Nodus Publikationen, 2014), pp. 149-54 (152-53).

38 Vannieuwenhuyze, Bram, "Allen dengenen die in der stad dienste sijn". Een overzicht van de stedelijke openbare ambten en diensten in het laatmiddeleeuwse Brussel 1229-1477, (unpublished master thesis, Gent University, 2002), p. 139.

39 Favresse, 'Esquisse', pp. 241-42.

40 Des Marez, *Organisation du travail*, pp. 165-66.

41 The identification of the craft guilds is possible thanks to the series of coats of arms illustrated in Henne, Alexandre, and Alphonse Wauters, *Histoire de la ville de Bruxelles*, new edition by Mina Martens (Brussels: Culture et civilisation, 1975), II, pp. 440-63.

42 Favresse, Félicien, 'Comment on choisissait les jurés de métier à Bruxelles pendant le Moyen Âge', in *Etudes sur les métiers bruxellois au Moyen Âge*, Centre d'Histoire économique et sociale (Brussels: Université libre de Bruxelles, Institut de sociologie, 1961), pp. 167-86 (182-86).

They regulated the behaviour of the craftsmen and ensured the rules of production were respected.⁴³ This particular point is emphasised in the manuscript, whilst also maintaining that the aim of this control was above all the protection of activities within the trades (fol. 9ᵛ: [...] *iura statutaque cuiusque officii seu artis custodiunt ac ne ars ulla corruptione in mercatorum fraudem ledatur preservantes*).

These two leading groups of representatives are meant to personify the whole urban population as they pay their respects to the princess. The relative vagueness in describing the role of the hundredmen and swornmen within city institutions is likely to have been deliberate. The image conveyed is of a society whose different sections were organised and managed for the benefit of public order and the smooth running of trade. As for politics, the manuscript text suggests that a sound consultation with the swornmen and the aldermen avoided confusion. The *superintendentes politice* mentioned in the text – that is, the city government – only consulted them on certain unspecified issues in order to avoid conflicts (fol. 9ᵛ: [...] *vitande multitudinis ac confusionis gratia ad consultandum!* [...]) and to ensure that the trades as a whole were not directly involved.

4.2 Southern Netherlandish, *The Festive Entry of Joanna of Castile into Brussels*, fol. 10ʳ (detail): *A Representative of the Guild of Saint Luke*, 1496, Berlin, SMPK, Kupferstichkabinett, ms 78 D5

The painting of these two groups emphasises social diversity in the variety of costumes worn. However, a number of minor details are worthy of note. The particular attention given to the painter in the procession seems to be a nod to the informed reader.

The author of the manuscript goes on to describe a series of six burlesque groups, in all probability presented by the military guilds, and perhaps associated with one of

---

43 Des Marez, *Organisation du travail*, pp. 169-72.

the rhetorical chambers or one of the parishes.[44] The carnation embroidered on the sleeves of the fife-player in the first scene (fol. 11^r) is a reference to the Great Guild of the Crossbow Bearers of Our-Lady. In the same scene, a fool is seen with a box and a spoon, the box possibly bearing the emblem of the archers or culverin-bearers. These *esbattements*, studied in greater depth by Laura Weigert, are typical examples of the participation of ordinary people in city celebrations, as opposed to the sophisticated *tableaux* presented later in the manuscript.[45] These are forms of entertainment and they included preposterous characters who brought laughter and jokes to a potentially poorly educated audience who was nonetheless devoted to the archduchess.[46] The positioning of these six groups subtly situated the military guilds, particularly the guild of Notre-Dame and perhaps those of the chambers of rhetoric at the interface between the masses and the city craft guilds on the one hand, and the highest-ranking dignitaries on the other. They thus incarnated in a jubilatory fashion the role of ideal intermediaries.

The Butchers: a Guild of Exception (fols 16^v-17^r)

Following the description of the *esbattements*, which is one of the only places in the manuscript where the urban landscape is represented (and we will come back to this later), the dramatic appearance of the young butchers cavorting on their horses cannot fail to surprise. We would rather have expected to see the rest of the procession of urban dignitaries. The incongruity was such that the former commentators of the manuscript have tended not to mention the presence of the butchers, or identified them as other urban figures more suited to this particular place in the organisation of the ceremony. Let us remember however that Jean Molinet had already mentioned the noteworthy role of the butchers when Philip the Fair entered Brussels in July 1495. On this occasion they had organised a hunt at the gates of the city, releasing their dogs to chase a stag and inviting the young prince to join them in their pursuit! This display was a way of showing to the new duke that as burghers of Brussels, they had the right to hunt and in their capacity as butchers, were noble enough to exercise this right *honnestement*, as Molinet wrote.[47] This charm offensive and demonstration of power was thus repeated in 1496 in front of Philip's new wife. This time, it was their tunic, matching the colours of the prince's costume, which sealed the alliance between the butchers and the dukes.[48] The text makes a point of noting that there were 36 butchers. Their energy and spirit conveyed in the text as well as in the

---

44 In relation to the involvement of the military guilds and chambers of rhetorics in the Joyous Entry, see article by Remco Sleiderink, and Amber Souleymane in this publication. With regards the participation of neighbourhoods and parishes in festivals and Entries, see Mareel, Samuel, *Voor vorst en stad. Rederijkerliteratuur en vorstenfeest in Vlaanderen en Brabant (1432-1561)*, (Amsterdam: Amsterdam University Press, 2010), pp. 78-94.
45 Weigert, *French Visual Culture*, pp. 61-70.
46 On this point see the contribution of Laura Weigert.
47 Doutrepont et Jodogne, *Chroniques de Jean Molinet*, I, p. 118.
48 The illustration indeed depicts the red vertical bands of the Castilian coat of arms. However, the green lines do not appear in the coat of arms, whereas the green and red are the colours of Brussels.

illustration in the movement of their horses and the tall fluttering feathers of their caps. Whereas the depiction of the other groups exudes calm and sobriety, every detail contributes to form a proud and potentially vindictive image of the butchers. Wealthy and influential, the butchers of Brussels had been in conflict with the city for decades. Feared instigators of socio-political struggles in the 14th century, they were seeking, from the middle of the 15th century onwards, to reaffirm a privilege granted to them first by Philip the Good in 1446, and then by Charles the Bold in 1467.[49] This privilege concerned the hereditary monopoly they wished to exercise within the butchering trade and the sale of meat in the market.[50] The city council and most of the other corporations considered this to be an extortionate request and one which was detrimental to the economic interests of the population. They opposed its implementation and this led to repeated violent outbreaks until the 1480s.[51] The presumed execution of one of their leaders by Maximilian in 1481 did not put an end to their actions.[52] The butchers unwaveringly followed their quest to impose this privilege by continually appealing to the prince and persuading him to grant them this request, in return for payment, until their demands were finally accepted in 1519.[53]

The place of the butchers in the Entry's portrayal is thus the result of a very particular power play. The ambitions of this corporation broke the unity of the guilds and pitted the prince and the city against one another. The author of the manuscript did not want and could not omit their presence, and thus assigned them instead an ambiguous position. They can be seen as belonging to the *esbattements* contingent, or as the forerunners of a long series of riders who, in the narrative, represent the city's political and legal professions.

The Magistrates on Horseback (fols 17^v-25^r)

In accordance with the socially hierarchically-ascending sequence of the procession we then see the sergeants, the messengers, the peacemakers (*apaiseurs* or *paysmakers*), the governors of the cloth guild, the secretaries, the counsellors of the Nations (craft guilds) and the receivers. They are the vanguard party of a unique group consisting of the 'First Member' of the city magistrature called the Law (*de Wet*),

---

49 Boffa, Serge, 'Réflexions sur la révolte des métiers bruxellois (22 juillet 1360)', in *Bruxelles et la vie urbaine. Archives-Art-Histoire. Recueil d'articles dédiés à la mémoire d'Arlette Smolar-Meynart (1938-2000)*, ed. by Frank Daelemans, and André Vanrie, 2 vols, (Archives et Bibliothèques de Belgique, numéro spécial 64, Brussels: KBR, 2001), I, pp. 163-85 (169-83); Thibaut Jacobs, 'Des hôpitaux de métiers à Bruxelles? Nouvelles perspectives sur la charité et la bienfaisance en milieu urbain à la fin du Moyen Âge', *Revue belge de Philologie et d'Histoire*, 91 (2013), 215-55 (234-35).

50 Billen, Claire, Chloé Deligne & David Kusman, 'Les bouchers bruxellois au bas Moyen Âge. Profils d'entrepreneurs', in *Patrons, gens d'affaires et banquiers, hommage à Ginette Kurgan-Van Hentenryk*, ed. by Serge Jaumain, et Kenneth Bertrams (Brussels: Le livre Timpermann, 2004), pp. 69-92.

51 Des Marez, *Organisation du travail*, pp. 85-93, 229.

52 Favresse, 'Documents relatifs à l'histoire politique intérieure', pp. 107-10: Pierre de Marbais, important leader of the 1477 revolt.

53 Des Marez, *Organisation du travail*, p. 94; and beyond: Bruneel, Claude, 'Sus au monopole des bouchers bruxellois: le franc marché du vendredi (1771-1787)', *Bijdragen tot de Geschiedenis*, 81 (1998), 115-25.

made up of seven aldermen, two burgomasters and the amman. They are followed by the burghers who accompany the burgomasters.

This cavalcade appears to be perfectly ordered. However, in reality, this arrangement was the culmination of a turbulent history, and those involved were well aware that the current state of affairs was potentially only a temporary one. In fact, the aims of the political struggles that had shaken Brussels society since at least the start of the 15th century were precisely aimed to reform the social order maintained by the representatives of the city's patrician families. The guilds, grouped together since 1421 into nine 'nations', as a means of political representation, had attempted, with varying degrees of success, to find a foothold within the city's institutions. However, it isn't always clear in which institutions they had succeeded in gaining a right of scrutiny (either by participating in the appointment of certain incumbents or by presenting some candidates for positions appointed by the aldermen). In this way, we know little about the 27 minor officers, described as sergeants or *knapen*, who served the aldermen and their tribunals and were the first to be presented to the princess (fols 17^v-18^r).[54] These officers were the lowest ranked members of this group within the procession. They are curiously referred to as *clientes* in the text. This is likely to signify that they were appointed by the aldermen and entirely at their command. Responsible for escorting the defendants to and from the courtroom, they were sword-bearers, as the illustration reveals. Their inferior status allows the author of the manuscript to make an evangelical allusion – *The last will be the first* (Matthew 20, 16) – thereby surreptitiously rewarding the archduchess with access to Paradise!

The sergeants are followed by the messengers or *boden*, who, we know, were appointed by the aldermen and the lineages from which they were chosen (fols 18^v-19^r).[55] Noteworthy is the unified colour of their coats depicted in the illustration. Like most officers, the city gave them cloth or a sum of money with which to make clothes, which revealed the prestige of Brussels. Their representation in the manuscript draws attention to their capacity to use a large diversity of languages: they are the symbol of the city's socially and geographically extensive relations with the outside world.

In contrast, it is mostly in the small patrician world of the city that the *apaiseurs* or *paysmakers* (fols 19^v-20^r) worked. They were responsible for quelling Brussels' chronic internal conflicts. As in all large towns, powerful families competed for influence, power and honour, resorting to affronts, assaults, violence, injuries and arson which led to endless cycles of revenge. The peacemakers' court was created in 1343. The ten members, chosen by the aldermen within the lineages, had to deal with conflicts passed on from one generation to the other, such as the feud between two branches of the Vander Noot family, or the conflict which opposed the Van den Heetvelde and de Mol parties, the repercussions of which were felt in different forms until the end of the 15th century.[56] In 1423, the *paysmakers'* tribunal

---

54 Vannieuwenhuyze, "Allen dengenen", p. 85.
55 Vannieuwenhuyze, "Allen dengenen", p. 86.
56 Smolar-Meynart, 'Les guerres privées et la cour des apaiseurs', pp. 237-54.

was no longer exclusively connected to the aldermen and the lineages. Henceforth they had eight members, half of whom had to be members of the guilds. This is the number represented in the manuscript. They are all dressed in red coats, the colour of justice. At least two judges were required to sit at the tribunal, one representing each 'obediance' (of lineages and guilds). At the time the peacemakers took part in the procession, their corporation was under considerable pressure to reduce the influence of the Nations. In 1481, Maximilian had already attempted to control the appointment of the peacemakers by the burgomaster who were not from patrician families. In 1509, the tribunal was once again entirely under patrician control.[57]

The following *Eight of the Guild* were also judges (fols 20^v-21^r). They sat at the city hall and their jurisdiction extended to litigation and all offences related to the textile industry and the clothing trade. Given that in a city like Brussels, these activities played a major economic role and employed a considerable number of artisans, the socio-political position of these judges is noteworthy. In addition, under the command of the guild's two deans, they also had extensive jurisdiction over the enforcement and seizure of property following debts involving transactions of cloth or raw materials in the textile industry, where advanced payments and credit were the norm.[58]

The *Eight* and the deans were appointed by the aldermen annually, like most commissions in Brussels at the time. From 1423, the position of guild administrators was evenly distributed among the patrician families and the craft guilds. However, between 1477 and 1480, around the time of the discord at the start of Mary of Burgundy's reign, all the guild commissions were exercised by the representatives of the Nations![59] This is a sign of the powerful tensions that must have been disrupting the running of this institution. Reinstating a shared responsibility between patricians and the craft guilds could not have been an easy process. For an institution so ubiquitous in the lives of most of the population of Brussels, the tensions present in the running of the guild must have had ongoing repercussions on civil peace. The text in the manuscript emphasises the role of the *Eight* in monitoring the quality of cloth and carrying out appeals when complaints were made. It also stresses the fluidity and stability of the textile trade in Brussels, an important aspect of the city's reputation.

The three groups to appear next in the procession were of a completely different order. They consisted of the city secretaries, the advisors of the Nations and the receivers. Being part of the city government, they were closely involved in the aldermen's legislative and judicial activities.

The author of the manuscript describes the presence of six secretaries (fols 21^v-22^r). This is in all likelihood an exaggeration. At the time of Joanna's

---

57 Van Honacker, Karin, 'Bestuurinstellingen van de stad Brussel (12de eeuw-1795)', in *De gewestelijke en lokale overheidsinstellingen in Brabant en Mechelen tot 1795*, ed. by Raymond Van Uytven, Claude Bruneel, Hilde Coppens, and Beatrijs Augustijn, 2 vols, Algemeen Rijksarchief in de provinciën, Studia 82 (Brussels: Algemeen Rijksarchief, 2000), II, pp. 393-461 (405).
58 Dickstein-Bernard, Claire, 'Actes du tribunal de la gilde drapière de Bruxelles 1333-1435', *Bulletin de la Commission royale pour la publication des Anciennes Lois et Ordonnances de Belgique*, 35 (1995), 1-43.
59 Dickstein-Bernard, 'Actes du tribunal de la gilde drapière', p. 6, n. 14.

Entry, there were in fact three secretaries and three sworn clerks.[60] They were from affluent backgrounds and sometimes began their careers in religious or charitable institutions.[61] Highly qualified and able to express themselves with ease in Latin as well as the vernacular languages spoken at the time, their role was crucial. The manuscript describes them in a very interesting way. The cloaks they wore were supplied by the city, making them easily recognisable. Closely connected to the magistrates, they drafted the aldermen's acts in the spirit they were conceived and wrote up the minutes of city council meetings which they attended and whose content they transmitted to the participating individuals and institutions. Thus, they were privy to secrets, and their political competence dictated how they made use of these. They composed and compiled records, leading the manuscript to state that they produced the annals (*decreta legislatorum annalibus annotantes*). This rather pompous way of describing their task reveals the sense of importance given to the secretaries. Bearers of knowledge *par excellence* and established in their profession for a long period, they thus recorded valuable elements of the city's memory and had the means to transmit it, a role to which the author of the manuscript had be particularly sensitive to.[62] Wasn't he also a city chronicler? Later in the manuscript, the somewhat unexpected importance given to the so-called *Boterpot* building, where the freedoms of the city were kept, undoubtedly echoes the importance given to the secretaries in the text.[63] Together, these two references no doubt aimed to show that, in Brussels, the memory and the rights of the city were well guarded.

It is only concern with hierarchical ranking that make it possible to understand why the author of the manuscript placed the advisors of the Nations after the secretaries and before the receivers (fols 22^v-23^r). Logically, they would have been placed further down in the manuscript, directly before the aldermen, who were in theory their colleagues within the Law (*de Wet*).

The six advisors of the Nations held seats in the city government since the uprising of 1421. An ordinance dated to 10th June 1423 states that they would be chosen by the lineages from a list of 27 men presented by the Nations to govern alongside the aldermen.[64] It is from this same list that the patricians also elected the burgomaster and the receivers of the trades, of whom we will talk about in a moment. The advisors were thus largely dependent on the oligarchic families that had governed Brussels since the 13th century. Furthermore, it was decided in 1480 that any candidate for a political mandate would need to prove the receipt of an annual income of at least

---

60 Vannieuwenhuyze, "Allen dengenen", p. 84.
61 Dickstein-Bernard, Claire, *La gestion financière d'une capitale à ses débuts: Bruxelles, 1334-1467*, Brussels: Annales de la Société royale d'Archéologie de Bruxelles, 54, 1977, p. 289.
62 Dumolyn, Jan, and Anne-Laure Van Bruaene, 'Urban Historiography in Late Medieval and Early Modern Europe', in *Urban History Writing in North-Western Europe (15th-16th Centuries)*, ed. by Bram Caers, Lisa Demets, and Tineke van Gassen, Studies in European Urban History, 47 (Turnhout: Brepols, 2019), pp. 7-24 (12-16).
63 On that point see here the contribution of Sasha Köhl, 'The Brussels Town Hall. A Worthy Emblem for a Capital City'.
64 Favresse, 'Esquisse de l'évolution constitutionnelle', pp. 231-32.

50 Rhine florins.[65] This directive introduced a long series of restrictions which sought to weaken the role of the guilds in city governance, a policy which went on for most of the 16th century. The text in this section of the manuscript is particularly unclear on the exact role of the advisors in the first member of the city government. They advised the aldermen and drafted some of their acts.[66] They were all workshop masters or wealthy entrepreneurs, appointed by leaders of the guilds and members of the Nations. The way the Nations were structured clearly favoured the less radical and more wealthy guilds. Some corporations never had an advisor to represent them.[67]

The receivers who succeeded in the procession were also chosen by the aldermen to whom they took an oath, and were also a constituent part of the Law (23ᵛ-24ʳ). This arrangement had existed in Brussels since 1334 and was initiated by the city, without the prince's involvement.[68] From 1421 – that is to say from the time the craft guilds took part in the city's governance – the aldermen appointed four rather than two receivers. This role was henceforth entrusted to two men from the lineages and two members of the guilds.[69] They did not have any decision-making power but their responsibilities required a great deal of expertise in negotiation, and they had a wide-ranging remit. Receivers were responsible for keeping accounts and presented their work to the aldermen, councillors and the ducal representative, the amman.[70] They did not lend money to the city; this responsibility fell to the money changer, a figure who does not appear in our document.[71] Nevertheless, the receivers were guarantors, using their personal collateral for payments owed by the city to its creditors. To be a receiver, it was therefore necessary to be rich and relatively free from the constraints of regular work. The position involved a great deal of responsibility. It was unpaid and required education, experience and financial means. Among the lineages, the receivers were often former aldermen.[72] The receivers from the guilds belonged to corporations of businessmen, such as silversmiths, butchers, haberdashers, armourers or saddlers. Among them were traders who supplied the court or entrepreneurs who played an active role in urban construction sites.[73] It is likely that their jobs and connections on the ground counterbalanced the political knowledge and the interpersonal skills of their patrician colleagues who had previous experience within city institutions. In the illustration, the receivers also wear a uniform, a rose-coloured coat which appears

---

65 Favresse, 'Esquisse de l'évolution constitutionnelle', p. 252. This ordinance had also attempted to eliminate the role of the guild advisors; a measure which was cancelled in 1481. See Godding, Philippe, 'L'adaptation de la justice échevinale aux besoins d'une ville en expansion: le cas de Bruxelles', in *Bruxelles et la vie urbaine. Archives-Art-Histoire. Recueil d'articles dédiés à la mémoire d'Arlette Smolar-Meynart (1938-2000)*, ed. by Frank Daelemans, and André Vanrie, 2 vols, (Archives et Bibliothèques de Belgique, numéro spécial 64, Brussels: KBR, 2001), I, pp. 29-72 (50).
66 On this point, Godding gives more accurate details than Favresse: Godding, 'L'adaptation de la justice échevinale', pp. 50-54.
67 Favresse, *L'avènement du régime démocratique*, pp. 287-89.
68 Dickstein-Bernard, *La gestion financière*, pp. 234-35.
69 Dickstein-Bernard, *La gestion financière*, p. 240.
70 Dickstein-Bernard, *La gestion financière*, pp. 260-90.
71 Dickstein-Bernard, *La gestion financière*, pp. 310-11.
72 Dickstein-Bernard, *La gestion financière*, pp. 243.
73 Dickstein-Bernard, *La gestion financière*, pp. 251-52.

to have been chosen to express their affiliation to the city. The importance of the receivers' status should not be underestimated. The comments on their presence in the manuscript, are concise yet strikingly indulgent. They credit the receivers with much more authority than they had in reality (fol. 23^v: [...] *administrantes rempublicam in materialibus; erarii publici dispensatores* [...]). Their place in the procession, immediately preceding the aldermen, was also intended to exalt their prestige.

Placed at the summit of the urban hierarchy, the seven aldermen appear last in the cavalcade, alongside the amman and the burgomasters (24^v-25^r). The aldermen were all from patrician families. They judged and legislated. They were the first magistrates of the city, the guardians of its law. Their role in city government has been traced back to the first third of the 12th century. They were appointed by the duke of Brabant on whose behalf their court acted. Their yearly appointment began in 1235.[74] At the turn of 14th century, the great landed families of Brussels organised themselves into 'lineages' *(geslachten)* in order to restrict access of the aldermen's judicial authorities to their members alone.[75] Despite the repeated uprisings of the guilds and the pressure exerted by rich families of the city, excluded from power throughout the 14th century, and despite the great regime change of 1421, the aldermen were in a way the guardians of the oligarchy within Brussel's political society. It should be noted that the manuscript does not make any reference to their administrative and managerial roles, even though these impacted on every aspect of public life. They are only represented in their role as keepers of justice. This made it possible to create a majestic unit of horsemen wearing the city coat, shouldered by the two burgomasters and the amman, without being encumbered by other members of the government, who were presented separately in the procession.

The aldermen's judgements, including the death penalty, were carried out in the name of the duke by the amman (*amptman*). The amman was the ducal officer, whose jurisdiction extended much beyond the aldermen's, encompassing a vast rural region around the city. The amman's role originated from the powers of the seigneurial mayor. The first ammans of Brussels are cited at the very end of the 12th century.[76] In the 14th century, when the city government demanded a right of scrutiny over the ducal administration, the amman had to swear an oath of allegiance to the city, as he did to the duke.[77] The amman presided over the court of the aldermen. In a city like Brussels, his powers were limited by the aldermen and the burghers who depended on them. In the middle of the 15th century, the amman of Brussels was appointed within the local nobility or the urban patriciate and was closely involved in party strife. The prince appointed and dismissed the amman in accordance with the alliances

---

74 Van Honacker, 'Bestuurinstellingen van de stad Brussel', pp. 393-404.
75 Martens, Mina, 'Note sur l'époque de fixation du nom des sept lignages bruxellois', *Cahiers Bruxellois*, 4 (1959), 173-93.
76 Kerremans, Charles, *Étude sur les circonscriptions judiciaires et administratives du Brabant et les officiers placés à leur tête par les ducs antérieurement à l'avènemement de la Maison de Bourgogne (1406)*, Mémoires de l'Académie royale de Belgique, Classe des Lettres et des Sciences morales et politiques 44, (Brussels: Palais des Académies, 1949), pp. 26-27.
77 Kerremans, *Étude sur les circonscriptions judiciaires*, p. 74.

of the moment.⁷⁸ This practice weakened the institution the amman represented. Undoubtedly, this is what allowed the author of the manuscript to abstain from conferring any particular significance to the amman's presence in the procession. The illustration does however place the amman in the centre of the picture, bearing a staff and wearing a red costume, the symbol of justice. Moreover, it might be that the author did not wish to draw undue attention to the representative of princely power when the premise of the procession was to show the good administration and independent authority of the city.

This contrasts strongly with the emphasis placed on the role of the two burgomasters, one representing the Nations and the other the lineages (since 1421), and even of the depiction of the aldermen.⁷⁹ The institution of the burgomasters expresses perfectly the politics of compromise that presided over the new constitution of Brussels in 1421, in that the burgomaster of the lineages was ultimately appointed by representatives of the Nations and vice versa for the burgomaster of the craft guilds.⁸⁰ The text appears to insist on the undisputed power of the burgomasters over the citizens of Brussels and the equity they sought in the exercise of judicial authorities, which allowed them to intervene in decisions made in the aldermen's court. They are described as mediators, as the true leaders of the burghers (*cives, oppidani*). The latter, represented in the following illustration (fols 25ᵛ-26ʳ) were very different to the 'masses' kneeling at the start of the procession. They accompanied the burgomasters. Young and old, the text suggests that the burghers of Brussels, experienced on horseback like their noble counterparts, offered the princess a splendid spectacle! In this way, the burghers and their two main representatives (the burgomasters of the guilds and the lineages), in their role as leaders of wonderfully functioning institutions and highly competent magistrates were thus placed at the very top of the symbolic ladder depicted in the Entry's portrayal.

This detailed description, concluded by the place of honour given to the burgomasters and the burghers who brought together the elite of the guilds and the noble families of Brussels makes no mention of an institution whose existence was, however, well established in 1496. This was the council composed of the aldermen, the burgomasters and the retired receivers. It was dominated by representatives of the lineages and formed the second member of government, alongside the Law (the first member of government) and the swornmen and the hundredmen (the third member). Originally an advisory body, this council had obtained prerogatives in fiscal matters since the 1460s.⁸¹ It would be foolhardy to attempt an explanation of this

---

78 The most egregious examples of this system can be observed between 1430 and 1469 when the family of Enghien occupied the function of amman. See Stein, Robert, 'Van publieke devotie naar besloten orde. De stichting van het klooster Scheut', *Millenium. Tijdschrift voor middeleeuwse studies*, 23 (2009), 12-37 (21-23); Bartier, 'Un document sur les prévarications', pp. 348-52.
79 Favresse, *L'avènement du régime démocratique*, pp. 226-28.
80 Favresse, *L'avènement du régime démocratique*, p. 228.
81 Favresse, 'Esquisse de l'évolution constitutionnelle', pp. 236-45. On the role of this institution in times of financial crisis, see Dickstein-Bernard, Claire, 'La voix de l'opposition au sein des institutions bruxelloises 1455-1467', in

omission. However, let us note nonetheless that it succeeds in highlighting even more clearly the omnipotent power of the Law, of the first member of government, the aldermen and burgomasters.

A Tribute to the Built Environment of the City and its Builders (fols 26ᵛ-27ʳ)

The city's excellence did not rely solely on its exemplary magistrates and fine burghers. The buildings, their beauty and design, and the built environment of the city as a whole all were crucial in consolidating its reputation.[82] The archduchess was thus invited to visit her Coudenberg palace, following a column lined with the countless figures paid to be present by the city in order to create an image of grandeur. Architects, builders, surveyors, sculptors and other craftsmen cite Brussels as a patron and developer.[83] Through a contemporary lens, it is strange to see in the manuscript the craftsmen and engineers who oversaw the construction of large monuments depicted alongside wall watchmen or *moddermeyer* (mud mayor). Yet, it does all cohere. Firstly, the city's magistrates and civil servants were all dressed in the colours of Brussels and held a torch bearing the city's red coat of arms. They had pledged an oath to the city and stood as equals. Secondly, from an ideological viewpoint, they were all contributors to the physical manifestation of an ideal city, a shared space, adorned with beautiful and carefully designed buildings, with roads and squares that were safe and clean, and with fountains that dispersed the miasma and nasty smells of the city.[84] It was by the light of the torches held aloft by all the creators of this comforting security that Joanna reached her residence.

At the very end of the 15ᵗʰ century, it is likely that the financial and demographic difficulties facing the city meant it was no longer possible to pay a large number of skilled craftsmen. It is at present accepted that Rogier van der Weyden (†1464) had no successor in his role as city painter.[85] Similarly, the contracts with the architects and master builders of the city hall or the large room (*Aula magna*) of the ducal palace, financed by the city, were not renewed with other builders, except on a one-off

---

Hommage au professeur Paul Bonenfant (1899-1965), Études d'histoire médiévale dédiées à sa mémoire par les anciens élèves de son séminaire à l'Université Libre de Bruxelles (Brussels: Université Libre de Bruxelles, 1965), pp. 479-500 (495-500).

82 Billen, Claire, and Chloé Deligne, 'Urban Space: Infrastructure, Technology and Power', in *City and Society in the Low Countries, 1100-1600*, ed. by Bruno Blondé, Marc Boone, Anne-Laure Van Bruaene (Cambridge: Cambridge University Press, 2018), pp. 162-91.

83 Geleyns, Piet, and Pierre Smars, 'Het ontwerpproces en zijn context: de bouwmeester, de opdrachtgever en het ambacht', in *Gotiek in het hertogdom Brabant*, ed. by Krista De Jonge, Piet Geleyns, Markus Hörsch (Leuven: Peeters, 2009), pp. 139-55 (143-45).

84 Coomans, Janna, *Community, Urban Health and Environment in Late Medieval Low Countries*, (Cambridge: Cambridge University Press, 2021).

85 Vannieuwenhuyze, "Allen dengenen", pp. 198-99.

4.3 Aert van den Bossche, *Triptych of the Martyrdom of Saint Crispin and Saint Crispinian for the Cobblers and Shoemakers of Brussels*, Brussels, oil on wood, 1490, Musée de la Ville de Bruxelles, K1977 1 et 2 © KIK-IRPA

basis.[86] It seems that corporations, churches and individuals were more active as benefactors at the time (Fig. 4.3) than city institutions.[87] Without the yearly accounts of Brussels, now partly lost, it is not possible to ascertain the actual number of people employed by the city responsible for maintaining its buildings, roads, fountains and firefighting services, or be clear about their respective functions. Perhaps there was a master-mason and master-carpenter, a slate roofer, a clock-maker and a locksmith.[88] There appears to have been 16 guards keeping watch at the gates and walls of the city. They were also watchers around the city hall, the tower of Saint-Nicholas and the tower of the Church of La Chapelle (*Kapellekerk*).[89] The manuscript makes a curious mention of the cries made by those on night patrols: (fol. 26ᵛ: [...] *clamatorum luminum et ignium qui singulis noctibus preconisantes hiis cautio adhibeantur* [...]). They did indeed swear to shout: *wacht uwe licht ende uwe vier* (watch over your lights and your fires!).[90] As for those responsible for the removal of garbage, they were at the head of a small department that also looked after the fountains.[91]

The assembled Escort of Military Guilds (fols 27ᵛ-31ʳ)

The four military guilds of Brussels participated in Joanna's Entry and escorted her in order to guarantee her safety.[92] The procession was led in the following order: the guild of the *coulevriniers* (culverin-bearers) or *arquebusiers* (arquebus-bearers) of Saint-Christophe, the archers' guild of Saint-Sébastien, the crossbowmen guild of Saint-Georges and the more prestigious guild of the Grand Serment de Notre-Dame.

The *couleuvriniers* or *arquebusiers* were light artillerymen (fols 27ᵛ-28ʳ). Unequivocal mention of the Brussels artillery is made from 1378 onwards and its existence resulted in a large expense for the city. Whereas in 1456, the city's artillery provided five master-gunners (*donderbusmeesteren*) and five culver-bearers (*colovermeesteren*), accompanied by four servants (*knechten*) for Philip the Good's expedition against Deventer, it appears that the princes did not rely on the city's artillery thereafter.[93] The Brussels' expedition against the castle of Beersel in 1488 during Philip of Cleves'

---

86 Dickstein-Bernard, Claire, 'La construction de *l'Aula magna* au palais du Coudenberg. Les préliminaires (1451-1452)', *Annales de la Société royale d'Archéologie de Bruxelles*, 67 (2006), 53-75 (55-64); Dickstein-Bernard, Claire, 'La construction de *l'Aula magna* au palais du Coudenberg, histoire du chantier (1452-1461?)', *Annales de la Société royale d'Archéologie de Bruxelles*, 68 (2007), 35-64.
87 Bücken, Véronique, 'La peinture à Bruxelles à la fin du XVe siècle. Fortune critique et méthodologie', in *L'Héritage de Rogier van der Weyden. La peinture à Bruxelles 1450-1520*, ed. by Véronique Bücken, et Griet Steyaert (Thielt: Lannoo, 2013), pp. 13-36 (22-24).
88 Vannieuwenhuyze, "Allen dengenen", pp. 191-94. There was a master mason in 1499-1500; Claire Dickstein-Bernard, 'La construction de l'Aula Magna', p. 59.
89 Dickstein-Bernard, 'La construction de l'Aula Magna', pp. 164, 166.
90 Dickstein-Bernard, 'La construction de l'Aula Magna', p. 165.
91 Deligne, Chloé, *Bruxelles et sa rivière. Genèse d'un territoire urbain (12ᵉ-18ᵉ siècle)*, Studies in European Urban History, 1, (Turnhout, Brepols, 2003), pp. 100-04.
92 The fencers' guild was active only from 1506.
93 Depreter, Michael, *De Gavre à Nancy (1453-1477). L'artillerie bourguignonne sur la voie de la 'modernité'*, Burgundica 18 (Turnhout: Brepols, 2011), p. 74; pp. 169-73.

revolt did make use of the artillery but only with mediocre success. Maximilian had taken advantage of the repression to confiscate artillery.[94] We therefore presume that, in the period we are dealing with here, the Brussels arsenal was only a shadow of its former self, despite the enthusiastic description by the author of the manuscript.

The archers' guild of Saint-Sébastien is only mentioned in passing, the text simply highlighting its perfect integration in the procession (fols 28ᵛ-29ʳ). In accordance with the culture of the times, the place of honour was given to the crossbowmen. The crossbow as a weapon was established as early as the 13th century within the burgher corporations. Efficient and more complex, it did not aim to supplant the lighter and faster traditional bow but its formidable power supported and strengthened the infantry.[95] It was a weapon widely used in siege warfare. The first mention of a group of crossbowmen in Brussels dates back to 1304, when the *gemeyne schutters* of the town were given a site for the construction of a chapel by the Saint-John's hospital.[96] A collective place of worship was certainly one of the very first steps in the creation of a corporation.

Let us note that several groups of crossbowmen subsequently coexisted. It's likely that each had its own social niche, which was more or less accepted by a city administration dominated by the major oligarchic families. In this way, the *Compagnons tireurs* of the Saint-Laurent district – a marshy area where market gardeners and launderers lived in the north-east of the city – were not allowed to continue as an independent organisation. In the first half of the 14th century, they were forced to merge with the first corporation and accept an inferior status within a guild which very quickly became elitist, referred to as a 'great' guild or *Gilde du Grand Serment*.[97] The grill motif on the cap badges of some of the participants in the procession may be a sign of the persistence of their collective memory (Fig. 4.4). Another group, founded later in the 1380s, managed to survive. Dedicated to Saint-Georges, it was present in the Entry's procession, just before the great guild (fols 29ᵛ-30ʳ). The great guild finally appeared at the end surrounding the young princess in a setting illuminated by the city hall and the sparkling costumes of the shooting corporations (fols 30ᵛ-31ʳ).

At the end of the 15th century, all the shooting corporations had a chapel in the sanctuary of the crossbowmen's great guild. Throughout the 15th century, the sanctuary had been rebuilt in majestic proportions.[98] Known as the Church of Our Blessed Lady of the Sablon (*Onze-lieve-Vrouw-ter-Zavelkerk* or *Notre-Dame du Sablon*), it was an elegant place of worship frequented by the court. It was at the centre of the organisation of the *Ommegang*, the great circular procession of Brussels started by

---

94 Vrancken, *Een papier strijd*, pp. 21-22; see also Léon Zylbergeld, 'L'artillerie de la ville de Bruxelles au milieu du XVe siècle d'après un inventaire de 1451-1452', *Revue belge d'Histoire militaire*, 23 (1980), 609-46.
95 Serdon, Valérie, *Armes du diable. Arcs et arbalètes au Moyen Âge* (Rennes: Presses Universitaires de Rennes, 2005).
96 Vanrie, André, 'L'église et son environnement', in *L'église Notre-Dame du Sablon*, ed. by Ministère de la Région de Bruxelles-Capitale, Direction des monuments et sites (Brussels: 2004), pp. 24-42.
97 Jacobs, 'Des hôpitaux de métiers à Bruxelles?', pp. 242-45.
98 De Clercq, Lode, and Frans Dopéré, 'Apport de la chronologie de la taille des pierres', in *L'église Notre-Dame du Sablon*, pp. 91-98.

4.4a/b Southern Netherlandish, *The Festive Entry of Joanna of Castile into Brussels*, a) fol. 29ʳ (detail): *A Crossbowman wearing a hat badge with a grill*, b) fol. 31ʳ (detail): *A Crossbowman wearing a hat badge with Notre Dame du Sablon and two additional Figures standing on a Boat*, 1496, Berlin, SMPK, Kupferstichkabinett, ms 78 D5

the crossbowmen in order to unify the urban population, the magistrates and the princes in their devotion to the miraculous statuette of the Virgin conserved at the Church of Our Blessed Lady of the Sablon.⁹⁹ Joanna's Entry seems to re-enact a kind of *Ommegang* procession. The escort of the Grand Serment closed the procession of Brussels' official institutions. As well as demonstrating their role in providing security of the archduchess, this promoted the authority of the crossbowmen's great guild over the city's rites of unity. In fact, the text clearly points out the subordinate and compliant position of the culverin-bearers, the archers and the crossbowmen of Saint-Georges, and the aloofness of the members of the Grand Serment, thus affirming their dominating status (Fig. 4.5).

One of the main aims of the military corporations was to organise regular practice in the use of weaponry, as well as maintaining a spirit of unity, devotion to the city and the development of displays.¹⁰⁰ Contrary to what we might have expected, the

---

99 Billen, Claire, 'La construction d'une centralité: Bruxelles dans le duché de Brabant au bas Moyen Âge', in *The Power of Space in Late Medieval and Early Modern Europe. The cities of Italy, Northern France and the Low Countries*, ed. by Marc Boone, and Martha C. Howell, Studies in European Urban History 30, (Turnhout: Brepols, 2013), pp. 183-95.

100 Crombie, Laura, *Archery and Crossbow Guilds in Medieval Flanders 1300-1500* (Woodbridge: The Boydell Press, 2016), pp. 128-35.

4.5 Brussels, collection of the Great Guild of the Crossbow: *Ornament for a processional stick representing the miraculous Statue of Onze-Lieve-Vrouw ten Zavel (Notre-Dame du Sablon) on a boat*, silver, composite object with three crossbows attached © J.-M. De Pelsemaeker, Centre Albert Marinus

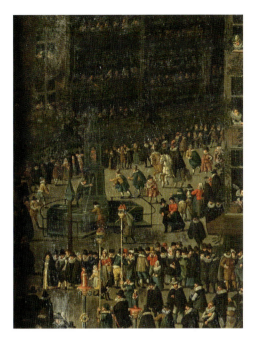

4.6 Denijs van Alsloot and workshop, *The Ommegang of 1615. Parade of craftsmen on the Brussels Grand-Place* (detail): *The Fountain on the Fish Market*, Brussels, Musées Royaux des Beaux-Arts de Belgique, inv. 170. Photo: J. Geleyns © RMFAB

manuscript makes little mention of the role of shooting corporations in defence and war, but insists instead on their role as guardians of law and order within the city itself, and their submission to the burgomasters' authority. This recurring message is thus repeated again here: Brussels is well governed, the security of the princes is ensured not only by an administration and a justice system which is well devised and functions harmoniously, but also by armed corps who are sworn to loyalty, experienced and disciplined, and able to mobilise at the slightest rumour.

There were many connections between the shooting guilds and the chambers of rhetoric. They both recruited members from the middle of the social spectrum, where the elite of the crafts and entrepreneurs had pride of place. The crossbowmen of Brussels put on theatrical performances and their organisation of the *Ommegang* included the *esbattements* and the performance of scenes.[101] There is little doubt that they were amongst the initiators of Joanna's Entry, as we indicated earlier. Let

---

101 Van Bruaene, Anne-Laure, *Om beters wille. Rederijkerskamers en de stedelijke cultuur in de Zuidelijke Nederlanden (1400-1650)*, Amsterdam: Amsterdam University Press, 2008, pp. 47, 93-94.

us note that the representation of the crossbowmen of Saint-Georges may reveal collusion with the chamber of rhetoric of the Lys (*De Lelie*), if the embroidery on the sleeves of the crossbowmen, unfortunately not fully legible, could be identified as a lily. The embroidery on the sleeves of certain protagonists in the procession, such as the jesters or the military guilds, provide clues in interpreting the manuscript. It is clearly replete with imperceptible details and subtle messages which can only be deciphered by readers who are aware of the codes used within Brussels society. It includes the suggestion of collaboration between the shooting guilds and the literary and painting associations in the signature of the organisers; the painters being put forward in the passages relating to the swornmen. These corporations were likely to be the originators of the manuscript, conserving those memories of the festivities where their knowledge and expertise had shone and echoed the city's great pride. From the start of the manuscript to its conclusion, Brussels appears with its patron saint, magistrates, burghers, technicians, rhetoricians and finally its splendid city hall and is presented as rich, unified, learned and devoted to its princes.

The first section of the manuscript does not reflect Joanna's welcoming procession as it really took place. It establishes, in a sophisticated succession rich with symbols, an inventory of the best of Brussels society. The literary circles at the head of the procession's organisation were responsible for bolstering the role of Brussels as a courtier city. The manuscript is a record of the ceremony but also an aid in this process, aiming to show that, despite its diversity, Brussels was an orderly city. These organisers later became the initiators of the guild of Our Lady of the Seven Sorrows which, in the same way as the *Ommegang* and the entries, aimed to unite all the privileged citizens of Brussels in a polite devotional practice that would reassure the princely powers.[102]

Conclusion

The manuscript we are concerned with is unique in more ways than one. It appears to be the only source identified to date documenting Joanna's Entry into Brussels, but is also unique in the fact that over half of the manuscript is devoted to the representation of the religious and civic bodies that enabled the city to run smoothly. These two aspects of the manuscript invite us firstly to contrast what may have happened in Brussels on December 9th 1496 and the account given in the manuscript, and secondly, to question the function of the oddly detailed initial section of the manuscript. What emerges is a sense that the discourse was aimed as much at the stakeholders in the city's public life as it was to the princess. Centred on the city itself,

---

102 Speakman-Sutch, Susie, and Anne-Laure van Bruaene, 'The Seven Sorrows of the Virgin Mary: Devotional Communication and Politics in the Burgundian-Habsburg Low Countries, c. 1490-1520', *Journal of Ecclesiastical History*, 61 (2010), 252-78; Speakman-Sutch, Susie, 'Patronage, Foundation History, and Ordinary Believers. The Membership Registry of the Brussels Seven Sorrows Confraternity', in *The Seven Sorrows Confraternity of Brussels. Drama, Ceremony and Art Patronage (16th-17th Centuries)*, ed. by Emily S. Thelen, Studies in European Urban History, 37 (Turnhout: Brepols, 2015), pp. 19-48.

the manuscript opens with a representation of Saint-Michel, the patron of the city of Brussels, and closes with a description of the extraordinary city hall. Gordon Kipling has already noted the relative importance placed on the princess in the representation of this very particular entry:

> What we get is the astonishing illustration which actually seeks to displace her from the center of attention (…) instead of singling her out of special attention, the artist has chosen to depict her surrounded by – indeed nearly obscured by – a group of torch-bearing military guildsmen (…) In fact, however, the artist is more interested in the guildsmen's special distinction than he is in hers.[103]

Whether through veiled references, the liberty taken in interpreting historic realities or in the selection of what could be shown and the calculated omissions, this first section of the manuscript sends a number of messages about everyone's place within a staged urban ideal. The author emphasises the upstanding, learned, competent and traditional character of the members of the institutions chosen to participate in the procession. These qualities are essential in the construction of an underlying discourse whereby Brussels was a unified and peaceful city where public order reigned. This performative discourse must be understood within the context of the profound unrest that had divided Brussels society for many decades. However, it could only be achieved by undermining the elements seen by the author of the manuscript as disruptive, i.e. the craftsmen, and to a lesser extent, the Brussels oligarchy, which is portrayed in a dominant rather than a dominating role. There is a deliberate emphasis placed on the institutions which succeeded in bringing together the patriciate, the elite of the crafts guilds and, where possible, the prince.

This discourse is all the more coherent if we acknowledge the fact that the procession, in company with the resulting manuscript, was orchestrated by the chambers of rhetoric and the military guilds, two bastions where the pride and unity of the city was cultivated. The connection between these two closely linked corporations is stressed – perhaps even celebrated – by the symbols on the clothing of some of their representatives.

One more element can be seen to contribute to this desire to represent the city as a unified body. In contrast to the classic accounts of the princely entries often related in the chronicles, our manuscript makes no allusion to a direct entry of the princess into the city escorted by officials.[104] On the contrary, the manuscript's illustrations appear to take all the different groups around the city, through a peripheral area dotted with a few emblematic buildings, a mill or an inn, a chapel, church or bridge, where it would futile to attempt to recognise existing buildings with any degree of

---

103 Kipling, 'Brussels, Joanna of Castile, and the Art of Theatrical Illustration (1496)', p. 233.
104 Whereas a princess' entry took the form of a circular procession around the city, the princes' entries took direct possession of the city, a reference to the princes taking possession of their wives, see the entry of Mary of Burgundy in Bruges: Karaskova, Olga, '*Panthasilia virgo in civitatem Tryona amicabiliter recepta fuit*. La Joyeuse Entrée de Marie de Bourgogne à Bruges en 1477', in *Marie de Bourgogne. Figure, principat et postérité d'une duchesse tardo-médiévale*, ed. by Michael Depreter, Jonathan Dumont, Elisabeth l'Estrange, and Samuel Mareel, Burgundica 31 (Turnhout: Brepols, 2021), pp. 103-14 (112).

certainty. The background sometimes evokes the defensive walls and towers of the city, highlighting that the groups represented were indeed beyond its confines. More than a linear route through the city, the author thus depicts a circumambulation that recalls the processions of unity such as the *Ommegang*, but on a city-wide scale.

The images and the text do however take differing viewpoints. While the artist invites the viewer into a peri-urban space moving seamlessly from hills to valley bottoms, the writer on the other hand presents the procession from the fixed standpoint of a spectator positioned near the *Grote Markt* (*Grand-Place*). In the first part of the manuscript, it is striking that the two illustrations which depart from the norm and represent an urban scene rather than a peri-urban one, depict, this time in a fairly realistic way, two iconic buildings of the city centre: the fountain of the fish market (fol.12^r) and the city hall (fol. 31^r). Whereas the representation of the city hall, the jewel of Brussels' political glory, is hardly surprising, the depiction of the fountain is rather more enigmatic (Fig. 4.6). Appearing in one of the six illustrations of the *esbattements*, the fountain was in fact located in the very heart of the butchers' district, close to the *Grand-Place*, on the main artery that traversed the city: the *Steenwech*. Later in the manuscript (fol. 56^r), a third cityscape is represented: the quays of Brussels' port. Together, these three images reflect the political, commercial and artisanal centres of the city, all endowed with an infrastructure which was both functional and aesthetic.

The organisers of Joanna's Entry and the authors of the manuscript thus created, in a multitude of ways, a discourse where the centrality of Brussels was as important as its unity. Both had to be brought together through a coalition of interests among the burgher elites, who would act in harmony with the princes.

REMCO SLEIDERINK AND AMBER SOULEYMANE

In unam pacis accordantiam

The Role of City Poet Jan Smeken and Other Rhetoricians in Organizing the Brussels Entry

▼ **ABSTRACT** In this contribution, we want to discuss the role that the Brussels rhetoricians played in the organization of joyous entries and other festivities such as the baptism of a princess. More specifically, we will show how Jan Smeken – who was the city poet from 1485 until his death in 1517 – and some of the rhetoricians closest to him (Johannes Pertcheval, Jan van den Dale) took the lead in the organization and how they involved the four chambers of rhetoric of Brussels, as well as the archers of the greater Crossbowmen's guild (who were very active culturally as well). Unfortunately, we do not have city accounts for December 1496, but the involvement of Smeken *cum suis* in festivities such as Joanna's entry is detailed in the city accounts from 1485-1486 and from 1497 onwards (the entries of Maximilian and Frederick III in 1486, the baptism of Eleanor in 1498, the arrival of young Charles in 1500). How central the contribution of Jan Smeken was, is shown by the first *tableau* in the entry of Joanna in 1496. The invention of music by Jubal and Tubal-Kain was depicted in a way that directly referred to the blazon of the city poet (an anvil with three hammers). The accompanying text states that this was done *in unam pacis accordantiam*. The same phrase, but in Dutch, was used in 1507 as the new slogan of *'t Mariacranske*, the chamber of rhetoric that arose from a merger of *De Lelie* (of Jan Smeken) and *De Violette* (of Jan van den Dale). With reference to the Leemans manuscript, we will argue that it were the rhetoricians who assured the artistic and theatrical unity of the joyous entry. These rhetoricians were mostly members from the middle class, but some belonged to the clergy.

▼ **KEYWORDS** Chambers of rhetoric, Jan Smeken, City Poet, Johannes Pertcheval, Jan van den Dale, *Ommegang*, Maximilian I, Frederick III, *tableaux vivants*

The illustrated manuscript of the entry of Joanna of Castile into Brussels in 1496 is highly remarkable and of great importance in imagining such a celebration in which the court and the city were in close contact.[1] However, to recover how such an entry was practically organized and who was involved behind the scenes, additional sources are needed. The Brussels city accounts are particularly valuable in this respect, even though they have not been preserved for the year of Joanna's entry. The twelve annual accounts that do survive – those from 1485-1486 and then from 1497 to 1507[2] – contain data on similar festivities. For example, the oldest city account contains information on the Joyous Entry of Maximilian, King of the Romans, into Brussels on 16 July 1486 as well as on the entry of Holy Roman Emperor Frederick III into Brussels on 21 July 1486. The accounts show that both shooting guilds and chambers of rhetoric were involved in the execution of the theatrical activities, and that the general organization was in the hands of a few of the members of the local chambers of rhetoric, including some clergymen. Towards the end of the fifteenth century, it was mainly the city poet who assumed the main coordinating role. This was Jan de Baertmakere alias Smeken, from whom a lot of literary work has survived, both in manuscript and in print. Supported by a few other rhetoricians he was able to leave his mark on the entry of 1496.

In this contribution, we will first briefly discuss the role that chambers of rhetoric and shooting guilds played in the cultural life of Brussels, especially based on the oldest city account (1485-1486). Next, we will take a closer look at the festivities around the entries of Maximilian and Frederick on 16 and 21 July 1486, respectively. The expenses that the city incurred for these entries already give an impression of how the entry of Joanna in 1496 will have been organized. In the paragraph that follows, this picture is supplemented by data from the period from June 1497 to August 1507. Interesting comparative material includes the celebrations organized in Brussels for the birth and baptism of Joanna's daughter Eleanor (November 1498) as well as for the festive entry of Philip the Fair (November 1503) and the return of Joanna in May 1504. At these and other festivities, the Brussels city poet Jan Smeken played a particularly important role in the organization. The fact that he had already taken on this role in 1496 is proven by the first *tableau vivant* that not only deals with the invention of music by the biblical figure Jubal, but also portrays the blazon of Jan Smeken – the blacksmith. At the end of this contribution, we will show how the organization of the entry of Joanna of Castile matched his literary and artistic capabilities and how he used his network to bring it to a successful conclusion.

---

1 Vandenbroeck, Paul, 'A Bride amidst Heroines, Fools and Savages: The Joyous Entry into Brussels by Joanna of Castile, 1496 (Berlin, Kupferstichkabinett, ms 78D5)', *Antwerp Royal Museum Annual* 2014, 153-94; Blockmans, Wim P., 'Le dialogue imaginaire entre princes et sujets: les joyeuses Entrées en Brabant en 1494 et 1496', *Publications du Centre Européen d'Études Bourguignonnes* 34 (1994), 37-53.
2 Brussels, Algemeen Rijksarchief, Inventaris van de Archieven van de Rekenkamer (V132) 30942, 30943, 30944, 30945, 30946, 30947, 12704, 30948, 30949, 30950, 30951, 30952. The city accounts can be accessed online via the website of the Rijksarchief: https://search.arch.be/nl/zoeken-naar-archieven/zoekresultaat/ead/index/eadid/BE-A0510_000014_802355_DUT/node/c%3A0.c%3A3.c%3A0.#c:0.c:3.c:0. For important excerpts of these accounts, from artistic and literary viewpoint, see Duverger, Jozef, *Brussel als kunstcentrum in de XIVe en XVe eeuw* (Antwerp: De Sikkel/ Ghent: Vyncke, 1935), pp. 64-69, 84-93.

Rhetoricians and Archers

In the course of the fifteenth century, chambers of rhetoric arose all over the Low Countries: confraternity-type chambers of burghers – predominantly belonging to the social middle class – who, often in competition with each other, engaged in theater, poetry, music and spectacle. Up until the beginning of the seventeenth century, the chambers of rhetoric would set the tone and define literary life in the Low Countries.[3] The oldest chamber of rhetoric may have been *Den Boeck* (The Book) in Brussels, founded in 1401, but it is not clear whether the chamber was already producing literary activities at that time (in any case, the society had good ties with the court and also had several musicians in its ranks).[4] The big breakthrough of the Netherlandish rhetoricians occurred in the second half of the fifteenth century. The chambers that were then established often bore the name of a flower, which then symbolically referred to Mary, Christ or a saint.[5]

5.1 Membership list of rhetoricians chamber *De Lelie* (The Lily) from early 1499, starting with Jan Smeken and Johannes Pertcheval, *Liber authenticus of the Seven Sorrows Confraternity of Brussels*, Brussels, Stadsarchief, hs. 3413, fol. 161ʳ

The Brussels city account of 1485-1486 shows that no less than four chambers of rhetoric were active in the city at that time: *Den Boeck* (also fashionably called *The Tijteloze* / The Daffodil), *De Violette* (The Violet), *De Corenbloem* (The Cornflower) and *De Lelie* (The Lily).[6] In the financial document, these chambers are mentioned mainly in relation to the performance of plays and *tableaux vivants* and the setting off of fireworks. For these activities, the city paid subsidies and, in some cases, even commissioned activities, especially for those activities where the city acted as host and had to show its best side.

---

3 Van Bruaene, Anne-Laure, '"A wonderfull tryumfe, for the wynnyng of a pryse": Guilds, Ritual, Theater, and the Urban Network in the Southern Low Countries, c. 1450-1650*', *Renaissance Quarterly* 59 (2006), 374-405 (p. 384).

4 Van Bruaene, Anne-Laure, 'Het Boek des Levens: Literaire corporaties, factiestrijd en de turbulente voorgeschiedenis van het Brusselse gezelschap Den Boeck (eerste helft van de 15de eeuw)', *Revue belge de Philologie et d'Histoire* 86 (2008), 335-50.

5 Van Bruaene, Anne-Laure, *Om beters wille: Rederijkerskamers en de stedelijke cultuur in de Zuidelijke Nederlanden (1400-1650)* (Amsterdam: Amsterdam University Press, 2008), p. 41.

6 See also the contribution by Wim Blockmans in this volume.

The rhetoricians were not the only ones in Brussels that concerned themselves with drama, *tableaux vivants* and fireworks. The Brussels shooting guilds were also active in this area. The most important shooting guild – the greater Crossbowmen's guild – had a remarkable reputation. Every year on the weekend before Pentecost, the greater Crossbowmen's guild organized a great procession, the *Ommegang*, during which a miraculous statue of Mary was carried from the archers' chapel – Our Lady of the Sablon – through the city. On that occasion, the archers also organized two performances of one of the *Bliscappen van Maria* (Joys of Mary). In all, there were seven Marian plays, each of which focused on and depicted a glorious moment in the life of Mary. Most *Ommegang* drama is highly visual, thus appealing to the eyes: the play's meaning or moral had to be interpreted through the images.[7] The *Bliscappen* were performed in a cycle that lasted seven years. This annual tradition of dramatic performances had existed since 1448 and would eventually continue until 1566, the year of the Iconoclast movement. The *Ommegang* was the largest annual festival in Brussels and the artistic activities surrounding it – including additional performances by the rhetoricians – were generously subsidized by the city. The city government considered these subsidies to be a good investment: through the excise on beer, the city earned a lot of money from the many spectators who came to the festival.[8]

The Entries of Maximilian and Frederick in 1486

The city account of 1485-1486 contains a separate section on the expenses incurred for the entries of the Roman King Maximilian and the Roman Emperor Frederick on 16 and 21 July 1486, respectively.[9] This is not the only source on these festivities. The Burgundian chronicler Jean Molinet relates that Maximilian's entry, for example, was accompanied by much merriment: 'plaisans esbas, esbatemens joyeulx, joyeusetéz nouvellez, nouvelletéz haultaines, haultains festoyemens et festes d'instrumens'. The city had commissioned some forty to fifty *tableaux vivants* for the occasion. Molinet does not describe them in detail but does indicate that they were 'hystoires bibliennes et morales' (Biblical and moralizing stories).[10]

The city accounts provide insight into the people and groups who conceived, organized and executed the activities surrounding the entries of Maximilian and

---

7 Ramakers, Bart, *Spelen en figuren: toneelkunst en processiecultuur in Oudenaarde tussen Middeleeuwen en Moderne tijd* (Amsterdam: Amsterdam University Press, 1994), p. 352.
8 Stein, Robert, 'The Bliscapen van Maria and the Brussels policy of annexation', *Publications du Centre Européen d'Études Bourguignonnes* 31 (1991), 139-51; Remco Sleiderink, 'The Brussels Plays of the Seven Sorrows', in *The Seven Sorrows Confraternity of Brussels: Drama, Ceremony, and Art Patronage (16th-17th Centuries)*, ed. by Emily S. Thelen, Studies in European Urban History 37 (Turnhout: Brepols, 2015), pp. 51-66 (pp. 63-65).
9 RK 30942, see pp. 113-24 for the expenses incurred for the entry of Maximilian, and pp. 124-32 for the expenses incurred for the entry of Frederick; Duverger, *Brussel als kunstcentrum*, pp. 85-86.
10 *Chroniques de Jean Molinet*, ed. by Georges Doutrepont, and Omer Jodogne, Collection des Anciens Auteurs Belges, 3 vols (Brussels: Palais des Académies, 1935-37), I (1935), pp. 525-26; see also Mareel, Samuel, *Voor vorst en stad: rederijkersliteratuur en vorstenfeest in Vlaanderen en Brabant (1432-1561)* (Amsterdam: Amsterdam University Press, 2010), p. 15; and Ramakers, *Spelen en figuren*, p. 180.

Frederick. For the *tableaux vivants* – referred to as 'person(n)agie' or 'person(n)atie' (character) – the city made payments to the four chambers of rhetoric in Brussels and at least three different guilds, including the greater Crossbowmen's guild.[11] What was shown is usually not mentioned, but the account does specify that a certain Jan Merchant provided a *tableau vivant* with *Parys, Venus ende Pallas* (Paris, Venus and Pallas) in front of the town hall. The characters of the *tableaux vivants* probably portrayed their scenes on so-called *kasttonelen*, basic stage façades with a triumphal arch that was divided into three (or more) compartments by means of partitions or curtains. Curtains were also used to cover and uncover the front of the stage. Unlike regular stages, the *kasttonelen* lacked a proscenium, a stage in front of the curtain.[12] Presumably, various images were shown on the stage.[13] Although a *tableau vivant* is usually a silent performance, speaking characters were not uncommon in the *tableaux* of the rhetoricians. Nor was it necessary for the characters to stand still.[14] The meaning of the *tableau* was usually explained textually, and often as well by a so-called *explicateur* (tropologist).[15] The city account of 1498-1499 shows that Merchant or 'Mertsant' collaborated with members of the local chambers of rhetoric in organizing the Brussels baptism of Eleanor. Presumably he himself was a member of a chamber or guild.[16] As part of the depiction of the *Judgement of Paris*, Juno will undoubtedly have been shown, and perhaps Mercury as well. After all, Venus, Juno, Pallas, Paris and Mercury were also shown together in a *tableau vivant* in 1496 (fol. 57[r] in the Berlin manuscript). It is very likely that Jan Merchant was then again involved in the depiction of the mythological scene. The explanation given in 1496 must have been different from that in 1486 for it would have been adapted to the visiting monarch.[17]

In addition to a *tableau vivant*, the greater Crossbowmen's guild, *Den Boeck* and *De Corenbloem* performed one play each in 1486.[18] The plays were probably

---

11 Duverger, *Brussel als kunstcentrum*, p. 85; see also Ramakers, *Spelen en figuren*, p. 180.
12 For an example of a *kasttoneel*, see the manuscript, particularly fol. 31[v], on which the use of the curtains is expounded as well. On the rhetoricians' stages, see also Hummelen, Willem M. H., 'Types and Methods of the Dutch Rhetoricians' Theatre', *The Third Globe. Symposium for the Reconstruction of the Globe Playhouse, Wayne State University, 1979*, ed. by Hodges, C. Walter, S. Schoenbaum, and Leonard Leone (Detroit: 1981), pp. 164-89, 233-35, 252-53.
13 Ramakers, *Spelen en figuren*, pp. 167-69, 170, 177-78.
14 Hummelen, Willem M. H., 'Het tableau vivant, de "toog", in de toneelspelen van de rederijkers' *Tijdschrift voor Nederlandse Taal- en Letterkunde* 108 (1992), 193-222 (pp. 200-01).
15 Pleij, Herman, '7 maart 1500: De Brusselse stadsdichter Jan Smeken is uitgezonden naar Gent om te berichten over de doopfeesten van Karel V – De rederijkerij als beschavingsinstituut', *Nederlandse literatuur, een geschiedenis*, ed. by M. A. Schenkeveld-Van der Dussen (Groningen: Nijhoff, 1993), pp. 121-25 (p. 122).
16 RK 30944, fol. 38[v]-39[r]; Duverger, *Brussel als kunstcentrum*, p. 87 (see also the next section of this contribution); de Keyser, Paul 'Nieuwe gegevens omtrent Colijn Caillieu (coellin), Jan de Bartmaker (smeken), Jan Steemaer (percheval) en Jan van den Dale', *Tijdschrift voor Nederlandse Taal- en Letterkunde* 53 (1934), 269-79 (p. 275).
17 For the *tableaux* of 1496 and the explanations given to it, see Legaré, Anne-Marie, 'L'entrée de Jeanne de Castille à Bruxelles: un programme iconographique au féminin', *Women at the Burgundian Court: Presence and Influence*, ed. by Dagmar Eichberger, Anne-Marie Legaré and Wim Hüsken, Burgundica 17 (Turnhout: Brepols, 2010), pp. 43-55 (pp. 52-53).
18 Duverger, *Brussel als kunstcentrum*, p. 85; see also Ramakers, *Spelen en figuren*, p. 180.

interrupted by *pausas* (intermissions), during which music was played.[19] In doing so, the long performances were made more pleasant to the spectators.[20] New stages were built for the occasion, but the city also borrowed stages from the Church of Our Lady of the Sablon. That church served as the chapel of the archers of the greater Crossbowmen's guild. These stages thus must have been also used for the *Ommegang* and the performances of the *Bliscappen*.[21] Possibly the stages were illuminated with candles and torches during performances in the evening, as was the case with entries in Brussels during the sixteenth century.[22]

For the general organization of the entry of 1486, the city rewarded five persons, all of whom are mentioned by name in the city account.[23] Three of them were priests, and at least two of those priests were demonstrably active in a chamber of rhetoric. It seems reasonable to assume that the five organizers all came from the world of the rhetoricians. Accordingly, it has been argued and demonstrated before that not only laymen were affiliated with chambers of rhetoric.[24] The fact that the clergymen's contribution in 1486 was so large suggests that it had a strong religious bias and required the expertise of priests. The largest fee, thirty shillings Brabant *groten*, went in 1486 to priest Jacob van Buyten, who appears in other sources as chaplain of the church of St. Nicholas. By contrast, an experienced Brussels artisan received fifteen pennies per working day; one shilling of Brabant *groten* consists of twelve pennies.[25] Unfortunately, there is not much more to tell about Van Buyten, not even about a possible relationship with the rhetoricians. In his will of 1507, he left a breviary and psalter to a fellow priest.[26]

More is known about Peter Volckaert, the priest who is mentioned in the account as the second organizer and who received twenty shillings for his contribution. Volckaert was a very active chaplain of the collegial church of St. Gudula and was – certainly at the end of his life – closely involved in Brussels rhetoricians' culture. The members of *'t Mariacranske* (The Garland of Mary), a chamber of rhetoric that arose in 1507 through the merger of *De Lelie* and *De Violette*, were present at his funeral in 1522, and in his legacy various religious books were found, handwritten and printed,

---

19 Ramakers, Bart, 'Walk, Talk, Sit, Quit? On What Happens in Netherlandish Rhetoricians' Plays', *Medieval Theatre Performance. Actors, Dancers, Automata and their Audiences*, ed. by Philip Butterworth and Katie Normington (Cambridge: D. S. Brewer, 2017), pp. 35-51 (pp. 46-47).
20 Kramer, Femke, 'Staging practice in Brussel, 1559: Lawsuit reports concerning *Het esbatement van de bervoete bruers*', *Formes teatrals de la tradició medieval*, ed. by Francesco Massip (Barcelona: Institut del Teatre), pp. 283-92 (p. 287).
21 Duverger, *Brussel als kunstcentrum*, pp. 84-85.
22 Kramer, 'Staging practice in Brussels', p. 287.
23 Duverger, *Brussel als kunstcentrum*, p. 85; Roobaert, Edmond, 'Priesters en rederijkers te Brussel in de eerste helft van de zestiende eeuw', *Spiegel der Letteren* 45.3 (2003), 267-94 (p. 270).
24 Roobaert, 'Priesters en rederijkers', passim. For (former) priests who were active as members of a chamber of rhetoric, see also Van Bruaene, *Om beters wille*, pp. 40, 51, 73, 83, 100, 106, 207, and Arjan van Dixhoorn, *Lustige geesten: Rederijkers in de Noordelijke Nederlanden (1480-1650)*, (Amsterdam: Amsterdam University Press, 2009), pp. 68, 84, 104, 254, 277, 287.
25 Sleiderink, Remco, 'De dichters Jan Smeken en Johannes Pertcheval en de devotie tot Onze Lieve Vrouw van de Zeven Weeën. Nieuwe gegevens uit de rekeningen van de Brusselse broederschap (1499-1516)', *Queeste* 19.1 (2012), 42-69 (pp. 46-47).
26 Roobaert, 'Priesters en rederijkers', pp. 270, 275-76.

as well as 'eenen cleynen sluytcorf ende daerinne vele oude papieren pauci valores van refereynen ende anderssins' (a small closing basket with therein many old papers of little value, refrains and otherwise).[27] The reference to refrains is interesting for that verse form is a very typical form of rhetoricians' literature.[28] The statutes of the Ghent chamber of rhetoric of *De Fonteine* (The Fountain) from 1448 – the oldest surviving statutes of a chamber of rhetoric – already stipulated that every three weeks the members of this chamber had to take part in an internal competition in which they had to compose a refrain based on an example that was put forward by a different member each time.[29] Moreover, prior to Maximilian's arrival in Brussels, Volckaert had travelled to Antwerp and Leuven to see how the king was received there. He was rewarded by the city council for this as well: it was very important for the city not to be inferior to the other cities.[30]

The third priest-organizer in 1486 was Anthonis de Vos and he received ten shillings for his contribution. De Vos earned his living as chaplain of the churches of St. Nicholas and St. Gudula. He was also active as a scribe of manuscripts for liturgy and choral singing. He possibly also wrote his own 'veerzen' (verses). He is mentioned first on the membership list of the chamber of rhetoric *De Lelie* from 1499.[31]

The fourth and fifth organizers of the 1486 entry were named Gheert van Gaesbeke and Abel Valcke and they were not priests.[32] For their role in the organization they each received the same amount as priest Anthonis de Vos. As yet, we have not been able to properly identify them. Presumably they were rhetoricians, but that is difficult to verify due to a lack of data: only for *De Lelie* and *De Violette* the membership list of 1486 can be reconstructed, and only to a limited extent.[33]

More Feasts for Joanna

To get a better view of the organization of the entry of Joanna of Castile in 1496, we can look not only at the celebrations surrounding the entries of Maximilian and Frederick, but also at the better documented festivities in the period that followed.

---

27 Roobaert, 'Priesters en rederijkers', pp. 270, 279-81 (quote on p. 281).
28 van Dixhoorn, Arjan, Samuel Mareel, and Bart Ramakers, 'The relevance of the Netherlandish rhetoricians', *Renaissance Studies* 32.1 (2018), 8-22 (p. 11).
29 Coigneau, Dirck, '9 december 1448: Het Gentse stadsbestuur keurt de statuten van de rederijkerskamer De Fonteine goed. Literaire bedrijvigheid in stads- en gildeverband', *Nederlandse literatuur, een geschiedenis*, ed. by Maria A. Schenkeveld-Van der Dussen (Groningen: Nijhoff, 1993), pp. 102-08 (pp. 106-07).
30 Roobaert, 'Priesters en rederijkers', pp. 270-71.
31 Roobaert, 'Priesters en rederijkers', pp. 270, 276-78.
32 Roobaert, 'Priesters en rederijkers', p. 270; Duverger, *Brussel als kunstcentrum*, p. 85, Duverger mistakenly read 'Valsche' instead of 'Valcke'.
33 A membership list of *De Lelie* from 1499 (plus later additions) is included in the *Liber Authenticus* of the Seven Sorrows Confraternity of Brussels (Stadsarchief Brussel, hs. 3413, fol. 161ʳ). The earliest membership list of *De Corenbloem* dates from *c.* 1520, see for edition Remco Sleiderink, 'De schandaleuze spelen van 1559 en de leden van *De Corenbloem*: Het socioprofessionele, literaire en religieuze profiel van de Brusselse rederijkerskamer', *Revue Belge de Philologie et d'Histoire* 92.3 (2014), 847-75 (p. 849).

Particularly informative is the consecutive series of city accounts from 24 June 1497 to 24 August 1507. This series thus opens barely six months after Joanna's entry. Here and there, the data from the accounts can be supplemented with descriptions of Brussels festivities by court chronicler Jean Molinet.

What emerges strongly from these city accounts is that Jan Smeken has played an increasingly important role in organizing feasts since his appointment as city poet in 1485. He is often mentioned in the company of two other rhetoricians of *De Lelie*, Johannes Pertcheval (the *prince* or the ceremonial figurehead of the chamber) and Hendrik De Lichte.[34] For example, when bonfires were lit in Brussels in August 1498 to mark the peace Philip the Fair had made with France, the coordination was in the hands of this trio.[35] As is the case with Jan Smeken, some of Johannes Pertcheval's literary work is still preserved, namely a 1493 translation of Olivier de la Marche's *Le Chevalier Délibére: Den camp vander doot*.[36] He was furthermore involved in the organization of the now-lost cycle of the Seven Sorrows of the Virgin Mary. Jan Smeken in particular must be seen as the author of these plays; Pertcheval was possibly the director.[37] Additionally, Pertcheval was a physician and pharmacist and annually produced an almanac by order of the city.[38]

5.2 Heraldic representation of the rhetoricians chamber *De Lelie* (The Lily) with its motto *Liefde groeit* (Love grows). Illustration made by Johannes Pertcheval in the *Liber authenticus of the Seven Sorrows Confraternity of Brussels*. Brussels, Stadsarchief, hs. 3413, fol. 1ʳ

Interesting comparative material offer the festivities surrounding the baptism of Eleanor, the first child of Joanna of Castile and Philip the Fair. The girl was born on the night of 15-16 October 1498. The baptism was celebrated a month and a half later, on 30 November. King Maximilian acted as one of the godfathers and had come

---

34 Sleiderink, Remco, 'Johannes Steemaer alias Pertcheval. De naam en faam van een Brusselse rederijker', *Want hi verkende dien name wale. Opstellen voor Willem Kuiper*, ed. by Marjolein Hogenbirk and Roel Zemel (Amsterdam: Stichting Neerlandistiek VU; Münster: Nodus Publikationen, 2014), pp. 149-54 (p. 150).
35 Duverger, *Brussel als kunstcentrum*, pp. 86-87.
36 See for edition Jan Pertcheval, *Den camp vander doot*, ed. by Gilbert Degroote, and A. J. J. Delen (Antwerp: De Seven Sinjoren; Amsterdam: Stichting 'Onze oude letteren', 1948).
37 Sleiderink, 'The Brussels Plays of the Seven Sorrows', pp. 55.
38 Sleiderink, 'Johannes Steemaer alias Pertcheval', p. 150.

to the city especially for the occasion.[39] For the part of the feast that was public, the city again called upon the three rhetoricians of De Lelie: Smeken, Pertcheval and De Lichte. For the occasion three others were added to the festive committee. One of them was Jan van den Dale, a painter who was associated with the chamber of rhetoric *De Violette* and of whom much literary work has been preserved.[40] The other two were Peter Verlichtere and Jan Merchant.[41] We had already seen that the latter was rewarded in 1486 for the portrayal of the *Judgement of Paris*. Presumably he and Peter Verlichtere were, like the other four, members of a chamber of rhetoric. It is noteworthy that now, unlike in 1486, no priests are part of the organizing committee. This suggests that the poets were familiar and experienced enough with the religious material to work it out independently, without the help of the clergy. The six organizers received a sheep and 36 jugs of wine as payment.

What could spectators experience in 1498? From the accounts and the description by Jean Molinet, we can deduct that between the Palace of Coudenberg and the church of St. Gudula, a wooden gallery was built with a large gate at the beginning and end, and sixteen smaller gates in between. At nightfall, the little Eleanor was carried past this in procession. Decorative lighting was installed along this route and the four chambers of rhetoric performed *tableaux vivants*. Among other things, Molinet speaks of a child representing a prophet. It had a scroll in its hand. Along the route, singing children could also be seen and heard. They represented angels and shepherds.[42] Thus, a link was made in the visual program of Jan Smeken *cum suis* between the birth of Eleanor and the birth of Christ. This was appropriate because by now the Advent season had arrived.

In addition to *tableaux vivants*, the chambers of rhetoric each performed a *spel van zinne* (morality play) on the occasion of Eleonora's baptism. They did this in competition with each other, following the tradition of such festivals. According to the city account, this competition was organized by the well-known trio: Smeken, Pertcheval and De Lichte. What exactly was displayed is not mentioned, but it seems obvious that it concerned so-called *presentspelen* (gift plays) in which symbolic gifts were presented to the newborn. The poets presumably appealed to both the verbal and visual aspects of drama for rhetoricians' drama had a strong musical bias on the one hand,[43] and on the other hand costumes, attributes, mimicry and gestures attributed to the play's central meaning or moral.[44] An example of such a *presentspel*

---

39 King Maximilian traveled to Brussels via Leuven. In October 1498, the city rewarded two men to see how the people of Leuven received the king. They were town pensioner Geert van (den) Hecke and rhetorician Johannes Pertcheval. See Roobaert, 'Priesters en rederijkers', p. 271.

40 Waterschoot, Werner, 'Jan van den Dale, "eenen vermaerden Retoricien"', *Tijdschrift voor Nederlandse Taal- en Letterkunde* 119.1 (2003), 265-78.

41 Duverger, *Brussel als kunstcentrum*, p. 87.

42 *Chroniques de Jean Molinet*, ed. by Georges Doutrepont, and Omer Jodogne, Collection des Anciens Auteurs Belges, 3 vols (Brussels: Palais des Académies, 1935-37), II (1935), pp. 450-52.

43 Moser, Nelleke, *De strijd voor rhetorica: poëtica en positie van rederijkers in Vlaanderen, Brabant, Zeeland en Holland tussen 1450 en 1620* (Amsterdam: Amsterdam University Press, 2001), pp. 98-99, 109.

44 Ramakers, Bart, 'Allegorisch toneel: Overlevering en benadering', *Spel en spektakel: Middeleeuws toneel in de Lage Landen*, ed. by Hans van Dijk and Bart Ramakers (Amsterdam: Prometheus, 2001), pp. 228-45 (p. 229).

is the one written by Colijn Caillieu in January 1480 on the occasion of the birth of Margaret of Austria, with which he made a link with the feast of Epiphany.[45] At the competition in November 1498, *De Lelie* won first prize, consisting of three sheep and eighteen jugs of wine. *De Lelie* and *De Corenbloem* shared the second and third prizes. Chamber of rhetoric *Den Boeck* finished fourth and received a consolation prize.[46]

The pattern outlined here is further confirmed in the accounts of the years that followed: whenever royal guests came to town, the rhetoricians organized the festivities, with which they were occasionally aided by the archers. *Tableaux vivants* are performed, and the chambers put on new plays in competition with each other, both *spelen van zinne*, prologues and farces. The organization is constantly in the hands of Jan Smeken, usually assisted by Johannes Pertcheval and Hendrik De Lichte. Sometimes these men are also sent to other cities to see what is organized there, such as Smeken in 1500 to Ghent at the baptism of Charles V and Smeken and Pertcheval in 1503 to Mechelen when Philip the Fair had returned from Spain and was welcomed in Mechelen. In each case, this took place in preparation for festivities that would take place in Brussels a little later.[47]

At the end of May 1504, Joanna was also welcomed back to Brussels. On behalf of the city, Smeken, Pertcheval and De Lichte organized a dramatic competition with prologues and farces in which rhetoricians and archers participated. The first prize this time was for the greater Crossbowmen's guild, the second prize being shared by *De Violette*, *De Lelie* and the shooting guild of the hand-bow. Additionally, under the direction of Smeken, Pertcheval and De Lichte, many *tableaux vivants* were once again performed. The trio also provided the accompanying texts 'in 't Walsche ende in 't Duytsche' (in French and in Dutch).[48]

The City Poet as Key Figure

The city accounts from 1497 onwards make it clear that Jan Smeken, Johannes Pertcheval and Hendrik De Lichte strongly influenced the Brussels festivities. All three of them were members of the chamber of rhetoric *De Lelie* and they also played a major role there. According to the membership list of *De Lelie* from 1499, Jan Smeken was the 'facteur' (the artistic leader) of the chamber in that year, and Johannes Pertcheval was the 'prinche'.[49]

The fact that Jan Smeken was able to play such a prominent role in the organization of Brussels festivities will, however, also have to do with his appointment as city poet in 1485. This appointment is mentioned in the oldest city account. It is noted that he took the place of Colijn Cailieu as Brussels city poet. He received the same

---

45 Mareel, *Voor vorst en stad*, pp. 156-65.
46 Duverger, *Brussel als kunstcentrum*, p. 87.
47 Mareel, *Voor vorst en stad*, p. 91; Rick de Leeuw & Remco Sleiderink, *Ik Jan Smeken* (Hannibal, 2017), pp. 102-03.
48 Duverger, *Brussel als kunstcentrum*, p. 91.
49 Brussels, Stadsarchief, hs. 3413 (*Liber Authenticus* of the Seven Sorrows Confraternity of Brussels) (on loan to the Stedelijk Museum), fol. 161[r].

substantial compensation of ninety shillings Brabant *groten*, which corresponded to about one third of the salary of a skilled artisan.[50] In addition, he received allowances for specific assignments, also in relation to princely entries and other public feasts.[51]

Smeken wrote many different literary works during his time as city poet. His body of work attests to his literary, dramatic and comic talents, his familiarity with mythology, and his ability to use literature to respond to political scenes. In addition to the cycle of the Seven Sorrows of the Virgin Mary, Smeken wrote another play with a devotional function, namely the *Spel vanden heilighen sacramente vander Nyeuwervaert* (the Play of the sacrament of Niervaart). He also wrote strophic poems, namely the *Spieghel der behoudenessen* (Mirror of salvation) (*c*. 1508), *Dwonder van claren ijse en snee* (The miracle of pure ice and snow) (1511) and a poem on the Brussels meeting of the Order of the Golden Fleece in 1516. His *Spieghel der behoudenessen* appears to be based on a *toogspel* (an allegorical play built on *tableaux vivants*). Smeken wrote secular drama too, including some now-lost *esbattementen* (short comic plays), and a number of plays that survive in manuscripts: the *Spel op hertoge Karle* (Play of Duke Charles) (possibly written in 1505) and *Hue Mars and Venus tsaemen bueleerden* (How Mars and Venus dallied together).[52]

The *Spel op hertoge Karle* has survived in the Leemans manuscript, which was compiled in the first half of the sixteenth century by the Brussels rhetorician Gielis Leemans. The manuscript consists of a collection of older texts that Leemans presumably copied from other manuscripts. In addition to Smeken's play, it contains a play of Caillieu, an anonymous rhetoricians' play, a poem by the Bruges rhetorician Anthonis de Roovere and an exemplary list of female figures from history, mythology and the Bible. The list was probably compiled with an iconographic aim: rhetoricians (and other artists) could draw on the descriptions in the manuscript for their dramatic depictions of historical, mythological and biblical women. Thus, the list encourages emulation.[53] Moreover, these descriptions seem to have been used for the *tableaux* that were performed in 1496.[54]

Colijn Caillieu was the first person to officially hold the position of Brussels city poet, and the 1474 decree of appointment shows that the city initially wanted to ensure that a talented rhetorician who contributed greatly to the name and fame of Brussels would not be tempted to move to another city.[55] There were no clear tasks

---

50 Ham, Laurens, Nina Geerdink, Johan Oosterman, Remco Sleiderink, and Sander Bax, 'Krijg je nog rente voor een lied? Stadsdichterschap als eer en verdienste door de eeuwen heen', *Nederlandse letterkunde* 25.1 (2020), 99-131 (p. 112); Sleiderink, 'De dichters Jan Smeken en Johannes Pertcheval', pp. 46-47.
51 Duverger, *Brussel als kunstcentrum*, p. 84. Although city accounts and other archival sources speak of 'rhetorician of the city' and 'factor of the city' (or some variation thereof), we use the term 'city poet' in this article. That term should be interpreted broadly. Indeed, the rhetoricians practiced many different genres. On this subject, see also Ham and others, 'Krijg je nog rente voor een lied?', pp. 101-04, 112.
52 Sleiderink, 'The Brussels Plays of the Seven Sorrows', pp. 52-62.
53 De Keyzer, Paul, 'Het rhetoricaal "exemplum". Bijdrage tot de iconologie van onze Rederijkers', in *Vooys voor De Vooys. Nieuwe Taalgids* (1953), 48-57; Saskia Buitink, '"Wt gelesen vrouwen om yn cameren te ordijneren". Over de Neuf Preuses (Verz. Leemans F.29V), in *Rapiarijs. Een afscheidsbundel voor Hans van Dijk*, ed. by Saskia Buitink, Alphonsus Maria Joseph van Buuren & I. Spijker (Utrecht: Ruygh-bewerp, 1987), pp. 23-25.
54 See also Mareel, *Voor vorst en stad*, pp. 93-94, 254-55, and the contribution by Wim Blockmans in this volume.
55 Mareel, *Voor vorst en stad*, pp. 95-96; Duverger, *Brussel als kunstcentrum*, p. 85.

attached to it yet. However, the accounts from 1497 onwards paint a different picture. Jan Smeken oversaw just about all the festivities organized by the city. He preferred to call upon the help of Johannes Pertcheval and Hendrik De Lichte, two rhetoricians with whom he also worked closely within the chamber of rhetoric *De Lelie*. This close relationship between the city poet and a specific chamber may have led to tensions. In a preserved oath of the city rhetorician ('den eedt vanden factuer deser stadt') (Brussels, c. 1529-33) the importance of the impartiality of the city poet is strongly emphasized:

> Ic gelove sekere ende zwere [...] dat ic onser liever vrouwen spel dwelck men jairlicx ter processien speelt sal doen ende hulpen spelen ende dat metten alder besten speelders die ic in die stadt in eenigen van den bloemen sal bevinden. Ende dat ic geen partyscap dragen en sal met eenigen vanden anderen bloemen maer metter eender cameren also familier sal syn als metten anderen.
>
>> I swear [...] that I will organize and help perform the play of Our Lady, which is performed annually during the procession, with the very best actors I can find in any of the flowers [chambers of rhetoric] of the city. And that I will not be partial in favor of one of the flowers, but that I will be as familiar with one chamber as I am with the others.

Specifically for the performance of the *Bliscappen* during the *Ommegang*, he must call upon the best actors of the city, regardless of the chambers of rhetoric they belonged to. It is possible that Jan Smeken's actions, who had been city poet continuously from 1485 until his death in 1517, had been perceived as too partisan. Especially considering his tendency to involve Pertcheval and De Lichte in organizing activities as well as the fact that city poets after Smeken's demise had to swear an oath, preventing them from doing just that.[56]

The first *tableau vivant* in the Berlin manuscript (fol. 32^r) suggests that Jan Smeken not only played an important coordinating role from 1497 onwards, but already at the 1496 entry of Joanna of Castile. That *tableau* dealt with the invention of music by the biblical character Jubal (or Tubal) when he heard his half-brother Tubal Cain, the inventor of the forge, beating on an anvil. However, the *tableau* does not depict one blacksmith, as in the Bible (Genesis 4:21-22), but rather three blacksmiths, each striking the anvil with a hammer. Scholars puzzled over this deviation from the Biblical story. They suspected influence from the similar story about Pythagoras as the inventor of harmony. After all, that story mentions several blacksmiths with hammers of different weights.[57] What was not realized, however, is that Jan Smeken had an important reason for deviating from the Biblical story. By showing three hammers, he made a link with his own blazon, which consisted of an anvil and three

---

56 Ham and others, 'Krijg je nog rente voor een lied?', p. 116; Edmond Roobaert, 'De Brusselse rederijkers in de 16de eeuw, hun plaats in het stadsgebeuren en hun beroepsactiviteiten', in *Eigen Schoon & De Brabander* 95 (2012), 541-94 (p. 590).

57 See particularly Tammen, Björn R., 'A Feast of the Arts: Joanna of Castile in Brussels 1496', *Early Music History* 30 (2011), 213-48 (pp. 222-26).

5.3 The *Liber authenticus* honors the four founding fathers of the Seven Sorrows Confraternity of Brussels. The second blazon – an anvil with three hammers – represents city poet Jan Smeken. Brussels, Stadsarchief, hs. 3413, fol. 159ᵛ-160ʳ

hammers. That blazon has survived in a manuscript by *De Lelie* from 1499, the *Liber Authenticus*. It is not difficult to imagine why Jan Smeken had chosen precisely that blazon. On the one hand, with that blazon he was indeed referring to the story of Pythagoras and the invention of harmony. In addition to *retorica*, *musica* was also central to *De Lelie*, so such a blazon was quite appropriate for the *factor* of the chamber. On the other hand, with this particular blazon he was referring to his own nickname. After all, in the local dialect Smeken could also be understood as *kleine smid* (little blacksmith).[58]

Ingeniously, city poet Jan Smeken had thus put his stamp on the first *tableau vivant* for the entry of Joanna of Castile. According to the Berlin manuscript, the explanation for the princess for this *tableau vivant* was that she could emulate Jubal. Just as the Biblical figure 'invented the sweet melody of music' 'in the middle of clammering hammers', so Joanna will unite her countless subjects 'in unam pacis accordantiam'. The latter was presumably a reference to a motto associated with the Brussels rhetoricians of *De Lelie*. When they merged with *De Violette* of *factor* Jan van

---

58 Sleiderink, Remco, 'De kleine smid', *Madoc. Tijdschrift over de Middeleeuwen* 31.2 (2017), 167-70.

den Dale in 1507, they did so at least with the motto 'in minlijck accoert'. This is the Dutch variant of 'in unam pacis accordantiam'.

The people of Brussels will undoubtedly have noticed that the city poet also put himself in the picture. In doing so, he more generally highlighted the role of the rhetoricians in the entry. Similarly, the last *tableau* showed the legend of St. Luke painting Mary and the Christ Child (fol. 59ʳ). Following this legend, St. Luke became the patron saint of the artists' guilds. This was thus a clear reference to the painters' guild, which had undoubtedly made an important contribution to the *tableaux vivants*. Often, the rhetoricians called upon the painters from their city to (help) construct *tableaux vivants* or paint stage scenes for entries and processions.[59] Double memberships also demonstrate that chambers of rhetoric and painters' guilds were strongly integrated: many a rhetorician was a member of the painters' guild in his city.[60]

The fact that not only Jan Smeken but also Johannes Pertcheval and Hendrik De Lichte put so much effort into the festivities surrounding the monarchs paid off greatly for their chamber. In 1499, *De Lelie* received permission to establish a chapter of the confraternity of the Seven Sorrows of Our Lady in Brussels.[61] This fraternity was technically dedicated to the devotion of the seven sorrowful moments in Mary's life, but was in practice also associated with Mary of Burgundy, who had died in 1482, and her son Philip the Fair. Thus, the fraternity essentially promoted the people's devotion of the young monarch. Remarkable about this specific chapter was that brothers and sisters did not have to pay a membership fee for enrolling. This meant that it was open to both the poor and the rich and thus reached a broad audience.[62]

Conclusion

From the city accounts it becomes clear that the Brussels rhetoricians played an important role in the organization of princely entries and other public feasts. The city poet, Jan Smeken, was a key figure in this respect. The rhetoricians contributed particularly to the theatrical activities of the festivities, namely with their *tableaux vivants* and *spelen van zinne*. For this they also regularly called upon the Brussels painters and archers. Thus, there was an artistic alliance between the city poet and the rhetoricians, painters and archers of the city. The city government's appreciation toward their efforts not only becomes clear from the many subsidies, but also from the chambers' position. That position gradually – after the chambers proofed their

---

59 Van Dixhoorn, *Lustige geesten*, p. 232.
60 Van Bruaene, *Om beters wille*, pp. 85, 124-27; Van Dixhoorn, *Lustige geesten*, pp. 114-15; Van Dixhoorn, Mareel and Ramakers, 'The relevance of the Netherlandish rhetoricians', p. 13.
61 Thelen, Emily S. (ed.), *The Seven Sorrows Confraternity of Brussels: Drama, Ceremony, and Art Patronage (16th-17th Centuries)* (Turnhout: Brepols, 2015).
62 Sutch, Susie Speakman, and Anne-Laure van Bruaene, 'The Seven Sorrows of the Virgin Mary: Devotional Communication and Politics in the Burgundian-Habsburg Low Countries, c. 1490-1520', *The Journal of Ecclesiastical History* 61.2 (2010), 252-78 (pp. 259, 262-63).

worth time and again – became more influential. With *De Lelie* being granted permission to establish a chapter of the confraternity of the Seven Sorrows, Smeken and his colleagues not only played a central role in the devotional practices of the Brussels townspeople through their plays, but also through the confraternity. And while in the 1480s priest-rhetoricians still made a major contribution to the organization of princely entries, by the end of that century it was mainly Smeken who pulled the strings. Of course, he was, as we have seen, more often than not assisted by his companions Johannes Pertcheval and Hendrik De Lichte. Thus, from the end of the fifteenth century onwards, the 'little blacksmith' became a central figure in Brussels' festive culture and devotional practices.

WIM BLOCKMANS

Role Models for a Queen's Daughter*

▼ **ABSTRACT** The advent in Brussels of princess Joanna, daughter of the 'Catholic Kings' of Spain, newly married to Philip of Habsburg, ruler of the Low Countries, was celebrated by a welcoming procession of the local corporations and a theatrical show along its route. The event was recorded in sixty water colour images with short descriptions in Latin, in a manuscript on paper. That is the oldest known pictorial representation of a complete princely entry in Europe. It is clearly structured in sections of three and its multiples, showing theatrical scenes and the clerical and civic groups in the procession. The following essay compares this celebration with preceding entries in Brabatine cities and identifies a series of *Nine Female Worthies* and some additonal stages. The motives in this entry are intended to celebrate the Brussels magistracy in a most elaborate way.

▼ **KEYWORDS** Heroines, Female Worthies, regal virtues, dynastic relations, Joyous Entries, urban competition

Symbolic Numbers

The manuscript presented in this volume is carefully constructed on the basis of numerical equilibria, mostly multiples of the number three. Though it may be a pure coincidence that this observation even applies to the ceremony's date 9/12/96, religious symbolism was deeply rooted in medieval minds. The total of sixty representations is divided in two halves, the first showing the procession of the city's corporations, starting with six groups of ecclesiastics, followed by six humoristic scenaries, *esbattements*; they are separated by torchbearers. The manuscript's second half displays the *tableaux vivants* set up in the streets, and at corners. The number nine appears to have been the starting point, as a given in the tradition of the Nine Worthies, which

---

* I like to thank Dagmar Eichberger most cordially for her initiative to launch and realize this edition, for her constant inspiration and formidable support.

A Spectacle for a Spanish Princess, ed. by Dagmar H. Eichberger, Burgundica, 35 (Turnhout: Brepols, 2023), pp. 123–142

might be considered as one of the event's leading themes. Their group, featuring on folios 43^r to 51^r, was preceded by nine scenes from the Old Testament, on folios 32^r to 40^r. The latter don't belong to a particular standardised and coherent series. Among the female characters, only Judith and Thecuites were heroic, while four women are shown kneeling, and getting married. The number of nine *tableaux* from the Old Testament seems to have been imposed for reasons of symmetry with the model of the Nine Worthies. After the latter group, three additional female characters from the Old Testament are displayed, Queen Saba coming to listen to the wisdom of King Salomo, prophetess Deborah encouraging Baruch to destroy his ennemies, while Jael was a vigourous heroine (fols 52^r, 54^r, 55^r). The total of twelve biblical components surrounding the *Neuf Preuses*[1] may have been meant to compensate the latter's exclusively pagan character.

The *Nine Female Worthies*

The Nine masculine Worthies, consisting of three groups of three heroes each, were very popular in written literature as well as in public representations. The triads became standardised by around 1400, including pagan/ancient, Jewish, and Christian/chivalric heroes. They appeared in Flanders by the end of the twelfth century, and were still staged for the entry held for Duke Charles the Bold in Douai in 1472.[2] Female versions appeared, inspired by Giovanni Boccaccio's *De claris mulieribus*, from 1361-62, a collection of 106 biographies of mythological, historical, and contemporary heroic ladies. The Brussels entry of 1496 featured no more than five of Boccaccio's famous women, namely Semiramis, Penthesilea, Tamyris, Juno, and Venus. A officer at the *Parlement de Paris* named Jehan le Fèvre appears to have invented the first series of nine amazones, virtuous and courageous women, somewhere between 1373 and 1387. He presented this work to a queen, probably Jeanne de Bourbon, King Charles V's spouse (d. 1378). Through her and her successor Isabeau of Bavaria, the theme became immediately popular at the royal court, especially in visual arts.[3]

The earliest known statues of both the nine male and female Worthies may have been those, larger than natural size, placed around 1387 in adjacent rooms in the

---

1 The female equivalent of the Nine masculine Worthies or chivalric role models, as explained in the subsequent paragraph.
2 Schroeder, Horst, *Der Topos der Nine Worthies in Literatur und bildender Kunst* (Göttingen: Vandenhoeck, 1971); van Anrooij, Wim, *Helden van Weleer. De negen besten in de Nederlanden (1300-1700)* (Amsterdam: AUP, 1997); Lecuppre-Desjardin, Élodie, *La ville des cérémonies. Essai sur la communication politique dans les anciens Pays-Bas bourguignons* (Turnhout: Brepols, 2004), pp. 272-76.
3 Sedlacek, Ingrid, *Die Neuf Preuses: Heldinnen des Spätmittelalters* (Marburg: Jonas, 1997), p. 55; Cassagnes-Brouquet, Sophie, 'Les Neuf Preuses, l'invention d'un nouveau thème iconographique dans le contexte de la Guerre de Cent ans', in *Le genre face aux mutations. Masculin et féminin, du Moyen Âge à nos jours*, ed. by Luc Capdevila and others (Rennes: PUR, 2003), pp. 279-89; Legaré, Anne-Marie, 'Joanna of Castile's Entry into Brussels: Viragos, Wise and Virtuous Women', in *Virtue Ethics for Women, 1250-1500*, ed. by Karen Green, and Constant J. Mews (Dordrecht: Springer, 2011), pp. 177-86; Legaré, Anne-Marie, 'L'Entrée de Jeanne de Castille à Bruxelles: un programme iconographique au féminin', in *Women at the Burgundian Court: Presence and Influence*, ed. by Dagmar Eichberger, Anne-Marie Legaré, and Wim Hüsken (Turnhout: Brepols, 2010), pp. 43-55.

castle of the fervent military leader Enguerrand de Coucy (1340-97).[4] Philip the Bold, the Duke of Burgundy (r. 1363-1404), had in 1389 a large tapestry repaired in Arras representing 'les Neuf Preux et les Neuf Preuses'. Ten years later, he ordered in Paris a series of tapestries, woven with gold-thread, showing the same subject.[5] His brother, Duke Jean de Berry, owned three tapestries of the Neuf Preuses, which were inherited by King Charles VI. Their nephew, Duke Louis d'Orléans (r. 1392-1407), purchased chimney statues of the *Neuf Preuses* for his castle in Pierrefonds, and then had the façade of his castle in Ferté-Milon (dép. Aisne) decorated by monumental sculptures of the *Nine Female Worthies*.[6]

In the current state of the research, it seems that a complete series of *Nine Female Worthies* was displayed in a public theatrical performance for the first time in Nevers, in 1456, for the entry of Isabel of Bourbon, spouse of Charles, then Count of Charolais, and soon-to-be mother of Mary of Burgundy. The show combined the nine exclusively mythological heroines with their male counterparts, composed in triads.[7]

The Burgundian courtier Philippe Bouton composed a *Miroir des Dames* (Ladies' Mirror) briefly after the birth of Philip the Fair on the 22nd of June 1478. In one copy, the frontispice shows him presenting it to his young mother, Mary of Burgundy, who is seated on a throne and surrounded by seventeen (the symbolic number[8]) ladies-in-waiting and numerous people on balconies.[9] A second copy belonged to Mary of Hungary's library. This author applied the model of triads of mythological, biblical, and Christian heroines to his selection of *Nine Female Worthies*. In the first two categories, he selected Penthesilea, Semiramis, and Tamaris, in the second Deborah, Esther, and Judith. These six ladies featured all in the Brussels entry, but none of the Christian heroines were chosen. The latter were Emperor Constantin's mother Helena, Gertrud of Saxony, and Clotilde, daughter of the king of Burgundy; this invention did not find many followers.[10] Obviously, there are no sufficient reasons to hypothesize any influencing by the court residing in Mechelen on the program of Joanna's entry in Brussels. Philip had been absent over the last months. Immediately after his return from the Habsburg lands, he got married and then became involved

---

4 The castle, located in the village Château de Coucy-le-Château-Auffrique, in the departement Aisne in Northwestern France, was considered to be the most awesome of its time. It was restored by Viollet-le-Duc but blown up by German troops in 1917.
5 Lestocquoy, Jean, *Deux siècles de l'histoire de la tapisserie*, 1300-1500 (Arras: Commission départ. des Monuments hist. du Pas-de-Calais, 1978), p. 34 and 37, cited by Cassagnes-Brouquet, 'Les Neuf Preuses'.
6 Sedlacek, *Neuf Preuses*, p. 190.
7 Legaré, 'Joanna', pp. 181-82, based on Sedlacek, *Die Neuf Preuses*, pp. 118, 153.
8 Stein, Robert, 'Seventeen: The Multiplicity of a Unity in the Low Countries', in *The Ideology of Burgundy. The Promotion of National Consciousness (1364-1565)*, ed. by D'Arcy Jonathan Dacre Boulton and Jan R. Veenstra (Leiden & Boston: Brill, 2006), pp. 223-85.
9 Reproduced in the exh. cat. *Bruges à Beaune. Marie, l'héritage de Bourgogne* (Paris: Somogy, 2000), p. 104.
10 Karaskova, Olga, 'Une princesse dans le miroir : Marie de Bourgogne est-elle la dédicatrice du *Miroir des Dames* de Philippe Bouton ?' in *Women, Art and Culture in Medieval and Early Renaissance Europe*, ed. by Cynthia J. Brown, and Anne-Marie Legaré (Turnhout: Brepols, 2016), pp. 291-308.

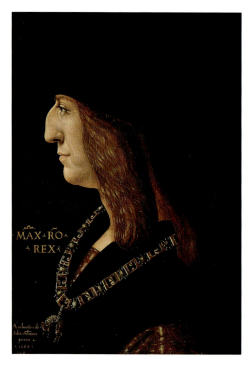

6.1 Ambrogio de Predis, *Maximilian as King of the Romans*, oil on wood, 44 × 30.3 cm, 1502, Vienna, Kunsthistorisches Museum, GG 4431 © Wikimedia Commons/ public domain

in political problems for which he had convened the States General in Breda, in the north of the duchy.[11]

In contrast to the *Nine Male Worthies*, no canon of their female counterparts had been established yet in the fifteenth century, and there was no established order. However, all *Nine Female Worthies* featuring in the Brussels entry had been shown on stages for the entry of Isabel of Bourbon in Nevers forty years earlier, though accompanied by their male counterparts. In the intermediate decades, no noticeable innovations were produced at the occasion of entries of princesses. Comparison with the extravagant celebration of Duke Charles's wedding with Margaret of York (1468), and her entry in Bruges, is complicated since the court, and especially chronicler Olivier de la Marche, kept firm control over the week-long program as well as over its written reports.[12] The nearest entry of a princess was that in Douai in November 1470, where Duchess Margaret of York and her stepdaughter Mary of Burgundy were received – under 'vilain temps', horrible weather conditions. Stages displayed references to her patron saint, and the program had an explicitly religious inspiration.[13]

Duke Charles spent most of the sharply increased taxation in wars, none of which produced any positive effect for the subjects. In 1477, Mary's inaugurations were overshadowed by the French invasions, local revolts, and the subjects' political claims.[14] The French attacks required further military investments, and when the States General had finally succeeded to conclude peace in 1482, new tensions arose, especially in Flanders, where resistance against Maximilian's autocratic style of

---

11 Cauchies, Jean-Marie, and Marie Van Eeckenrode, '"Recevoir madame l'archiduchesse pour faire incontinent ses nopces…". Gouvernants et gouvernés autour du mariage de Philippe le Beau et de Jeanne de Castille dans les Pays-Bas (1496-1501)', in *L'héritière, le prince étranger et le pays. Le mariage de Jean l'Aveugle et d'Élisabeth*, ed. by Michel Pauly (Luxembourg: CLUDEM, 2013), pp. 263-77.
12 Blockmans, Wim P., and Esther Donckers, 'Self-Representation of Court and City in Flanders and Brabant in the Fifteenth and Early Sixteenth Centuries', in *Showing Status. Representation of Social Positions in the Late Middle Ages*, ed. by Wim Blockmans, and Antheun Janse (Turnhout: Brepols, 1999), p. 98.
13 Lecuppre-Desjardin, *La ville des cérémonies*, pp. 287-90, 373.
14 *1477. Le privilège général et les privilèges régionaux de Marie de Bourgogne pour les Pays-Bas*, ed. by Wim P. Blockmans (Kortrijk: UGA, 1985).

government led to nine years of internal military conflict. In 1488, the Roman King was held prisoner for more than three months in Bruges, which explains his harsh feelings against that county.[15] The court moved to a safe residence in Mechelen. It was therefore with great relief and real enthusiasm, that the people of the Low Countries welcomed the peace-loving Philip, their 'natural prince', as their new ruler. In 1496, new enthusiasm prevailed, the economy recovered, booming in Antwerp and its region. While the county of Flanders had suffered heavily from revolts and repression, and its trade was hampered by blockades, Brabant profited from the shift of activities.

Preceding Joyous Entries

In August 1493, Maximilian's father Emperor Frederick III died, to be succeded by his son, the Roman King (Fig. 6.1). The States General requested him to send a delegate to conduct the inauguration ceremonies in the various territories for his son archduke Philip, who had reached his majority.[16] Maximilian agreed, but he wanted to keep control himself. He insisted to come personally to the Low Countries to be sure that the privileges would be excluded from the oath-takings that his first spouse Mary of Burgundy had conceded during the dramatic months following her father's dead on the battlefield in January 1477.

6.2 Ambrogio de Predis, *Bianca Maria Sforza*, oil on poplar, 51 × 32.5 cm, c. 1493, Washington, National Gallery of Art, Widener Collection, 1942.9.53 © Wikimedia Commons / public domain

Maximilian arrived in August 1494 at the court in Mechelen, accompanied by his newly-wed spouse Bianca Maria Sforza (Fig. 6.2). The Four Members of Flanders[17] sent notable delegations to Leuven to show reverence to the Roman King, and to observe the lengthy negotiations he had with the Estates of Brabant concerning the terms of his son's inauguration. That mattered in particular, as the duchy of Brabant

---

15 Blockmans, Wim P., 'Autocratie ou polyarchie? La lutte pour le pouvoir politique en Flandre de 1482 à 1492, d'après des documents inédits', *Bulletin de la Commission royale d'Histoire*, CXL, (1973), pp. 257-368.
16 Wellens, Robert, *Les Etats Généraux des Pays-Bas des origines à la fin du règne de Philippe le Beau (1464-1506)*, (Heule: UGA, 1974), pp. 233-34.
17 That is the consortium of the governments of the three capital cities, Ghent, Bruges, and Ypres, and the wealthy rural district around Bruges, conducting the negotiations for all matters concerning the 'third estate'.

had developed over two centuries an elaborate tradition of solemnly issued inauguration charters, named after the Joyous Entry event, the *Blijde Inkomst*. Moreover, he made sure that Philip would not swear his inaugural oaths in person in the county of Flanders, as a revenge for their refusal to recognize him, Maximilian, as regent after Mary's death in 1482. This was a matter of lengthy debates in the States General, the Estates of Flanders, and the city of Ghent, but the king remained inflexible, just conceding that inauguration by procuration would not be regarded as a precedent.[18]

The secretary and historiographer of the Saxonian Elector Frederick the Wise, Georg Spalatin (1484-1545) left a lively description of the celebrations in several cities, from August to December 1494. The level of detail suggests that he was informed by eyewitnesses belonging to the Roman King's following. On the 6th of August, Duchess-dowager Margaret of York, Archduke Philip and his sister Margaret (having returned from France, where her betrothal to the dauphin had been disrupted) rode into the fields to welcome Queen Bianca and introduced her into the lavishly decorated streets of the residence city Mechelen.

> All the bells were ringing when the priests, monks, clerics and all the able-bodied people, young and old, went out of the city walls in procession to meet the queen and conduct her within the walls. [...] The celebration lasted from eight to ten in the evening. [...]
> Hundreds of great wood fires and pitch tons, thousands of torches and candles were lit in the streets, on the market square, on the façades of houses and towers. There was so much light that one could see as well as by daylight.
> As it is accustomed in this country, in the queen's honour, the citizens of Mechelen had organized, in the streets where she would pass, lots of plays and marvelous and rare stories, ancient, new as well as saintly ones. They showed many ornaments and costly display.[19]

On the 16th of August, a similar reception was held in Antwerp, 'with extraordinary plays, fires and light'. The historiographer decribed at length the beautiful procession and the gorgeous theatrical representations displayed at Leuven to celebrate Our Lady's Nativity, on the 7th and 8th of September. The next day, Philip had to ride out of the city, to be solemnly entered under his father's guidance. He had to climb on a stage erected on the square in front of the town hall, and 'make a great number of promises in front of the princes and the people of Brabant' in order to be recognized and sworn as the 'rightful and natural prince'.[20] The observer did not mention that

---

18 Wiesflecker, Hermann, *Kaiser Maximilian I.*, vol. I, Munich: Oldenbourg, 1971), pp. 378-85; Blockmans, Wim P., and Walter Prevenier, *The Promised Lands. The Low Countries under Burgundian Rule, 1369-1530* (Philadelphia: Pennsylvania UP, 1999), pp. 206-07; Blockmans, Wim P., *De volksvertegenwoordiging in Vlaanderen in de overgang van middeleeuwen naar nieuwe tijden (1384-1506)* (Brussels: Academy, 1978), pp. 316-18; *Handelingen van de Leden en van de Staten van Vlaanderen. Regeringen van Maria van Bourgondië en Philips de Schone*, vol. II, ed. by Wim P. Blockmans (Brussels: Academy, 1982), pp. 678-97; Jean-Marie Cauchies, *Philippe le Beau. Le dernier duc de Bourgogne* (Turnhout: Brepols, 2003), pp. 32-40.
19 Spalatin, Georg, *Historischer Nachlaß und Briefe*, ed. by Christoph G. Neudecker, and L. Preller (Jena: Mauke, 1851), pp. 226-27.
20 Spalatin, *Historischer Nachlaß*, pp. 228-29.

the Estates of Brabant had been negotiating during three weeks on the terms of the inauguration charter, nor did he pay much attention to the constitutional character of the ceremony, held in the city which was considered to be the oldest capital of the duchy of Brabant. Mary's *Blijde Inkomst* (Joyous Entry) of 1477 entailed 108 articles, of which 63 had to be deleted in the version sworn by Philip in 1494.[21] The report related instead that Maximilian participated twice in public festivities in Mechelen, on the 12th to preside over a tournament on the market square, and another one on the 18th which Queen Bianca attended as well. The latter was held at the occasion of the marriage of his captain Wolfgang Polheim to a local lady. In the evening, a great dancing party took place on the market square,

> where everybody danced in his own way, mixing people from the High Lands with those of the Low Countries and Waloons [...]. The king and several of his people put on masks and joined the dancing in their special disguise.[22]

On the 5th of October, Maximilian conducted Philip to his inauguration in Antwerp, which was a marquisate, deserving an inauguration in its own right. The reciprocal oaths were sworn on a stage on the market square, in front of 'all the people'. The observer was deeply impressed by the spectacle,

> at the entry of the great market, of an angel coming down from heaven bringing a sword to the young prince, as a sign of his personal rulership, implying the protection and defence of his lands and his peoples.

The ceremony was followed by more tournaments, banquets and balls.[23] With the inaugurations in Leuven and Antwerp, the duchy of Brabant and the integrated marquisate of Antwerp, the highest ranking principality in the Low Countries had seen their privileges confirmed in so far as they dated from before 1477. Philip – probably still under Maximilian's influence – showed less consideration for the other territories. The Estates of Zeeland and Holland were pressurized to accept the inauguration without more ado in towns near the border with Brabant, on the 6th of November in Reimerswaal, and on the 12th of December in Geertruidenberg. At that moment, he refused performing the customary tour through the counties to confirm or adapt all kinds of local privileges, as Maximilian had demonstrated in his quality of spouse from March and April 1478.[24] Philip sent delegates to the Estates of Flanders in Ghent on the 26th of December to swear the observance of the privileges dating from before 1477, but he did it in person for the county of Hainaut, on the 31st in Mons, and on the 3rd of January 1495 in Valenciennes. The seigniory of Mechelen had him inaugurated on the 27th of March, the county of Namur on the 17th of May. Brussels enjoyed the special honour to be the first individual city (after the

---

21 Vrancken, Valerie, *De Blijde Inkomsten van de Brabantse hertogen* (Brussels: ASP, 2019), pp. 77-79, 350-56.
22 Vrancken, *De Blijde Inkomsten*, pp. 230-31.
23 Vrancken, *De Blijde Inkomsten*, pp. 232-34.
24 Smit, J. G., *Vorst en Onderdaan. Studies over Holland en Zeeland in de late Middeleeuwen* (Leuven: Peeters, 1995), pp. 229-33.

marquisate of Valenciennes) to see her privileges confirmed on the 21st of July 1495. Only in 1497 would Philip visit the most important towns of Flanders and Holland.[25]

Maximilian had more reasons for spending months in the Low Countries in 1494, as he attempted with military force to bring the duchy of Guelders under his direct rule, which he failed to achieve. On the other hand, he liked to travel around in these territories, which were far more populated and richer than his Austrian and Tyrolian dynastic lands. The average volume of expenditure of the Burgundian principalities amounted to the quadruple of those in his homelands.[26] Moreover, he enjoyed the traditional chivalric lifestyle and showing off his status. He may have been impressed by the spectacular events organized in his and his family's honour in the relatively large and prosperous cities in Brabant. He is known to have made great efforts in spreading his reputation as widely as possible by using the new printing techniques. He financially supported humanistic scholars with assistants, and invested in the writing of his autobiography and having it illustrated by dozens of woodcuts by Hans Burgkmair and others. He was very keen on widely communicating his political achievements and ideals, and preserving them for posterity in monuments, images, and texts.[27] Maximilian was certainly not unique in his days in paying great attention to his propaganda. Queen Isabella of Castile similarly loved pomp and circumstance in processions and entries, and the celebration of victories. She employed chroniclers who disseminated the good news and engaged in re-writing history as well as having them published in print.[28]

The Rhetoricians' Tradition

In several cities of the Low Countries, particularly in Arras and Valenciennes, confraternities or companies of musicians and other performers emerged as early as the thirteenth century, partly in the context of religious celebrations. In the fourteenth century, the composition of literary texts in the vernacular languages became the mission of a growing number of such voluntary confraternities of citizens.[29] From the mid-fifteenth century onwards, urban governments recognized the statutes of these 'rhetoricians' and fostered such companies ever more, some purely literary, others lyrical and performing plays, also in inter-urban competitions. Their organizational set-up was similar to that of companies of archers and crossbowmen, who were just as eager to participate in regional competitions. Three scenes in the manuscript depicting Joanna's entry in Brussels show precisely these 'guilds' at the end of the

---

25 Cauchies, *Philippe*, 34-36.
26 Körner, Martin, 'Expenditure', in *Economic Systems and State Finance*, ed. by Richard Bonney (Oxford: Clarendon, 1995), pp. 399-400.
27 Silver, Larry, *Marketing Maximilian: The Visual Ideology of a Holy Roman Emperor* (Princeton: Princeton UP, 2008); Müller, Hans-Dirk, 'Literatur und Kunst unter Maximilian I.', in *Kaiser Maximilian I. Bewahrer und Reformer*, ed. by Georg Schmidt-von Rhein (Ramstein: Paqué, 2002), pp. 141-51.
28 Tremlett, Giles, *Isabella of Castile. Europe's First Great Queen* (London: Bloomsbury, 2017), pp. 148-51.
29 van Bruaene, Anne-Laure, *Om beters wille. Rederijkerskamers en de stedelijke cultuur in de Zuidelijke Nederlanden (1400-1650)* (Amsterdam: AUP, 2008), pp. 27-41.

procession; the second is said to have silenced the turmoil of the masses, the third is protecting the princess (fols 29ʳ-31ʳ).

By then, the major cities of Flanders and Brabant had several companies in their midst. The Ghent aldermen, for example, recognized statutes of new rhetoricians' companies in 1448, 1458, 1469, and 1484. Membership grew in the hundreds for each of them, they recruited members of the local elite, honorary members and some high officers of the prince, or their close relatives. The low amount of the yearly fee made access feasible for ordinary skilled craftsmen. In Brussels, the earliest mention of a 'Chamber of Rhetoricians' was that in 1417 of *Den boeck* (The book); they owned a house for their meetings. The second, named *De corenbloem* (The cornflower) was mentioned in 1479, having a room at their disposal in the Butchers' Hall, and in 1485-86 their own house. In that year, the chambers 'The lily' (*De Lelie*) and 'The violet' (*De Violette*) received a subsidy for presenting 'a character' during the entry of Maximilian who was elected Roman King in February 1486 and crowned in April.[30] Maximilian and Philip demonstrated their particular sympathy for the rhetoricians' activities in the wording of the participants' safe-conduct for a contest organized by the chamber 'The lily' in Brussels in May 1493, which was open for productions in French as well as in Dutch:

> en faveur de Rethoricke, qui es le seuil de toutes Recreation et Joyeulx passetemps … pour esmouvoir les cuers et coraiges des hommes a Joye et Recreacion.[31]

> favouring Rhetorics, which is the threshold to all kinds of Recreation and Joyous leisure… bringing Joy and Recreation to the hearts and courage of all people.

It was probably Maximilian, whose lively interest in literature and theatrical performances I noted above, who had particularly favoured activities of Rhetoricians' chambers in Brussels. In this endeavour he was assisted by courtiers like Olivier de la Marche, who had been the master-mind in the week-long festivities in Bruges at the occasion of the wedding of Duke Charles and Margaret of York in 1468. Several prominent councillors supported the idea, while they had sponsored activities of rhetoricians in their own seigneuries in Brabant, especially John II and John III, lords of Bergen-op-Zoom, Engelbert of Nassau, marquess of Antwerp and lord of Breda and Diest, and Guillaune de Croÿ, lord of Aarschot.[32] Maximilian and Philip formally initiated the creation of an overarching 'sovereign chamber of rhetorics' in the Dutch-speaking territories. For that purpose, they convened a meeting of representatives of all chambers in Mechelen on the first of May 1493, directly following a well-attended meeting of the States General. This connection revealed the political

---

30 van Bruaene, *Om beters wille*, pp. 42-51; see the overview on www.dbnl.org/tekst/brua.
31 van Bruaene, *Om beters wille*, pp. 221, 234.
32 Biographies by Paul de Win and Robert Wellens in *Les Chevaliers de l'Ordre de la Toison d'or au XVᵉ siècle*, ed. by Raphael de Smedt (Frankfurt: Lang, 2000), pp. 180-83, 216-20, 247-49; W. H. Van Ham, *Macht en gezag in het Markiezaat. Een politiek-institutionele studie over stad en land van Bergen-op-Zoom (1477-1583)* (Hilversum: Verloren, 2000), pp. 87-91.

intention behind the cultural initiative, namely controlling the public representations to avoid the dissemination of oppositional messages, as it happened during the revolt in Flanders during the preceding decade. Thirteen Brabantine chambers participated in the meeting and just four Flemish ones, and one from Holland; those of Ghent, Bruges and Ypres were not represented. Three years later, the first inter-regional competition of rhetoricians in Antwerp included thirteen chambers of Brabant and Flanders each, and one from Zeeland and Holland each. Maximilian was busy in the Empire, the negative feelings about the revolt had faded away, and Philip had been emancipated.[33]

The Brussels magistrate paid a regular salary to the official city rhetorician, who was Colijn Caillieu for the years 1474-85, and Jan Smeken from 1485 till his death in 1517. A manuscript compiled in the 1520s by a rhetorician named Gielis Leemans comprised three plays related to the courtly context. The first is an anonymous play composed for an entry in Brussels, probably in 1466, of Charles of Charolais, then stadholder-general for his debilitated father. The second one is by Colijn celebrating princess Margaret of Austria's birth or baptism on the 10th of January 1480, and the third is by Jan Smeken, expressing the fear that Joanna, as the designated queen of Castile, and her eldest son Charles might leave the country, an issue that was at stake around 1505. As shown in Raymond Fagel's essay in this volume, Joanna had spent more than half of her years in the Low Low Countries in the Coudenberg palace in Brussels until 1501. The city's interest was thus at stake here, as well as the harmonious relations between the court, the local government and the whole citizenry.[34] The same manuscript also contains an allegorical poem on the death of Charles the Bold by the Bruges rhetorician Anthonis de Roovere (c. 1430-82) and a sort of exemplum list of mythological subjects. This may well have inspired the designers of Joanna's Entry, as that did show the personages he described, as well as their outlook.

> excellent ... goddesses or princesses to
> be displayed in the chambers, selected from
> various books, be it in harness, in
> triumph or naked.[35]

The first category lists seven naked characters, among whom Venus, Juno, and Pallas featured as a stage in the 1496 entry (fol. 57^r). Then follow 'Women in harness, first the ix Worthies', who are all the same heroines as those shown in the entry, albeit in a different order. The comment on the characters is abbreviated in the Leemans manuscript, and corresponds fairly well with the descriptions in the manuscript of

---

33 Van Bruaene, *Om beters wille*, 63-66, 73-76.
34 Mareel, Samuel, 'Theatre and Politics in Brussels at the time of Philip the Fair: The Leemans Collection', in *Books in Transition at the time of Philip the Fair*, ed. by Hanno Wijsman and others (Turnhout: Brepols, 2010), pp. 213-30.
35 De Keyzer, Piet, 'Het rhetoricaal "exemplum". Bijdrage tot de iconologie van onze Rederijkers', in *Vooys voor De Vooys. Nieuwe Taalgids* (1953), 48-57, esp. p. 54. I am grateful to Professor Remco Sleiderink for sharing this reference with this volume's contributors.

the entry. The greatest discrepancy concerns Semiramis, of whom the 1496 comment tells that she 'had this peculiar habit that whenever she received an unwelcome message, she did not brush her hair until the case had been decided, with weapons or by peaceful means' (fol. 46^v). The version in the Leemans manuscript mentions that she slaid Yonastron, 'and did not brush her hair until she had submitted her cities or enemies'.

Nineteen Heroines

Overall, however, it is clear that the *Nine Female Worthies* belonged to the standard repertoire of the Brussels rhetoricians around 1500. Thereafter, the Leemans manuscript enumerates another set of nine ladies, nymphs or muses, which is followed by a long list drawn 'from the Bible and other books'. The first three, Judith, Jael, and Tecuites, all feature in the 1496 entry; the last three also are to be noted:

- *Die Maegt van Vranckrycke* (France's Virgin), Joanna of Arc
- *Die conyngynne van Spaengyen* (The Queen of Spain), Isabella of Castile
- *Yacoba van Hollant*, Jacqueline of Bavaria.[36]

Joan of Arc's name circulated already as a heroine, and Isabella, Joanna's mother, Queen of Castile (1451, r. 1474-1504), staged in the Brussels entry of 1496, was one of her admirers. The latter was evidently chosen, because she was Joanna's mother and the first queen regnant in her own right in Europe, but also because of the spectacular submission of the kingdom of Granada in 1492. She occupied a central place in the Brussels show, between the nine biblical stages and the Nine Worthies. That intersection comprised two *tableaux*, the first being a representation of Astyages, King of the Medes in the sixth century BCE, dreaming that a vine would grow from his daughter Mandane's womb and cover the whole world (fol. 41^r). The Greek historiographers Herodotos and Xenophon report that she married the Persian King Cambyses; their son Cyrus would indeed overthrow his grandfather Astyages.[37] The Brussels rhetorician bluntly formulated this analogy as follows: 'So, Philip's fatherland hopes for offspring from Joanna of Spain's womb' (fol. 41^v).

More explicit is the extensive comment on the representation of Queen Isabella, holding her sword upright and a shield with her heraldic arms, receiving Granada's ruler Boabdil's homage (fol. 41^v).[38]

---

36 De Keyzer, 'Het rhetoricaal "exemplum"', p. 56.
37 Pelling, Christopher, 'The Urine and the Vine: Astyages' Dreams at Herodotos 1.107-8': https://www.cais-soas.com/CAIS/History/madha/astyages_dreams.htm (consulted on 1 June 2023).
38 In reality, Boabdil was captured during a raid in April 1483, and had to accept his submission as Isabella's vassal and ally, kneeling and kissing her hand, leaving his small son in her custody and promise to join her in the war against his own father, then still Granada's ruler. On 2 January 1492, when he had to give up the exhausted city after months of siege, the pre-established ritual let him leave the Alhambra on a mule, accompanied by fifty of his retainers, mimicking to dismount for Isabella and her son Juan on horseback. She, however, did not want to humiliate him and magnanimously granted him free departure with his son, then nine years old: Tremlett, *Isabella of Castile*, pp. 206-08, 249-50.

Elizabeth Regina Johanne nostre mater Inclitissima que (ut scema prefert) garnapolitanum regem pro genibus supplicem habens famosissima illa victoria quam non tam suorum armis quam suo animo cui par numquam extitit et obsidionis diuturnitate eventuum belli diversitate ac rei magnitudine novem subsequentium ac omnium illustrium feminarum quas unquam vel muse vel hystorie celebres cecinere gloriam famamque oblitterans immortales reportavit triumphos quos cum verbis musisve minime vel silentio predicare indultum est.

> Isabella, worthy of every praise, the renowned mother of our Joanna, who – having the King of Granada begging on his knees (as the depiction shows), belittling the glory and fame of all nine following illustrious women who have been praised in poems and famous stories with this well-known victory, not only because of the weapons of her army, but also because of her spirit, of which the like has never been found, and the length of the siege, the changes in successes during the war end the magnitude of the case – gained eternal triumphs that one may praise with words or poems, or in silence.

The upward position of the sword was meaningful: it referred to the war she and her husband Ferdinand had waged since 1481 against the last Moorish kingdom in Iberia, as they had sworn to do in their marriage contract of 1469.[39] Isabella was proclaimed queen regnant of Castile on the central square of Segovia on 13 December 1474, and she swore to protect her people, to respect the church and 'the privileges and freedoms that the *hidalgos* (knights), cities and other places enjoy'. Thereafter, she strode through the streets, preceded by a single gentleman holding a bare sword with the hilt upwards. On the day of her inauguration, the young queen demonstrated her royal judicial power in this unprecedented way.[40]

Isabella's stage can be interpreted as one of the central themes of the whole entry: Joanna's mother is even greater than the famous Nine Worthies, not so much by her armed force, as through her fortitude and the vigour of her spirit. As a young queen, she immediately demonstrated her extraordinary qualities as a ruler: her fortitude, clear strategic as well as tactical insight, voluntarism, and courage, even in the heat of military operations. She chose her spouse herself, against the will of her half-brother King Enrique IV (1425-74). She decidedly acted to push her claim to the throne which was contested on dubious grounds by him and his followers. The grandees opposed her outspoken character, and launched a civil war out of fear that she would strengthen royal power. In the first two years of her reign, she was moreover confronted with an invasion by a strong Portuguese army. She overcame all these challenges, in a remarkable understanding with her husband King Ferdinand, her second cousin.[41] Their next major challenge was the eleven years' war against the kingdom of Granada, in which her role, even close to the military operations, was decisive. The royal couple took their son Juan and daughter Joanna with them during

---

39 Tremlett, *Isabella of Castile*, p. 196.
40 Tremlett, *Isabella of Castile*, pp. 95-96.
41 Tremlett, *Isabella of Castile*, pp. 128-48.

the greater part of the eight months' siege of the city in 1491, which must have made a deep impression, especially on twelve-years-old Joanna.[42]

It that line of thought, the Nine Worthies are not presented here as role models for Joanna, nor has any comment suggested an analogy between them and her. Their visual representations are standardised and simply displaying three characters against a black background. All the Worthies were harnessed – though that is not visible in the representation of Penthesilea, the last queen of the amazons -, holding a sword and a shield, assisted by two young ladies, one bearing the heroine's pennon, the other her helmet. Lampeto, Queen of the amazons, is the only one holding a halberd and her sword in the scabbard. Three Worthies are holding their sword upright as in the case of Queen Isabella (Deiphilis, Tamaris, and Teuca), probably because they were the only ones of whom was said that they obtained great military victories. Five of the Worthies are represented bearing a crown: Semiramis as Empress of Babylon, Lampeto and Penthesilea, queens of the amazons, Tamaris, and Teuca, the latter 'bearing the sceptre over the Illyrians'.

In the order of the display in 1496, the Nine Worthies can thus be identified by their concise descriptions.

> **Deiphilis**: destroyed Thebe, together with her sister Argina.
> **Sinope**: erroneously presented here as Queen of the amazons, she was not defeated by Hercules.
> **Hippolyta** and her sister **Menelopa** (following): they successfully fought against Hercules and Theseus, and conquered Greece.
> **Semiramis**: Empress of Babylon, she waited brushing her hair until she had solved problems by arms or peacefully.
> **Lampeto**: Queen of the amazons, victoriously coming from the north through Europe, she founded many and great cities.
> **Tamaris**: called 'queen', subdued King Cyrus of Persia and Medea with his 30,000 soldiers; because of his blood-thirsty character, she had his head drowned in a womb filled with blood.
> **Teuca**: Queen of the Illyrians, gained the victory over Roman legions.
> **Penthesilea**: Queen of the amazons, fought with love for Hector against the Troyans.

Regal Qualities

In striking contrast to the comments accompanying the preceding and the following representations, the *Nine Female Worthies* were just presented with praise for their military achievements, fighting spirit, and leadership, without any explicit reference to Joanna being made. Queen Isabella's presentation made it even clear that *her* qualities were far superior to those of the celebrated Worthies, since her victory rested more on

---

42 Tremlett, *Isabella of Castile*, pp. 196-231, 240-48.

her spiritual leadership than on the vicissitudes of war. The seven scenarios following the *Worthies* provided gentle counsels to Joanna regarding the classical triad of wisdom, love, and force, and some made associations with her marriage. The structure is less systematic than in the two preceding sections comprising nine stages each, but we can still distinguish three biblical characters (bringing their total to twelve), and two stages representing three ladies each. Anne-Marie Legaré pointed out that the coherence of this group of stages is to be found in the general admonishing of the virtues represented by the three classical goddesses Venus (love, *luxuria* (lust), and fertility), Juno (power), and Pallas (wisdom).[43] These three corresponded to the biblical exempla: just as Queen Saba came to listen, kneeling, to the wise King Salomo, Joanna is advised to listen to the wise Philip. Prophetess Deborah shows her persuasive power and Jael her physical force, and so 'Joan of Spain shall batter the heads of our enemies with the nail of her exquisite power' (folio 54^v).

The next stage of the Three virgins (fols 55^v-56^r) is a simple association with the three deities in the following *tableau* of the three goddesses. The central virgin is angling, holding at her rod a white dove that is carrying the imperial crown. This visual representation is rather different from the text that associates Emperor Henry IV (r. 1054-1105) who gave his daughter in marriage to Godfrey the Bearded, first Duke of Brabant (r. 1095-1139), with King Ferdinand of Aragon giving his daughter Joanna in marriage to Philip, Duke of Brabant. The crown at the angling-rod clearly was the closed imperial model, which may be interpreted as a speculation that Philip might at some point wear it. His father was painstakingly trying to persuade the pope to crown himself emperor, which never materialized. However, Philip and Joanna's two sons, Charles and Ferdinand, would become emperor, and their three daughters, Eleonora of Portugal and France, Mary of Hungary, and Catherina of England became queens.

The representation in between the three stages with biblical characters consists of three scenes showing the exchange of portraits between young princes, named Florencius and Meriana who fell heavily in love after seeing each other's portraits, and subsequently married. So, too, did the portraits of Philip and Joanna spark a mutual love, resulting in a memorable union (fol. 53^r). This stage reflects the far more glorious stage on folio 39 showing the marriage of Rebecca and Isaac, also split in three scenes and moreover headed by the Trinity and numerous torches. It can be seen as leading to the penultimate one labelled as 'Domus delicie et iocunditatis' (The House of Pleasure and Merry-making), where the jester points at the loving couple, who are surrounded by a merry company dancing, drinking, making music, and playing (fol. 58^r).

---

43 Legaré, 'Joanna of Castile's Entry', pp. 182-85; Legaré, 'L'entrée de Jeanne', pp. 53-54.

The Milanese Connection

The description in the text on fol. 52ᵛ, explaining the marriage of Florencius and Meriana, raises a problem of identification of the principal agents in what was evidently meant to be a reference to a historical precedent.

> Hoc scemate representatur Qui uti figure facierum florentii ducis mediolanensis et meriane filie regis Castillie mutuo presentate amorem in alterutrum excandescere fecerunt exque hiis dicti matrimonium contraxerunt Sic vise Philippi Johanneque ymagines amorem vicissim reconciliantes celebres nuptias effecerunt.
>
> This depiction displays how Florentius, the Duke of Milan, and Meriana, the daughter of the King of Castile, fell heavily in love after seeing each other's portraits, and subsequently married. So, too, did the portraits of Philip and Joanna spark a mutual love, resulting in a memorable union.

Until now, nobody suggested an identification of that princely couple, and the issue is complicated indeed. Milan has been elevated to a duchy in 1395, but in the subsequent century none of the dukes was named Florentius. Similarly, no king of Castile had a daughter named Meriana, neither can any marriage be traced between a Castilian royal descendant and a duke of Milan.[44] Was this representation then a pure invention of the spirited Brussels rhetoricians? That idea has to be rejected since it would have meant a blame to the daughter of the regnant Queen Isabella of Castile, whose character was shown with the highest praise just eleven stages earlier in the procession. My hypothesis is instead that the designers made a reference to a real event in recent history, but were mistaken about the persons' names and the princess's dynastic affiliation.

The only marriage between a duke of Milan and a princess of a Spanish royal house was that between the young Duke Gian Galeazzo Sforza (1469-94) and Isabella of Aragon (1470-1524), who was the daughter of Alfonso II, King of Naples in succession to his father Alfonso V/I the Magnanimous, King of Aragon and Naples (1394, r. 1416-1448), Joanna's paternal grandfather (and Isabella's great-uncle).[45] That marriage was intended to consolidate the Holy League formed in 1454 by the major political entities in Italy, including Naples and Milan, as a reaction to the Turkish conquest of Constantinople, the year before. King Ferdinand of Aragon (1452, r. 1478-1516), Joanna's father, and Duke Galeazzo of Milan (r. 1466-1476), Gian Galeazzo's uncle, had agreed to this marriage in 1470. It was celebrated in person in the Dome of Milan on 2ⁿᵈ February 1489 and was accompanied by a great theatrical performance entitled *Il Paradiso*, displaying sets and costumes designed by Leonardo da Vinci.[46] It was a representation of the seven planets orbiting around Isabella of Aragon and praising her. In addition to the acknowledgment of her physical beauty, Isabella was also noted for having an energetic personality, similar to

---

44 Sokop, Brigitte, *Stammtafeln europäischer Herrscherhäuser* (Vienna: Böhlau, 1993), p. 53.
45 Sokop, *Stammtafeln*.
46 Nicholl, Charles, *Leonardo Da Vinci: The Flights of the Mind* (London: Penguin, 2005).

her Castilian namesake, Queen Isabella. The young duke, however, was evicted by his uncle Ludovico 'il Moro' who had ruled as a regent during the past thirteen years and had no intention at all to see his role diminished by his sickly young nephew, who died in 1494. So, in contrast to the impression given in the Brussels *tableau vivant*, the Milanese marriage had been all but a happy one.

Yet another dynastic link was relevant in this context, namely the marriage negotiated in 1493 between Roman King Maximilian (Philip's father) and Ludovico Sforza. The latter became the effective ruler of the duchy of Milan after his brother's assassination in 1476, as regent for his nephew Gian Galeazzo, then seven years old. He tried to consolidate his position by strengthening his links with Maximilian to whom he offered his niece Bianca Maria (1472-1510) as a bride, accompanied with an impressive gift of 300,000 ducats. Moreover, they agreed on another 100,000 ducats in return for the Roman King's investiture which bestowed legitimacy on Ludovico as Duke of Milan. Ludovico's enfeoffment with the duchy of Milan was effectuated in April 1495, a few months after the legitimate successor's death. Maximilian was constantly short of money, which he spent primarily on his mostly symbolic military exploits, and he was looking forward to extending his descendancy. The marriage was concluded by procuration in Milan, and the new queen arrived in Innsbruck in December 1493, after a difficult journey over the Alpine passes. The reception in her new lands contrasted sharply with the triumphal procession that had brought her in gilded carriages from the Milanese castle to the Dome, where the archbishop had crowned her. Maximilian did not rush to meet her, making her wait till March 1494. Moreover, the German princes disapproved the new queen's low descendancy from a condottiere with the reputation of cruelty. Maximilian's hope for extension of his progeniture did not materialize, and the relations between the consorts never turned to happiness.[47] The scenery representing the marriage between a young Duke of Milan and a princess from a Spanish royal house must have referred to Joanna's second cousin Isabella of Aragon and Gian Galeazzo Sforza, the cousin of Bianca Maria, Maximilian's new bride. The close relations between the houses of Castile-Aragon and that of Burgundy-Habsburg, demonstrated by the marriages of Maximilian's children Philip and Margaret with children of the Catholic Kings, were just as fresh in the peoples' memories as Maximilian's marriage with the Milanese princess.

In the summer and autumn of 1494, Maximilian did take his young bride Bianca Maria to the festivities in the cities of Brabant. It was a common practice that members of urban governments as well as rhetoricians went to see inaugural celebrations in other cities, to match their own plans with them. We can hypothesize that Brussels rhetoricians observed with keen interest the festivities described above in nearby Mechelen, Leuven, and Antwerp, which were attended by Maximilian and Bianca

---

47 Wiesflecker, Hermann, *Kaiser Maximilian I.*, vol. I (Munich: Oldenbourg, 1971), pp. 363-72; Rill, Gerhard, 'Bianca Maria Sforza', in *Die Habsburger*, ed. by Brigitte Hamann (Vienna: Ueberreuter, 1988), pp. 66-68. Unterholzner, Daniela, *Bianca Maria Sforza (1472-1510): herrschaftliche Handlungsspielräume einer Königin vor dem Hintergrund von Hof, Familie und Dynastie*, (PhD, University of Innsbruck, 2015), online: https://diglib.uibk.ac.at/ulbtirolhs/content/structure/761506, pp. 36-54.

Maria. There, they might have heard about the marriage, just five years earlier, of the young Gian Galeazzo Sforza and Isabella of Aragon. They might have misunderstood – or just imagined – the names of the couple, but they correctly referred to a young duke of Milan married to a daughter of a king belonging to a Spanish royal house. Moreover, this marriage implied a reference to the union to the Habsburg dynasty and that of Aragon, whose head was Joanna's father, King Ferdinand. This was the type of analogies people liked in those days.

Messages

The opposition against Maximilian's autocratic rule had been most virulent in Flanders, starting already in 1480, and lasting until the submission after years-long military confrontations, by the end of 1492.[48] Maximilian was hated for his ongoing financial claims for military enterprises that did not at all serve the common interest. Foreign soldiers had devastated the lands, ruined the cities, and after some twenty years of wars and revolts, people above all longed for peace. The 1480s were moreover characterized by extremely high grain prices in Western Europe generally, economic blockades and disturbances of trade through political conflicts. Brabant had suffered less from a decade of generalized economic crisis than the coastal principalities Flanders, Zeeland, and Holland. Brussels had become the main ducal residence since Duke Philip the Good's later years. Mary preferred Ghent and Bruges, but since the Flemish revolt, Mechelen was chosen in the mid-1480s as a safe heaven. The court's residence and the location of the high court of justice (Great council) and the council of finances made Mechelen a central point of attraction.[49] From 1497 onwards, however, that is since Philip and Joanna's marriage, Brussels became the favorite residence, since the palace on the Coudenberg was more accommodating. This can be demonstrated by the places where the States General were convened: from November 1488 to November 1501, 25 meetings were held, of which only three times a city outside Brabant and Mechelen (geographically included in the duchy) was chosen. Brussels became the absolute favourite from 1497 onwards, hosting 14 meetings, while Mechelen had been leading until 1496 with 9 sessions.[50]

Ceremonial entries, especially those for Philip's inauguration, were held in Leuven, the oldest capital, Antwerp, the margraviate, and Mechelen, the residence. The double marriage of Maximilians's son and daughter with the second daughter and the only son of the Spanish royal couple, agreed upon on 20 January 1495, were celebrated by procuration in Mechelen, on 5 November of that year.[51] Semi-political events such as the meetings of the chambers of rhetoric, were first held in Mechelen,

---

48 Blockmans, 'Autocratie ou polyarchie?', 257-368.
49 Prevenier, Walter, 'Mechelen circa 1500. A Cosmopolitan Biotope for Social Elites and non-Conformists', in *Women of Distinction. Margaret of York – Margaret of Austria*, ed. by Dagmar Eichberger (Leuven: Davidsfonds, 2005), pp. 31-41.
50 Wellens, *Etats Généraux*, pp. 464-505.
51 Cauchies, *Philippe*, pp. 45-48.

Brussels, and Antwerp. Leuven seemed to lose in the competition, the smaller towns in northern Brabant were visited only occasionally, especially since Maximilian's attempts to conquer Guelders. The choice of the small town of Lier for Philip and Joanna's marriage, half-way between Antwerp and Mechelen, does not seem self-evident after these precedents. It population was relatively small and decreased from *c.* 7000 in 1437 to *c.* 5100 inhabitants in 1496 as the economic activities declined. In 1480, 97 houses were left unoccupied, which created opportunities to host the numerous Spanish guests who accompanied Joanna, and who would return with Philip's sister Margaret to marry Joanna's brother Juan.[52] Lier hosted two meetings of the States General, in 1489 and 1497, but each of them in combination with other locations. The reconstruction of the spire, the nave and the transept of the main church, dedicated to St. Gummarus, has been underway since 1475, and the works continued on the choir. The relics of the local saint were venerated for his assistance for women's fertility. In that year, Duchess Margaret of York undertook a pilgrimage to this place of devotion, without result; as a widow, she participated in the procession on the 11th of October 1477.[53] She might have persisted in her belief and advised the young couple in that direction. Philip himself returned from a long journey through the German lands only three days before the celebration of the marriage, which makes it unlikely that he would have had a great impact on the logistics of the celebration. The most probable factor may have been the bishop of Cambrai, to whose diocese northern Brabant belonged, Henry of Bergen (Berghes). He might have preferred to celebrate the marriage mass in this splendid church where the relics of Saint Gummarus were revered. As the eldest son of John II (1449-1502), Lord of Bergen-op-Zoom, Henry had been duchess-dowager Margaret of York's court chaplain since 1479, he was bishop from 1480 to his death in 1502. He acted as chancellor of the Order of the Golden Fleece, and as the first councillor of Philip. He sponsored his secretary, Desiderius Erasmus, for his study of theology in Paris. His father and his brother John III (1452-1532) were prominent members of the Burgundian and Habsburg courts, owning property in Lier and its environment.[54] John III had been incorporated in the Order of the Golden Fleece in 1481, he acted as chamberlain for Philip since 1485, and became his first councillor and warden of the seal in 1493. Bishop Henry and his brother John may have considered further competition between the Brabantine capitals undesirable for the occasion to which a great number of Spanish visitors would attend.

This sensitive symbolic competition was also expressed in the emblematic buildings, as exemplified in the building history of the town halls of Leuven and Brussels.[55] The latter's spire was unique in the Low Countries, both by its design and its height; the illustration and a lengthy description in the entry's manuscript made this point

---

52 Aerts, Erik, and Herman van der Wee, *Geschiedenis van Lier. Welvaart en samenleving van het ontstaan van de stad tot de Eerste Wereldoorlog*² (Lier: vzw. Gilde Heren van Lier, 2019), pp. 125-26, 171, 181.
53 Blockmans, Wim P., 'The Devotion of a Lonely Duchess', in *Margaret of York, Simon Marmion, and The Visions of Tondal*, ed. by Thomas Kren (Malibu: The J. Paul Getty Museum, 1992), pp. 36, 42-43.
54 Friendly communication with professor Erik Aerts.
55 See the contribution by Sascha Köhl in this volume.

crystal-clear (fols 31ʳ and 63ᵛ). Mechelen might have challenged Brussels' architectural supremacy by planning a spire of 168 meters high for its main church, but it gave up at exactly the same height of 97 meters as the Brussels spire. The booming metropolis Antwerp was constructing the largest church of the Low Countries and far beyond, with seven aisles and no less than five spires – as many as the Tournai cathedral. By 1530, its only achieved spire would reach 123 meters, but in 1496 that was not attained yet. In this competitive setting, none of the larger cities would have had a reason to be offended by the choice for Lier for the princely marriage, a small, loyal and calm town.

Brussels would, however, have its revenge on 9 December 1496. The first and the last stages of the entry may be considered as the identification marks of the rhetoricians, musicians, and painters who designed the whole procession and performed in it. Tubal, who invented music amidst the noises of a blacksmith's shop, is associated with Joanna's mission to 'unite countless souls into one peace agreement covering thirty countries', the number of Philip's lordships, of which the coats-of-arms are displayed on folio 61ʳ. Preceding the coats-of-arms of the ten kingdoms belonging to Joanna's dynasty (fol. 60ʳ), the last *tableau* depicts St. Luke painting Mary, amidst angels singing and playing instruments. The comment here suggests that God sent Joanna to Brabant to be embraced. The artists, musicians, painters, and rhetoricians conveyed the message welcoming the princess into the city where Margaret was born, her sister-in-law and expected queen of Spain. She would be warmly welcomed in March 1497 entering Burgos in dusk, 1.500 torches lit in the streets, and candles burning in the windows of the houses.[56] The Brussels rhetoricians were the first to create a program entirely focused on female characters as role models for the ideal princess-consort. The message to Joanna was the expectation that she would bring unity and peace to the Habsburg lands, be a loving wife, listen to Philip's wisdom and encourage him with the power of her good counsel, to bring him offspring, and possibly an even larger empire, maybe even the imperial crown. All this followed the praise of the city, its institutions, corporations, and its magnificent town hall, signaling that Brussels would be the ideal residence. Joanna followed that advice.

---

56 Tremlett, *Isabella*, p. 394.

DAGMAR EICHBERGER

Arguing with the Old Testament

Moral and Political Lessons for Princess Joanna of Castile

▼ **ABSTRACT** In Part Two of the entry organized in honour of Joanna of Castile twenty-eight *tableaux vivants* were erected on the streets of the city of Brussels. Twelve of them are dedicated to themes from the Old Testament. After an introductory presentation evoking the harmonious coexistence of the individual dominions, the focus is on exemplary women who made a name for themselves through courage, wisdom or virtue. In the Latin texts, a direct reference is established between the biblical story and Joanna of Castile. Several wedding scenes respond to the recent marriage of the Spanish princess to Archduke Philip the Fair in Lier (Brabant). Reference is made to the territories that Joanna acquired through the dynastic connection. Particular emphasis is placed on Joanna's willingness to defend her country against potential enemies.

▼ **KEYWORDS** Marriage, peace, chastity, wisdom, strength, courage, Mary of Burgundy, Philip the Fair, Maximilian I, Brabant.

This essay deals with twelve *tableaux vivants* or stage sets in the festive entry of Joanna of Castile that depict scenes from the Old Testament.[1] My aim is to examine what messages the city wanted to send to the princess and how this was achieved both through texts and images. Of the twenty-eight stages in total that make up the second part of the Berlin manuscript, about half deal with accounts from antiquity, such as *Mandane and King Astyages* (fol. 41^r), or, occasionally, with historical figures from the present such as *Queen Isabella of Castile* (fol. 42^r). The enumeration of belligerent amazons and additional heroic women from the past occupy nine stages in all (fol. 43^r-51^r).[2] The ten Old Testament women whose stories are told in this festive

---

1 I wish to thank the following colleagues for their helpful comments: Wim Blockmans, Alison Kettering, Samuel Mareel and Helga Kaiser-Minn.
2 See the essay by Wim Blockmans in this volume.

entry are: Judith, Jael, Tecuites, Deborah, Sara, Michal, Rebecca, Esther, the Queen of Sheba and the unnamed daughter of a Pharaoh.

Over the last twenty years, the role of the Old Testament in fifteenth and sixteenth-century art has increasingly been studied by art historians. In her essay 'The Old Testament as a moral Code', Ilja Veldman shows that the stories from the Old Testament provided people with both reprehensive and laudable examples. For this reason, the Bible was considered a suitable text for giving individuals guidelines for their behaviour.[3] The growing importance of the Old Testament is further discussed in Peter van den Coelen's exhibition catalogue *Patriarchs, Angels and Prophets. The Old Testament in Netherlandish Printmaking from Lukas van Leyden to Rembrandt*.[4] Yvonne Bleyerveld concentrates on the 'Power of Women' topos, emphasizing that women were believed to have an extraordinary influence on men, either good or bad.[5] The Dutch artist Lucas van Leyden (1494-1533) is one of the earliest Netherlandish artists dealing extensively with Old Testament stories in prints and paintings, thus being a trailblazer for the growing significance of the Old Testament in the Arts.[6]

As the chronicler Jean Molinet (1435-1507) reports, Old Testament themes were often used in festive entries dating from the last quarter of the fifteenth century. Neil Murphy points out, that Molinet repeatedly 'couches his descriptions of triumphal entries into re-conquered towns with biblical allusions'.[7] In his description of the 1490 entry into Vienna he compares Maximilian, King of the Romans, with David who freed the children of Israel from slavery in Egypt.[8] When Philip the Fair entered the city of Brussels in 1495, the city decorated the streets with thirty-five stages, mostly depicting Old Testament scenes, taken from the five books of Moses.[9] Molinet does not specify which themes were chosen for Philip but comments in a more general way that they were '[...] very fitting for the arrival and reception of my

---

3 She explained her ideas by investigating fifteenth- and sixteenth-century images that illustrated the Decalogue or Ten Commandments, see: Veldman, Ilja, 'The Old Testament as a Moral Code', *Simiolus* 23 (1995), pp. 215-39, republished in *Images for Eye and Soul: Function and Meaning in Netherlandish Prints (1450-1650)* (Leiden: Primavera, 2006), pp. 119-50.
4 Amsterdam, Museum Het Rembrandthuis, 1996 (Leiden: Primavera).
5 Bleyerveld, Yvonne, *Hoe bedriechlijck dat die vrouwen zijn. Vrouwenlisten in de beeldende kunst in de Nederlanden circa 1350-1650* (Leiden: Primavera, 2000); Bleyerveld, Yvonne, 'Chaste, Obedient and Devout: Biblical Women as Patterns of Virtue in Netherlandish and German Graphic Art, c. 1500-1750', *Simiolus* 28 (2000-2001), 219-50.
6 Gibson, Walter, 'Lucas van Leyden and the Old Testament', *Print Collector's Newsletter* XIV (1983), 127-30; Smith, Elise Lawton, 'Women and the Moral Argument of Lucas van Leyden's Dance around the Golden Calf', *Art History* 15 (1992), 296-316; Vogelaar, Christiaan (ed.), *Lucas van Leyden en de Renaissance* (Antwerp: Ludion, 2011).
7 Murphy, Neil, 'Between Court and Town: Ceremonial Entries in the *Chroniques* of Jean Molinet', *Burgundica* (2013), 159.
8 Molinet, Jean, *Chroniques* (1474-1506), ed. by Georges Doutrepont and Omer Jodogne, 3 vols (Brussels: Palais des Académies, 1935), vol. II, p. 187: "[...] car ilz se disoyent estre comme les enffans d'Israel quittes et delivréz de égiptienne servitude [...]".
9 Molinet, *Chroniques* (1474-1506), vol. II, p. 418: [fol. 352] "Les rues de la ville, par lesqueles il debvoit passer, estoyent ric(h)ement tendues, et les quarfours d'icelles notamblement aornéz d'histoires, jusque au nombre de trente chinq, fondées sur les livres de Moyse, fort bien appropries à la venue et reception de mondit seigneur et decorées des armes et blasons, tant de lui comme de madame Marguerite; puis arrivèrent à son hostel de Coberghe, environ .IX. heures de nuit".

aforesaid Lord'. The choice of Old Testaments scenes thus follows a well-established tradition and deserves to be looked at separately.

The programme that was drawn up for the 1496 event deals with themes that were tailored to a young princess from the Spanish royal family. With this set of twenty-eight stages, the city of Brussels wished to present specific ideas about the role of women in family and society, as they seemed fit for the occasion. As will be shown in the following discussions, the Latin text on the verso and the image on the recto page are always closely linked. In this context the question arises as to whether the Old Testament was seen exclusively as a moral guide to proper behaviour, or whether these stories fulfilled more than one function. Unlike the New Testament, this part of the Bible contains many dramatic stories taken from life, that give multiple insights into the human condition.

The first stage which opens up the series of Old Testament scenes, concentrates on two male protagonists, Jubal[10] and his half-brother Tubal Cain.[11]

Jubal and Tubal Cain: The Invention of Sweet Harmony (fols 31^v-32^r)

The inscriptions on the frame of the first theatre stage names two men that come from the same family. In Genesis 4. 21-22 Jubal (here wrongly called Tubal) is characterized as a lyre or flute player, whereas Tubal Cain is identified as a blacksmith or as an artisan handling metal objects. The Latin text on the opposite page (fol. 31^v) reads as follows:

> Primo hoc scemate Representatur Qui uti medio sonantium malleorum dulcem musices melodiam Jubal seu tubal adinvenit Sic Johanna hyspanie gravi auctoritate quam in triginta patrias accepit mille millium animos in unam pacis accordantiam adunabit.
>
>> This first depiction displays how – in the middle of clammering hammers – Jubal or Tubal invented the sweet melody of music. So Joanna of Spain will unite countless souls in one agreement of peace with the great power she received over thirty countries.

The musicologist Björn Tammen has analysed the stage set on fol. 32^v with an eye both to the biblical account and its interpretation through high-medieval theologians, such as Petrus Comestor (1100-1178) and others.[12] Tammen identified the kneeling man, who is holding a leaf with musical notes on his knee with Jubal, named INVENTOR MUSICE (the inventor of music) on the upper stage frame. He is portrayed as getting an inspiration while listening to his half-brother Tubal Cain, hammering on an

---

10 Gertz, Jan Christian, 'Jubal' (2014), *Das wissenschaftliche Bibellexikon im Internet*: https://www.bibelwissenschaft.de/stichwort/22848/
11 Gertz, Jan Christian, 'Tubal-Kain' (2014), https://www.bibelwissenschaft.de/stichwort/36274/; Vandenbroeck, Paul, 'A Bride amidst Heroines, Fools and Savages. The Joyous Entry into Brussels by Joanna of Castile, 1496 (Berlin, Kupferstichkabinett, ms 78D5)', *Jaarboek. Koninklijk Museum voor Schone Kunsten* 2012, 182-83.
12 Tammen, Björn, 'A Feast of the Arts: Joanna of Castile in Brussels, 1496', *Early Music History* 30 (2011), 222-24.

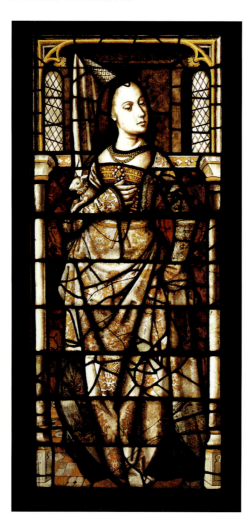

7.1 Southern Netherlandish, *Duchess Mary of Burgundy*, stained-glass window from the Holy Blood Chapel in Bruges, 182.9 × 77.5 cm (framed), c. 1496-1500, London, Victoria & Albert Museum © V&A

anvil together with two more man. Tammen is particularly concerned with assessing the role of musical performances in this and other entries of the period.[13] He makes an effort to link the guild of musicians (St Job) with the painters' guild (St Luke) and the Brussels chambers of rhetoric, arguing that this entry was in fact a concerted effort by all three groups: music – painting – literature.[14] Remco Sleiderink and Amber Souleymane have put forward the idea, that the city poet and rhetorician Jan Smeken (= *little blacksmith*) played a prominent role in the opening stage because he had a leading position in the group organizing this entry. His coat of arms consisted of an anvil and three hammers, which explain the emphasis on Tubal Cain, who is given a central position in the first stage of the entry.[15] The notion of sweet music is expressed by supporting figures: one woman playing the viola da Gamba, one man playing the recorder and a second woman holding a sheet of music in her hand as if starting to sing.

The various interpretations that have been brought forward in regard to this first *tableau vivant* – whether considered to be a mute performance or one with sound – show that these living images are open to interpretation and allow different readings. In my view, too little attention has been paid to the message in the second part of the Latin text: 'So, Joanna of Spain will unite countless souls in one agreement of peace with the great power she received over thirty countries'. A direct link is created between 'the sweet melody of music' and Joanna's power to unite in peace thirty countries that have come under her rule as a consequence of her

---

13 Ibid., section II., pp. 222-26; pp. 232-34.
14 Ibid., section VI., pp. 240-45.
15 *Liber authenticus*, begun 1499, Brussels, city archive, Historisch Archief, ms 3413, reproduced in: De Leeuw, Rick, and Remco Sleiderink, *Ik Jan Smeken* (Bruges: Hannibal, 2017), p. 20; see also Remco Sleiderink's and Amber Souleymane's contribution in this volume.

marriage to Philip the Fair. These countries are mentioned again in conjunction with another stage, the story of Rebecca and Isaac on fol. 39ʳ. The Latin text on fol. 38ᵛ explains:

> Sic Illustrissima Johanna per claros ambatiatores ex hyspania cum insigni classe profecta Inque lira brabantie opido mellifluo archiduci Philippo suo sponso letanter offenso solempni matrimonio gratisque himineis previis ab eodem in throno xxx patriarum quem piissime memorie gloriosa eius mater maria liquerat amorosissime collocata extitit.
>
> > So the illustrious Joanna, accompanied by renowned ambassadors, departed from Spain with a fleet, and after she happily met the sweet Archduke Philip, her spouse, in Lier, a town in Brabant, in a solemn marriage-ritual and with pleasing wedding-songs, she was placed lovingly by him on the throne of the thirty countries that his glorious mother Mary, now deceased, left him.

Joanna is explicitly described as the female heir to the territories under the rule of her mother-in-law, the late Duchess Mary of Burgundy (Fig. 7.1). At the very end of the manuscript (fol. 61ʳ), the thirty coats of arms that are mentioned on fol. 31ᵛ are listed in five registers with six armorial shields each. The alliance crest, which was used by Philip's family for generations, is placed underneath a gothic pediment at the top of the page. It combines the Duchy of Burgundy with the Duchy of Brabant, the Free County of Burgundy and the County of Flanders. The thirty territories are named on fol. 61ʳ as follows:

> [row 1] Archduchy Austria (*Austria*), Duchy of Burgundy (*bourgondia*), Duchy of Lorraine (*lotharingia*), Duchy of Brabant (*brabantia*), Duchy of Styria (*Stiria*)[16], Duchy of Carinthia (*Carinthia*)[17]
>
> [row 2] Duchy of Carniola (*Carniola*)[18], Duchy of Limburg (*limburgia*), Duchy of Luxemburg (*lutzenburg*), County of Guelders (*Gheldria*), County of Habsburg (*habsburgia*), County of Flanders (*Flandria*)
>
> [row 3] County of Tyrol (*Thyriolia*), County of Artois (*Arthesia*), Free County of Burgundy (*bourgondia*), County of Hainault (*hannonia*), Landgraviate Alsace (*Alzatia*), Margraviate Burgau (*burgonia*)
>
> [row 4] Margraviate Antwerp (*Marcio Sancti Imperii*), County of Holland (*hollandia*), County of Zeeland (*zeelandia*), County of Pfirt (*Ferrete*), County of Kyburg (*Kyburgia*), County of Namur (*namuria*)
>
> [row 5] County of Zutphen (*Zuthphania*), Lordship of Frisia (*Frisia*), Lordship Windisch Mark (*Sclavonia*), Lordship Pordenone (*portusuaonia*), Lordship of Salins (*Salina*), Lordship of Mechelen (*Mechlina*).

The shields are organized in hierarchical order, starting off with the Archduchy of Austria and finishing with the Lordship of Mechelen. The significance of these

---

16 In German: Steiermark.
17 In German: Kärnten.
18 In German: Krain.

7.2 Jan van Battel, *Heraldic Triptych with Archduke Charles as Spanish King*, oil on wood, 88 × 57 cm (central panel); 90 × 25 cm (wings) c. 1517-18 © Musea Erfgoed Mechelen, inv. No. S/0010

territories is expressed even more clearly in a triptych made for Charles V in 1517-18 by the Mechelen painter Jan van Battel (Fig. 7.2).[19] Some twenty-five years later, Emperor Charles V commissioned a modern copy of this triptych with sixty-five armorial shields for his Spanish correspondence office (Fig. 7.3).[20] Many of the coats of arms listed in the festive entry are to be found in these two triptychs indicating that they were considered core territories.

The two folios with the coats of arms of Joanna (fol. 60^r) and Philip (fol. 61^r) are reminiscent of a similar project undertaken in Innsbruck by Archduke Maximilian

---

19 Jan van Battel's version of this triptych, dating from 1517-18, still exists in Mechelen, Museum Hof van Busleyden; see: Hüsken, Wim, 'Kunstwerk in de kijker (XII): Jan van Battel, Triptiek met Karel van Habsburg, koning van Spanje, Stedelijke Musea Mechelen, inv. Nr. S/0010', *Mededelingenblad Koninklijke Kring voor Oudheidkunde Letteren en Kunst van Mechelen* 45/4 (2014), 14-17; Kruip, Marjolijn, 'Jan van Battel (1477-1557), heraldische schilder in Mechelen. Kunstenaar, werken en nieuwe vondsten', *Handelingen van de Koninklijke Kring voor Oudheidkunde, Letteren en Kunst van Mechelen* 119 (2015), 105-13.

20 Triptych of Charles V with the coats of arms of his territories, after Jan van Battel, c. 1540-50, Berlin, Deutsches Historisches Museum, Gm 2003/71; see: Beneke, Sabine (ed.), *Im Atelier der Geschichte. Gemälde bis 1918 aus der Sammlung des Deutschen Historischen Museums*, cat. no. 10: 'Wappentafel aus dem spanischen Korrespondenzbüro Kaiser Karls V', pp. 35-36 (Dresden: Stiftung Deutsches Historisches Museum/ Sandstein, 2012) https://www.dhm.de/mediathek/kaiser-karl-v/wappentafel/.

7.3 Anonymous, after Jan van Battel, *Heraldic Triptych with Emperor Charles V*, oil on wood, c. 1540-50, Berlin, Deutsches Historisches Museum, Gm 2003/71 © bpk / Deutsches Historisches Museum / Arne Psille

(Fig. 7.4).[21] In 1496 his court architect Niklas Türing the Elder († 1517) was commissioned with the construction of a tower that decorated the entrance to the imperial precinct in the city of Innsbruck. His court painter, Jörg Kölderer (1465/70-1540), decorated the façade with the fifty-four coats of arms of countries that Maximilian I owned or claimed for his dynasty. The royal coats of arms of Maximilian I and his wife Bianca Maria Sforza were placed at the top of the structure. It can thus be assumed that the coats of arms of Philip the Fair and Joanna of Castile were displayed somewhere along the processional way, possibly close to the townhall of Brussels or to Coudenberg palace.

The first *tableau vivant* in Part Two of the Berlin manuscript expresses the city's hope for peace and harmony in the Burgundian Netherlands and beyond after years of conflict and civil war.[22] In the Latin text the young princess Joanna is assigned the

---

21 Lüken, Sven, 'Kaiser Maximilian I. und seine Ehrenpforte', *Zeitschrift für Kunstgeschichte* 61 (1998), 456-57.
22 See essay by Claire Billen and Chloé Deligne in this volume.

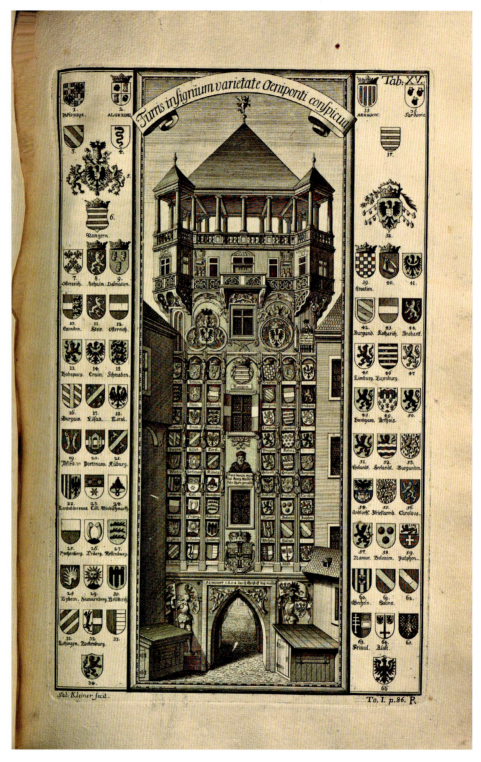

7.4 Salomon Kleiner, *Heraldic tower in Innsbruck (1496-99)*, engraving, 36,5 × 22,4 cm, c. 1496-1500, in *Monumenta Augustae Domus Austriacae*, ed. by Herrgott Marquart (Vienna: L. J. Kaliwoda, 1760) vol. 1, Pl. XV. https://onb.digital/result/10A89A1F

role of peacemaker.[23] Through her powerful position as Philip the Fair's spouse, she is expected to contribute to the peaceful coexistence between the individual territories.

The next set of stages present examples from the Old Testament that illustrate the influence of women on political events and family history.

Judith beheads the Babylonian Commander Holofernes (fols 32ᵛ-33ʳ)

The killing of Holofernes by Judith is one of the most popular scenes demonstrating the power of women in overcoming enemies of the chosen people (Judith 8-16). In a desperate situation, the beautiful widow Judith decided to go to the enemy's camp in the interest of the besieged city of Bethulia. Because Holofernes desired her, he invited her into his tent and drank wine excessively. After he lost control of himself, Judith cut off his head and took it in a sack back to Bethulia to present it to her people as proof. In the biblical account she says: 'See here, the head of Holofernes, the commander of the Assyrian army, and here is the canopy beneath which he lay in his drunken stupor. The Lord has struck him down by the hand of a woman' (Judith 13. 15)."[24] On fol. 32ᵛ the Latin text in the Berlin manuscript repeats this message and advises Joanna to follow Judith's model:

> Hoc scemate Representatur Qui uti Judith holofernem ad nichilum redigens proprio ense interfecit populumque suum israel redemit Sic illustrissima domina nostra Johanna quitquit adversi est perimens populum suum liberabit.
>> This depiction displays how Judith reduced Holofernes to nothing by killing him at his own sword, thereby liberating Israel, her people. So our most illustrious Lady Joanna will save her people by eliminating all that is unbeneficial to them.

The Marriage of Tobias and Sara (fols 33ᵛ-35ʳ)

The Book of Tobit tells the story of Tobias, and how he is given in marriage to his distant relative Sara (Tobit 4-11)[25]. It is astonishing that Tobias' father is given a prominent role in the design of the first stage, sitting on a throne, holding a staff in his hand. The Latin text on fol. 33ᵛ provides the answer:

> Hoc scemate Representatur Qui uti Senior Thobias tobie filio suo saram Raguelis filiam uxorem asscivit Sic Romanorum rex Johannam hyspanie filiam filio suo Philippo invictissimo conthoralem adoptavit.

---

23 On the role of women as peacemakers see: Dumont, Jonathan, Laure Fagnart, Pierre-Gilles Girault, and Nicolas Le Roux, eds, *La paix des Dames: 1529* (Tours: Presses universitaires François-Rabelais, 2021).
24 Schmitz, Barbara, 'Judit / Juditbuch' (2006), WiBiLex https://www.bibelwissenschaft.de/stichwort/10395/.
25 Mühling, Anke, 'Sarai/ Sara' (2009), WiBiLex https://www.bibelwissenschaft.de/stichwort/26065/; ibid., Nichlas, Tobias, 'Tobit/ Tobitbuch' (2005), https://www.bibelwissenschaft.de/stichwort/12080/.

7.5 Southern Netherlandish, *Archduke Maximilian, King of the Romans*, Stained glass window from the Holy Blood Chapel in Bruges, 182.9 × 77.5 cm (framed), London, Victoria and Albert Museum
© V&A

This depiction displays how Tobias the Elder took Raguel's daughter Sara to wed his son Tobias. So the King of the Romans chose Joanna, Spain's daughter, to become the wife of his son, the invincible Philip.

In this case, it was evidently the intention of the city of Brussels, to present Archduke Maximilian, King of the Romans, in a favourable light (Fig. 7.5). As head of family, he is personally credited with choosing a Spanish princess as bride for his son. Sara is portrayed in both scenes as a splendidly dressed princess with a crown, to make the correspondence with Joanna even more convincing. In September 1488, under the leadership of Philip of Cleve, the city of Brussels had played a significant role in the uprising against Maximilian.[26] By giving Tobit-Maximilian such a prominent role in this *tableau vivant*, the city attempts to strike a conciliatory note and generate a positive mood. The way Tobias the Elder is portrayed is reminiscent of the image of Maximilian as King of the Romans on a gold coin dating from 1487 (Fig. 7.6).

In the sequence of the biblical account, the second scene (fol. 35^r) takes place before Tobias' and Sara's return journey to Nineveh. The young couple is portrayed at a crucial moment of the biblical story, when they spend the first night of their marriage immersed in prayer, in order to protect themselves against the devil's attack. The archangel Raphael fends off Asmodeus who intends to kill the bridegroom as had happened before. The scene

---

26 See the essay by Claire Billen and Chloé Deligne in this volume. Haemers, Jelle, 'Philippe de Clèves et la Flandre. La position d'un aristocrate au cœur d'une revolte urbaine (1477-1492)', in *Entre la ville, la noblesse et l'État: Philippe de Clèves (1456-1528), homme politique et bibliophile*, ed. by Jelle Haemers, Céline Van Hoorebeeck & Hanno Wijsman, Burgundica 13, (Turnhout: Brepols, 2007), pp. 21-99; Vrancken, Valerie, 'Opstand en dialoog in laatmiddeleeuws Brabant. Vier documenten uit de Brusselse opstand tegen Maximiliaan van Oostenrijk (1488-1489)', *Bulletin de la Commission Royale* vol. 181 (2015), 209-66.

7.6a/b *Maximilian I as King of the Romans*, Real d'Or, coin, gold, diameter: 38,9 mm, 1487, recto: °MAXIMILIAИVS*DEI*GRA*ROMAИORV*REX*SEP'*AVG' – verso: TEИE*MEИSVRAM*ET*RESPICE*FIИEM*MCCCCLXXXVII Vienna, KHM, MK 23ba © KHM-Museumsverband

takes place in the bedroom of the newly-wed couple. The Latin on fol. 34ᵛ text reads as follows:

> Hoc scemate Representatur Qui uti Raphael angelus saram et tobiam casto amore orationibusque previis ab asmodeo salvavit Sic angelo ductore Johanna maris pericula sulcans philippo conjungenda brabantie applicuit.
>
> This depiction displays how the angel Raphael safeguarded Sara and Tobias against Asmodeus through chastity and prayer. So an angel guided Joanna across the perilous seas to Brabant to marry Philip.

In the early modern period, the story of Sara and Tobias plays a significant role as an *exemplum* of bridal choice and happy marriage.[27] In the Latin inscription, particular emphasis is placed on the chastity and godliness of the young couple. The reference to the princess's perilous voyage has less to do with the biblical narrative itself than with recent events in the life of the Spanish princess. Joanna's fleet first had to make an emergency landing in England and, later on, the ship with her trousseau sank off the coast of Holland.[28]

---

27 In a wedding motet by Orlando di Lasso, one of three sections is dedicated entirely to this story; see: Eichberger, Dagmar, 'Esther – Susanna – Judith. Drei tugendhafte Frauen des Alten Testaments im dritten Teil der Hochzeitsmotette *Gratia sola Dei*', *Troja. Jahrbuch für Renaissancemusik* 15 (2016), 143-59.
28 See Annemarie Jordan Gschwend's essay in this volume.

Abimelech killed by a Woman named Thecuites (fols 35ᵛ-36ʳ)

Abimelech, King of Sichem, had laid siege to Thebez and entered the city. The residents had fled into a citadel within the city which Abimelech planned to burn. The text in Judges 9. 53 says: 'A certain woman threw an upper millstone upon Abimelech's head, and crushed his skull'. In the miniature she is referred to as 'Mulier Tecuites'. The Latin text (fol. 35ᵛ) accompanying the image refers to this story in the following way:

> Hoc scemate Representatur Qui uti mulier Thecuites desuper fragmento mole abimelech excerebrans vita privavit Sic illustrissima domina nostra Johanna arxi austrie, Burgundie Brabancie [etc] innixa letales inimicos conterere habebit.
>
>> This depiction displays how a woman, Thecuites, took the life of Abimelech by crushing his skull with a stone from the citywall. So our most illustrious Lady Joanna, leaning on the bulwark of Austria, Burgundy, Brabant, etc. shall crush our deadly enemies.

This scene shows extreme brutality and much blood flows from the head of the dying assailant. The Bible text additionally addresses the fact that Abimelech considered it a special disgrace to be killed by a woman (Judges 9. 54). Thus, the strength and power of women is underlined even further, as the so-called 'weaker sex' is capable of defeating a male army commander. It is remarkable that the author of the Latin text refers to the 'bulwark Austria, Burgundy and Brabant' in the same breath. After having been involved in civil war with Maximilian and his allies, this can be understood as another attempt to underline the unity of the different territories that are now ruled by his son, Archduke Philip the Fair.

King Solomon and the Daughter of the Pharaoh (fols 36ᵛ-37ʳ)

In the first book of Kings (1 Kings 3. 1) one can read: 'Solomon allied himself by marriage with Pharaoh, King of Egypt. He married the daughter of Pharaoh and brought her to the city of David, until he should finish building his own house, and the house of the Lord, and the wall around Jerusalem'. The alliance through marriage is seen as a sign of the wealth and power of the Hebrew monarchy, for Pharaohs' daughters did not ordinarily marry outside of their own family. Consequently, the Latin text on fol. 36ᵛ equals Philip the Fair with King Solomon and Joanna with the daughter of the Pharaoh:

> Hoc scemate Representatur Qui uti Salomon sapientissimus filiam pharaonis regis egypti in uxorem suscepit Sic immenso gaudio philippus austrie prudentissimus filiam hyspanie exertis brachiis excepit ac fovit.
>
>> This depiction displays how Salomon the Wise once received the daughter of Pharaoh, the King of Egypt, in marriage. So the clever Philip of Austria

received the daughter of Spain with unmeasurable joy into his open arms and cherished her.

In the miniature, King Solomon holds a golden sceptre in his right hand and welcomes the daughter of the Pharaoh who respectfully kneels in front of him. The bride from Egypt wears a crown and is dressed in rich clothes, made from green velvet cloth-of-gold with a pomegranate pattern, similar to the textiles worn by Joanna on her journey to the Netherlands.[29]

King David marries Michal (fols 37^v-38^r)

The Bible gives little space to the marriage between David and Michal, King Saul's daughter.[30] More important is the ongoing conflict between the young David and his mischievous father-in-law. Saul wanted to trap David by demanding the foreskins of one hundred Philistines as bridal price (1 Samuel 18. 21-28). This is, however, not the subject of the *tableau vivant* in the entry of Joanna of Castile. The Latin text on fol. 37^v reads:

> Hoc scemate Representatur Qui uti Abner marescallus exercitus quon dam saul regis uxorem michol in ebron david regi reduxit Sic dominus admiraldus hyspanie Johannam filiam castillie hyspanie [etc] Philippo coniugem in brabantia adduxit.
>
> This depiction displays how Abner, marshal in the army of the former King Saul, accompanied Michal to Hebron to marry King David. So a Spanish admiral brought Joanna, daughter of Castile, Spain, etc., to Brabant to marry Philip.

While Abner was the commander of King Saul's army, David did not yet have a royal title at the time of his wedding with Michal. Nevertheless, David is portrayed with sceptre and crown on the Brussels' stage, thus giving him a higher social standing. At this point, Philip the Fair, Joanna's bridegroom, only held the title of Archduke. Michal was the daughter of a king and thus compares well with Princess Joanna. The Latin texts praises the Spanish admiral who brought Joanna to Brabant. Paul Vandenbroeck suggested that this is a reference to Admiral Don Fadrique Enríquez (1465-1538) who accompanied Joanna on her journey to the Netherlands.[31]

---

29 Bonito Fanelli, Rosalia, 'The Pomegranate Pattern in Italian Renaissance Textiles: Origins and Influence', *Textile Society of America* (1994)–https://digitalcommons.unl.edu/tsaconf/1042/.
30 Fischer, Alexander Achilles, 'David' (2009), WiBiLex; David (AT) https://www.bibelwissenschaft.de/stichwort/16233/; Schmidt, Uta, 'Michal' (2008), https://www.bibelwissenschaft.de/stichwort/27673/; Arneth, Martin, 'Abner' (2007), https://www.bibelwissenschaft.de/stichwort/12276/
31 Vandenbroeck, 'A Bride amidst Heroines', 174; Macpherson, Ian, and Angus MacKay, *Love, Religion, and Politics in Fifteenth Century Spain* (Leiden: Brill, 1998); Conti, Santiago Fernández, 'Carlos V y la alta nobleza castellana: el almirante don Fadrique Enríquez', Congreso Internacional *Carlos V y la quiebra del humanismo político en Europa (1530-1558)* (Madrid, 3-6 de julio de 2000) (Madrid: Sociedad Estatal para la Conmemoración de los Centenarios de Felipe II y Carlos V, 2001), vol. 2, p. 29-51.

The Marriage of Rebecca with Isaac (fols 38ᵛ-39ʳ)

The *tableau vivant* depicted on fol. 39ʳ is undoubtedly the most magnificent stage of all twenty-eight; the sophistication of its scenography is emphasized in the Latin text (fol. 38ᵛ):

> Hiis tribus scematibus In una scena desuper sexaginta rutilantibus flambis prominentibus unacum speculis decentissime compositis representatur Qui uti Rebecca per eleazerem servum seniorem domus abrahe ex mesopotamia ysaac cum nutrice et familia uxor accita Ipsique vultum pallio operiens in agro obviam facta demumque per eundem in tabernaculum matris sue introducta fuit [...]
>
>> These three depictions – on a single stage with sixty luminous torches burning from above together with aptly placed mirrors – display how Rebecca is brought back from Mesopotamia with a wet-nurse and her family by Eliezer, an old servant in the house of Abraham, to marry Isaac. She approached him on a field while she covered her face with a veil. Finally, she was led by him into his mother's tent.

In contrast to all other scenes, this stage operates on two levels. The lower level which described the events happening on earth is divided by three, thus forming a narrative triptych.

The first segment shows Rebecca and Isaac meeting for the first time.[32] As described in Genesis 25. 65, the chaste bride lifts her veil to cover her face; this was understood as a gesture of humility. The third section depicts the marriage of the couple by a priest, who joins their hands in accordance with the Catholic rite. In this scenario, the couple has changed position and Rebecca is now wearing a crown.

Less easy to decipher is the scene in the centre. Abraham, the father of Isaac, meets Eliezer, his messenger, who points towards heaven with his right hand. In the upper panel, the Trinity with God the Father, the Son and the Holy Ghost is joined by Mary depicted as Queen of Heaven and kneeling in adoration before Christ. The inscription on the frame refers to Song of Solomon 3. 4: 'Inveni quem diligit anima mea, Canticorum 3' (I found him whom my soul loves). In the medieval interpretation of the text, the bridegroom was usually identified with Christ and the bride either with the Church, the single soul or the Virgin Mary.[33] In this *tableau* a bridge is built between the heavenly couple, Christ and Mary, and the earthly couple, Isaac and Rebecca. The accompanying text mentions that Isaac lead his wife into his mother's tent to consummate the marriage (Genesis 24. 67). The second part of the Latin inscription (fol. 38ᵛ) refers specifically to the wedding celebrations of Philip and Joan in Lier, which makes the parallelism of the events even more obvious: "So the illustrious Joanna [...] departed from Spain with a fleet, and after she happily

---

32 Klein, Renate Andrea, 'Rebekka' (2009), https://www.bibelwissenschaft.de/stichwort/32823/; Michel, Andreas, 'Isaak' (2007), https://www.bibelwissenschaft.de/stichwort/21862/.

33 Kaiser, Otto, *Einleitung in das Alte Testament – Eine Einführung in ihre Ergebnisse und Probleme*, snd. ed. (Gütersloh: Mohn, 1970), p. 286.

met the sweet Archduke Philip, her spouse, in Lier, a town in Brabant, in a solemn marriage-ritual and with pleasing wedding-songs, she was placed lovingly by him on the throne of the thirty countries that his glorious mother Mary, now deceased, left him."

Only very few of the inscriptions are so detailed that they mention the place, Lier, and the province, Brabant, by name. The mention of the thirty estates that Joanna inherits from Mary of Burgundy, her deceased mother-in-law, also underlines the contemporary significance of the events portrayed on this stage.

Queen Esther asks King Ahasuerus to save her People (fols 39^v-40^r)

The story of the Persian King Ahasuerus and his Jewish wife Esther concentrates on the moment when Esther steps in front of her husband to inform him about the plot against the Jewish people that had been organized by Haman, his counsellor.[34] On the left, Ahasuerus is seated on an elevated throne and wears a crown. It was forbidden on pain of death to appear before the king without being invited to do so. To prepare herself and increase her chance of survival, Esther dressed herself royally, also wearing a crown. She then took the risk of approaching the throne, kneeling in front of her husband in order to voice her concern. In the second scene, the king points to Esther with his sceptre and thus gives her life. She is now able to safe her people by exposing the treason. This scene is depicted many times in art and is understood as a sign of divine grace (Esther 4. 11; 5. 2).[35] The Latin text (fol. 39^v) sums up the story as follows:

> Hoc scemate representatur Qui uti Hester regina Judaicam plebem ab insidiis Aman mardochaeumque eximens liberavit Sic Johanna hyspanie populum suum a malivolis tutabit. Et sicut assuerus rex persarum hester reginam judaici generis mitius a terra levavit. Sic archidux Austrie Philippus Johannam hyspanie cordialitius amplexus fuit.
>
>> This depiction displays how Queen Esther guarded the Jewish people and Mordecai against Haman's treachery and saved them. So Joanna of Spain shall protect her people against those who wish them ill. And, as Ahasuerus, King of the Persians, gently raised Esther, Queen of the Jewish Tribe, so Philip, Archduke of Austria, very warmly embraced Joanna of Spain.

Again, Joanna is called upon to protect her people against potential enemies. Philip's role is to give his wife a benevolent welcome, as King Ahasuerus did. This seems to suggest that he is expected to support his wife in similar matters.

---

34 Franke, Birgit, *Assuerus und Esther am Burgunderhof. Zur Rezeption des Buches Esther in den Niederlanden (1450 bis 1530)* (Berlin: Mann, 1998).
35 Brünenberg-Bußwolder, Esther, 'Ester/ Esterbuch' (2006). WiBiLex- https://www.bibelwissenschaft.de/stichwort/17832/.

The first nine stages with scenes from the Old Testament are followed by a *tableau vivant* with a story from ancient history, transmitted by Herodotus. The image on fol. 41^v depicts the dream of King Astyages, who felt threatened by the exceptional fertility of his daughter Madanes.[36] The following ten stages are occupied by nine combative heroines of antiquity (fol. 42^v-51).[37] Six of them are characterized as queens, Semiramis even carries the title of empress (*Imperatrix*). These women are preceded by Queen Isabella of Castile, the famous mother of Princess Joanna (fol. 41^r), who was still alive at the time of the Brussels entry.

The Queen of Sheba honours the Wisdom of King Solomon (fols 52^v-53^r)

On fol. 53^r, another scene from the Old Testament is added to the festive parade through the city of Brussels. King Solomon appears in the centre of the stage, sitting on a throne. In the foreground, two richly dressed ladies kneel and present the king with precious golden vessels – one is identified as Queen of Sheba (*Regina Saba*).[38] The Queen of Sheba, whose name is not stated in the bible, came to Jerusalem 'with a very great retinue, with camels bearing spices, and very much gold, and precious stones' (1 Kings 10. 2). She tested Solomon's wisdom by asking him difficult questions. After Solomon answered them to her satisfaction, they exchanged gifts and she returned to her country. The Latin text on fol. 51^v reads as follows:

> Hoc scemate Representatur Qui uti regina Saba regem salomonem (sapientie eius gracia) a longinquis cum muneribus visitavit. Sic Johanna hyspanie Philippum sagacissimum cum virgineo pudore ac donis honorem perpetuum impendere venit.
>
>> This depiction displays how the Queen of Sheba honoured King Solomon (because of his wisdom) with exotic gifts from her far-off country. So Joanna came with virginal timidity and gifts to pay lasting tribute to the wise Philip.

The interpretation given in the Latin text underlines two aspects, the virginal purity of the Spanish princess and the wisdom of her husband. In passing it is mentioned, that Joanna honoured Philip with gifts. The research undertaken by Annemarie Jordan Gschwend has shown how much money the Spanish crown was prepared to spend on the royal furnishings of their daughter.[39] Expensive jewels,

---

36 [40^v] Hoc scemate Representatur Qui uti ex mandanes filia rex astrages vineam florentem totam terram tegentem vidit. Sic philippi patria prolem uberem ex johanna hyspanie speravit. (This depiction displays how King Astyages saw a flowering vine that covered the whole earth growing from his daughter Mandane. So Philip's fatherland hoped for many children from Joanna of Spain.)
37 See the essay by Wim Blockmans in this volume. The nine heroines are: Deiphilis, Queen Sinopis, (Queen) Hippolyta, Melanopa, Empress Semiramis, Queen Lampeto, Queen Tomyris, Queen Teuta and Queen Penthesilea.
38 Stein, Peter, 'Saba' (2014), WiBiLex https://www.bibelwissenschaft.de/stichwort/25250/.
39 See Annemarie Jordan Gschwend's essay in this volume.

silverware, objects made of precious metal and rich clothes were among the treasures she was to bring with her to the Netherlands. In this light, the choice of the subject makes sense. Quite obviously, Philip the Fair hoped for financial advantages by marrying a Spanish princess from the house of Trastámara.

The Prophetess Deborah supports Commander Baruch (fols 53ᵛ-54ʳ)

In Judges 4, Deborah is characterized as a wise woman who is described as a prophetess and as a female judge giving advice to the Israelites.[40] She functions as the mouthpiece of God. In the song of Deborah (Judges 5) she tells Barak (*Baruch*) to fight against the Canaanite commander Sisera and supports him by accompanying him to Mount Tabor.[41] This fight is depicted on the stage, as well as Deborah's prayer to God. The text on fol. 53ᵛ reads as follows:

> Hoc scemate Representatur Qui uti baruch ex inimicis oratione Delbore prophetisse victoriam reportavit Sic fernandus hyspanorum rex instantia Elizabeth eius regine ex garnato et adversariis victor evasit.
>
>> This depiction displays how Baruch once conquered his enemies thanks to the prayers of the prophetess Deborah. So Ferdinand, King of the Spaniards, conquered Granada and defeated his foes through the persistence of his Queen Isabella.

The parallel drawn between Baruch in the Old Testament and Joanna's father, King Ferdinand of Aragon (Fig. 7.7), points to two men who defeated the enemy but were only capable of doing so because of the strength of the woman at their side, one being Deborah, the other being Queen Isabella of Castile (Fig. 7.7). The text is designed to flatter the young princess but also alerts her to the possibility of influencing her husband in a critical moment.

Jael kills the Canaanite Commander Sisera (fols 54ᵛ-55ʳ)

While the Book of Judges reports that the battle is fought and the enemy was destroyed, the military commander Sisera was not killed by Barak but by Jael, the wife of the Kenite Heber (Judges 5. 25-27).[42] She succeeded in killing Sisera by using a trick and thus contributed significantly to the victory of Israelite tribes over Canaan. She took Sisera into her tent as he fled and killed him by piercing a tent peg through his temple. The image is explained on fol. 54ᵛ as follows:

---

40 Eder, Sigrid, 'Debora / Deboralied' (2009), WiBiLex http://www.bibelwissenschaft.de/stichwort/16245/.
41 Eder, Sigrid, 'Barak' (2008), WiBiLex http://www.bibelwissenschaft.de/stichwort/14506/.
42 Neef, Heinz-Dieter, 'Jael' (2006), WiBiLex http://www.bibelwissenschaft.de/stichwort/22055/.

7.7 Spanish, *Queen Isabella of Castile and King Ferdinand II of Aragon*, oil on wood, a) 37.5 × 26.9 cm, b) 37.35 × 27 cm, London, Royal Collection Trust, RCIN 403445 and 403448. Royal Collection Trust / © His Majesty King Charles III 2023

> Hoc scemate Representatur Qui uti Jahel mulier egregia Sizare Tempora clavo perforavit. Sic Johanna hyspanie capita inimicorum nostrorum clavo discretissime auctoritatis sue dolabit.
>
> > This depiction displays how Jael, an outstanding woman, pierced Sisera's temple with a nail. So Joanna of Spain shall batter the heads of our enemies with the nail of her exquisite power.

The comparison between Jael and Joanna is very drastic indeed and has a strong combative quality to it. Again, the power of women is referred to, here in symbolic rather than in physical form. The performance on stage is very lively and vivid, a lot of blood flows over Sisera's face and the three women that accompany Jael express their horror through raising their hands.

7.8 Erhard Schön, *Six of twelve Famous Women from the Old Testament*, two woodcuts, 19,8 × 38,2 cm, *c*. 1530, woodcut no. 2: Ruth, Michal, Abigail, Judith, Esther und Susanna. © The Trustees of the British Museum

Which Old Testament Women were chosen for Joanna's Entry?

In the Old Testament there are many female figures that made a name for themselves.[43] Nevertheless, the organizers of the Brussels' entry selected nine particular heroines. The stories either focus on women who performed heroic deeds, such as freeing their people from the enemy (Judith, Thecuites, Jael, Esther), or they directed the light on courtship and marriage negotiations (Sara, Michal, Rebecca, Pharaoh's daughter). Susanna, Bathsheba or Abigail are not mentioned in the Brussels entry, as their life story was not considered appropriate to the occasion. A third element addressed in this entry, is the role of the wife as a wise counsellor and peacemaker (Debora).

In the course of the sixteenth century, a canon of famous women established itself and was reproduced in numerous graphic series.[44] In 1530, Erhard Schön designed two woodcuts that show six famous Old Testament women each. The first print lists Eve, Sarah, Rebecca, Rachel, Leah and Jael; the second print shows Ruth, Michal, Abigail, Judith, Esther and Susanna (Fig. 7.8).[45] Of these twelve women, only six are represented in the Brussels' entry. Further series with a similar choice of heroines were produced in the later sixteenth century by Jost Amman and Maarten van Heemskerck.

---

43 Sölle, Dorothee, Joe H. Kircherger, Anne-Marie Schnieper, and Emil M. Bührer, *Große Frauen der Bibel in Bild und Text* (Osterfildern: Schwabenverlag, 2004); Fischer, Irmtraud, 'Frauen in der Literatur (AT)' (2008), WiBiLex http://www.bibelwissenschaft.de/stichwort/42334/.
44 Eichberger, 'Esther – Susanna – Judith', p. 147, fn. 12-15.
45 Schön, Erhard, *Zwölf berühmte Frauen des Alten Testaments*, two woodcuts (20,1 × 78 cm), *c*. 1530, a) Eva, Sara, Rebecca, Rachel, Lea, Jael, and b) Ruth, Michal, Abigail, Judith, Esther und Susanna; see: Mielke, Ursula, *Hollstein's German Engravings, Etchings and Woodcuts 1400-1700*, vol. 47: Erhard Schön, Amsterdam 2000, pp. 86-89, cat. no. 66; https://www.britishmuseum.org/collection/object/P_1923-1119-1 and https://www.britishmuseum.org/collection/object/P_1909-0612-7.

It is not known whether such lists of Old Testament women existed already in the fifteenth century and might have served as a guide for the organizers.

In principle, the programme could have focussed on women from antiquity and ancient history. Giovanni Boccaccio's (1313-1375) famous treatise *De Mulieribus Claris* was a wide-spread compendium on famous women and had been translated into French by the early fifteenth century.[46] Of the one hundred-and-six women listed in his account, only two appear in the Brussels entry, Semiramis (fol. 47^r) and Penthesilea (fol. 51^r), which suggests that this text was irrelevant for the programme designers.

Political Context and Relevance

In three of the Old Testament scenes, direct reference is made to the territories that Joanna gained through her marriage with Philip the Fair. On fol. 31^v, Joanna is admonished to work for peace in the Habsburg-Burgundian lands; on fol. 38^v, Joanna is told that Philip 'placed her lovingly on the throne of the thirty countries that his glorious mother Mary left him'. On fol. 35^v, the three countries owned jointly by Philip and Joanna – Austria, Burgundy and Brabant – are treated as a political unit that is capable of crushing the enemy. But who is the enemy the programme is referring to? Bethany Aram suggests that this is a reference to the French, who had occupied Brussels in 1489.[47]

While the text emphasizes the importance of the thirty lands brought into the marriage by Philip, no mention is made in the Latin text of the bountiful dowry contributed by the Spanish princess. On fol. 53^r the Queen of Sheba showers King Solomon with gifts; this is as close as the programme gets to commenting on the immense material and political wealth that Joanna brought into the marriage. In a visual manner, fol. 60^r depicts the coats-of-arms of ten kingdoms under Spanish rule: Castile, Leon, Aragon, Sicily, Granada, Galicia, Toledo, Valencia, Mallorca and Sardinia. As will become clear later in history, these territories were passed on to Charles, the male successor from this dynastic union.

While Joanna takes centre stage in virtually every commentary to the twelve Old Testament stages under discussion, Philip is mostly addressed as her consort. There is talk of 'the invincible Philip' (fol. 33^v), 'the clever Philip' (fol. 36^v), the 'sweet Archduke' (fol. 38^v) and the 'wise Philip' (fol. 52^v). More importantly, he is equalled with famous men such as King Solomon (fol. 36^v) and King Ahasuerus (fol. 39^v).

Despite the fact that Philip the Fair did not accompany his young wife on this occasion, the city of Brussels made sure the duke of Brabant was honoured in the appropriate manner. Similarly, the Latin text refer to Maximilian, Joanna's father-in-law,

---

46 Brown, Cynthia, 'Women Famous and Infamous: Court Controversies About Female Virtues', in *The Queen's Library. Image-Making at the Court of Anne of Brittany, 1477-1514* (Philadelphia: University of Pennsylvania Press, 2011), pp. 108-80.

47 Aram, Bethany, *Juana the Mad. Sovereignty and Dynasty in Renaissance Europe* (Baltimore: The Johns Hopkins University Press, 2005), p. 40.

by comparing him to Tobias the Elder (fol. 33ᵛ). Ferdinand of Aragon and Isabella of Castile, Joanna's parents, are put on a par with Baruch and Deborah (fol. 53ᵛ). The emphasis on the male relatives corresponds to the introductory paragraph (fol. 2ʳ) in which Joanna is characterized in the following way:

> Quo Egregios animos novitatumque cupidos quam exertis brachiis pronis affectibus patulisque ymmo precordiis insignis Bruxellarum ducatus Brabantie opidi cives quinto ydus decembris anni nonagesimisexti in occursum serenissime Johanne gloriosissimi fernandi hyspanie Castillie, [etc.] regis Illustrissimi Philippi archiducis Austrie Romanorum regis Maximiliani semper augusti […]
>
>> For it to be no longer concealed from excellent minds who are keen on novelties, how the citizens of the prominent city of Brussels, in the duchy of Brabant, on 9 December 1496 went to meet their most beloved ruler, the serene Joanna, daughter of the glorious Ferdinand, King of Spain, Castile, etc., married to the illustrious Philip, Archduke of Austria, son of the King of the Romans Maximilian, semper Augustus […]

The interpretations of the individual stages have shown that many of the Old Testament scenes carry moral lessons. Humility, respect, piety and modesty are described as desirable qualities in a female consort. In the same way, however, the strength of the princess, her ability for diplomacy and her wisdom are emphasized. A woman's political power is, to a large extent, defined by the territories she holds. It seems that the city of Brussels emphasized these aspects in order to prepare the comparatively inexperienced Spanish princess for her office with the intention of to strengthening her back in times of adversity.

LAURA WEIGERT

To move the hearts and spirits of men towards joy and recreation

The Entry of Joanna of Castile as Entertainment*

▼ **ABSTRACT** This article turns to Berlin ms 78 D5 for clues to an experience of Joanna of Castile's entry as entertainment and spectacle, one that moved beyond the processional route and into the city. It focuses on the series of pictures of the 'entertainers' who accompanied the procession and on three intriguing stagings of female figures and amorous themes. Looking closely at details within the pictures, it makes a new argument about the collaboration between rhetorician chambers and shooting guilds— in addition to the political elite, craft guilds, and inhabitants—in this event in honour of Joanna of Castile. The article also contributes to a broader understanding of fifteenth-century civic entertainment and performance traditions.

▼ **KEYWORDS** Entertainment, spectacle, fools, competitions, pyrotechnics, militia guilds, chamber of rhetoric, wild women, wild men, *Judgement of Paris*.

Berlin ms 78 D5 is an exceptional manuscript. Not only is it the earliest extant illustrated commemorative account of a civic entry, it also offers a glimpse of what was considered 'entertainment' at the time. The expansive nature of the term has challenged historians. A multiplicity of words convey the general idea: amusement, enjoyment, delight, interlude, festival, game, diversion, pleasure, recreation, distrac-

---

* My thanks to Dagmar Eichberger, whose invitation to return to this exceptional manuscript has reminded me that one always sees more when one looks again. Chloé Deligne and Remco Sleiderink generously shared their own work and extremely helpful bibliography. The title's quote comes from a description of the contribution of rhetorician chambers' activities in order to justify their safe passage to a contest in 1493 (cited in Blockman's essay in this volume and in Van Bruaene, Anne-Laure, *Om beters wille: Rederijkerskamers en de stedelijke cultuur in de Zuidelijke Nederlanden (1400-1650)* (Amsterdam: Amsterdam University Press, 2008), p. 234. My translation.

A Spectacle for a Spanish Princess, ed. by Dagmar H. Eichberger, Burgundica, 35 (Turnhout: Brepols, 2023), pp. 165–180

8.1 Southern Netherlandish, *The Festive Entry of Joanna of Castile into Brussels*, fol. 30ʳ (detail): Crossbow Bearers, 1496, Berlin, SMPK, Kupferstichkabinett, ms. 78 D5

tion, pastime, and play.[1] In an article on the early history of the term, Władysław Tatarkiewicz, identifies two of its features: entertainment exceeds the utilitarian to produce pleasure and amusement; its purpose is to amuse an audience, rather than just oneself.[2] The term *joyeuse entrée* (joyous entry) captures the sense of pleasure that was central to the experience of such an event. This feeling is also evoked in the manuscript. What the citizens of Brussels presented on that day is succinctly summed up as 'the most earnest vows, the most festive applause, and the most delightful joys'. Clearly, for the organizers, spectators, and participants, the success of the entry did not just lie in its 'tropological' message. Above and beyond moralizing or instructing, Joanna's entry astonished and amused. Moreover, the event was not limited to the adornment of the processional route but expanded into the urban environment.[3] Experienced as spectacle and entertainment, Joanna's entry provided 'joy and recreation'.

This article seeks to bring to the front and centre the elusive activities such spectacular entertainment encompassed and the sensations it sought to elicit. All too often art and cultural historians reduce their objects of study to what they identify as an overarching message or internal meaning. Moreover, the two-dimensional pages between the bindings of a manuscript tend to flatten and reduce the historical record. The book format has encouraged us to read texts and pictures as part of a linear sequence, one that progresses as we turn from one page to the next. In the case of Joanna's entry, however, what was considered entertainment and spectacle exceeded the bounds of the manuscript's pictorial and textual record, as well as the spatial and temporal bounds of the procession itself. Looking closely at clues within the manuscript, we can begin to recover traces of this multidimensional experience and to situate it in relation to a broader civic performance culture.

One picture serves to anchor and historicize this discussion of entertainment in Brussels. In a key moment in the procession, the princess arrives in the city,

---

1 Symes, Carol, *A Common Stage: Theater and Public Life in Medieval Arras* (Ithaca, NY: Cornell University Press, 2007), pp. 11-12; Van Bruaene, Anne-Laure, *Om beters wille: Rederijkerskamers en de stedelijke cultuur in de Zuidelijke Nederlanden (1400-1650)* (Amsterdam: Amsterdam University Press, 2008), p. 134.

2 Tatarkiewicz, Władysław, 'Theatrica, the Science of Entertainment: From the XIIth to the XVIIth Century', *Journal of the History of Ideas* 26 (1965), 263-72.

3 For an example, we might turn to William FitzStephen's early description of London. The activities that turned London into a 'source of delight and diversion' ranged from saints' lives and miracle plays to tournaments, processions, simulated battles, hunting, and athletic contests, s. Fitzstephen, William, *Descriptio Nobilissimae Civitatis Londoniae*, in Stowe, John, *A Survey of London*, ed. by Charles Lethbridge Kingsford, (Oxford: Clarendon, 1908), II, pp. 218-29.

accompanied by the greater Crossbowmen's guild (Fig. 8.1). She appears seated on a mule, her body facing forward, her head slightly turned to the side, followed by another woman also on a mule.⁴ Joanna is clothed in a golden gown. A white cloth appears through slits in the gown's sleeves and hangs down from her right arm; a gold-trimmed crimson mantle skirts her waist and extends over the mule's body.⁵ These female figures are elevated above the guild members, who walk in front of, beside and behind the mules. The city hall with its magnificent spire and facade, both depicted in significant detail, appears on the left.⁶ This topographic reference locates the scene in the Grand Place. Three levels of the tower are adorned with torches: red and yellow flames burn brightly; smoke wafts upwards. Larger painted flames, also in red and yellow, unfurl from the torches held by the members of the guild, torches which surround the princess in a forest of wax, fire, and emblems of the guild. The Crossbowmen's clothing is similarly luxurious: cloaks of half blue and half red, with collars of various colours.

8.2 Southern Netherlandish, *The Festive Entry of Joanna of Castile into Brussels*, fol. 29ʳ (detail): *Members of the Archers Guild of Saint Sebastian with silver ornaments on their sleeves*, 1496, Berlin, SMPK Kupferstichkabinett, ms. 78 D5

The text (fol. 30ᵛ) accompanying the picture underscores the spectacular nature of the Crossbowmen's clothing and the brilliance of their torches.

> quorum singuli suis vestium intersigniis gemmatarum phaleratharumque manicarum fulgure choruscantes cum ardentibus facibus tumultuose popularium multitudini tale silentium incusserunt ut et vicissim visendi notandique presentibus adminiculo hiisq[ue] ac posteris miraculo fuisse potuerit.

> All of them (with their coats of arms on their clothing, glittering with bright jewels and shining ornaments that adorn the long sleeves of their tunics, with burning torches) caused such a silence among the mass of people, so that they in turn, notable and remarkable, could be an encouragement for the people present, and a source of amazement for them and posterity.

The 'official symbols' mentioned in the text appear on the sleeves of three of the Crossbowmen. The left arms of three of the members of the greater Crossbowman's society who precede Joanna of Castile are adorned with the symbol and namesake of one of the four rhetorician's chambers in Brussels *De Violetten*, a configuration of

---

4 Thanks to Raymond Fagel for specifying the species.
5 On Joanna's clothing, please see Annemarie Jordan Gschwend's article in this volume.
6 Köhl, Sascha, *Das Brüsseler Rathaus: Repräsentationsbau für Rat, Stadt und Land* (Petersberg: Imhof, 2019); see Sascha Köhl's essay in this volume as well.

8.3 Southern Netherlandish, *The Festive Entry of Joanna of Castile into Brussels*, fol. 11ʳ (detail): A Fool whose sleeve is decorated with three red flowers and crossbows, 1496, Berlin, SMPK, Kupferstichkabinett, ms. 78 D5

carnations and crossbows (Fig. 8.2). The lower Crossbowmen, depicted on the previous page, also appear 'with uniforms with their own official symbols'. The lilies and crossbows on their arm link them to a second rhetorician chamber in Brussels, *De Lelie* (Fig. 8.3).[7] We learn of their effect on the crowd. When the Crossbowmen appeared, they 'caused silence'.

As the preeminent militia organization in Brussels, the greater Crossbowmen had the honour of accompanying Joanna into the city.[8] The prominence of the Crossbowmen in the procession also makes sense when we consider the guild's contribution to the annual *Ommegang*. Dedicated to Our Blessed Lady of the Sablon, it was the most important procession in Brussels. The Crossbowmen's guild was the main organizer; it was tasked and remunerated for the plays about the miracles associated with the statue of the Virgin; its members carried the miraculous statue itself in the procession.[9] The picture recalls this event. The mule on which the princess rides is obscured by the guild members; the picture creates a visual parallel between the princess and the statue of the virgin they carried in the *Ommegang*. On this festive occasion, and for Joanna's entry as well, three of the members process barefoot as a sign of their humility. The Brussels Greater Crossbowmen's guild was also responsible for the inter-city shooting competitions the city hosted, during which participating militia guilds took part in more playful forms of performance. In 1483 the Crossbowmen organized *schiet-en esbatementspelen* (games of shooting and diversion, amusement, play) in Brussels. In addition to the display of shooting skills, these large gatherings incorporated pyrotechnics and performances, which could include scripted words and were referred to as *jeux* or *esbatements* (diversions, amusements, plays).[10] The crossbow as activity was referred

---

7 Van Bruaene, *Repertorium* https://www.dbnl.org/tekst/brua002repe01_01/brua002repe01_01_0061.php
8 Petitjean, O., *Historique de l'ancien grand serment royal et noble des arbalétriers de Notre-Dame du Sablon* (Brussels: Imprimerie du Marais, 1963); Wauters, Alphonse, *Notice Historique sur les anciens serments ou guildes d'arbalétriers, d'archers, d'arquebusiers et d'escrimeurs de Bruxelles* (Brussels: Briard, 1848); Crombie, Laura, *Archery and Crossbow Guilds in Medieval Flanders, 1300-1500*, Woodbridge: The Boydell Press, 2016; La Fons de Mélicocq, Alfonse, 'Les Archers, les arbalétriers et les arquebusiers du Nord de la France', *Archives historiques et littéraire du Nord de la France et du midi de la Belgique*, ser. III, t. I (1850), pp. 500-09.
9 In 1448 the magistrate paid them for bringing "the miraculous image of the Virgin of Sablon to life in plays" (Trowbridge, Mark, 'Art and Ommegangen: Paintings, Processions, and Dramas in the Late-Medieval Low Countries' (unpublished doctoral thesis, New York University, 2000), 216).
10 Arnade, Peter J., *Realms of Ritual Burgundian Ceremony and Civic Life in Late Medieval Ghent* (Ithaka, NY: Cornell University Press, 1996), p. 81; Steenbergen, Gerard Jo, *Het landjuweel van de rederijkers* (Leuven: Davidsfonds, 1950), pp. 46-57.

to in the fifteenth century as 'the very joyous and the very honourable game'. Entertainment in a broad sense was thereby associated with the purpose of the guild, which brought together the various meanings of the term, including game, sport, and play.

The picture confirms, moreover, that the Crossbowmen collaborated with the rhetorician chambers in these entertainment events. That the rhetoricians' chambers played a role in the orchestration of the procession has been assumed, given their literary involvement in civic ceremony. The themes of virtuous and heroic women, depicted in Joanna's entry, were part of their repertoire, those 'excellent women and princesses to be ordinated in 'chambers' from diverse books, be it in armor, in triumph or naked'.[11] These exempla of female behaviour fulfilled the edifying purpose of the rhetoricians; their source in classical themes corresponded with the educational project and focus of civic chambers of rhetoric. Björn Tammen has argued that the depiction of Jubal and Tubal Cain in the first staging refers directly to the rhetoricians in Brussels.[12] The former is credited with the invention of music; the latter with the arts of metal. The staging links the two crafts: the sounds of Tubal Cain's hammers inspired the proportions on which Jubal based his music. Tammen's argument is that the staging refers generally to poetry and music, the two arts closely allied within medieval conceptions of rhetoric. In this respect it can be considered an origin myth or portrait of rhetoric and a general reference to rhetoricians in the city.[13]

The references to *De Violetten* and *De Lelie* on the Crossbowmen's sleeves allow us to be more specific about the groups directly involved in the procession and also to appreciate one of the vital and essential goals of the entertainment rhetorician chambers provided. The rhetoricians are associated not just with the books and learning from which they culled their themes but also with the performative arts of spoken poetry and music. In their association with the Crossbowmen guilds, the rhetorican chambers exceeded the educational text-based definition of rhetoric. *De Violette* and *De Lelie* were responsible for the 'personages' (arrangements of human and inanimate figures) at Maximilian's entry into Brussels in 1486.[14] In 1507 the two groups fused into a single chamber. In 1493 *De Lelie* organized a rhetorician contest in Brussels; the chamber was known for its pipers, who played before Maximilian.[15] The

---

11 *Liber Authenticus*; list of women in 'chambers' from the Leemans manuscript, c. 1520, fol. 29ᵛ; *Rapiarijs. Een afscheidsbundel voor Hans van Dijk*, ed. by Buitink, Saskia, Alphonse M. J. van Buuren, and I. Spijker, *Ruyghbewerp* 16, Utrecht: Instituut De Vooys voor Nederlandse Taal en Letterkunde, 1987, 23-25; De Keyzer, Piet, 'Het rhetoricaal "exemplum". Bijdrage tot de iconologie van onze Rederijkers', in *Vooys voor De Vooys. Huldenummer van de Nieuwe Taalgids* (Groningen 1953), 48-57; I thank Remco Sleiderink for these references; please see his article in this volume.
12 Tammen, Björn, 'A Feast of the Arts: Joanna of Castille in Brussels, 1496', *Early Music History* 30, 213-48. Willem Blockmans made this suggestion in his 1994 article, reprinted in 1998.
13 I have suggested elsewhere that the pictures of Tubal Cain at the start of the stagings and Saint Luke at the end bring together more generally the variety of crafts and individuals involved in the entry. It is a civic portrait of intermedial collaboration between artists and artisans, s. Weigert, Laura, *French Visual Culture* (Cambridge: Cambridge University Press, 2015, pp. 71-73.
14 '*Personage*' is often translated as *tableau vivant* when used in the context of entry ceremonies. For a discussion of the term and its implications for a historically informed understanding of medieval performance traditions, please see: Weigert, *French Visual Culture*, pp. 26-27, pp. 45-46, and pp. 122-23.
15 van Bruaene, *Repertorium*. https://www.dbnl.org/tekst/brua002repe01_01/brua002repe01_01_0061.php

function of the activities of rhetorician chambers was described in Maximilian and Philip's assurance of safe conduct for participants as, 'le seuil de toutes Recreacion et Joyeulx passetemps…pour esmouvoir les cuers et coraiges des hommes a Joye et Recreacion'. (the gateway to all recreation and joyous pastimes…to move the hearts and spirits of men towards joy and recreation)[16]

The Crossbowmen's guilds and the rhetorician chambers collaborated towards the orchestration of organized entertainment in Brussels. They both contributed to the promotion and enhancement of shooting and dramatic contests; they both employed a variety of entertainers.[17] For the inter-city shooting competitions and the later competitions the rhetoricians hosted, prizes were given for the best entry procession, which could include dancers and musicians, the best pyrotechnics, and the best fools.[18] Entrances of each participating city, including musicians, banners, and stagings into these competitions became part of competitions themselves. A day was set aside for these entrances, later they could take two or even three days. In 1440 in Ghent, Brussels won best entry. 'The ten wonderfully dressed marksmen from Brussels came by horse and were accompanied by a carriage and forty confreres on foot; they were followed by a group of 350 men on foot, dressed half blue and half red and in their turn followed by 380 other men in rich civil dress'. The Crossbow competition in Ghent in 1498 is well documented in the *Excellent Chronicle*, with a poem describing the entrances. Brussels was considered the best entry (from outside of Flanders). It included 'a wagon with jesters, and a further fifty wagons with pipers and flowers, and a wagon with towers'. In Brabant prizes were given in different categories: the best fool on land, on rope, and even on water.[19] Brussels received prizes in both these categories.

With the flames emitted from the torches on the city hall, the picture alludes to the spectacular pyrotechnics that were central to the emotional experience of the entry. The procession took place at night. The artisans walk on either side of the road, 'subduing the darkness and the crowds that are pressing together with their density and torches'. After the identification of the last staging, a paragraph sums up the significance of the light display of the event (fol. 62^r):

> Notandum quod Ignium Immensitas diversarum materiarum luminumque eciam supra tecta mirabili ingenio instructorum qui ipsum opidum adinstar carbonis vivi accenderant (pro eo quod nichil deliciarum eorum effigies visui afferunt) nulla scemata ponuntur eorum tamen eam fuisse copiam aspectumque credatis que et si non troye carthaginisque incendia excessere nil tamen eis vicinius similiusve (eo dumtaxat quod non tam diu arsere) unquam visum fuerit.

---

16 (My translation), see: van Bruaene, *Om beters wille*, p. 221 and p. 234 and Wim Blockmans, essay in this volume.
17 Henne, Alexandre, and Alphonse Wauters, *Histoire de la Ville de Bruxelles* (Brussels: Perichon, 1845) I, pp. 110, 234, 236, 286, 315-16; Trowbridge, 'Art and Ommegangen', pp. 309-18.
18 Arnade, 'Realms of Ritual', pp. 67-83; Crombie, 'From War to Peace', pp. 271-76; de Schrijver, Marc, and Christian Dothée, *Les concours de tir à l'arbalète des guildes médiévales* (Antwerp: Antwerps Museum en Archief den Crans, 1979), unpaginated.
19 Wauters, 'Notice historique', pp. 24-28.

It should be noted that the brightness of the fires and the torches of diverse materials, which were even placed on rooftops with great ingenuity and made the city glow like on fire, cannot be captured in the depictions (because images cannot convey their splendour to our eyes). You must believe, however, that these fires were so great in number and their effect so spectacular that, while the fires of Troy and Carthage may have been greater, nothing has ever resembled them more closely and similarly (even though they burned much shorter).

8.4 Southern Netherlandish, *The Festive Entry of Joanna of Castile into Brussels*, fol. 11ʳ (detail): *A fool in striped garments*, Berlin, 1496, SPKB, Kupferstichkabinett, ms. 78 D5

As the concluding text claims, Brussels was lit up on that night to rival the burning of Troy and Carthage. Over the course of the entry ceremonies, the entire city became a brilliant spectacle.[20] The makers acknowledge the insufficiency of their medium to capture the impact of this aspect of the procession. The fires and torches, appealing directly to the audience's senses, 'can't be captured in pictures'. As Élodie Lecuppre-Desjardin argues, the emotion that such light phenomena elicited was fundamental to the political and social power of ritual.[21]

Other pages that form the manuscript's verbal and pictorial description of Joanna's entry provide clues to features that would have characterized Brussels' prize-winning entertainers. Six full-page miniatures document their presence in the entry: two represent wild men and women; three show jesters or fools; one includes masked bagpipers pulled in a sled. Sandwiched between the group-portraits of the governing secular and religious institutions within the city the antics and costumes of these figures seem to contrast with the overall political message of the event. Their masks and elaborate costumes blur the boundary between the human and the non-human. The figures on the sled have human bodies and birds' heads; one of the fools has the beak of a bird and the ears of an ass. The wild men and women are clothed in fur and sport tails.

The first group of fools confirms their association with the Crossbowmen and the *Violetten* (fol. 11ʳ) Displayed on the sleeve of the fool closest to the picture plane are three miniature crossbows below a bunch of red carnations (Fig. 8.4). This 'official symbol' becomes the focal point of the composition, proclaiming the figures' association with both the Greater Crossbowmen and the *Violetten*. The connection between these figures of fools and other militia groups is also suggested in the picture. The red and green stripes worn by the figure on the right connect him to the group of youths, who appear on the following page (fol. 17ʳ). The fool in the back left hand side of the

---

20 For the use of light in entry ceremonies, please see: Lecuppre-Desjardin, Élodie, 'Les lumières de la ville: recherche sur l'utilisation de la lumière dans les cérémonies bourguignonnes (XIVᵉ-XVᵉ siècles)', *Revue Historique* 301 (1999), 23-43.
21 Lecuppre-Desjardin, 'Les lumières', p. 43.

8.5 Southern Netherlandish, *The Festive Entry of Joanna of Castile into Brussels*, fol. 13ʳ (detail): *An Ethiopian Princess on a mule, accompanied by wild women*, 1496, Berlin, SMPK, Kupferstichkabinett, ms. 78 D5

group is also linked directly to a prominent militia guild in the city (Fig. 8.4). The intersecting arrows painted on the box which the figure beats with a spoon, and which reappears on his sleeve, refer to the insignia that appears on the sleeve of members of the Archers' guild. The attire of the figure playing the bellows recalls the monastic idiom upon which associations generally responsible for festive occasions drew. As opposed to the secular clerical hierarchy that was inverted in the liturgical celebration of the Feast of Fools, in which a bishop led festivities, these groups inverted the monastic hirearchy, designating an Abbot as their leader.[22]

The depictions of entertainers that accompanied Joanna's procession into Brussels emphasize the gestural capacity of the human body. In a choreographed dance the wild men stretch their bodies in opposing directions, straining to strike each other with their clubs or to join their outstretched limbs in a circular round (fol. 15ʳ). The children mock with their hand gestures. The directionality of the procession does not confine them; their antics extend into the surrounding countryside. Finally, the body's ability to produce music is highlighted by the choice of wind instruments – flute, bagpipe, bellows – and the adornment of their costumes. The bells stitched into the eared hoods of two of the fools and onto the bellows, and the wooden clogs worn by one of them would also have contributed to the noise that the group made. Their gestures are capacious and dynamic, suggesting that they often exceeded the border of the road upon which the procession travels; the continual sounds they created would have pervaded the spaces through which they moved.

This cluster of pictures also calls attention to the way inversion, humour, and parody structured such performances. For instance, the red and green stripes worn by one of the fools not only aligns him with but also makes fun of the official clothing of the 'youths'; the club-wielding wild men mock the way the urban militia groups carry their arms. The parody of Joanna's arrival in the city in the group of wild women escorting a princess is carefully conceived and orchestrated (fol. 13ʳ). The two images are compositionally and visually similar, except they reverse the skin colour of the two princesses, one referred to simply as the 'Ethiopian Princess', and the colour of their mules (Fig. 8.5). The red coat of arms that dangles from the miniature tree, held jointly by the Ethiopian Princess and one of the wild women, resembles those hanging from the torches of the members of the Crossbowmen's guild. The figure clad as a monk parodies the monastic orders. Moreover, the bellows he holds, which in Latin is

---

22 Davis, Natalie Zemon, 'The Reasons of Misrule', in *Society and Culture in Early Modern France*, ed. by Davis, Natalie Zemon, (Stanford: Stanford University Press, 1975), p. 102; Harris, Max, *Sacred Folly: A New History of the Feast of Fools* (Ithaka, Cornell University Press, 2011), p. 241.

follis (fool), is traditionally associated with the hot air that fills the empty-headed fool. The fool on horseback holds the same instrument.

The accompanying texts further specify the mode of performance represented in the six images. The authors chose Latin words that bring to mind the language used in antiquarian accounts of the 'theatre' of antiquity. They call the group of four fools leading the procession *mimes* and refer to the performer who follows them as a *hystrio*, the same words Isidore of Seville used to refer to actors.[23] Like contemporary antiquarian texts, the model of role-playing these individuals engage is based on imitation, disguise, and dissimulation.[24] The *mimes* 'disguise themselves'; the bagpipers 'cover their faces'; those who accompany the Ethiopian on horseback 'simulate wild women'; their male counterparts 'counterfeit' wild men 'by an art of a composite nature'.[25] The description of the wild men acknowledges that their mode of disguise involved costumes, masks, as well as gestures and characterizes their performance not as a skill but as an *art*.

Such classical references would be familiar to the chambers of rhetoric in the late fifteenth century, but the entertainment they provided was also geared towards less intellectualized exercises. Recreation was understood as what provoked laughter. A prize was given in Antwerp in the 1496 landjuweel for 'd'alder plaisanste, 't vreughdelijcxste ende vremste estattement ...[which] meest beruerende 't volck tot lachene' (the most humorous, delightful and exotic diversion...which most moved the people to laughter).[26] The authors of Joanna's manuscript praise this quality of the performances. The *hystrio* and the fool on horseback provoked 'many laughs from the people'; the wild men produced 'a quite pleasant distraction (called forth an approving nod)'; the bagpipers created 'a most agreeable harmony'. The laughter the performers elicit is one that 'even the *gods* can't refuse'.

Pleasure that comes from entertainment is evoked directly and indirectly in the three penultimate depictions of the twenty-eight processional stagings depicted in the manuscript. These three processional stagings are particularly resistant to summation in terms of a moralizing or didactic message. They conjure up that distinctive feature of entertainment, one which exceeds the utilitarian, one which produces pleasure. The text refers to the intended response to these stagings, a response which cannot be characterized as a single message. Each picture, moreover, alludes specifically to the broader spatial contours and spectacular dimensions of Joanna's *joyeuse entrée*. As a group they offer important clues for the ways the procession moved into the urban geography of Brussels and for what counted as entertainment at the time.

The first of the sequence strikingly illustrates the inadequacy of both the text and the pictures to capture the effect of these stagings on contemporary audiences.

---

[23] Isidore of Seville, *Chronica* XVII, 43, ed. by Martín, José Carlos, CCSL, 112 (Turnhout: Brepols, 2003).
[24] For instance, Raoul de Praelles' fifteenth-century translation and gloss of Augustine's *City of God* describes these actors as 'gens desguisez', who 'contrefaisoient les personages' (text transcribed by Hedeman, Anne D., in *Medieval Manuscripts, Their Makers and Users, a special issue of Viator in honor of Richard and Mary Rouse* (Turnhout: Brepols, 2011), pp. 27-50, Appendix 2, p. 40.
[25] Berlin, Kupferstichkabinett, ms 78 D5, fols 12^v, 13^v, 14^v and 15^v.
[26] Van Bruaene, *Om beters wille*, p. 234.

The inscription on the frame states simply, *Tres Virgines* (Three Virgins) (fol. 56^r). Three richly clad female figures are seated on the scaffolding. The two side figures gesture and turn their heads towards the one in the centre, who wears a more ornate gown of golden brocade embroidered with a patterned motif in red, matching the colour of her cap. The central figure extends a rod, which breaches the picture frame to reappear again in the implied space in front of the scaffolding. At its end is a miniature canopy from which a dove appears, dangling a crown in its claws. As Wim Blockmans points out in this volume, the text does not correspond with the picture.[27] The text adds a narrative content to the scene, identifying it as Emperor Henry IV offering his daughter's hand in marriage to the first duke of Brabant. Aside from the historical inaccuracy of the identification (given the dates, it couldn't be Henry IV), the picture does not depict a king/emperor presenting his daughter. The curious misidentification of the staging could be an attempt by the text's authors to ascribe meaning to a group of figures whose purpose was primarily to delight the eyes. Like the burning flames throughout the city which cannot be 'captured in words', the experience these figures were meant to elicit exceeded verbal articulation. Such figures were there to produce pleasure and joy.

The presence of 'maidens' either alone or in groups of three formed part of the adornment and entertainment in shooting competitions. For one inter-city shooting competition, 'the Tournai crossbowmen brought with them three lithe and gracious virgins in a fine garden who presented the guilds with their prizes'.[28] Might the *Tres Virgines* be repurposed for the granting of prizes to the crowning of a princess? I have suggested elsewhere that this staging illustrates a moment in which Joanna would have interacted with the figures in the staging. She would be crowned as she passed.[29] Looking closely at the picture thereby offers a case of the processional performance broaching the depicted frame of the staging. Moreover, we are given a glimpse into the city of Brussels. The scaffolding is angled to allow the picture to incorporate an expanse of cobblestone streets. A canal, accessible by a series of steps and on which boats transporting barrels are docked, cuts through the streets on either side. Two barrels lie on the side of the canal closer to the staging; the opposite side of the canal includes the facades of two buildings, a stretch of the city wall, and a towered gateway. Here, the picture suggests another way that the processional stagings expanded into and interacted with the urban environment.

The next picture suggests a similar expansion beyond the theatrical frame of the scaffolding into the city. It depicts a version of the story of *Paris and the Golden Apple* (fol. 57^r). Situated within the elevated wooden platform are figures of the three goddesses, covered only by ornamented headdresses in red, blue, and a shade of purple, their long hair, and the diaphanous veils draped around the arms of one and held in the hands of another. The position of the figures and their pose provide three

---

27 See Wim Blockmans' essay in this volume.
28 Cited in Brown, Andrew, and Graeme Small, *Court and Civic Society in the Burgundian Low Countries* (Manchester: Manchester University Press), 2007.
29 Weigert, *French Visual Culture*, pp. 42-43, p. 53.

perspectives on these bodies and highlight different body parts. On the left, we see the figure's backside, her left hand resting on her hip. The central figure adopts the *Venus pudica* pose, her right hand slightly cupped under her left breast, her right hand holding the veil that covers her genitalia. On the right, the latter are revealed, as the figure lowers the veil held in her two hands. A low wall of painted or actual bricks separates the goddesses from the figures of Paris lounging on the left, his head on his helmet, and Mercury, standing on the right with the golden apple in his hand.

The figures are static, however the movement of the goddesses is implied by the circular ramp on which they stand and the door, which opens on the left through which the figures will pass, to return into view through the doorway on the right, now closed. Indeed, this detail and the water emitted from the spouts of the fountain are clues to the assemblage's construction. Water flows into a large basin from three spouts at the top of a round column at its centre, setting the three figures in motion. Their rotation before viewers and around the fountain would probably have been triggered by a hydraulic mechanism linked to the circulation of water through pipes, hidden from view, into the fountain. This was not the first time that female figures were associated with the circulation of liquids in civic entertainment in Brussels. In 1444 the Brussels Crossbowmen hosted and organized a 'grand tir' (great shoot) in their city. A remarkable and central element in the ornamentation for this event was a sculpted female figure, spraying wine from a breast, erected in the Grand-Place.[30]

In addition to evoking the role such water devices played in the Crossbowmen's entertainment, the fountain at the centre of the staging might highlight the cities' masters in hydraulics and express pride in its fountains. Chloé Deligne has argued that the Brussels *Ommegang* procession incorporated the *mannequin pis* fountain, which is also included in Denis van Alsloot's painting of the event.[31] Such an incorporation of one of the city's fountains into an entry staging took place in 1549 when a figure representing Mary of Hungary appeared with the goddesses Diana and Athena at the fountain in the *Marché aux Herbes*.[32] In the case of the *Judgment of Paris*, the use of an actual fountain as the centrepiece of the staging is an intriguing possibility. In so doing, the staging would have incorporated a fixture in the urban landscape and a central geographic landmark. The picture of the *Judgment of Paris* would serve to locate the staging in the cityscape of Brussels. It would invoke, once again, the broader urban spatial environment which the procession encompassed.

The picture also recalls the amorous content of the plays that would have been performed in conjunction with an entry. Such plays took place either the same day or on subsequent days of the procession. The *Judgement of Paris* could be perceived both as one of a series of stagings and in relation to a longer performance of a play. In so doing, it interrupted the continuous flow of the procession with an evocation

---

30 'En 1444, entre autres, il y eut sur la grand'place, qui était ornée d'allées d'arbres fruitiers et où l'on voyait une statue de femme jetant du vin par le sein, une grande joûte dont cinq joyaux d'or furent les prix', in Henne, and Wauters, *Histoire de la ville de Bruxelles*, 1, pp. 249-50.
31 Deligne, Chloé, 'Manneken-Pis dans l'espace bruxellois du Moyen Âge: distribution d'eau et centralité urbaine', forthcoming.
32 Trowbridge, 'Art and Ommegangen', p. 219.

of the expanded temporal experience of watching a play. The picture might even conjure up a specific performance of a well-known play, 'How Mars and Venus Dallied Together'. Brussels' chief rhetorician, Jan Smeken, composed the script, which tells a story involving the three goddesses. Smeken served as city poet of Brussels (1485-1517) and factor of *De Lelie*. The script is preserved in a sixteenth-century manuscript.[33] One interpretation of the play considers it a metaphor for the social body. In the play, such mismatched couples represent the opposite of civic cohesion. Amorous sexual relations are presented as necessary and also enjoyable, when the partners are suitably matched. When they are not – as in the case of Venus and Vulcan – they prevent not only the fulfilment of desire but also harmony and peace. The *sinnekens* (moralizing personifications) in the play, called *Love's Thought* and *Eye's Desire* point to the moralizing stance to which the audience was directed. Yet these figures offered 'potential for ambivalence', participat[ing] vigorously in the growth of love, or lust, between the two protagonists'.[34] The play's performance was thereby also directed at the audience's experience of that very pleasure; it provided 'eye's delight'.

'Amorous' subjects like this one were the common subject matter for the *esbatement* in shooting competitions.[35] The civic function of these plays is expressed succinctly in a rare reference to the goal of contemporary entertainment. In this case the inhabitants gathered to watch an amorous play 'in recreation and consolation of melancholy and in honor and profit of the city'.[36] The numerous plays relating to the goddess of love, in particular, allowed an audience to experience the 'harmonising or appeasing qualities ascribed to Venus and their benevolent consequences'.[37] These contemporary archival references confirm that civic performances organized by rhetorician chambers, among other urban groups, were considered to serve beyond a moralizing or educational function. Entertainment was medicine for the social body.

According to contemporary accounts, the theme of the three goddesses was particularly efficacious in the pleasure it provided spectators. For instance, a similar configuration appeared when Joanna of Castile's husband Philip the Handsome made his *joyeuse entrée* into Antwerp in 1494. To quote a chronicler of the time, 'the staging that most pleased the people was the one that represented the story of the three god-

---

33 'How Mars and Venus dallied together', in *For Pleasure and Profit: Six Dutch Rhetoricians Plays*, ed. and trans. by Strietman, Elsa, and Peter Happé (Tempe: Arizona Center for Medieval and Renaissance Studies, 2013), van Dijk, Hans, and Femke Kramer, 'Hue Mars en Venus tsaemen bueleerden. Het overspel van Mars en Venus', in *Europees toneel van Middeleeuwen naar Renaissance*, ed. by Gosman, Martin, (Groningen: Boekwerk, 1991), 229-302.
34 Strietman and Happé, 'How Mars and Venus dallied together', VIII.
35 van Herk, Anke, *Fabels van liefde: Het mythologisch-amoureuze toneel van de rederijkers (1475-1621)* (Amsterdam: Amsterdam University Press, 2012).
36 van Bruaene, Anne-Laure, 'A wonderfull tryumfe, for the wynnyng of a pryse': Guilds, Ritual, Theater, and the Urban Network in the Southern Low Countries, *c.* 1450-1650', *Renaissance Quarterly* 59 (2006), 385.
37 Strietman, and Happé, 'How Mars and Venus dallied together', p. 1.

desses, which was composed of female figures who were naked and enlivened'.³⁸ To return to the information in the picture of the staging for Joanna's entry, the rotating figures in Brussels allowed participants to perceive sculpted and human bodies from all sides. The female body became a site of artistic and technological demonstration of hydraulic technology of craftsmen in Brussels and a site of pleasurable looking.

Sensual pleasure itself, as well as the pleasure of observing people partaking in it, is evoked in the last of the cluster of three stagings. Within the boxlike structure and between the parted curtains of the picture, five well-dressed couples of men and women engage in pleasurable activities. Beginning on the lower left, a seated woman holds a sleeping man's head in her lap. At the centre, a couple dances, while another on the right plays a board game, probably backgammon. Above on the right another couple stands, while a woman offers them food on a platter and a male servant refills the man's glass. A musician serenades the group with a flute and drum. The fool, holding a double headed bauble points at the last couple, whose awkward embrace suggests that the woman is led unwillingly towards the bed in the left-hand corner behind them. The intricate headboard and red covering resemble the furnishing of the bed in the staging of Sarah and Tobias (fol. 35ʳ). To its right and behind the figures, a textile-covered buffet contains what appears to be a helmet and other vessels, relating to the refreshments served or the display of luxury festive tableware and precious metal prizes.³⁹ The venue in which these vignettes of love making, feasting, and gaming take place is identified in the inscription above: *Domus Delicie et Iocunditatis*, the House of Pleasure and Joy. The accompanying text reads (fol. 57ᵛ):

> Hoc scemate representatur Qui uti hii deliciosi cunctis se voluptatibus occupaverunt sic occasione coniunctionis Philippi et Johanne ducum omnibus tristiciis sese singuli exuentes cunctis iocis indulserunt.
>
> > This depiction displays how these hedonists have abandoned themselves in all kinds of pleasures. So have all – on the occasion of the marriage of their Duke and Duchess Philip and Joanna – laid aside all sadness and devoted themselves to all manners of merriment.

Combined with the written text, the page highlights the multiple purposes – both didactic and pleasurable – of the entry procession. On the one hand, the staging could send a moralizing message. The same cluster of events appears, for instance, in depictions of wayward youths, like in the story of the Prodigal Son.⁴⁰ The activities taking place in a 'house of pleasure' would serve as negative exempla, the opposite of the virtues of the princess and of the virtuous love she and her new husband shared. Within the bookish culture of the rhetorician chambers, the staging might

---

38 Jean Molinet, '1494, l'Entrée de Philippe le Beau à Anvers', in *Chroniques de Jean Molinet*, ed. J.-A. Buchon, V, pp. 14-15, (Paris: Verdière,1828); see also Blockmans, Wim, 'Le dialogue imaginaire entre princes et sujets: les joyeuses entrées en Brabant en 1494 et en 1496', in *A la cour de Bourgogne. Le duc, son entourage, son train*, ed. by Jean-Marie Cauchies (Turnhout: Brepols, 1998), pp. 160-61.
39 On prizes, see: Crombie, 'From War to Peace', pp. 186-88.
40 See for example the thirteenth-century windows at Chartres and Bourges (Kemp, Wolfgang, *Sermo Corporeus: Die Erzählung der mittelalterlichen Glasfenster* (Munich: Schirmer-Mosel, 1987).

have conveyed a more specific, albeit esoteric, moralizing message. It would be an image of Babylon, culled from the images crafted in the Book of Revelation, and updated to a fifteenth-century context.[41]

On the other hand, however, the picture itself does not suggest disdain or disgust at the activities depicted. The figures are quite staid in their exchanges; their clothing resembles that of wealthy burgers. The text, moreover, suggests that the activities depicted here correspond with those in which inhabitants engaged during Joanna's entry into Brussels. The painted vignettes capture the pursuits that would have taken place in a contemporary tavern or brothel. Brothels and taverns were ubiquitous in Brussels, as in other late medieval cities.[42] Also important for our interpretation of the picture is that the Roman King Sigismund's entourage had their entrance fee to brothels waived during their trip to the Council of Constance.[43] The social function brothels served on specific occasions and more generally for the urban population was accepted and understood. The female figures in the staging for Joanna's entry would be playing the roles of prostitutes, referred to also as 'daughters of joy'.[44]

The presence of the helmet might be a further clue that the women performing in the tavern scene were themselves engaged in prostitution. The only helmets featured in the sequence of stagings are those held by female figures. Given this fact, it is plausible to associate the helmet with the female figures in the house of pleasure. Might this connection be an indication of the identity of the performers in the sequence of stagings? Surprisingly little historical work has been done on the identity of these actors or those who participated in the entertainment accompanying shooting and rhetoricians' competitions. There is isolated evidence of prostitutes performing in such events in the fifteenth century. King Albert II, for instance, was greeted at the city gates of Vienna by prostitutes in 1438. In 1471 in Nuremberg prostitutes were part of a performance skit, involving Emperor Frederick III. The women captured the emperor with a golden chain, then released him in exchange for a ransom.[45] Élodie Lecuppre Desjardin raised the possibility that the staging of Paris and the three Goddesses at the 1468 entrance of Charles the Bold into Lille cast prostitutes in the roles of Venus, Juno, and Athena.[46]

'The House of Pleasure and Joy' points more directly than any of the other pictures or words in the manuscript to what was considered the general restorative purpose of entertainment. Yet the picture and the staging to which it refers would have accommodated a range of associations. The time of Joanna's entry was a moment of transformation in the social acceptability and civic support for these institutions.

---

41 For a brilliant discussion of such contemporary updating of the sinful city and the moral ambiguities of the passage, see: Moss, Candida, and Liane Feldman, 'The New Jerusalem: Wealth, Ancient Building Projects and Revelation 21-22', *New Testament Studies* 66 (2020), pp. 351-66.
42 Spindler, Eric, 'Were Medieval Prostitutes Marginals? Evidence from Sluis, 1387-1440', *Revue Belge de Philologie et d'Histoire/Belgisch Tijdschrift voor Filologie en Geschiedenis* 87 (2009), 239-72.
43 Page, Jamie, *Prostitution and Subjectivity in Late Medieval Germany* (Oxford: Oxford University Press, 2021), 10.
44 Rossiaud, Jacques, *Medieval Prostitution*, trans. by Lydia Cochrane (New York: Blackwell, 1988), p. 69.
45 Page, *Prostitution and Subjectivity*, 10.
46 Suggestion communicated in conversation with author.

The result was a criminalization of houses of pleasure and the women who worked there.[47] The picture might hint at the moralizing gloss on houses of pleasure, while retaining an ambiguity and allowing for spectators to feel amused and entertained. Indeed, such a moral outlook remained in the background as justification and pretext for entertainment. It continues in some current history writing on fifteenth-century urban culture.

Finally, the picture and accompanying text indicate that the event of the entry spilled out into the city streets. The text refers not to the staging itself but to the enjoyment experienced by the people of Brussels at the time of the entry. What it seems to imply is that taverns or brothels were open for business at this time and that the inhabitants took full advantage, 'devoting themselves to all manner of merriment'. Given the text, therefore, the staging depicts not an isolated scene on a scaffold but the kinds of merriment that went on throughout Brussels. The picture looks outwards onto the city, condensing in one picture activities happening at different locations during the entry. Such a reading allows us to expand the one dimensionality of the picture and the spatial and temporal linearity of the procession, duplicated in the succession of pages of the manuscript, to encompass the broader urban environment in which it took place. The entire city became a spectacle and the site for entertainment.

We come full circle back to the picture of the crossbowmen as they transport the princess into the city, against the backdrop of the town hall alit with torches. The bright lights of the city combined with the sounds of merrymaking from the taverns and brothels produced a multi-dimensional, multi-sensory experience. Entertainment on this occasion encompassed and infused the city and its inhabitants. Looking closely at the manuscript's text and pictures and situating what we observe in relation to the broader performance culture in which militia guilds and rhetorician chambers participated, we can recover traces of what was appreciated as entertainment at the time. We can begin to imagine the sights, sounds, smells, and experiences the organizers of Joanna's entry considered so important.

---

47 Beate Schuster's term is the 'new moralism' of the 1400s and early 1500s (Schuster, Beate, *Die freien Frauen: Dirnen und Frauenhäuser im 15. und 16. Jahrhundert* (Frankfurt: Campus, 1995), pp. 316-50); Page, Jamie, 'Masculinity and Prostitution in Medieval German Literature', *Speculum* 94 (2019), 744-45; Bousmar, Eric, 'Marguerite d'York et les putains de Mons, entre charité dévôte et offensive moralisatrice (1481-1485). Autour d'une Fondation de Repenties', in *Marguerite d'York et son temps*, ed. Jean-Marie Cauchies, Publication du Centre européen d'études bourguignonnes XIVᵉ-XVIᵉ siècles, vol. 44, (Neuchâtel: 2004), pp. 81-102.

SASCHA KÖHL

The Brussels Town Hall

A Worthy Emblem for a Capital City

▼ **ABSTRACT** The Berlin manuscript of Joanna's entry into Brussels concludes with an elaborate description of the city's town hall, one of the most magnificent municipal buildings in late medieval Europe. The description is an exceptional document in many respects. It is a particularly early example of a description of a secular building and, as such, an important testimony to the perception and interpretation of architecture at the dawn of the early modern period. This essay provides the first detailed analysis of the town hall's description. It examines the role of this Latin text within the manuscript as a whole. The appearance, perception and meaning of the town hall in the years around 1500 are equally addressed. To conclude, the building's significance in the context of Joanna's entry is discussed.

▼ **KEYWORDS** town hall, architectural description, fountains, encomium, Rogier van der Weyden, Trajan and Herkinbald, Boterpot, civic archive, bulbous spires, Brabant

Over the last thirty years, the illustrated manuscript of the entry of Joanna of Castile into Brussels has attracted the interest of researchers from a wide range of disciplines. It has been subject to studies dealing with the iconography of the *tableaux vivants*, theatrical and musical aspects, or historical contexts and political messages.[1] The significance of the manuscript as a source for architectural history, however, has

---

1 Blockmans, Wim P., 'La Joyeuse Entrée de Jeanne de Castille à Bruxelles en 1496', in *España y Holanda*, ed. by Jan Lechner, and Harm den Boer (Amsterdam: Rodopi, 1995), pp. 27-42; Kipling, Gordon, 'Brussels, Juana of Castile and the Art of Theatrical Illustration (1496)', *Leeds Studies in English*, n.s., 32 (2001), 229-53; Eichberger, Dagmar, 'Illustrierte Festzüge für das Haus Habsburg-Burgund: Idee und Wirklichkeit', in *Hofkultur in Frankreich und Europa im Spätmittelalter. La culture de cour en France et en Europe à la fin du Moyen Âge*, ed. by Christian Freigang, and Jean-Claude Schmitt (Berlin: Akademie-Verlag, 2005), pp. 73-98; Legaré, Anne-Marie, 'L'entrée de Jeanne de Castille à Bruxelles: un programme iconographique au féminin', in *Women at the Burgundian court. Presence and Influence*, ed. by Dagmar Eichberger, Anne-Marie Legaré, and Wim Hüsken (Turnhout: Brepols, 2010), pp. 43-55; Tammen, Björn, 'A Feast of the Arts: Joanna of Castile in Brussels, 1496', *Early Music History*, 30 (2011), 213-48.

hitherto been overlooked. The booklet concludes with an elaborate description of the Brussels town hall, which constitutes by far the longest section of text in the entire manuscript (fols 63^r-63^v). It is an important testimony to the perception, description and interpretation of architecture at the dawn of the early modern period. Moreover, the text was originally intended to be accompanied by an illustration of the town hall, which has since been lost – or was never executed. Thus, the portrait(s) of the town hall, serving as an emblem for Brussels, formed a counterpart at the end of the book to the city's coat of arms with Saint Michael on folio 1^v.

On the one hand, it might come as a surprise that the town hall is given such a prominent place in a booklet written for documenting an ephemeral entry ceremony. On the other hand, the town hall was not only the most prestigious municipal building in Brussels (Fig. 9.1), it was also of central importance during the *joyeuses entrées*. Its façade usually formed the backdrop for the constitutional acts of such a ceremony: the reciprocal oaths of allegiance between the duke on the balcony and the citizens gathering on the Grand Place. Even though Joanna did not take such an oath herself, it is most likely that the town hall also served as an important stage during her official entry and that the magistrate gave Joanna a similarly festive reception in this building as has, for instance, been documented for her grandson, Philip II of Spain, in 1549.[2]

Nevertheless, the description of the town hall in this manuscript constitutes a noteworthy, if not an extraordinary source. Up to this time, comparably extensive descriptions of secular buildings were very rare north of the Alps.[3] For example, no eulogies had yet been dedicated to the magnificent town halls in the Burgundian Netherlands as would be the case two centuries later with the baroque town hall of Amsterdam.[4] The only available written evidence of the contemporary perception of the late gothic town halls is therefore provided by the interesting, but mostly brief accounts of foreign visitors. Even more unusual than the description of a secular building, however, was its pictorial representation. It is true that the tower of the Brussels town hall attracted the interest of painters early on; soon after its completion in 1455, it was repeatedly depicted in the background of religious paintings (Fig. 9.2), once even in a miniature in a ducal privilege book depicting the silhouette of Brus-

---

2 Calvete de Estrella, Juan Cristóbal, *El felicissimo viaje d'el muy alto y muy Poderoso Principe Don Phelippe* (Antwerp: Nucio, 1552), fol. 91^v; an earlier festive reception of a duke in the town hall is, for instance, also documented for Philip of Saint Pol in 1427, see Galesloot, Louis, 'Notes extraites des anciens comptes de la ville de Bruxelles', *Bulletin de la Commission royale d'Histoire*, second series, 9 (1867), 475-500 (485); for the entry of Joanna in the context of the ducal entries in the cities of Brabant see Blockmans, 'La Joyeuse Entrée', pp. 28-32.

3 A very early comprehensive description of a city and its various buildings was written by Jean de Jandun for Paris in 1323. However, it remained an exceptional work for a long time: Jean de Jandun, 'Tractatus de Laudibus Parisius', in *Paris et ses historiens aux XIVe et XVe siècles*, ed. by Antoine Le Roux de Lincy (Paris: Imprimerie impériale, 1867), pp. 32-79; see also Freigang, Christian, 'Zur Wahrnehmung regional spezifischer Architekturidiome in mittelalterlichen Diskursen', in *Kunst und Religion. Architektur und Kunst im Mittelalter. Beitrage einer Forschungsgruppe*, ed. by Uta Maria Bräuer, Emanuel S. Klinkenberg, and Jeroen Westerman (Utrecht: Clavis, 2005), pp. 14-33 (27).

4 Van den Vondel, Joost, *Inwydinge van 't stadthuis t'Amsterdam*, ed. by Marijke Spies, and others (Muiderberg: Dick Coutinho, 1982).

9.1 Brussels, *town hall*, built in two stages between 1401 and 1455 © Sascha Köhl

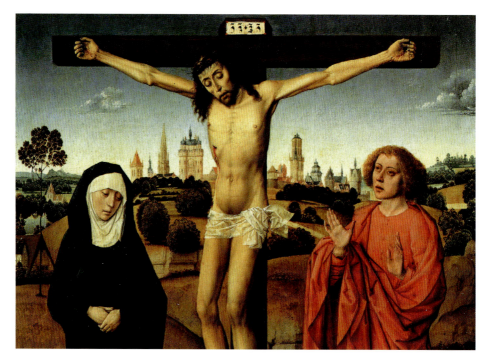

9.2 Southern Netherlandish (circle of Dieric Bouts), *Crucifixion* (detail): *several towers of Brussels*, oil on wood, 88 × 71cm, c. 1470/80, Berlin, SPKB, Gemäldegalerie © Goedleven, La Grand-Place de Bruxelles, p. 48

sels.[5] Autonomous views of the whole building, however, have not survived from this period. It was not until the middle of the sixteenth century that the town hall, like other secular buildings in the Netherlands, was depicted in its overall appearance in drawings, paintings, or engravings (Fig. 9.3).[6] Therefore, regardless of the question of execution, the very intention of such a drawing remains remarkable. However, this task would have been a great challenge even for artists more talented than our moderately skilled draughtsman, for it is not mere hyperbole when the description states

---

5 A brief overview of early pictorial representations of the town hall is provided by Köhl, Sascha, *Das Brüsseler Rathaus. Repräsentationsbau für Rat, Stadt und Land* (Petersberg: Imhof, 2019), pp. 60-62; see also the various images and essays in *Met passer en penseel. Brussel en het oude hertogdom Brabant in beeld*, ed. by Véronique Van de Kerckhof, Helena Bussers, and Véronique Bücken, exh. cat., Brussels, Koninklijke Musea voor Schone Kunsten (Brussels: Dexia, 2000).

6 The earliest surviving depiction of the entire square façade of the town hall is the engraving by Melchisedech van Hooren from 1565 (who also created a corresponding depiction of the Antwerp town hall at about the same time). Slightly earlier in date, from around the middle of the sixteenth century, are the first depictions of Coudenberg Palace in Brussels. In addition, several painted depictions of entire church buildings have been produced in the Netherlands since the early sixteenth century. However, according to Meischke, these are often related to ongoing construction work and therefore show projects rather than portraits of the buildings; see: Meischke, Ruud, *De gothische bouwtraditie. Studies over opdrachtgevers en bouwmeesters in de Nederlanden* (Bekking: Amersfoort 1988), pp. 157-60.

that it was almost impossible to capture the magnificent appearance of this building in words or pictures.

Moreover, it was neither an empty cliché nor parochial pride to claim that the town hall was incomparable, for many contemporary visitors shared this view.[7] Even the far-travelled Castilian Pero Tafur, who stayed in Brussels in 1438, wrote about the town hall that it was the 'best' (i.e., probably the most magnificent) house he had ever seen – and this despite the fact that at the time of his visit only part of the building that Joanna would later see was already standing.[8] The construction of the town hall essentially took place in two stages. First of all, the L-shaped eastern part of the building complex was erected from 1401 onwards. This comprises the left wing of the square façade, including the lower parts of the tower, as well as the adjoining wing on rue Charles Buls. It was not until 1444, six years after Tafur's visit, that the second major building campaign started. The young Charles the Bold laid the foundation stone of the right wing of the square façade, and from 1449 onwards the upper storeys of the tower were built. The crowning of the spire with the figure of the city's patron saint, St Michael, in 1455, marked the completion of the construction work.[9] However, it remained, as we shall see, only a provisional completion.

This building, as it appeared in the later fifteenth century, was indeed unprecedented. In Brabant, as in the other parts of the Low Countries, most cities, including the commercial metropolis of Antwerp, were content with modest town halls until well into the sixteenth century. It is true that Leuven, Brussels' perennial rival, had a similarly magnificent town hall built from 1448 onwards, which, like its Brussels counterpart, was distinguished by a richly articulated façade.[10] The Brussels town hall, however, surpassed this rival (as well as the older model at Bruges) by its size and, even more, by its tower. This tower was exceptional in many respects. Firstly, there was no tradition of such town hall towers in Brabant.[11] Consequently, there was no proper function for the tower in Brussels: neither the municipal archives nor the bells were housed in there. An even more exceptional feature of the tower, however,

---

7 Martens, Mina, 'Initiation à une rencontre', in *La Grand-Place de Bruxelles* (Brussels: Vokaer, 3rd ed., 1974), pp. 53-90 (70-72).
8 Tafur, Pero, *Andanças é viajes de Pero Tafur por diversas partes del mundo avidos* (Madrid: Ginesta, 1874), p. 247.
9 For the history of the construction see Köhl, *Das Brüsseler Rathaus*, pp. 64-73, and (except for the construction of the main tower) Maesschalck, Alfonsine, and Jos Viaene, *Het stadhuis van Brussel* (Kessel-Lo: self-published, 1960); see also various articles in *L'hôtel de Ville de Bruxelles – Bilan de trois années d'études du bâti*, ed. by Vincent Heymans (= *Studia Bruxellae*, 12, 2018/1), in particular Philippe Sosnowska, and others, 'L'Hôtel de Ville de Bruxelles. Apport de l'archéologie à la compréhension d'un édifice majeur au travers d'une étude des maçonneries gothiques', pp. 43-75; the authors of the latter article argue that the construction of the wing along rue Charles Buls, although already underway in 1405, may have stretched into the second quarter of the fifteenth century.
10 Maesschalck, Alfonsine, and Jos Viaene, 'Het Stadhuis van Leuven', *Arca Lovaniensis*, 6 (1977), 7-255; Köhl, *Das Brüsseler Rathaus*, pp. 149-52.
11 In contrast to northern France, Flanders and Hainaut, there was also no tradition of building belfries in Brabant. An exception was the fourteenth-century tower of the former cloth hall in Lier (which was converted into a *stadhuis* in the early fifteenth century). However, this tower was neither designated as a belfry nor was it used like Flemish belfries; see Van Uytven, Raymond, 'Flämische Belfriede und südniederländische städtische Bauwerke im Mittelalter. Symbol und Mythos', in *Information, Kommunikation und Selbstdarstellung in mittelalterlichen Gemeinden*, ed. by Alfred Haverkamp (Munich: Oldenbourg, 1998), pp. 125-59.

9.3 Melchisedech van Hooren, *The town hall of Brussels*, engraving, 1565
© Bibliothèque Royale de Belgique | Koninklijke Bibliotheek van België

was its design. Up to that time, similarly tall and ornate towers had only been built for churches, such as the cathedral towers of Utrecht and Cambrai, both built in the fourteenth century. With the latter, once part of the *ecclesia matrix* of Brussels but destroyed around 1800, the town hall tower also shares the design feature of an openwork tracery spire. However, in both its overall structure and in many details, the Brussels tower is more closely related to the most ambitious contemporary towers in the Upper German regions between Strasbourg and Vienna.[12] In Brabant, the town hall tower was a pioneering work that stimulated a tower-building competition of

---

12 Kayser, Christian, '"Brüsseler Spitze" – The tower of Brussels town hall in the context of late medieval openwork spires', in *L'hôtel de Ville de Bruxelles – Bilan de trois années d'études du bâti*, ed. by Vincent Heymans (= *Studia Bruxellae*, 12, 2018/1), pp. 149-78.

unprecedented scale – but, significantly, only among church towers. This is further evidence of how extraordinary, even 'incomparable' this town hall was. At the end of this contribution, we will return to the question of why such a building was erected in Brussels – and what it had to do with Joanna. First, however, we will get to know three other features of the town hall that the author of the description considers equally unique: the fountains, the paintings, and finally another tower.

Fountains of the Town Hall and the City: a building Description as City Encomium?

A most peculiar feature of the town hall, admired by many authors, was its fountains, which even supplied the upper floors of the building with fresh water. These amenities delighted not only the magistrates, but also illustrious guests. Philip II of Spain, for instance, retired to the interior of the town hall after his entry to relax at the fountains and refresh himself with their clear water.[13] Depending on the written source, there may have been at least twelve, if not thirty-six fountains in the entire town hall complex at that time.[14] How proud the Brussels city fathers were of these fountains is proven not least by the remarkably detailed and vivid description of their practical and, notably, their sanitary use in the booklet. Unfortunately, all these fountains have disappeared today. Only the much younger baroque fountains in the town hall's courtyard (1714) remind us of this often neglected but very interesting aspect of the building's history.

The fountains of the town hall are in many ways representative of the now lost wealth of fountains in medieval Brussels.[15] All that remains of these fountains are a few early modern successors, such as today's most popular fountain, whose predecessor was mentioned as early as the fifteenth century as the *fonteyne dmenneken pist*.[16] Yet the most important fountain in the Middle Ages was the one on the Grand-Place, built in the fourteenth century.[17] Still admired by an Italian traveller as a *fontana bellissima* in 1517/18,[18] it was replaced by a Renaissance-style fountain only half a century later. Thanks to a detailed description from around 1400, we at least have an idea of its original appearance: it was a tower-like construction of

---

13 Calvete de Estrella, *El felicissimo viaje*, fol. 91ᵛ.
14 Calvete de Estrella mentions 12 fountains (fol. 91ᵛ), but according to Antonio de Beatis, who visited Brussels in 1517/18, there were as many as 36 fountains in the town hall; see De Beatis, Antonio, *Die Reise des Kardinals Luigi d'Aragona durch Deutschland, die Niederlande, Frankreich und Oberitalien, 1517-1518*, ed. by Ludwig von Pastor (Freiburg: Herder, 1905), p. 116.
15 On the fountains in medieval Brussels see Deligne, Chloé, 'Édilité et politique. Les fontaines urbaines dans les Pays-Bas méridionaux au Moyen Âge', *Histoire urbaine*, 22 (2008), 77-96; Deligne, Chloé, *Bruxelles et sa rivière. Genèse d'un territoire urbain (12ᵉ-18ᵉ siècle)* (Turnhout: Brepols, 2003), pp. 115-23.
16 The quote is from the *Percquement boeck mette taitsen*, a fifteenth century cartulary: Archives de la Ville de Bruxelles, Archives Anciennes, Cartulary IX, fol. 121ᵛ; it is, obviously, the predecessor of the fountain of Manneken Pis, whose famous figure was created by Jérôme Duquesnoy the Elder in 1619.
17 On the medieval fountain on the Grand-Place see Deligne, 'Édilité et politique', pp. 85-87.
18 De Beatis, *Die Reise*, p. 116.

9.4 Frans Hogenberg and Joris Bruin, *Bruxella*, coloured woodcut, 1572 © Bibliothèque Royale de Belgique | Koninklijke Bibliotheek van België

more than ten metres, crowned with a figure of St Michael.[19] Hence, it must have appeared as a miniature version (and anticipation) of the town hall tower built some decades later. As an ensemble, all these fountains not only served to embellish the squares and streets. They were also a symbol of Brussels' much-lauded public water supply system. The city maintained an elaborate network of conduits that, starting from the high-lying quarters, supplied fresh water to large parts of the city and fed the numerous fountains in and around the town hall.[20] This abundance of fresh water and the vast number of public fountains were clearly a source of pride for the city, as evidenced by the title of the Braun and Hogenberg plan, which probably reaches back to

---

19 Deligne, 'Édilité et politique', pp. 86-87; although a fountain on the Grand-Place is first mentioned in 1302, Deligne plausibly assumes that the fountain described around 1400 was constructed in the later fourteenth century. It may be added that a possible predecessor (or successor) of this fountain, also dating from the fourteenth century, was found on the market square in front of the town hall of Aachen. This richly decorated, tower-like construction was also replaced by an early modern fountain. The connection between Aachen and Brussels is interesting because it is also manifest in the design of the town hall buildings (see the last section of this contribution). On the fountain in Aachen see Walter, Barbara, 'Fons Vitae und Zeichen städtischen Rechts. Mittelalterliche Stadtbrunnen im Heiligen Römischen Reich' (unpublished doctoral thesis, Albrecht-Ludwigs-Universität Freiburg i. Br., 2015); https://nbn-resolving.org/urn:nbn:de:bsz:25-freidok-1514243), pp. 81-85.

20 Deligne, *Bruxelles et sa rivière*, pp. 83-130.

the early sixteenth century: *Bruxella, urbs aulicorum frequentia, fontium copia, magnificentia principalis aulae, civicae domus [...] nobilissima* (Fig. 9.4).[21] Brussels, in short, was famous for its palace, the court, its town hall – and the fountains.

By mentioning the building's sophisticated water supply system, the town hall description thus implicitly alludes to a famous feature of the entire city. This leads us to a general observation about the role of this description within the manuscript. It is striking that, on the one hand, the city's social groups and political bodies are presented at length and in detail in this booklet.[22] As to the physical city, on the other hand, with its squares and buildings, its many sights and amenities praised by various travellers: all this is neither described nor depicted.[23] Thus, the elaborate description of the town hall seems to compensate for the neglect of other buildings in the manuscript. Moreover, in one passage it explicitly links the magnificence of this building to the excellence of the entire city. Are we therefore dealing with a city encomium in the guise of a building description? It is worth noting that the oldest surviving encomium of Brussels dates from exactly the same period, around 1500.[24] It testifies to a revival of this literary genre which had begun in the fifteenth century, instigated by humanist pioneers such as Leonardo Bruni for Florence or Enea Silvio Piccolomini for the cities north of the Alps.[25] By dealing with past and present, with buildings, institutions, and the people, the Brussels encomium unfolds, despite its brevity, a comprehensive panorama of the city. The text is characterized by the combination of precise descriptions with an overarching and omnipresent symbolism of the number seven (which was to become popular in early modern Brussels). As might be expected, the encomium, too, particularly praises both the 'most excellent' town hall and the city's fountains – among which the seven *fontes principales* stand out.

If the description of the town hall was indeed meant to imply, as proposed here, a praise of the entire city, then it would be an important early document taking a new perspective on town halls. In the cities of the preceding period, the idea of the town hall as a monument representing the municipality was reflected neither in

---

21 Deligne has already referred to this title in this context (Deligne, p. 123). The map by Braun and Hogenberg was published in 1572, but the author of the title seems to have been the Leuven professor Adrianus Barlandus, who had already died in 1538.
22 See the contribution by Billen and Deligne in this volume.
23 One of the few exceptions to this is the (rather sketchy) depiction of the town hall as the background of Joanna's arrival at the *Grote Markt* (*Grand-Place*) on fol. 31ʳ.
24 It is found in a partial copy, probably made in the early sixteenth century, of the *Roedt Privilegie boeck*, a Brussels cartulary for important charters. The copy is now kept in the Royal Library in Brussels (ms 17157-17161) and contains charters from 1477 to 1506, introduced by the city encomium along with a genealogy of the dukes of Brabant, beginning with Adam. The encomium is published in full in Wauters, Alphonse, *Ville de Bruxelles. Inventaire des cartulaires et autres registres faisant partie des archives anciennes de la ville* (Brussels: Bartsoen, 1888), pp. 85-87 (followed by a French translation of the Latin text); the idea that the appreciative description of the Brussels town hall may have been intended as a praise of the whole city was already expressed by Dagmar Eichberger in her brief analysis of the manuscript in Eichberger, 'Illustrierte Festzüge', p. 78.
25 Although some praising descriptions of individual cities have survived from the Middle Ages, it was not until the fifteenth century, in the context of humanism, that this genre underwent an important revival in many cities across large parts of Europe; see Meyer, Carla, *Die Stadt als Thema. Nürnbergs Entdeckung in Texten um 1500* (Ostfildern: Thorbecke, 2009), pp. 245-322.

written sources nor in pictorial representations. Hence, the seals of Netherlandish cities may show representations of various buildings – of churches, steeples, and city gates – but they never depict town halls.[26] It is also hard to imagine that the city leaders and citizens of Mechelen, for example, having built the unprecedented tower of St Rumbold since 1452, saw their city represented in their modest aldermen's house (which was systematically ignored in all visitor accounts). In this light, the description of the Brussels town hall appears once again to be a remarkable document. It is an early literary testimony to the interpretative model according to which the appearance of a town hall reflects the significance and wealth of a city as well as essential structures and features of its political community. It was not until 1500 that this perspective on town halls gained ground in the Netherlandish cities and led to an unprecedented boom in new town hall buildings.[27] In the 1560s, Antwerp too finally had a magnificent town hall built that corresponded to the importance of this metropolis.[28]

The Paintings by Rogier van der Weyden: Instruction and optical Illusion

Probably the most famous attractions of the Brussels town hall were the paintings in the so-called Golden Chamber, created by the city painter Rogier van der Weyden (whose name, however, as are all artists' names, is not revealed in the manuscript). Unfortunately, none of these paintings have survived. They fell victim to the bombardment of Brussels by Louis XIV's troops in 1695.[29] Large parts of the town hall's façades and even its filigree tower withstood the bombardment, but the interior of the building was largely destroyed by subsequent fires. Rogier's panel paintings were lost, like numerous other works by great painters such as Coxie, Rubens, and van Dyck. During the reconstruction of the town hall, the exterior of this venerable building was restored *conform de gothische maniere* and the layout of rooms on the bel étage remained largely unchanged as well.[30] The decoration of the rooms, however, had to be completely renewed after 1695. Today, the town hall's interior is essentially

---

26 The only known example from the Netherlands of a city seal supposed to show a town hall is the oldest seal (late twelfth century) of the small town of Vilvoorde nearby Brussels. However, it is unlikely that this seal actually depicts a town hall or an equivalent building – more than 100 years before Brussels acquired a first aldermen's house. The building depicted probably represents a castle; Köhl, *Das Brüsseler Rathaus*, p. 53.
27 Köhl, pp. 143-71.
28 This is also how Guicciardini puts it in his contemporaneous description of the city: Guicciardini, Lodovico, *Descrittione di tutti i Paesi Bassi* (Antwerp: Silvius, 1567), p. 81; Bevers, Holm, *Das Rathaus von Antwerpen (1561-1565). Architektur und Figurenprogramm* (Hildesheim: Olms, 1985).
29 See the various contributions in *Rond het bombardement von Brussel van 1695. Verwoesting en wederopstanding*, ed. by Arlette Smolar-Meynart (= *Het Tijdschrift van het Gemeentekrediet*, 51, 1997/1).
30 The quotation is found in the files concerning the reconstruction of the town hall: Archives de la Ville de Bruxelles, Liasse 504.

characterized by the interventions of the nineteenth century, when, for example, the two main halls on the *bel étage* were given a neo-Gothic makeover.[31]

The famous 'Golden Chamber', the smaller of the two principal halls, was the most important room in the entire town hall.[32] It served a variety of purposes, for example as a place for major political ceremonies and, above all, for the meetings of the municipal high court, the so-called *Vierschaar*. It was here that the aldermen passed sentences of death. The fact that this court resided in a splendidly furnished room on the *bel étage* was more unusual than it might appear at first sight. The location of a *Vierschaar* was usually a large sober hall on the ground-floor that opened directly onto the public space in order to create – or at least symbolize – the publicity of a trial.[33] In the Golden Chamber, this symbolic openness is reflected in the large windows facing the square and in the opening of the doors during trials. However, due to its location on an upper-floor hall, accessible via interior staircases and intermediate rooms, the distance between the municipal court and the urban community was considerably increased. As a counterpoint to this, the chamber was decorated with a series of monumental paintings with a clear message. They demonstrate that while the judges may physically withdraw from the public sphere, they cannot shake off their responsibility to judge fairly and impartially.

On one side of the chamber, above the aldermen's bench on the east wall, was a painting of the Last Judgement, mentioned as early as 1422.[34] Depictions of this subject were part of the decoration of many medieval courtrooms. They admonished the jury members to judge fairly by reminding them that they themselves will be judged one day.[35] Rogier's cycle of paintings was displayed on the opposite wall. Created from the 1430s onwards and probably completed no earlier than 1450, these paintings were among the first and most famous examples of *exempla iustitiae*, i.e., history paintings on the subject of justice, which adorned many town halls in the Low Countries from the fifteenth century onwards.[36] Due to detailed descriptions of Rogier's paintings and copies made in different media, we at least know their iconography and composition.[37] Two different sets of themes were depicted: on the

---

31 On the alterations of the town hall in the nineteenth century, see Jacqmin, Yves, and Quentin Demeure, *L'Hôtel de Ville de Bruxelles* (Brussels: Musée de la Ville de Bruxelles, 2011).
32 On the disposition, decoration and various uses of the town hall rooms around 1500, see Köhl, *Das Brüsseler Rathaus*, pp. 110-21; on the 'Golden Chamber' in particular pp. 113-15.
33 The traditional location of the Vierschaar is well preserved in the medieval town hall (behind a baroque façade) of 's-Hertogenbosch in North Brabant.
34 De Ridder, Juliaan, *Gerechtigheidstaferelen voor schepenhuizen in de zuidelijke Nederlanden in de 14de, 15de en 16de eeuw* (Brussels: Paleis der Academiën, 1989), p. 39.
35 Albrecht, Stephan, *Mittelalterliche Rathäuser in Deutschland. Architektur und Funktion* (Darmstadt: WBG, 2004), p. 15.
36 On painted *exempla iustitiae* in general and Rogier's Brussels panels in particular see de Ridder, *Gerechtigheidstaferelen*; Martyn, Georges, 'Painted *Exempla Iustitiae* in the Southern Netherlands', in *Symbolische Kommunikation vor Gericht in der Frühen Neuzeit*, ed. by Reiner Schulze (Berlin: Duncker & Humblot, 2006), pp. 335-56; see also the various contributions in the exh. cat. *De kunst van het recht. Drie eeuwen gerechtigheid in beeld*, ed. by Stefan Huygebaert, and others, exh. cat. Bruges, Groeningemuseum (Tielt: Lannoo, 2016).
37 Of particular importance are the tapestries of the Bishop of Lausanne, Georges de Saluzzo, which are now kept in the Historical Museum in Bern. They probably adapted Rogier's composition quite faithfully; see Cetto, Anna Maria, *Der Berner Traian- und Herkinbald-Teppich* (Bern: Bernisches Historisches Museum, 1966), pp. 23-34; the

9.5 Southern Netherlandish (after Rogier van der Weyden), *The Justice of Trajan and Herkinbald* (detail): *The Justice of Herkinbald*, tapestry, c. 1440/50, Bern, Historisches Museum © Buri and Stücky-Schürer, *Burgundische Tapisserien*, p. 43

one hand, the *Justice of the Roman Emperor Trajan*, who had one of his soldiers executed shortly before setting off to war, and on the other hand, the *Justice of the legendary Christian Count Herkinbald*, who condemned and executed his nephew with his own hands. However, the paintings showed not only the acts of justice, but also scenes of miracles in which God manifested his appreciation of these judges. The second panel of the Trajan legend, for example, depicted how Pope Gregory the Great, half a millennium after Trajan's death, was to find an incorrupt tongue in the emperor's skull – the very tongue that had spoken many righteous sentences. Therefore, these images served not only as historical exempla, but also as reminders of the relationship between the aldermen's judging and their being judged before God.

---

most important written source is Calvete de Estrella's detailed report on the paintings, which also reproduces the explanatory texts at the bottom of the pictures; Calvete de Estrella, *El felicissimo viaje*, fols 91^v-94^r.

The Golden Chamber's paintings are exemplary of the iconography of medieval town halls in several respects:[38] firstly, because the pictorial and sculptural cycles of town halls aimed less at self-representation of the office holders meeting in these rooms than at the exaltation of the offices entrusted to them; secondly, because these cycles mostly depict universal subjects without any obvious reference to a specific urban, civic, or local context. These subjects were as suitable for paintings in the town hall of Brussels as for a tapestry in a bishop's residence in the Vaud, the Trajan and Herkinbald tapestry made for the bishop of Lausanne, now kept in Bern, being a quite faithful contemporary copy (Fig. 9.5).[39] In other medieval town halls, pictures with universally valid themes equally predominated: these could be based on ancient, biblical, or legendary materials, their protagonists were rulers, prophets, or saints, and they conveyed norms and values that were equally relevant for people of different estates. References to particular urban or local contexts appeared at best in subordinate details of these paintings. Above all, however, such references can be found in another visual genre in which one might least expect them: in the sequence of dynastic portraits – either paintings or sculptures – that decorated many town halls from this period. In the selection and arrangement of the princes depicted, these cycles revealed a specific urban perspective on territorial history.[40] We will return to this point later.

Equipped with such magnificent artworks with a consensual iconography, the Brussels town hall was frequently visited by the dukes and their guests. The paintings by Rogier in particular were a must-see for all visitors, including Albrecht Dürer in 1520. If we look at the accounts of visitors, we find that before the middle of the sixteenth century, all authors emphasize the high quality of the paintings, especially their illusory effects, enticing the beholders to touch them. Some authors also mention Rogier as the creator of these paintings. None of these authors, however, refer to the subjects depicted.[41] Whether this is due to chance or the brevity of the accounts, these texts are in any case early evidence of an increasing appreciation of art works and artistic skills per se. In addition, they prove that Rogier's panels enjoyed a fame shared only by Van Eyck's Ghent altarpiece.[42] This may give us an idea of how serious the loss of these paintings is, not least for the appropriate assessment of Rogier's oeuvre today.

---

38 A comprehensive study of the medieval iconography of town halls north of the Alps is a desideratum. A brief introduction to the topic is provided by Albrecht, Stephan, 'Rathaus', in *Handbuch der politischen Ikonographie*, ed. by Uwe Fleckner, Martin Warnke, and Hendrik Ziegler, 2 vols (Munich: Beck, 2011), II, pp. 273-79; see also Köhl, Sascha, 'Die Lücken füllen? Zur Repräsentation von „Geschichtsbildern" in und an Rathäusern niederländischer Residenzstädte', in *Geschichtsbilder in Residenzstädten des späten Mittelalters und der frühen Neuzeit. Präsentationen – Räume – Argumente – Praktiken*, ed. by Gerhard Fouquet, and others (Vienna: Böhlau, 2021), pp. 245-70 (248-52).

39 Cetto, *Der Berner Traian- und Herkinbald-Teppich*, pp. 35-40.

40 Köhl, 'Die Lücken füllen', pp. 254-70.

41 The first account of a visit to the town hall, which also deals with the subjects of Rogier's paintings, is found in Calvete de Estrella's book, published in 1552: Calvete de Estrella, *El felicissimo viaje*, fols 91ᵛ-94ʳ.

42 Reynolds, Catherine, 'Bruxelles et la peinture narrative', in: *L'héritage de Rogier van der Weyden. La peinture à Bruxelles 1450-1520*, ed. by Véronique Bücken, and Griet Steyaert, exh. cat., Brussels, Musées royaux des Beaux-Arts (Tielt: Lannoo, 2013), pp. 49-65 (49); on the fame of Jan van Eyck and his Ghent altarpiece in the late fifteenth and sixteenth centuries see Hindriks, Sandra, *Der vlaemsche Apelles – Jan van Eycks früher Ruhm*

The Stone Tower: State of the Art(s) and Archive of the Estates (?)

The bombardment of 1695 hit the rear parts of the town hall complex particularly hard. Various buildings on this site – depicted in some seventeenth century images (Fig. 9.6) – were largely demolished and completely replaced by a uniform baroque building. Among the destroyed buildings in this area, the cloth hall, built as early as 1352 to 1362, was distinguished not only by its size, but also by its striking early 'shed roof'.[43] Next to the cloth hall was another remarkable, even enigmatic building with an unusual roof. It is the so-called *Boterpot* (butter pot), whose name, documented since the seventeenth century, refers to its significant roof shape.[44] This edifice, which is located at the western corner of the town hall complex and whose function as an archive has been documented since 1614, is undoubtedly identical with that western tower which the description praises for its ornate appearance and refers to as the repository of privileges. It is precisely in this passage that our author deviates from the usual scheme of descriptions of the Brussels town hall. While all other authors primarily praise the main tower facing the square as an elegant, artful or 'wonderfully transparent' construction,[45] our author mentions this tower with only a few words. He even underestimates the tower's height by far – which is rather unusual for this literary genre. Instead, he is all the more enthusiastic about the small tower at the back of the town hall, ignored by all other authors. But what is the reason for that?

Unfortunately, we know very little about this tower, not even when it was built. Mina Martens assumed that the tower dates from the early fifteenth century, as the municipality had acquired land in this area in the years around 1400.[46] By contrast, the author of the present essay previously argued – at that time still unaware of the building description analysed here – for a later construction date: around or even after 1500.[47] The latter dating is supported by some advanced architectural forms, which are quite accurately reproduced both in an engraving from the mid-seventeenth century and in a recently rediscovered painting from 1616 (Fig. 9.7).[48] According

---

und die niederländische Renaissance (Petersberg: Imhof, 2019); Kemperdick, Stephan, 'Die Geschichte des Genter Altars', in *Der Genter Altar der Brüder van Eyck. Geschichte und Würdigung*, ed. by Stephan Kemperdick, and Johannes Rößler, exh. cat. Berlin, SMPK, Gemäldegalerie, (Petersberg: Imhof, 2014), pp. 8-69; on the increasing appreciation of artistic skills and aesthetic aspects of artworks in the context of the Mechelen court of the early sixteenth century see Eichberger, Dagmar, *Leben mit Kunst – Wirken durch Kunst. Sammelwesen und Hofkunst unter Margarete von Österreich, Regentin der Niederlande* (Turnhout: Brepols, 2002), pp. 345-67.

43 Dickstein-Bernard, Claire, 'Une ville en expansion (1291-1374)', in *Histoire de Bruxelles*, ed. by Mina Martens (Toulouse: Privat, 1976), pp. 99-138 (113-14).

44 Des Marez, Guillaume, *Guide Illustré de Bruxelles. Monuments Civils et Réligieux* (Brussels: Touring Club Royale de Belgique, 1979; first edition from 1918), pp. 18-19; Martens, 'Initiation à une rencontre', p. 65.; Charles Pergameni, *Les archives historiques de la ville de Bruxelles. Notices et inventaires* (Brussels: Wauthoz-Legrand, 1943), p. X.

45 Albrecht Dürer, for example, praises the tower as a *herrlichen durchsichtigen thurn* ('magnificent transparent tower'); Dürer, Albrecht, *Tagebuch der Reise in die Niederlande*, ed. by Fedja Anzelewsky (Zurich: Seefeld, 1988), p. 15.

46 Martens, 'Initiation à une rencontre', p. 65.

47 Köhl, *Das Brüsseler Rathaus*, p. 201, no. 574.

48 The engraving is by Abraham Santvoort; it shows the building complex from an unusual lateral perspective. The painting is by David Noveliers and measures 118 × 327 cm; it shows the lateral town hall façade as the

9.6 Abraham van Santvoort, *town hall of Brussels, bird's eye view of the building complex depicting the Boterpot on the right*, engraving, c. 1650 © *Les maisons de la Grand-Place*, p. 197

9.7 David Noveliers, *Parade of Giants and of the Horse Bayard* (detail), panel painting, 1616, Spain, private collection

to these images, the tower rose with two lavishly decorated storeys above a plain ground floor. Remarkably, there are a number of structural differences between the two upper storeys. The first floor had a rectangular ground plan, while the second floor had a squared shape; a peculiar small half-storey bay with a monopitch roof mediated between the rectangle and the square. Furthermore, the two storeys differ from each other regarding the articulation of the façade: while on the lower storey, superimposed tabernacles frame large (and mostly blind) tracery windows, the upper storey appears to be tightly structured by slender columns. Perhaps these differences indicate a change of plan, but they may also result from a two-stage construction process, with the lower storey having been built together with the identically designed annex building to the right. A precise dating of the tower's lower storeys seems impossible; even their construction in the early fifteenth century, as suggested by Martens, could well be. The upper storey appears stylistically far more advanced due to its colonnaded structure. It was only after 1500 that façades of public buildings were frequently articulated in this way. Examples of this are the *Maison du Roi* or *Broodhuis* in Brussels (from 1515) and the town hall in Zoutleeuw (from 1526).⁴⁹ In contrast to these two buildings, however, the columns of the *Boterpot* do not bear flat arches, but a kind of cornice, which gives the façade an almost classical appearance – despite the elongated proportions of the columns. Does this façade, which appears both peculiar and advanced, really date from the fifteenth century – or is it the result of alterations to the tower in the decades after 1500? We do not know.

The distinctive butter-pot roof, too, could have been built after 1500. However, there is some evidence that the author of the description had precisely this roof in mind when he wrote that the tower was built (*structa*) *and* roofed (*tecta*) in an admirable way. In general, roofs of this kind were not entirely new in the Low Countries around 1500.⁵⁰ In the decades before, different variants of bulbous spires had already been erected, at a very early date, around 1440, on the octagonal baptistery chapel of St Martin's in Halle (near Brussels). Later in date are several towers in Bruges, such as the one of the Jerusalem Church, built around 1470 as an interpretation of the Church of the Holy Sepulchre, and the towers of the Chapel of St Basil and the Holy Blood (built shortly before 1496) (Fig. 9.8), in which the highly venerated relic of the Holy Blood was kept.⁵¹ In all these cases, the extraordinary roof shapes obviously referred to buildings in the Holy Land. Inspiration for these motifs and their design may have come from contemporary painters, who enriched their silhouettes of Jerusalem with many domed buildings – some of them fantasy architectures, others precise portraits of real buildings such as the Church of the Holy Sepulchre or the Dome of the Rock.⁵² In the case of the *Boterpot*, however, there is no obvious link to Jerusalem. Accordingly, its façade lacked those clearly historicizing or orientalising forms that

---

background for the spectacles of the *Ommegang* in the Rue Tête d'Or. This painting belongs to a famous series depicting the celebrations of the *Ommegang* of 1615. It is now in a private collection and was only recently (re)discovered and published by Sabine van Sprang; see van Sprang, Sabine, *Denijs van Alsloot (vers 1568-1625/26). Peintre paysagiste au service de la cour des archiducs Albert et Isabelle*, 2 vols (Turnhout: Brepols, 2014), II: *Les festivités du Papegai en 1615 à Bruxelles*, cat. F4 (pp. 332-35 and 447-48); I owe thanks to Sabine van Sprang (Academia Belgica, Rome) and Jean-Paul Heerbrant (Centre Albert Marinus, Woluwe-Saint-Lambert) for their helpful information and advice.

49 De Jonge, Krista, 'Bouwen in de stad', in *Gotiek in het hertogdom Brabant*, ed. by Krista de Jonge, Piet Geleyns, and Markus Hörsch (Leuven: Peeters, 2009), pp. 101-36 (124-30); on the town hall of Zoutleeuw see Meischke, Ruud, 'De stedelijke bouwopgaven tussen 1450 en 1500', in *Keldermans. Een architectonisch netwerk in de Nederlanden*, ed. by Herman Janse, and others (The Hague: Staatsuitgeverij, 1987), pp. 87-103 (96-97); on the Maison du Roi see Frieda van Tyghem, 'Bestuursgebouwen van Keldermans in Brabant en Vlaanderen', in *Keldermans. Een architectonisch netwerk*, pp. 105-30 (105-09).

50 De Jonge, Krista 'La toiture pyramidale à bulbe, signe identitaire de l'architecture Habsbourg d'origine brabançonne au XVIᵉ siècle', in *Toits d'Europe. Formes, structures, décors et usages du toit à l'époque moderne (XVᵉ-XVIIᵉ siècle)*, ed. by Monique Chatenet, and Alexandre Gady (Paris: Picard, 2016), pp. 25-46.

51 It is a Romanesque double chapel whose upper storey, together with the towers, was rebuilt in the second half of the fifteenth century. Exact construction dates have not been handed down, but a source from 1496, referring to the upper chapel, mentions new stained-glass windows with portraits of Flemish counts *in de nieuwe cappelle daer de thoorenkens op staen*; Gailliard, Jean, *Recherches historiques sur la chapelle du Saint-Sang* (Bruges: Gailliard, 1846), p. 99.

52 Moore, Kathryn Blair, *The Architecture of the Christian Holy Land. Reception from Late Antiquity through the Renaissance* (Cambridge: University Press, 2017), pp. 169-82; Born, Wolfgang, 'The Introduction of the Bulbous Dome into Gothic Architecture and its Subsequent Development', *Speculum*, 19/2 (1944), 208-21 (209-10); De Jonge, 'La toiture pyramidale', pp. 30-32.

9.8 Bruges, *Chapel of St Basil and the Holy Blood*, 12th and 15th centuries © Sascha Köhl

characterize both the painted towers of Jerusalem and the above-mentioned towers in Bruges.

In the secular context, similar bulbous spires were much rarer in the fifteenth century. It is true that they became fashionable among the Brabant nobility around 1500 (Fig. 9.9), but none of the bulbous spires erected for noble residences can be reliably dated before 1500.[53] Moreover, the roof of the *Boterpot* differed from most of these spires in a detail that may seem negligible but points to a fundamentally

---

53 De Jonge, 'La toiture pyramidale', p. 27; unfortunately, we do not have exact construction dates for the probably most prominent early examples of such towers of a noble residence: the towers of the Brussels court of Nassau, which was built from the 1480s into the sixteenth century (and largely demolished in the eighteenth century); see Meijering, Stefan, and Bram Vannieuwenhuyze, 'Het Brusselse hof van Nassau. De oprichting van een laatmiddeleeuwse stadsresidentie', *Revue belge de philologie et d'histoire*, 88/2 (2010), 349-76; at exactly the same time as in the Netherlands, the first towers with bulbous roofs were built at the noble residences in France; Guillaume, Jean, 'Architectures imaginaires et "nouvelles inventions". L'apparition des toits cintrés en France au XVIe siècle', in *Toits d'Europe. Formes, structures, décors et usages du toit à l'époque moderne (XVe-XVIIe siècle)*, ed. by Monique Chatenet, and Alexandre Gady (Paris: Picard, 2016), pp. 9-24 (9-11).

different construction: the ridges of its roof were accentuated by sturdy, crocketed ribs. Such ribs are rarely found on the wooden spires of Brabant's noble residences, but frequently on bulbous stone spires built in the fifteenth and early sixteenth centuries in a wider European context between Vienna and London.[54] One of the most beautiful towers of this kind, however, was neither made of stone nor designed by an architect: it is the tower of St Barbara on the St John triptych by the painter Hans Memling (1479) (Fig. 9.10). This architectural bijou may seem familiar to us in more than one respect, most notably with its colonnaded upper storey and the curved stone roof with crocketed ribs. This tower was more than a mere attribute of the saint. A closer look reveals that it was also a sacramental tower, which held a monstrance.[55] It served both symbolically and compositionally as a counterpart to the Christ lamb on the opposite side of the painting. Thus, a reference to the holy sites would again be conceivable. In its overall appearance, however, Barbara's tower differs markedly from the towers that, for example, dominate the cityscape of Jerusalem on Memling's Turin panorama of Christ's Passion. While most of these towers were clearly outdated or exotic in style, Barbara's tower appears as a contemporary gothic interpretation of such towers, combining iconographic motifs with formal inventions in a pioneering architectural synthesis. This raises the questions of whether Memling (who must have known Brussels very well) was referring to existing buildings such as the *Boterpot* – or, vice versa, whether the creations of Memling and his colleagues inspired the architects of the time. Of course, it requires profound professional knowledge to translate into

9.9 Heverlee, *Arenberg castle*, 15th and 16th centuries © Wikimedia Commons

---

54 A particularly early and elaborate example is the bulbous openwork tracery spire of St. Maria am Gestade in Vienna, built in the 1420s. Similar but smaller openwork spires are found on the turrets of Cologne town hall (stair turret of the tower, c. 1414) and Passau Cathedral ('Stephanstürmchen', last third of the fifteenth century), while a massive, domed stone spire was planned for the tower of St Bartholomew in Frankfurt from the first half of the fifteenth century. The spires of the turrets of King's College Chapel in Cambridge and the tower-like buttresses of Westminster Abbey's Lady Chapel are massive as well. These English examples were created in the early sixteenth century, in an environment in which many Netherlandish artists were active.

55 Lane, Barbara G., *Hans Memling. Master Painter in Fifteenth-century Bruges* (London: Harvey Miller, 2009), pp. 179-86; Memling – or a workshop that collaborated with him – later used the motif of the bulbous spire (again) in another key work for St John's Hospital in Bruges, albeit in miniature format: bulbous spires are found on the pinnacles of the St Ursula shrine (1489); see Lobelle-Caluwé, Hilde, 'Het Ursulaschrijn van Hans Memling. Ontwerp, constructie en oorspronkelijk uitzicht', in *Hans Memling*, ed. by Dirk de Vos, 2 vols, exh. cat., Bruges, Groeningemuseum (Brussels: Ludion, 1994), II: Essays, pp. 89-100.

stone what the painters invented on panels, paper, or parchment, unburdened by structural concerns. Nevertheless, the painters' impact on architects has hardly ever been as strong as in this generation, when many painters were able to render architecture with unprecedented precision and sought to design complex architectural forms with boundless creativity.[56]

We can therefore conclude that the tower praised in the description for its stone roof (*sine aliquo ligno*) seems to be largely identical to the *Boterpot* as it appeared in reproductions dating from the seventeenth century. The tower would thus be a testimony to the growing interest in such bulbous roofs that found expression in various artistic disciplines from the early fifteenth century onwards. In view of the advanced design of the tower's upper parts, however, these were probably not built considerably earlier than 1496. This would still make the roof a remarkably early example of such a bulbous spire in a secular context – created in a still experimental phase immediately before a limited repertory of types for such spires became established. The prominent position of the tower in the town hall description, in which it explicitly represented the artistic life of Brussels in general, may therefore be due to the fact that it was considered a

9.10 Hans Memling, *St John Altarpiece*, central panel, (detail): *St Barbara sitting next to her tower*, oil on wood, 1479, Bruges, Sint-Janshospitaal / Memlingmuseum, photo: Alexey Yakovlev © Wikimedia Commons

---

56 It is true that the relationship between painting and architecture had already been very close in the second half of the thirteenth century, when painters (as well as artists from other disciplines) adopted the formal repertoire of the Rayonnant style. In contrast to the situation in the later fifteenth century, however, the painters had then been mostly or exclusively the receiving party in this interdisciplinary relationship. On the exchange between painters and architects in the Netherlands in the fifteenth and early sixteenth centuries, especially with regard to architectural design, see Wilson, Christopher, *The Gothic Cathedral. The architecture of the great church, 1130-1530* (London: Thames & Hudson, 1990), pp. 246-47; Campbell, Lorne, 'Rogier as a designer of works of art in Media other than oil on panel', in *Rogier van der Weyden in context*, ed. by Lorne Campbell, and others (Paris: Peeters, 2012), pp. 23-43 (23-24); Kavaler, Matt, *Renaissance Gothic. Architecture and the Arts in Northern Europe. 1470-1540* (New Haven: Yale University Press, 2012), pp. 242-55; see also the various essays by Stephan Hoppe, which, while mostly devoted to the meaning of representation or reinterpretation of historical architecture, also address the interdisciplinary exchange between painting and architecture in general; see, for example, Hoppe, Stephan, 'Translating the Past. Local Romanesque Architecture in Germany and its Fifteenth-Century Reinterpretation', in *The Quest for an Appropriate Past in Literature, Art and Architecture*, ed. by Karl A. E. Enenkel, and Konrad A. Ottenheym (Leiden: Brill, 2019), pp. 511-85.

contemporary creation. The message was that forty years after the completion of the town hall's main tower and thirty years after Rogier's death, Brussels was still a vibrant artistic hub.

However, the special attention that the description pays to this tower may also stem from its use, which is mentioned only in passing, but hardly by chance: the tower served as an archive of privileges. This function as a repository of precious documents might also explain its fireproof construction and the small number of windows. While it was common to store the municipal documents in massive, vaulted towers, it was rather unusual to build a tower that served only (or mainly) this purpose. In most places in Brabant, the magistrates used existing towers, especially church towers.[57] In Brussels, too, important privileges were kept in the tower of the parish church of St Nicholas and in the treasury of the collegiate church of St Michael and Gudula, at least until the Calvinist episode around 1580.[58] Why, then, did the magistrate build another (and particularly splendid) tower for the municipal archive? We do not have an answer to this question – perhaps because it is the wrong question. We should bear in mind that the Brussels town hall was the central meeting place not only for the representatives of the municipality, but also for those of the Estates of the duchy. The Estates' magnificent assembly hall in the town hall's Baroque wing, built exactly on the former site of the *Boterpot*, is a reminder of this. Since the 1480s at the latest, the prelates, the nobility, and the cities of Brabant each had their own room in the town hall complex.[59] By this time, Brussels was also already the place where documents relevant to the entire duchy and its Estates were collected and preserved.[60] Brussels received, for example, one of the two original charters of the 'Great Privilege' of 1477 issued for Brabant.[61] We do not know where exactly these documents were kept, but the *Boterpot* seems to be a suitable place. Might it be possible, then, that this tower served to store not just *any* privileges, but also, and especially, *the* Great Privilege along with other fundamental charters of the duchy?

While we cannot determine the exact function of this tower, there is little doubt that the reference to its archival use in the description was intended to remind the princess of those privileges that had been granted by the dukes, but repeatedly

---

57 Van Uytven, 'Flämische Belfriede', pp. 126-28; in Flanders and northern France, it was often the belfry that was used for this purpose.
58 Pergameni, *Les archives historiques*, p. X.
59 The chambers of the prelates, nobles and cities are mentioned several times in the few surviving city accounts from this period, which date from between 1485 and 1507 (National Archives of Belgium, Chambre des comptes / Rekenkamer, 30.942-30.952); see for the use of Brussels town hall as a meeting place of the Estates of Brabant, Köhl, *Das Brüsseler Rathaus*, p. 119, and Wils, Lode, 'De werking van de Staten van Brabant omstreeks 1550-1650 volgens Leuvense Archiefbronnen', *Standen en Landen*, 5 (1953), 3-19 (6).
60 For this reason, many medieval documents of the Estates of Brabant were destroyed in the bombardment of 1695; see Damen, Mario, 'Prelaten, edelen en steden. De samenstelling van de Staten van Brabant in de vijftiende eeuw', *Bulletin de la Commission royale d'histoire. Académie royale de Belgique*, 182 (2016), 5-274 (7); Augustyn, Beatrijs, 'Staten van Brabant', in *De gewestelijke en lokale overheidsinstellingen in Brabant en Mechelen*, ed. by Raymond Van Uytven, and others, 2 vols (Brussels: Algemeen Rijksarchief, 2000), I, pp. 97-132 (129).
61 *1477. Le privilège général et les privilèges régionaux de Marie de Bourgogne pour les Pays-Bas*, ed. by Wim Blockmans (Kortrijk-Heule: UGA, 1985), p. 86, and the essay by Raymond Van Uytven, '1477 in Brabant', in Blockmans, pp. 253-85 (280).

violated in the preceding troubled period.[62] With the subtle reference to these privileges and the less subtle praise of the city's arsenal, Brussels presents itself as a self-confident city that, for all its loyalty, is ready to defend its rights.

Conclusion: a warm Welcome for the City's most distinguished Resident

However, the description (and the entire manuscript) concludes with some particularly warm words addressed directly to the Princess – final words of welcome from the traditional and, as many people in Brussels hoped, future seat of power. At the time of Joanna's arrival, Brussels had housed the main ducal residence in Brabant for at least two centuries and was also one of the most important cities of the Burgundian dukes for more than sixty years.[63] This was of crucial importance for Brussels, as it was both a central component of the city's identity and an essential basis for the urban economy. However, its status as a residence city remained contested throughout the fifteenth century. The still largely itinerant dukes often stayed in other major cities such as Bruges, Ghent, and Lille, and in the last decades of the century, Mechelen in particular gained importance both as a ducal residence and as a seat of administration. Therefore, Joanna's entry must also be seen against this background of an open competition for the status of 'capital city'.

For much of the fifteenth century, the magistrate of Brussels pursued a policy that Robert Stein has termed *residentiepolitiek*:[64] Due to the constantly changing political and dynastic constellations in this period, the magistrate had to make ever new efforts to convince the dukes to reside in Brussels. One of the city's main strategies for attracting the dukes was to pay for their building projects as well as for those of their courtiers and the administration. Thus, Brussels not only financed the extension of the ducal gardens and the construction of the majestic palace hall, but also subsidized the residences of influential families such as the Croÿ (1459) and the Nassau (1480s). In the same year as Joanna arrived, the magistrate provided the chancellor of Brabant with a new residence in the city.[65] However, Brussels' various campaigns to promote itself as the ideal residence city were not limited to such acts of generosity towards the dukes, courtiers and officials; they also affected the city's self-conception and

---

62 *Histoire du Brabant du duché à nos jours*, ed. by Raymond van Uytven, and others (Zwolle: Waanders, 2004), pp. 219-20.
63 Dickstein-Bernard, Claire, 'Bruxelles résidence princière (1375-1500)', in *Histoire de Bruxelles*, ed. by Mina Martens (Toulouse: Privat, 1976), pp. 139-65; Billen, Claire, 'Bruxelles première ville du Brabant, capitale de fait des Pays-Bas', in *Bruxelles*, ed. by Claire Billen, and Jean-Marie Duvosquel, pp. 58-69; van Uytven, Raymond, 'De opgang van een hoofdstad', in *Met passer en penseel*, pp. 129-32; Stein, Robert, 'Brussel: de Coudenberg. De groei van een regeringscentrum', in *Plaatsen van herinnering. Nederland van prehistorie tot Beeldenstorm*, ed. by Wim Blockmans, and Herman Pleij, (Amsterdam: Bakker, 2007), pp. 326-37.
64 Stein, Robert, *Politiek en historiografie. Het ontstaansmilieu van Brabantse kronieken in de eerste helft van de vijftiende eeuw* (Leuven: Peeters, 1994).
65 Dickstein-Bernard, 'Bruxelles résidence princière', pp. 152-54; on the building of the new chancellery, see Henne, Alexandre, and Alphonse Wauters, *Histoire de la ville de Bruxelles*, 3 vols (Brussels: Périchon, 1845), III, p. 293.

self-representation. The magistrate commissioned various historiographical, literary, and theatrical works and thus made ample use of various media and performances (not least during the ducal entries) to convey the idea of Brussels as the traditional centre of an ancient and noble duchy to the widest possible audience.[66]

It was precisely in this historical context that the Brussels town hall was built.[67] The foundation stone was laid in 1401, shortly before the (foreseeable) arrival of the Burgundian dynasty in Brabant. Plans for the extension of the building, on the other hand, have been documented since the 1430s, after the duchy had fallen to Philip the Good and Brussels suddenly found itself in an intensified competitive situation among the ducal residences in the Burgundian Netherlands. By building a town hall that was without equal in these territories, the Brussels magistrate sent a message that was hard to miss. This message would have been even more explicit, however, if an important component of the town hall had been realized in toto: the cycle of life-size sculptures on the façade. Most of the tabernacles, which are now filled with figures from the nineteenth and twentieth centuries, initially remained empty.[68] By the middle of the sixteenth century, only a couple of sculptures had been executed on the right corner turret (which did not survive either the bombardment of 1695 or the subsequent reconstruction). According to the pictorial sources of the seventeenth century (Figs 9.6, 9.7 and 9.11), their clothing and attributes, as well as the coats of arms under their feet, indicate that they represented rulers, probably dukes and duchesses of Brabant. This would correspond to the common iconography of such sculptural cycles in the wider region, most of which were dedicated to the territory or realm represented by a series of lords, princes, or kings.[69]

The first of these sculptural cycles was probably made for the town hall of Aachen in the third quarter of the fourteenth century.[70] Representing kings and emperors, these figures refer equally to the building's history as Charlemagne's former palace, to its function as a stage for coronation ceremonies, and to the city's status as the first of the imperial cities. A few years later, another magnificent town hall with a

---

66 Stein, Robert, 'Cultuur en politiek in Brussel. Wat beoogde het Brusselse stadsbestuur bij de annexatie van de plaatselijke Ommegang?', in *Op belofte van Profijt. Stadsliteratuur en burgermoraal in de Nederlandse letterkunde van de middeleeuwen*, ed. by Herman Pleij, and others (Amsterdam: Prometheus, 1991), pp. 228-43; Pleij, 'Cultuur in context. Het spel van Menych Sympel (1466) als spiegel van de Brusselse politieke verhoudingen', *Bijdragen en mededelingen betreffende de geschiedenis der Nederlanden*, 113 (1998), 289-321; Sleiderink, Remco, 'Grootse ambities. Culturele initiatieven van de stad Brussel ten tijde van Filips de Goede', in *De Macht van het schone woord. Literatuur in Brussel van de 14de tot de 18de eeuw*, ed. by Jozef Janssens, and Remco Sleiderink (Leuven: Davidsfonds, 2003), pp. 106-23.
67 On the history of the construction, see Köhl, *Das Brüsseler Rathaus*, pp. 64-73, on the historical context, pp. 143-48, and Köhl, Sascha, 'Brussels town hall in context. Architectural models, historical background, political strategies', in *L'hôtel de Ville de Bruxelles – Bilan de trois années d'études du bâti*, ed. by Vincent Heymans (= *Studia Bruxellae*, 12, 2018), pp. 236-54.
68 *Les sentinelles de l'histoire. Le décor sculpté des façades de l'hôtel de ville de Bruxelles*, ed. by Vincent Heymans (Brussels: Ville de Bruxelles, 2000).
69 On sculptural cycles of gothic town halls in general and the possible plans for the Brussels cycle in particular, see Köhl, 'Die Lücken füllen', pp. 254-70.
70 Albrecht, *Mittelalterliche Rathäuser*, pp. 144-50; Judith Ley, 'Das Rathaus der Freien Reichsstadt Aachen. Der Umbau der karolingischen Aula Regia zum gotischen Krönungspalast', in *Rathäuser und andere kommunale Bauten*, ed. by Michael Goer (Marburg: Jonas, 2010), pp. 159-74; Köhl, *Das Brüsseler Rathaus*, pp. 129-33.

9.11 *The town hall of Brussels* (detail): *The right corner of the town hall with figures of rulers*, engraving, in Puteanus, *Bruxella* (1646)

similar sculptural cycle was built in Bruges.[71] Construction began in 1376, on the eve of the dynastic transition to the House of Burgundy. The figures on the façade mainly represented the counts of Flanders, starting with Baldwin Iron Arm, who was revered in Bruges as a founding father of the county with special ties to the city. There is therefore little doubt about the message of this cycle: Bruges is the traditional centre of an ancient and largely independent county. In the following decades, as the dukes of Burgundy inherited or usurped more and more Netherlandish principalities, the example of Bruges town hall was adopted by many other capitals of neighbouring territories, such as Leuven in Brabant, Middelburg in Zeeland, Mons in Hainaut, and Arras in Artois. All of these cities constructed magnificent town halls, characterized by elaborately decorated façades with many tabernacles reserved for sculptures. In many instances, these tabernacles remained empty, but wherever they were filled with sculptures, as was the case with the town hall of Middelburg, these figures mainly represented a sequence of local rulers. These outstanding town halls were thus primarily

---

71 *600 jaar Brugs stadhuis. 1376-1976*, ed. by André Vandewalle, Guillaume Michiels, and Ant Michiels (Brussels: Bank Brussel Lambert, 1976), pp. 7-10; Janssens de Bisthoven, Alin, 'Het beeldhouwwerk van het Brugsche stadhuis', *Gentsche bijdragen tot de kunstgeschiedenis*, 10 (1944), 7-81; Köhl, *Das Brüsseler Rathaus*, pp. 133-37; Köhl, 'Die Lücken füllen', pp. 254-58.

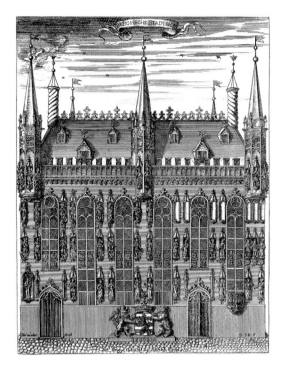

9.12 *Façade of the Bruges town hall with the counts' statues*, engraving, in Danckaert, *Stadhuys* (1711)

manifestations of the pre-eminence of the cities within the respective principality.[72] However, all of them were surpassed by Brussels, which – according to its self-image and ambitions – strove to outdo not only its fiercest rival in Brabant, Leuven, but also all other cities in the Netherlands.

This town hall must also have made a strong impression on Joanna. The arrival of the princess on the *Grote Markt* (*Grand-Place*) was the triumphant climax of the entry ceremony. The brightly lit town hall offered the princess a final, particularly imposing image of the entire city: the building united many of Brussels' amenities and virtues, embodied the city's loyal yet self-confident attitude, and demonstrated its paramount importance in the Netherlands. The message of the town hall seems to have been received, as well as the description's final request that the Princess may always appreciate 'all this': the town hall, the city, and the citizens. Joanna indeed resided predominantly in Brussels,[73] and her son, Charles V, eventually made the city a centre of

---

72 Köhl, *Das Brüsseler Rathaus*, pp. 152-62; Wim Blockmans, and Walter Prevenier already pointed in this direction in their overview of the history of the Burgundian Netherlands, interpreting the town halls of Bruges and Brussels as a proclamation of the cities' primacy in Flanders and Brabant respectively: Blockmans, Wim, and Walter Prevenier, *The Promised Lands. The Low Countries under Burgundian Rule* (Philadelphia: Pennsylvania University Press, 1999), pp. 220-21.

73 See the contribution by Raymond Fagel in this volume.

Netherlandish and, to a certain extent, European politics.[74] It goes without saying, that the city leaders of the fifteenth century could not have foreseen this development. However, thanks to their ambitious policy, they paved the way for Brussels to become a European metropolis and provided the city with a town hall that befitted this status.

---

74 Billen, 'Bruxelles première ville', pp. 62-65; Wellens, Robert, 'La domination espagnole (1506-1700)', in *Histoire de Bruxelles*, ed. by Mina Martens (Toulouse: Privat, 1976), pp. 193-232 (193-96).

ANNE-MARIE LEGARÉ

Illustrating Contemporary Events in Watercolour on Paper[*]

A New Genre of Memorial Books

▼ **ABSTRACT** The use of paper in combination with watercolours and pen drawings might seem a surprising choice for illustrating the Entry of Joanna of Castile into Brussels. It is however a common choice when documenting unique events as quickly as possible, allowing to escape the heavy technical constraints of working on vellum. The focus of this article is to present a few manuscripts from the fifteenth and sixteenth centuries, coming from different regional contexts – Flanders, the Holy Roman Empire, Provence, Lorraine – which belong to a similar genre of books, that encompasses historical or political events with strong performative elements. The books' physical appearance is an additional characteristic as they are mostly large, written on paper and executed in a fast and energetic style by using coloured drawings. Such manuscripts were often works produced with the high nobility and the upper middle classes in mind. Joanna's Entry manuscript is a telling testimony to this endeavour as the chosen genre – coloured pen drawing on paper – was considered more than worthy for this significant occasion.

▼ **KEYWORDS** Paper, watercolour, drawings, style, Flanders, the Holy Roman Empire, Provence, Lorraine, high nobility, performative events.

The manuscript of the *Entry of Joanna of Castile* made in Brussels in 1496 is in perfect condition. It survived from the vicissitudes of time despite the fragility of its support, paper. The use of paper in combination with watercolour drawings might seem surprising at first sight. It is however a frequent choice when intending to document

---

[*] I would like to thank Jane Davison, Susie Speakman Sutch, and Dagmar Eichberger for their comments and for helping to improve the English version of this essay.

A Spectacle for a Spanish Princess, ed. by Dagmar H. Eichberger, Burgundica, 35 (Turnhout: Brepols, 2023), pp. 207–226

unique events as quickly as possible. Such events could be political or ephemeral[1], often related to theatre and performance, which incorporate significant elements of orality, such as dialogues and recitations, together with gestures.[2]

For a long time, this type of work on paper was judged as a minor form, sober and without luxury, and therefore cheap.[3] Such negative assessments, based on purely economic considerations, were rightly rejected in favour of aesthetic values.[4] Nowadays we speak of 'pen drawings coloured with washes' or 'transparent gouache'.[5] We now use a terminology that is less pejorative than in the past, avoiding unfortunate expressions such as 'bad figures', 'mediocre' or even 'coarse miniatures', as can be found in eighteenth century inventories.[6] The technique used for the illustrations of this manuscript is, on the contrary, very refined, in some places displaying highlights painted in either gold or silver. The gold is mainly applied to the ceremonial dress of Joanna of Castile in the miniature of her official entry (Fig. 10.1). Shell gold is found on the badges worn on the hats of several participants. It is also often used to highlight a queen or king in mythological or Old Testament scenes. Silver is more difficult to detect because of oxidation which has completely blackened the surface. The now unsightly features must be imagined by the viewer as images with many touches of light that would provide the whole picture with shimmering effects. It should be noted that silver is also used for the insignia on the sleeves of the shooters' guilds. Recourse to paper and watercolour made it possible to escape the technical constraints of working with opaque gouache on vellum to provide a product that was rapidly available. Books executed in this genre would first and foremost have a documentary value, capturing a political and/or theatrical event, ephemeral but quickly crystallised into descriptions and images in such a way that they could be effectively imprinted in the memory.[7] My intention here is to present a few manuscripts from the fifteenth and sixteenth centuries, coming from different regional contexts – Flanders,

---

1 Eichberger, Dagmar, 'The *Tableau vivant*, an Ephemeral Art Form in Burgundian Civic Festivities', *Parergon*, 6 (1988), 37-64, http://archiv.ub.uni-heidelberg.de/artdok/869/.
2 Weigert, Laura, '"Vocamus Personagias": The Enlivened Figures of Ephemeral Stagings', in *French Visual Culture and the Making of Medieval Theater*, ed. by Laura Weigert (New York: Cambridge University Press, 2015), pp. 27-73.
3 For a good summary of the issue, see Lavenus, Marielle, 'Lecture renouvelée des miniatures du Maître de Wavrin: *L'Histoire de Gérard de Nevers* du manuscrit Bruxelles, KBR, ms 9631' (unpublished doctoral thesis, University of Lille, 2021), pp. 3-7.
4 This is the position adopted by Pascal Schandel in his pioneering study of the Master of Wavrin: Schandel, Pascal, 'Le maître de Wavrin et les miniaturistes lillois à l'époque de Philippe le Bon et de Charles le Téméraire' (unpublished doctoral thesis, University of Strasbourg, 1997). François Avril had already noticed it: '[C]e qui procédait peut-être à l'origine de contraintes matérielles se transforma peu à peu en parti-pris esthétique', see Avril, François, and Nicole Reynaud, eds, *Les manuscrits à peinture en France (1440-1520)*, (Paris, BnF, 1993), pp. 98-99.
5 See the introduction by Dagmar Eichberger.
6 Legaré, Anne-Marie, 'Les cent quatorze manuscrits de Bourgogne choisis par le Comte d'Argenson pour le roi Louis XV', *Bulletin du bibliophile*, 2 (1998), 289, 316, 317 and 318. Unfortunately, such unthinking value judgements still appear in some of the current BnF entries describing the watercolour drawings of the Master of Wavrin.
7 Lalou, Élizabeth, and Darwin Smith, 'Pour une typologie des manuscrits du théâtre médiéval', in *Le Théâtre de la cité dans l'Europe médiévale*, ed. by Jean-Claude Aubailly (Stuttgart: Heinz), pp. 569-79.

10.1 Southern Netherlandish, *The Festive Entry of Joanna of Castile into Brussels*, fol. 31^r: *Joanna of Castile and the members of the Great Crossbow guild reach the Grand-Place in Brussels*, coloured pen drawings, 1496, Berlin, SMPK, Kupferstichkabinett, ms. 78 D5 © SMPK

Germany, Provence, Lorraine. These case studies belong to a similar genre of books, that encompasses historical or political events with strong performative elements. The books' physical appearance is an additional characteristic as they are mostly large, written on paper and executed in a fast and energetic style by using pen drawings enhanced by watercolour.

The *Excellente Cronike van Vlaenderen*

The *Excellente Cronike van Vlaenderen* or *Chronike van den Lande van Vlaendre* of 1480 lends itself well to a first comparison with Joanna's *Entry*. This chronicle deals with the history of the foresters and the counts of Flanders since 613.[8] It is dedicated to Mary of Burgundy and Maximilian of Austria and to their children Philip the Fair and Margaret of Austria, the future regent of the Netherlands. The author, probably the Bruges rhetorician Anthonis de Roovere (*c*. 1430-1482), set to work around 1480.[9] Numerous manuscripts and printed copies of this *Cronike* testify to its importance.[10] Seven of the preserved manuscripts contain drawings with washes.[11] Did any of these belong to Mary of Burgundy? Although there is no evidence that Mary herself owned a copy of the *Cronike*, she may have been aware of the work, as Anthonis de Roovere was well introduced to the ducal family. From 1466 onwards, for example, Charles the Bold had him paid a yearly annuity of six Flemish pounds for services rendered, but especially for writing and presenting moralities, entertainments and other joyful works of rhetoric.[12] In 1468 he helped to organise the festivities ordered for the marriage of Charles to Margaret of York, and in 1477 he was responsible for the creation of three *tableaux vivants* for the Joyous Entry of Mary of Burgundy into Bruges. Unfortunately, the *tableaux vivants*, which have now disappeared, have left no iconographical traces, but it is conceivable that the manuscript of the *Entry of Joanna*

---

8 See the recent study by Demets, Lisa, *Onvoltooid verleden. De handschriften van de Excellente Cronike van Vlaenderen in de laatmiddeleeuwse Vlaamse steden* (Hilversum: Verloren, 2020).

9 On this *Chronicle* and its author, see Oosterman, Johan, 'Anthonis de Roovere. Het werk: overlevering, toeschrijving en plaatsbepaling', *Jaarboek De Fonteine* (1995-1996), 29-104; Johan Oosterman, 'De Excellente cronike van Vlaenderen en Anthonis de Roovere', *Tijdschrift voor Nederlandse Taal- en Letterkunde*, 118 (2002), 22-37. On the Douai library manuscript in particular, see Vandekerckhove, Simon, 'De Chronike van den lande van Vlaendre: Studie van het handschrift en uitgave van fol. 148^v tot fol. 415$^{v'}$ (unpublished Master thesis, University of Ghent, 2006-2007), 172-73. http://lib.ugent.be/fulltxt/RUG01/001/311/469/RUG01-001311469_2010_0001_AC.pdf.

10 In 1531, Willem Vorsterman produced another edition in Antwerp.

11 Douai, Bibliothèque Marceline Desbordes-Valmore, ms 1110; Bruges, Openbare Bibliotheek, Historisch Fonds, ms 436 and ms 437; Brussels, KBR, ms 13073-74; New York, Morgan Library & Museum, ms M 435; The Hague, KB, ms 132 A 13; Paris, BnF, ms Néerlandais 106; see Haufricht, Jocelyne, 'Les ducs de Bourgogne, comtes de Flandre, selon les enluminures de la *Chronike van den lande van Vlaendre* (fin XVe siècle)', *Publications du Centre Européen d'Études Bourguignonnes* 37 (1997), 87-114 (88); Karaskova, Olga, 'Marie de Bourgogne et le Grand Héritage: L'iconographie princière face aux défis d'un pouvoir en transition (1477-1530)' (unpublished doctoral thesis, University of Lille, 2014) http://www.theses.fr/2014LIL30019.

12 Coigneau, Dirk, 'Roovere, Anthonis de', in *De Nederlandse en Vlaamse auteurs van middeleeuwen tot heden met inbegrip van de Friese auteurs*, ed. by Gerrit Jan van Bork, and Pieter Jozias Verkruijsse (De Haan: Weesp, 1985), p. 498 https://www.dbnl.org/tekst/bork001nede01_01/index.php; Oosterman, 'Anthonis de Roovere', p. 34.

of Castile, although it is dated some twenty years later, may have employed similar devices (scaffoldings, mansions, curtains, etc.).

In the *Excellente Cronike*, the solemn event of Mary of Burgundy's Joyous Entry is strongly emphasised in the first four coloured drawings immortalising the highlights of her reign (Fig. 10.2).[13] To open the chapter on Margaret of Austria's mother, the artist provides a scene of a highly heraldic nature. He uses a rather limited palette, corresponding to the heraldic colours of the seventeen coats of arms of the various territories inherited by Mary.[14] These shields cover the top of the image, in the manner of a frame surrounding a gold-plated niche that emphasises the crown and the portrait of the duchess. She is riding side saddle on a white horse protected by a rich carapace bearing her arms, ready for the hunt, as is indicated by the falcon on her right hand.[15] Less dynamic and more discreet is the portrait of Joanna of Castile, also riding side saddle on a black mule, overlooking the representatives of the Crossbowmen's Guild. They are quite busy launching the procession and lightening the way with their torches, while the tower of the town hall shines brightly. The most intense heraldic moment in Joanna's *Entry* is not connected to the portrait of the princess in the middle of the book. One has to go to the very end of the manuscript to view two miniatures (fols 60^r and 61^r) which present a double display of shields with the intention of including Joanna of Castile in the Habsburg dynasty.

Amazingly close to the Berlin manuscript are the style and technique used by another artist in a copy on paper of the *Excellente Cronike*, today held in the Morgan Library & Museum (Fig. 10.3).[16] In comparable ways, both artists resort to pen drawings coloured with blue washes for the skies while their volumes and forms are delimitated by silver lines which, with time, lost their glimmering aspect and turned black and stiff through oxidation. It is worth mentioning that many aspects of the techniques used by these artists relate directly to those developed for colouring printed illustrations.[17]

---

13 Bruges, OB 437, fol. 361^v, see *Women of Distinction, Margaret of York / Margaret of Austria*, ed. by Dagmar Eichberger (Leuven: Davidsfonds, 2005), p. 69, cat. no. 2 (Ann Kelders).
14 On the ideological dimension of number XVII (17), see Stein, Robert, 'Seventeen: the multiplicity of a unity in the Low Countries', in *The Ideology of Burgundy: The Promotion of National Consciousness, 1364-1565*, ed. by D'Arcy Jonathan Dacre Boulton, and Jan R. Veenstra (Leiden: Brill, 2006), pp. 223-85.
15 Karaskova, 'Marie de Bourgogne et le Grand Héritage'.
16 New York, Morgan Library & Museum, ms M. 435, fol. 352^v, Bruges, *c*. 1490. I would like to thank Dagmar Eichberger for suggesting this comparison.
17 In an email exchange with Dagmar Eichberger (27 February 2023), Nadine Orenstein from the Metropolitan Museum, New York considered the possibility that these were artists who specialized in colouring prints and/or drawings on paper.

10.2 Southern Netherlandish, *De Excellente Cronike van Vlaenderen* fol. 361ᵛ: *Mary of Burgundy on horseback*, coloured drawing on paper, c. 1480, Bruges, Openbare Bibliotheek, ms 437
© Openbare Bibliotheek

10.3 Southern Netherlandish, *De Excellente Cronike van Vlaenderen*, fol. 352ᵛ: *Charles the Bold at the Battlefield of Nancy*, drawing, watercolour and lead point on paper, Bruges, c. 1484, 28 × 21 cm, New York, Morgan Library, ms M.435. © The Morgan Library & Museum, New York

Collecting and Displaying Relics in Bamberg around 1508/1509

At the beginning of Joanna's *Entry*, several miniatures are devoted to the processions of various civic groups entering Brussels. These show codicological and stylistic affinities with illustrated commemorative works such as the Bamberg *Heiltumsbuch* (illustrated book of relics) of 1508/1509.[18] Its formal aspects – format, paper support and watercolour – also suggest this relatedness.[19] Following the 133 illustrations of variously shaped reliquaries,[20] the manuscript ends with two full-page illustrations with coloured pen drawings.[21] The one on folio 36^r shows the procession of the relics of the Holy Roman Emperor Henry II, patron saint of Bamberg Cathedral (Fig. 10.4a/b).[22] A compact crowd, coming from the cathedral, follows the procession of the heavy reliquary, supported by men dressed in rich clothing, which probably indicates their status in the city. On the reverse of the previous leaf (fol. 35^v), the knight holding the banner of St George seems to play the same role as St Michael (fol. 1^v) who occupies a privileged position at the very beginning of Joanna's *Entry*, being the patron saint of Brussels. Although the figure of St George is relegated to the very end of the *Heiltumsbuch*, his symbolic presence is attested to from the very first miniature (fol. 2^r) by the banners of the patron saint and the Roman emperor (Fig. 10.5). We are thus presented with two ways of immortalising an event considered memorable by a civic elite in the case of the Brussels *Entry*, and a religious elite in the case of the Bamberg *Heiltumsbuch*.

---

18 London, British Library, Add ms 15689. For a full description of the digitized manuscript (online) http://www.bl.uk/manuscripts/FullDisplay.aspx?ref=Add_MS_1568; see also: Baumgärtel-Fleischmann, Renate, *Das Bamberger Heiltum von 1508/1509* [British Library London, Add MS 15689] (Bamberg: Historischer Verein, 1998).
19 Its format is quite a bit larger: 48 × 32 cm compared to 35,6 × 25 cm for Joanna's *Entry*.
20 The manuscript itemizes the relics of Bamberg Cathedral and those of nearby churches: St Stephen, St James and St Gangolf, and the Benedictine monastery of Michelsberg.
21 The manuscript was perhaps executed by Wolf Katzheimer (b. 1450, d. 1509), an artist employed by the bishop of Bamberg. On this artist, see the entry by Stolberg-Wernigerode, Otto zu, in *Neue deutsche Biographie*, vol. 11 (Berlin: Duncker & Humblot, 1977).
22 Holy Roman Emperor Henry II (b. 973, d. 1024) and his wife Cunigunde of Luxembourg (b. 975, d. 1040), were canonized as saints in 1146 and 1200 respectively.

ILLUSTRATING CONTEMPORARY EVENTS IN WATERCOLOUR ON PAPER 215

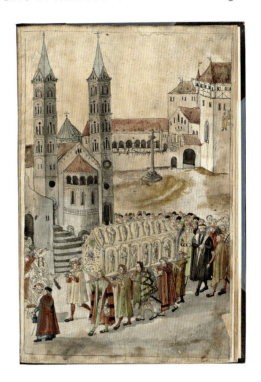

10.4a/b German, *Bamberg Heiltumsbuch*: doublespread, a) fol. 35ᵛ: *A Man in full Armour, holding a Banner with Saint George*, b) fol. 36ʳ: *A Reliquary Procession for Relics of Henry II before Bamberg Cathedral*, paper, pen drawings with watercolour, 48 × 32 cm, 1508-1509, London, British Library, Add ms 15689 © The British Library Board

10.5 German, *Bamberg Heiltumsbuch*, fol. 2ʳ: *Banners of St George and the Holy Roman Emperor Henry II*, paper, pen drawings with watercolour, 48 × 32 cm, 1508-1509, London, British Library, Add ms 15689, © The British Library Board

In the Entourage of King René d'Anjou

Let us now turn to the court of René d'Anjou, in Angers, where an exceptional production of manuscripts developed, aiming to etch into the memory important ephemeral spectacles of political dimensions. Compared to the Angevine court, the Burgundian court has left a less rich textual and iconographic legacy: the texts are few and the archives rare, or still in need of exploration, but in reality, the spectacles must have been just as numerous.[23] These magnificent and frequent performances in France and Burgundy were an efficient means of reinforcing the authority of princes. The theatrical and at the same time emotional nature of these public rituals encouraged communication and strengthened the bonds between the prince – or princess – and his or her subjects.[24]

From the middle of the fifteenth century onwards, René d'Anjou[25], one of the most cultured princes of his time, developed numerous theatrical forms likely to have a spectacular effect.[26] They may be rituals of tournaments and *pas d'armes* (passage of arms), or *mysteries, farces, sotties, mauresques* and *debates*.[27] This is the case, for example, with the *Pas de Saumur*.

Between entertainment and ceremony, the *Pas de Saumur* was part of the great jousts given at the Angevin court of René d'Anjou between 1445 and 1449.[28] It took place in 1446 at the foot of the castle of Saumur, bringing together about one-hundred participants. The manuscript copy preserved in Saint Petersburg is the only one known to have been illustrated (Fig. 10.6).[29] The narrative is accompanied by a description of the ceremonial, from the clashes between the two opponents to the clothing of the combatants and the main settings. The text also discusses the symbolic role and significance of the courtly weapons used. The author of the *Pas*,

---

23 Ferré, Rose-Marie, *René d'Anjou et les arts. Le jeu des mots et des images* (Turnhout: Brepols, 2012), p. 68, note 6.
24 Blockmans, Wim, and Esther Donckers, 'Self-Representation of Court and City in Flanders and Brabant in the Fifteenth and Early Sixteenth Centuries', in *Showing Status: Representations of Social Positions in the Late Middle Ages*, ed. by Wim Blockmans, and Antheunis Janse (Turnhout: Brepols, 1999), pp. 81-111.
25 Coulet, Noël, Anne Planche, and Françoise Robin, *Le roi René. Le prince, le mécène, l'écrivain, le mythe* (Aix-en-Provence: Edisud, 1982); Robin, Françoise, *La cour d'Anjou-Provence. La vie artistique sous le règne du roi René* (Paris: Picard, 1985); de Mérindol, Christian, *Le roi René et la seconde maison d'Anjou. Emblématique, art, histoire* (Paris: Léopard d'Or, 1987); *Le roi René dans tous ses États*, ed. by Jean-Michel Matz, and Élisabeth Verry (Paris: Ed. du Patrimoine, 2009), pp. 149-83; Bouchet, Florence, 'Introduction au personnage de René d'Anjou: poète ou politique?', in *René d'Anjou, écrivain et mécène (1409-1480)*, ed. by Florence Bouchet (Turnhout: Brepols, 2011), pp. 13-21; Bianciotto, Gabriel, 'Passion du livre et des lettres à la cour du roi René', in *Splendeur de l'enluminure. Le roi René et ses livres*, ed. by Marc-Édouard Gautier (Paris: Actes Sud, 2010), pp. 85-104.
26 This definition was established by Koopmans, Jelle, and Darwin Smith, in 'Un théâtre *français* du Moyen Âge?', *Médiévales* 59 (2010), 5-16. http://journals.openedition.org/medievales/6055.
27 On these performances, designed for entertainment but always accompanied by a speech of the prince, see Desprez-Masson, Marie-Claude, 'Jean du Prier: intertextualité, théâtre et politique à la cour d'Anjou-Provence', in *Les Arts et les lettres en Provence au temps du roi René*, ed. by Chantal Connochie-Bourgne, and Valérie Gontero-Lauze (Aix-en-Provence: Presses Univ. de Provence, 2013), pp. 209-29.
28 De Mérindol, Christian, *Les Fêtes de chevalerie à la cour du roi René* (Paris: Ed. du C.T.H.S., 1993), p. 5.
29 Saint Petersburg, National Library of Russia, Saltykov-Chtchedrine, ms Fr. F. p. XIV, 4, fol. 24ᵛ, Rose-Marie Ferré, 'Relation du pas de Saumur tenu en 1446', in Gautier, *Splendeur de l'enluminure*, entry no. 12, pp. 244-47; see also: Morrison, Elizabeth and Anne D. Hedeman, eds, *Imagining the Past. History in Manuscript Painting, 1250-1500*, exh. cat. (Los Angeles: J. P. Getty Museum, 2010), cat. no. 46 (Anne D. Hedeman), pp. 249-51).

10.6 French, *Pas de Saumur* (The Book of Tournaments for René d'Anjou) fol. 24ᵛ: *The Fight between King René and the Duke of Alençon*, pen drawings with washes, 36 × 27 cm, c. 1470, Saint Petersburg, National Library of Russia, Saltykov-Chtchedrine, ms Fr. F. p. XIV, 4 © Morrison, *Imagining the Past*, p. 250

still unknown up to this day, states himself that he is presenting a text with a strong political meaning and that the *pas d'armes* should not be seen as mere entertainment but rather as a celebration of chivalric values.[30]

The preserved copy of the *Pas de Saumur* was produced in the 1470s, more than twenty-five years after the actual performance, on the basis of a lost original that was contemporary with the event and was illuminated in *circa* 1446, perhaps by King René's favourite painter Barthélemy d'Eyck.[31] The text of the Saint Petersburg copy does not provide any information on its recipient or the context of its production. Isabelle de Lorraine, the first wife of René d'Anjou, may have been the first owner before her death in 1453.

Comparing the *Entry of Joanna of Castile* with the *Pas de Saumur* brings to the fore some interesting affinities. Firstly, the two manuscripts resemble each other physically, sharing roughly the same format – 36 by 27 cm for the *Pas* and 35,6 by 25 cm for the *Entry*. They both make use of a paper support on which each artist has created illustrations that make use of the technique of pen drawing and watercolour. In the *Pas*, the vigorous pen drawings, enhanced with bright colours, occupy more than the upper half of the page, while the lower half is reserved for text in two columns. The style of these drawings is dynamic and very graphic, giving movement and character to the riders and their horses depicted in various poses.[32] The relationship between text and image is therefore not always well established in this manuscript. The layout of Joanna's *Entry* on the other hand maintains the strongest possible link between text and illustration. All of this is done by a simple structure, maintaining a close connection between the descriptive paragraph and the corresponding watercolour drawing. In each case a diptych is created by combining a written commentary on the verso with a full-page miniature on the opposite page.

The organisation of text and images in Joanna's *Entry* thus favours a uniform layout. The considerable contrast with the *Pas de Saumur* is even more striking in René d'Anjou's *Livre des Tournois* (Fig. 10.7) in which no similar structure can be identified. One navigates through a flexible, even erratic organisation of the iconographic programme, between numerous decorated double pages, occasionally interrupted by several empty leaves. The miniatures sometimes extend to the edge of the page as if they were going to spill over into the void. The imposing size of the manuscript – 385 by 300 mm – as well as the paper support and the use of the heightened drawing technique make it another candidate for the genre of the 'memorial or commemorative manuscript'.

---

30 An interesting comparison could be made with the *Livre des faits de Jacques de Lalaing* which lists the knight's chivalric 'deeds' and values in an account completed thirty years after his death. The text has recently been translated into English. See *A Chivalric Life. The Book of the Deeds of Messire Jacques de Lalaing*, trad. Rosalind Brown-Grant, and Mario Damen (Woodbridge: Boydell, 2022); Bianciotto, 'Passion du livre et des lettres', p. 91.
31 Ferré, *René d'Anjou et les arts*, p. 67.
32 However, some of the characters' postures are repeated from one sheet to the next without any real understanding of how they meet the needs of the narrative, see Ferré, *Relation du pas de Saumur*, pp. 244-45.

10.7 Provencal, Barthélemy d'Eyck, *Livre des Tournois* (King René's Tournament book), fol. 103ᵛ: *The award ceremony*, coloured pen drawings on paper, 36 × 25,9 cm, c. 1460, Paris, Bibliothèque nationale de France, ms Français 2695
© Source gallica.bnf.fr / BnF

The *Livre des Tournois* of René d'Anjou (Paris, BnF, ms fr. 2695)[33] combines various customs followed in Germany, Flanders and the kingdom of France. It proposes an ideal imaginary tournament during which two opposing camps, that of the Duke of Brittany and that of the Duke of Bourbon, confront each other. It takes place in the manner of a liturgical *ordo*, regulating the coronation ceremony.[34] In contrast to

---

33 *Le Livre des Tournois du Roi René de la Bibliothèque nationale (ms Français 2695)*, introduction by François Avril (Paris: Herscher, 1986); see also Sturgeon, Justin, *Text and image in René d'Anjou's 'Livre des Tournois': constructing authority and identity in fifteenth-century court culture*, presented with a critical edition of BnF, ms français 2695 (Woodbridge: Boydell, 2022).

34 Avril and Reynaud, *Les manuscrits à peinture en France*, entry no. 127 (François Avril), pp. 235-36.

similar treatises, René d'Anjou's *Livre des Tournois* is here distinguished by the presence of a cycle of narrative illustrations that allow us to visually follow the progression of the event. In these drawings, crowds of people occasionally spread over two pages. The drawings are enhanced with watercolour and laid out in a way that is unusual and rare in French manuscript production of the period. Like Joanna's *Entry*, manuscript Français 2695 is an original, soberly written manuscript on paper that has been illustrated with simple watercolour drawings.[35] In spite of the particular technique used, François Avril recognised the hand of the great Barthélemy d'Eyck in his maturity around 1460. For him, the fact that a paper medium with coloured drawing was preferred is not surprising at all, when considering that Barthélemy d'Eyck was trained in the Dutch-Rhenish region, where heightened drawings were used frequently.

Emperor Maximilian's *Freydal*

A wonderful late example is *The Book of Tournaments of Emperor Maximilian I*, or *Freydal Tournament Book*, an exceptional manuscript written on paper and lavishly illustrated with pen drawings and watercolour over black chalk on laid paper. The images were executed by southern German artists, at the request of the Emperor Maximilian I between 1512 and 1515 (Fig. 10.8).[36] The three-volume work contains 255 fascinating miniatures of the tournaments of the young Freydal, the alter ego of Maximilian I (1459-1519), who played an important role in the development of this pastime at the beginning of the Renaissance. At the age of eighteen, during a visit to the Burgundian court to meet his future wife Mary of Burgundy, he was very impressed by the splendid parties and tournaments that were intended to demonstrate the court's magnificence. Tournaments were far more than entertainment, but rather an integral part of the political mission of a prince which is why Maximilian commissioned the prestigious *Freydal* manuscript.[37]

---

35 Paul Durrieu regarded it as a kind of model for the dedication copy made for Charles du Maine. Otto Pächt, on the other hand, saw it as a copy based on a lost original from which the Flemish copies produced later were derived. François Avril has taken the opposite view and considers Fr. 2695 to be the original 'minute' on the basis of the undeniably superior illustrations, which would thus be the source of all other known copies. See Avril and Reynaud, *Les manuscrits à peinture en France*, p. 235.

36 Vienna, Kunsthistorisches Museum, Kunstkammer, inv. no. 5073. Krause, Stefan, *Freydal. Medieval Games. The Book of Tournaments of Emperor Maximilian I* (Cologne: Taschen, 2019).

37 On the sporting and political dimension of the tournament, see Beaufort, Christian, 'The Court Tournament', in *A la búsqueda del Toisón de Oro. La Europa de los Príncipes. La Europa de las ciudades*, ed. by Eduard Mira, and An Delva (Almudin: Generalitat Valenciana, 2007), pp. 541-45.

10.8 Southern German, *Freydal, the Book of Tournaments of Emperor Maximilian I*, fol. 17^r: *Freydal fighting Count Wolfgang von Fürstenberg*, paper, coloured pen drawings, 1512-1515, Vienna, Kunsthistorisches Museum, inv. no. Kunstkammer 5073 © KHM-Museumsverein

Le Songe du Pastourel

Let us turn to the *Songe du Pastourel*, a text in which the weight of politics is also quite significant.[38] Composed by Jean du Prier around 1477,[39] it relates the victory of Duke René II of Lorraine, on 5 January 1477, before Nancy, a battle which mortally wounded his enemy, the Duke of Burgundy Charles the Bold, and which legitimately re-established René II as Duke of Lorraine.[40] The *Songe* was probably performed before the tomb of the Duke of Burgundy, perhaps on 5 January 1478, in the collegiate church of Saint-Georges in Nancy, where his funeral took place and where the Dukes of Lorraine were buried. As René II of Lorraine had neither a court artist nor an appointed copyist at that time, it is likely that the text of the *Songe du Pastourel* was composed at the request of King René and probably according to his instructions before he died in 1480. The surviving illuminated copy can be dated to around 1515, that is more than twenty-five years after he passed away. It is probably not the original dedication copy owned by René II of Lorraine, but could have been executed at the request of Antoine de Lorraine, his son and successor.

The sumptuous Vienna copy is adorned with magnificent washes of transparent gouache over light brown ink and with numerous white reserves.[41] Executed on parchment, fifty-eight of these drawings appear as large images in the middle of the page, framed at the top and bottom by two stanzas written in a dovetailed cartouche (Fig. 10.9). Eleven other pages bear more rapidly executed images in watercolour, distributed on either side of the unframed stanzas showing the sleeping poet and the objects of his dream. For François Avril, the artist was probably a painter who was rarely involved in manuscript illumination and can therefore not be called a professional illuminator. Alternatively, he applied the bold and effective technique of pen drawings enhanced with watercolours.[42]

---

38 Vienna, Österreichische Nationalbibliothek, ms 2556, coloured drawings on parchment, 380 × 295 mm, see: Chmelarz, Eduard, 'Le *Songe du Pastourel* von Jean du Prier', *Jahrbuch der Kunsthistorischen Sammlungen des Allerhöchsten Kaiserhauses* 13 (1892), 226-66; Pächt, Otto, and Dagmar Thoss, *Die Illuminierten Handschriften der Österreichischen Nationalbibliothek. Französische Schule II*, 2 vols (Vienna: Österreichische Akad. d. Wiss., 1977), pp. 102-10, ill. 242-61; Avril and Reynaud, *Les manuscrits à peintures en France*, pp. 385-87; Brachmann, Christoph, *Memoria Fama Historia* (Berlin: Mann, 2006), pp. 244-322.

39 The work takes the form of a poem of about 1200 eight-line verses. Christoph Brachman has argued that the text was composed between 1480 and 1490 while Jean du Prier was employed at the court of René II of Lorraine in Nancy; Brachmann, *Memoria, Fama Historia*, chapt. VI, pp. 223-29.

40 On this text and its political dimension, see Brachmann, Christoph, 'Le 'Songe du Pastourel' de Jean du Prier: 'Une chronique allégorisée au service de la mémoire lorraine de la bataille de Nancy (5 janvier 1477)', in *La Culture de cour en France et en Europe à la fin du Moyen Âge*, ed. by Christian Freigang, and Jean-Claude Schmitt (Berlin: Akademieverlag, 2005), pp. 403-30; Marie-Claude Desprez-Masson has studied these conflicts in detail: see Desprez-Masson, Marie-Claude, *Le Songe du Pastourel de Jean du Prier. Poésie et politique* (Montréal: CERES, 1989); Desprez-Masson, 'Jean du Prier: intertextualité, théâtre et politique', p. 209.

41 The large paintings measure approximately 25 × 21,4 cm and the manuscript 38 × 29,5 cm.

42 Avril and Reynaud, *Les manuscrits à peintures en France*, p. 387. Nicole Reynaud was the first to attempt to identify the illuminator from accounts that mention a certain Hugues de La Faye, employed as painter to Antoine de Lorraine since 1511. He was also the Duke's *valet de chambre*, then 'concierge' of the ducal palace in Nancy until his death in 1539.

10.9 Lorraine, Jean du Prier, *Le songe du Pastourel*, fol. 8ᵛ: *The author in his bedroom, in the foreground an illustration of his dream of a sick man with two doctors*, coloured drawings on parchment, 38 × 29,5cm, c. 1515, Vienna, Österreichische Nationalbibliothek, ms 2556 © ÖNB

The *Songe* is a poem in eight-line stanzas extolling the military successes of René II over Charles the Bold and the fatal battle of 1477. This triumph is important because it was subsequently at the centre of René II's propaganda. Marie-Claude Desprez-Masson has shown that the *Songe* was first considered as an ephemeral work of art, as a text intended for theatrical performance. At the behest of Antoine (1508-1544), son of René II, Jean du Prier transformed the original into a more durable form, and, at the same time, made it more lavish by adding a cycle of sumptuous watercolours.[43] This may explain why parchment was used as support instead of paper which is

---

43 Brachmann, '"Le Songe du Pastourel" de Jean du Prier', p. 409.

normally preferred for this type of work. In short, the aim may have been to produce a work of art for private consumption rather than for public use. Furthermore, as suggested by Christoph Brachmann, Antoine may have used images to explain a text composed of allegories that had become hermetic and incomprehensible over time. This transposition into images would then be the key to the interpretation and memorisation of this text by later generations.

Conclusion

The stylistic analysis of manuscripts with coloured pen drawings on paper is a challenge for research in so far as there have been few studies on this genre to date. Lieselotte Saurma-Jeltsch was able to prove that Diebold Lauber's workshop in Hagenau was a large production site for the manufacture of such artefacts in the Upper Rhine region.[44] As far as the manuscripts at the court of Emperor Maximilian I are concerned (e.g. *Freydal, Weißkunig*, fishing- and hunting manuals), there are now several publications available which prove the great significance of this type of manuscript at the Habsburg court.[45] For the Burgundian Netherlands, no comparable study is yet available that would allow us to place the *Entry of Joanna of Castile* in a larger context. The comparison with five manuscripts from the region north of the Alps has shown that such manuscripts were often works produced with the high nobility and the upper middle classes in mind. This alternative type of composition, which employed a more spontaneous and rapid method of execution, was used for chronicles, historical treatises, and for texts that served the *memoria* of a city or a dynasty. In contrast, luxury manuscripts with opaque colours and gold leaf on parchment represent an entirely different genre that was preferred for instance for precious books of hours and illustrated choir books.

When commissioning the Berlin manuscript, the city of Brussels opted for a large format. It is a well-structured manuscript with 63 folio pages, combining full-page illustrations on the recto with explanatory texts on the preceding verso. The first part of the manuscript depicts various representatives of the city of Brussels moving towards the Spanish princess in an open landscape. Although the individual images are framed, they still allow for a free and unrestrained painting style. The pale brown underdrawings are accentuated by darker pen strokes and modelled with watercolours. In this way, vivid portraits of the leading corporations of Brussels' society are created. The city government wanted to present itself to the princess in the best possible light. The second part of the manuscript reproduces various stages with programmatic themes that had been set up along the processional route. Due to their fixed structure with wooden frames and textile curtains, these representations seem altogether more static than the images in the first part of the *Entry of Joanna*

---

44 Saurma-Jeltsch, Lieselotte E., *Spätformen mittelalterlicher Buchherstellung: Bilderhandschriften aus der Werkstatt Diebold Laubers in Hagenau*, 2 vols (Wiesbaden: Reichert, 2001).
45 Silver, Larry, *Marketing Maximilian. The Visual Ideology of a Holy Roman Emperor* (Princeton: Princeton University Press, 2008).

of Castile into Brussels manuscript. Nevertheless, the scenes on stage are often of an extraordinary liveliness.

There is no doubt that the Brussels painters' guild was involved in the design of the festivities. Their patron, St Luke, appears as the painter of the Virgin Mary on the last stage (fol. 59^r). However, which painter or which workshop made the coloured drawings for this manuscript is still a mystery, because no written records on this event have been preserved in the city's archives. The *Entry of Joanna of Castile into Brussels* manuscript is the first illustrated account of a municipal pageant in the Netherlands, written more than twenty years before Archduke Charles' festive entry into Bruges in 1515. The city of Brussels opted for a paper manuscript with coloured pen drawings. For Charles' entry, an illuminated manuscript on vellum was made at the command of the Habsburg family. Even though Joanna of Castile appears in only one illustration herself (fol. 31^r), she is the main addressee of this event. The artistic means of the time were used to curry the favour of the young princess in the hope of winning her over to adopt the city of Brussels as the seat of her principal residence. *Joanna's Entry* manuscript is a telling testimony to this endeavour and the chosen genre – coloured pen drawing on paper – was considered more than worthy for this significant occasion.

DAGMAR EICHBERGER

Manuscript 78 D5

A Codicological Description

Berlin, Staatliche Museen Preußischer Kulturbesitz, Kupferstichkabinett, ms 78 D5
Brussels, after 9 December 1496
Southern Netherlandish, Paper, (I) + 63[1] + (I), 35,6 × 25 cm
<u>Watermark</u>: Gothic P similar to Briquet 8531 (Wescher)[2], Piccard's inventory lists nos 1024 and 1025 (Abteilung III)[3]
<u>Pen drawings</u> enhanced with watercolour and gouache, shell gold and silver colour
<u>Latin text</u> written in *Burgundica bastarda* or *gothica hybrida*, with rubrications
Rebound in veal skin in the first half of the 19th century by Charles Lewis[4] (Boese 1966[5]), middle-brown leather with blind tooling and embossed pattern (Fig. 11.1)
On the end paper, an English inscription in pencil: 'Bound by C. Lewis 2-0-0'.
On the spine:
    L'ENTRÉE DE LA REINE JEANNE DANS LA VILLE DE BRUXELLES
<u>Provenance</u>:
Collection William Thomas Beckford (1760-1844): no. 218[6]; Collection Alexander Hamilton Douglas (1767-1852): no. 353; Kupferstichkabinett Berlin, no. 148; information entered on 9 August 1884 into the acquisition book of that year[7]; the same information is noted in pencil on the flyleaf: 'Erw. 148-1884'

---

1 An entry in pencil on the flyleaf in the front states: '57 without front + 2 pp of arms'; the flyleaf at the end of the book has another English inscription in pencil, stating: '58 plates'. This number is incorrect. The date of these annotations is unclear, but they probably stem from the time before the manuscript was auctioned off by the last English owner.
2 Wescher, Paul, *Beschreibendes Verzeichnis der Miniaturen – Handschriften und Einzelblätter – des Kupferstichkabinetts der Staatlichen Museen Berlin* (Leipzig: Weber, 1931), pp. 179-80.
3 I am most grateful to Ann Kelders (KBR) who helped me identifying this reference.
4 Lee, Sidney (ed.), 'Lewis, Charles (1786-1836)', in *Dictionary of National Biography*, vol. 33 (London: Smith, Elder & Co, 1883), see: https://en.wikisource.org/wiki/Dictionary_of_National_Biography,_1885-1900/Lewis,_Charles_(1786-1836).
5 Boese, Helmut, *Die lateinischen Handschriften der Sammlung Hamilton zu Berlin* (Wiesbaden: Harrassowitz, 1966), cat. no. 353, pp. 168-69.
6 Wescher, *Beschreibendes Verzeichnis*, p. 179.
7 https://www.smb.museum/museen-einrichtungen/kupferstichkabinett/sammeln-forschen/erwerbungsbuecher/

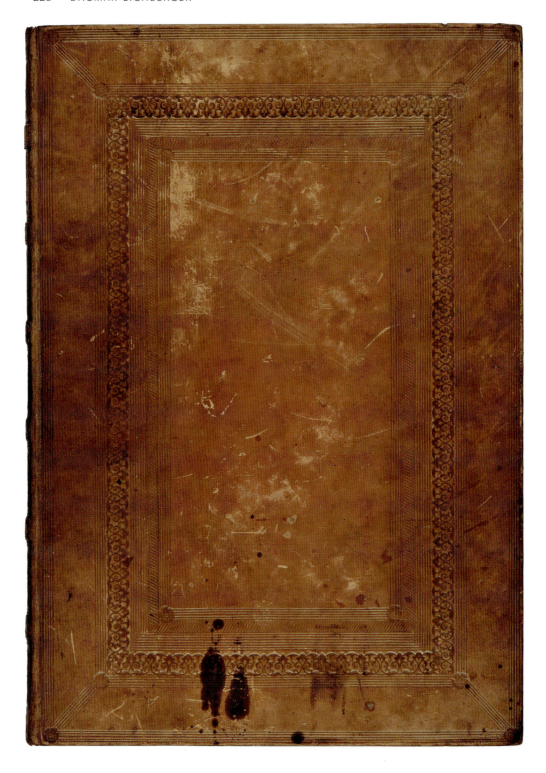

11.1 Berlin, Kupferstichkabinett, ms 78 D5, 19th century binding, photo: Dietmar Katz

Fol. 1ʳ: '148-1884' and the K-K-K stamp of the 'Königliches Kupferstichkabinett'[8] (Fig. 11.2)

This text will shed light on the codicology of the manuscript 78 D5 and provide a detailed physical description of the manuscript in its current early nineteenth-century binding.

The Berlin manuscript is made of paper and measures 35,6 by 25 cm. It consists of sixty-three folios plus one fly-sheet at the beginning and one at the end. Unfortunately, the individual gatherings cannot be determined as its current binding is extremely tight and does not allow for a more detailed structural analysis. The numbering in pencil – always at the top of the recto page – counts from 1 to 63.[9] Based on the analysis of text and images, as undertaken by the authors of this volume, it seems that the manuscript is almost complete. Only the wording at the beginning of the final description of the Brussels townhall (fol. 63ʳ) suggest that the manuscript once contained an illustration of this renowned civic monument.[10]

11.2 Berlin, Kupferstichkabinett, ms 78 D5, fol. 1ʳ: stamp of the 'Königliches Kupferstichkabinett' with the inscription '148-1884', photo: Dietmar Katz

> Hoc scemate quod sequetur Representatur Egregia ac incomparabilis domus consulum sive reipublice opidi Bruxellensis que pro facie seu anteriori parte ut patet (quantum ars admisit) protracta est cuius situs commoditas ornatus amplitudo sumptuositas omnisque (supra quam cogitari possit) architecture genus arsque sicut nec representari sic nec exprimi possunt quid nimirum cum nec visus perstringere sufficiat.

> The following depiction displays the wonderful and unrivalled town hall of Brussels. The facade has been rendered (insofar as the artwork allows). The pleasantness of the location, the decorations, size, opulence and architectural style and artistry (which far exceed one's expectations) cannot be captured in an illustration or in words. And no wonder, for the eye is incapable of taking it all in.

Most of the folios in manuscript 78 D5 are in very good condition. The sixty-one neatly framed images, as well as the blocks of written text, are intact. A detail analysis of the margins of individual folios points to the fact that the manuscript must have suffered some damage before it was bound in the early nineteenth century. Narrow stripes of paper have been applied to reinforce the outer margins of folios 2, 7 and 51; a similar treatment was used for the inner margins of folios 2 and 11.

---

8 Lugt, Frits, *Les Marques de Collections de Dessins & d'Estampes | Fondation Custodia* (The Hague: Nijhoff, 1956), no. L 1634; see http://www.marquesdecollections.fr/detail.cfm/marque/8036).
9 It cannot be ascertained when this numbering was added.
10 See the article by Sascha Köhl in this volume.

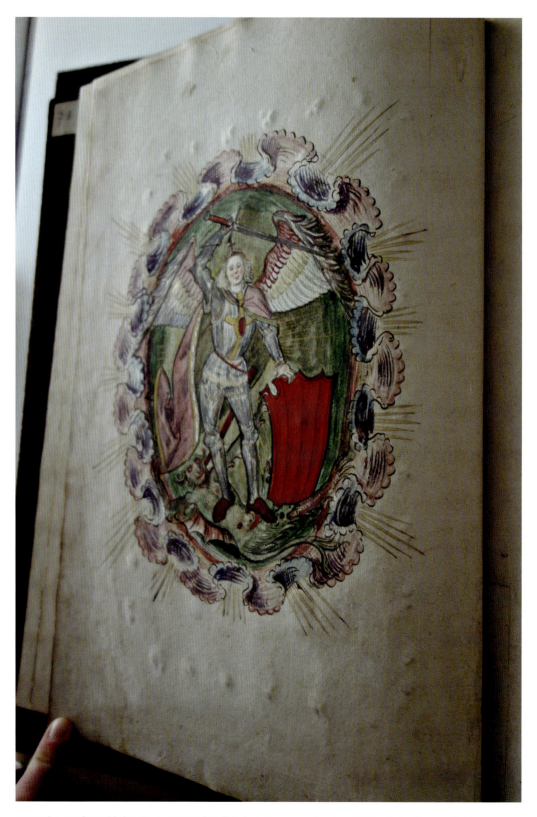

11.3 Berlin, Kupferstichkabinett, ms 78 D5, fol. 1ᵛ: indentations seen in raking light, photo: Dagmar Eichberger

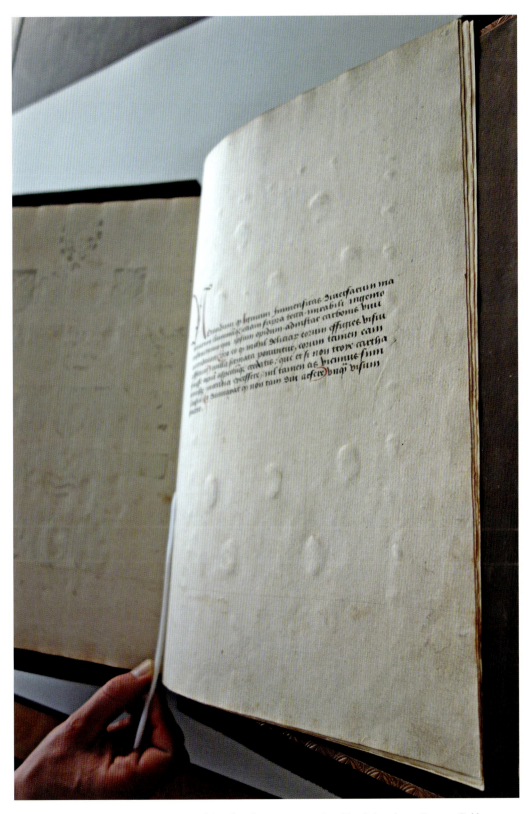

11.4 Berlin, Kupferstichkabinett, ms 78 D5, fol. 62ʳ: indentations seen in raking light, photo: Dagmar Eichberger

11.5 Berlin, Kupferstichkabinett, ms 78 D5, watermark 'P' on fol. 5ʳ, photo: Luise Maul

Some additional evidence points to the possibility that the manuscript was kept in an unbound state for some time. By using raking light, the Berlin paper conservator Luise Maul detected unusual indentation on several layers of paper (Fig. 11.3 and 11.4). These indentations appear at the beginning and end of the manuscript. One can detect these marks on approximately six layers of paper, both at the beginning and the end of the book. The indentations create an almost rectangular pattern on each, as if the unbound paper manuscript had been placed between two book covers with metal buttons or jewels that pressed against the medium.

The Berlin manuscript shows the consistent use of hand-made paper with the watermark 'P'. The watermark on fol. 5 measures 5,9 cm by 2,2 cm (Fig. 11.5).[11] The so-called Piccard database characterizes this watermark as: letter P, with split shaft, two-contoured, without crossbar. Exactly the same paper has been identified by Gerhard Piccard in a document dating from 1497 that is kept in the Ghent State Archive (*Rijksarchief*).[12] Another example can be found in the accounts of the City of Mechelen, dating from 1497 (*Stadsarchief*).[13] It can thus be assumed that the Berlin manuscript was made of paper coming from the same paper mill as these two archival documents. Inge van Wegens recently suggested that the Brussels region became a centre of paper production in the second half of the fifteenth century with several mills being situated in Linkebeek, right on the southern border of modern Brussels.[14] This evidence supports the hypothesis that the manuscript under discussion was manufactured in the Brussels region not long after the festive entry.

Pen Drawings with Watercolour and Gouache

The artists who produced the images in the Berlin manuscript are unknown. Given the difference in quality, we have to expect the involvement of a leading artist who was assisted by several hands. The painting process consisted of several steps.[15] The medium used for the first sketches was pale-brown ink employed to outline the figures, animals, landscapes and buildings. Transparent washes or watercolours supplemented these drawings in varying density. At a later stage, black or dark brown ink was employed for accentuating certain elements, such as facial features, the outlines of the human body or the limbs of the horses. It is precisely in the depiction of the horses that the mastery of the leading artist becomes apparent. The animals are depicted in different views, often foreshortened, standing, moving forwards and rearing up.[16]

Shell gold was used to emphasize the wealth of individual participants, starting with the clothes and the headdress of Princess Joanna of Castile (Fig. 11.6) and

---

11 I am most grateful to Luise Maul, the paper conservator of the Berlin Kupferstichkabinett, who provided me with the information used in this section; Piccard, Gerhard, *Wasserzeichen Buchstabe P* (Stuttgart: Kohlhammer, 1977), 3 vols: 'Buchstabe P, Schaftfuß gespalten, ohne Querzeichen'; see also the database in the Hauptstaatsarchiv Stuttgart, https://www.piccard-online.de/start.php.
12 This information comes from the *Raad van Vlaanderen 2430*, see: Hauptstaatsarchiv Stuttgart, Bestand J 340, Wasserzeichensammlung Piccard, Nr. 107978; I am grateful to Ann Kelders from the Royal Library in Brussels who has identified these two comparative examples (email from 7 March, 2023).
13 *Stadsrekeningen*, see: Hauptstaatsarchiv Stuttgart, Bestand J 340, Wasserzeichensammlung Piccard, Nr. 107976.
14 Van Wegens, Inge, 'Paper consumption and the foundation of the first paper mills in the Low Countries, 13th –15th century', in *Papier im mittelalterlichen Europa. Herstellung und Gebrauch*, ed. by Carla Meyer, Sandra Schultz und Bernd Schneidmüller (Berlin: De Gruyter, 2017), pp. 71-92, esp. 78-84.
15 Luise Maul kindly helped me to identify this technique; see the article by Anne-Marie Legaré for the genre of books in which this technique is to be found most frequently.
16 I would like to thank Nadine Orenstein for her assessment of these drawings (conversation on 22 February, 2023). She suggests that the colouring was done by artists who were trained to colour woodcuts, in German called 'Briefmaler'.

11.6 Berlin, Kupferstichkabinett, ms 78 D5, fol. 31ʳ: *Joanna's dress with highlights in gold pigment*, photo: Dagmar Eichberger

finishing with the badges worn by certain members of the shooters' guilds.[17] Silver paint was employed to characterize the armour of archangel Michael (fol. 1ᵛ) and to characterize the emblems of several members of chambers of rhetoricians or shooter guilds (fol. 29ʳ). Unfortunately, the irreversible oxidation process reduced the shimmering effect that this colouring must have initially created.

The sophistication and versatility in using this painting technique becomes evident on the page with the coats of arms of eleven kingdoms under Spanish rule (fol. 60ʳ). These shields are painted in an opaque medium in order to adequately characterize the kingdoms which they represent. The young female figures who hold the

---

17 These details can only be seen in raking light as was shown by Luise Maul; see also the article by Claire Billen and Chloé Deligne.

11.7 Berlin, Kupferstichkabinett, ms 78 D5, fol. 2ʳ: *rubrications*, photo: Dietmar Katz

shields are executed in a very loose, watery style. Together with their crowns and costly dresses, this creates an effect of elegance and beauty.

Many pages within this manuscript have been structured by a grid of two vertical lines and occasionally also a horizontal line to map out the spaces reserved for the illustration and the block of text.

The text was written by a scribe using a font called *Burgundica bastarda* or *gothica hybrida*. The beginning of each paragraph is embellished by a larger, rubricated letter. In three instances (Fig. 11.7), the first letter is written in an even more elaborate calligraphic style as it was popular at the end of the fifteenth century.[18]

Within the individual blocks of text, certain words were highlighted by red lines; this applies to important personalities such as Joanna, Philip the Fair, Emperor Maximilian I or to significant members of the Brussels community, as well as to respective locations within Brussels and Brabant.

---

18 König, Eberhard, *Das Kalligraphiebuch der Maria von Burgund. Brüssel, Bibliothèque royale de Belgique, ms II 845* (Luzern: Quaternio, 2015).

HELGA KAISER-MINN

Manuscript 78 D5

Short Descriptions of the Miniatures

Fol. 1ᵛ: The illuminated account of Joanna's festive entry is preceded by the image of the armed Archangel Michael, the patron saint of Brussels. Surrounded by an oval aureole of clouds, he stands with a raised sword on the body of the defeated devil, stretched out on the ground.

PART Ia: The Welcoming Procession for Joanna of Castile

Fol. 3ʳ: The procession is led by three Dominican teachers, the foremost of whom carrying the processional cross with the red *vexillum*. Their former students, clerics of different age groups follow in rows of two. In the distance one can see some buildings. The Latin text on fol. 2ᵛ refers to the students of Brussels embodying the city's intellectual potential.

Fol. 4ʳ: In a hilly landscape, a group of Carmelite monks participate in the procession, clad in white choir robes worn over a brown habit. The first monk carries the processional cross with the red banner. Fol. 3ᵛ underlines their venerable zeal which poured their chaste and spiritual embrace over the archducal spouse.

Fol. 5ʳ: The Carmelites are followed by the Minorites, wearing grey-brown habits. A young monk carries the processional cross with the *vexillum*. The caption on fol. 4ᵛ describes the Friars Minor's great popularity among Brussels's population.

Fol. 6ʳ: Next in line are secular chaplains in white robes; some of them are wearing brown fur stoles. In the background, between the hills, appears a church. On fol. 5ᵛ, the chaplains are described as having a regal demeanour, a worldly as well as a clerical solemnity and nevertheless devotedness. They meet the young princess, filled with joy.

Fol. 7ʳ: This image represents a group of regular canons from the monastery in the Sonian Forest. They wear a grey-brown habit and black stoles. Fol. 6ᵛ mentions the foundation of their monastery in the vicinity of the archducal court. The canons present themselves piously before the princess.

Fol. 8ʳ: Also, the canons of the Church of Saint Gudula take part in the procession, welcoming the young princess. They wear white linen surplices over long red or blue tunics and grey-brown mantles. Some have the hood pulled over the head. One of them is carrying a book in his hand. According to the author of the Latin text on fol. 7ᵛ, the dignified facial expressions of these canons, combined with their alacrity, authority, and earnestness, show the spectators something more than human.

Fol. 9ʳ: The so-called Hundredmen are accompanied by a squadron of Tenthmen and open the civic part of the procession. Each of them carries a burning torch. It is said that they take care of any disturbances and protect the city from fire and enemies. They are the first of the common people coming to meet Joanna.

Fol. 10ʳ: Next in line are the Sworn or Deans holding burning torches decorated with guild badges. The individual emblems refer to the cobblers, armourers, brewers, locksmiths, ragmen, haberdashers and painters. Placed in front are representatives of the Guild of St Luke, who were involved in preparing the decorations for the festive entry. At the far left, a bridge leads across a river. On fol. 9ᵛ the author states that these men have an important mediating function as leaders of the common people; the municipality consults them to avoid confusion.

PART Ib: A Series of six Burlesque Groups serving as an Intermezzo

Fol. 11ʳ: In this image, four jesters produce an exotic soundscape by playing the flute, bagpipes, bellows, spoon and box. The man with the bellows is dressed like a monk. The emblem on the sleeve of the fool in the front is probably a reference to the Great Guild of the Crossbow Bearers of *Onze-Lieve-Vrouw ten Zavel* (*Notre-Dame du Sablon*). The motive on the wooden box might be that of the Archers or Culverin-Bearers. The scene takes place in front of an inn. Fol. 10ᵛ comments that these mimes were concealing their true identity and went to welcome Joanna while playing various musical instruments.

Fol. 12ʳ: *Hystrio* represents a mentally handicapped man in a red coat who is pursued by a group of boys teasing him. He has put on a straw hat with three skimpy feathers and holds up a club with both hands as if it was a burning torch. The square with a fountain in its centre has been identified as the Brussels fish market. Hystrio gives expression to his pious veneration by continuously singing *Kyrie Eleison, most illustrious lord*; the meaning of this scene remains vague, even to the author of the Latin text (fol. 11ᵛ).

Fol. 13ʳ: A nobly dressed Ethiopian woman with a dark complexion rides side-saddle on a white horse. She is accompanied by seven actors disguised as wild men (or wild women). In her left hand, the Ethiopian woman holds a little tree with three armorial shields in red. The wild men hold up their clubs as if they were torches. One of them reins in the horse that starts to gallop. Fol. 12ᵛ comments that Ethiopia brings a gift to the young princess.

Fol. 14ʳ: A pipe-smoking fool, holding a *marotte* (a stick with a carved head on it) in his left hand and bellows in his right, rides on a chair that has been placed on the back of a grey horse instead of a saddle. On fol. 13ᵛ, it is noted that this scene made the audience laugh.

Fol. 15ʳ: Four actors costumed as wild men hit each other with clubs. On fol. 14ᵛ, another reaction of the audience is commented on. It is said that the audience nodded in agreement.

Fol. 16ʳ: This image represents five musicians playing bagpipes. All of them are wearing bright red caps and white masks. The sleigh is pulled by a white horse carrying another masked man. A castle with crenelated towers can be seen in the background. The commentator on fol. 15ᵛ reports that the masked individuals created a pleasant harmony with their musical performances.

PART Ic: Ten Civic Groups riding on Horses

Fol. 17ʳ: At the head of the next section, the young butchers burst forth on their barely restrained horses. They wear elegant garments in green and red and caps with luxuriant feather decorations. Carelessly they swing their burning torches. With their youthful spirit they show eager enthusiasm and verve, as the author notes on fol. 16ᵛ.

Fol. 18ʳ: Six mounted sergeants follow steadily in what is called an 'orderly fashion'. Responsible for order and apprehending law-violators, they are equipped with a sword, as the illustration shows. On the left, a church appears in the background. As is stated on fol. 17ᵛ these officers are the lowest-ranking members among the various representatives of the guilds but they will be the first to meet the princess.

Fol. 19ʳ: Eight messengers move forward with burning torches in their hands. A fenced-in forest with a gate appears in the background. On fol. 18ᵛ, the author reports appreciatively that the young messengers, multilingual as they are, are sent on public and secret missions and often act as heralds.

Fol. 20ʳ: Eight peacemakers in bright red robes are next to follow. On fol. 19ᵛ, the commentator explains that these men are empowered to settle disputes without the involvement of the legislature.

Fol. 21ʳ: This image depicts the so-called Eight (representatives of the guild), who manage the civic wool industry. They are wearing grey coats as well as black, grey, and red headdresses. A watermill can be seen in the background. The Latin text on fol. 20ᵛ reports that they have the authority to monitor and sanction irregularities and disputes in the textile industry.

Fol. 22ʳ: The next group consists of six city secretaries dressed in light red coats and black or red caps. The text on fol. 21ᵛ comments that they both keep records and act as advisors to the magistrates.

MANUSCRIPT 78 D5: SHORT DESCRIPTIONS OF THE MINIATURES 243

Fol. 23ʳ: Next in line are six guild advisors on horseback, dressed in light-red coats. In the distance, one can see a castle. It is said that these men advise the aldermen and legislators and bear testimony to their activities.

Fol. 24ʳ: The next group comprises six receivers in light-red coats. On fol. 23ᵛ, they are called the treasurers of the public finances. On the horizon, the skyline of a city can be seen.

Fol. 25ʳ: The amman and the two burgomasters (mayors) are accompanied by seven swornmen (aldermen). Together they form the city's magistrate. The amman in the centre is bearing a staff and is wearing a red costume, a symbol of justice. As the ducal officer he presides over the court of the aldermen, who ensure that justice is done. The mayors, in turn, warrant that neither a too strict nor too lenient approach is taken. The aldermen and the mayors all wear rose-coloured city-coats. In the background appears the silhouette of a church.

Fol. 26ʳ: The burgomaster is accompanied by a large group of older and younger citizens, all moving forward on horseback. As skilful horsemen, they show the illustrious princess the wonderful wealth of her chosen citizens.

PART Id: Six Civic Society Groups walking on Foot holding Torches in their Hands

Fol. 27ʳ: A selection of professionals working for the city move along the street in two rows of four. They are specialized officials and artists appointed by the city, controllers of public works, craftsmen and artists who are considered the best in their trade, such as land surveyors, master builders, sculptors, municipal clerks, tower guards, gatekeepers, night watchmen, street sweepers and lantern-lighters. All of them are clad in blue coats and carry torches decorated with red emblems.

Fol. 28ʳ: The next group represents the Culverin Bearers from the Guild of Saint Christopher. The cross-shaped ornaments on their sleeves identify them as such. The text on fol. 27ᵛ explains that these men have the task of providing the prince and the city with quick and safe protection; the same applies for the three guilds that follow.

Fol. 29ʳ: This group of eight archers, clad in coats half-red and half-blue, parade in rows of two; their torches are hung with coats of arms. On their sleeves, two crossed arrows point to their association.

Fol. 30ʳ: This group represents nine members of the Crossbow Guild of Saint George wearing brown coats and caps with badges. The emblem on their sleeve consists of a flower in a vase from which hang two crossbows. In the background, one can see a watermill.

Fol. 31ʳ: The Great Guild of Crossbow Bearers concludes the procession in Part I. Their coats are divided into red and blue, and their long sleeves are adorned with the guild's emblem. As the oldest, largest, and most privileged of all four guilds, they have the honourable task of protecting the ruling couple and the nobility. Princess Joanna arrives at the *Grote Markt* (*Grand Place*) riding her richly adorned black mule on a side saddle. A lady from her retinue accompanies her. In the background, the Brussels City Hall can be seen, its gigantic tower illuminated with burning torches.

PART II: Twenty-eight *tableaux vivants*

Fol. 32ʳ-59ʳ show the wooden scaffolding with stages erected on Brussels street corners for the festive entry. The curtains open on demand, and several figures set themselves in motion with appropriate gestures and props. These so-called 'Living Images' (*tableaux vivants*) present a principal character or story relevant to Princess Joanna. In the Latin text, on the opposite folio, the educated reader is presented with an analogy to her person, origins, or family history.

Fol. 32ʳ: The inscriptions on the front of the stage refer to Tubal / Tubal Cain, the inventor of all metalwork (Genesis 4.21-22) – here incorrectly called inventor of music. In the foreground, to the right, three young men (one of them Tubal) are hitting a red-hot iron lying on an anvil with three large hammers. On the left, a bearded man with a sheet of music on his right leg (Jubal, the inventor of music, Genesis 4.21) notes down the different tones produced by the hammers. In a reflective pose, he has put his left hand to his temple as if recognising the harmonies that are being unintentionally created. The invention of music is further thematised by eight men and women in courtly dress playing music in the background. The text on fol. 31ᵛ expresses the hope that Joanna will bring together in sweet harmony all the territories in her realm.

Fol. 33ʳ: Judith beheads Holofernes (Judith 13.7-10) while he is lying asleep on his bed. The Israelite woman brandishes his own sword to cut off his head with the intention of putting it into the sack held open by a servant. Holofernes' guards at the front of the stage are oblivious to duty. On fol. 32ᵛ, Joanna is called upon – like Judith – to save her people by eliminating all that is unbeneficial to them.

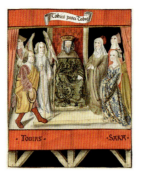

Fol. 34ʳ: Blind Tobit (Tobit 6-11) is enthroned at the centre of the stage, presented here like a ruler with a crown and staff. Sara stands in front of her father-in-law, wearing a crown and a sumptuous dress. Tobias approaches the throne from the left, guided by the archangel Raphael, who – unrecognised by all – served as his travelling companion and protected the young couple. The audience is told that the King of the Romans (that is Maximilian I) chose Joanna as a wife for Philip the Fair, as Tobit did for his son.

Fol. 35ʳ: Tobias and Sara kneel in prayer before their bridal bed, where all night they implore God for protection from the attacks of the devil called Asmodeus. Raphael vanquishes the devil who attempts to reach for them. Fol. 34ᵛ makes the following connection: just as Raphael protected Sara and Tobias, so Joanna was led through the dangerous sea by a guardian angel to meet her bridegroom in Brabant.

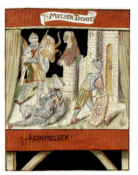

Fol. 36ʳ: From the city wall, a brave woman called Thecuites causes a millstone to fall on Abimelech, the commander of the enemy army, who is surrounded by three of his soldiers. He bleeds to death with his head crushed (Judges 9.54). On fol. 35ᵛ, Joanna is encouraged to crush her enemies in the same manner, from the bulwark of her lands.

Fol. 37ʳ: In the presence of nine court officials and three female attendants of the Pharaoh's daughter, King Solomon approaches his future wife with a sceptre in his hand, giving her his left hand in marriage (1 Kings 3.1). On fol. 36ᵛ, Philip the Fair is compared with King Solomon as he also received his future wife with open arms.

Fol. 38ʳ: Abner, David's field captain, lifts his cap and presents Michal to his master as his future wife. Michal, a beautifully dressed young woman, has humbly fallen on her knees (1 Samuel 18.21-28). The analogy to this Old Testament story is that of a Spanish admiral who safely brought Joanna of Castile to Brabant to marry Philip the Fair (fol. 37ʳ).

Fol. 39ʳ: This elaborate stage, designed as a triptych with carved gothic ornamentation, shows a heavenly zone with the Trinity, Virgin Mary and two angels. The earthly zone consists of a three-partite stage that curtains can close off. In the centre, Abraham instructs his servant Eliezer to woo Rebecca. Eliezer points upwards with his right hand to Mary, who kneels before Christ, dressed as the Queen of Heaven. The inscription on the frame indicates that Christ is to be understood as her bridegroom and Mary as the bride of the Song of Songs. Thereby a reference is established to the earthly bride Rebecca and her bridegroom Isaac, whose meeting is depicted in the left compartment (Genesis 24.67). The section on the right shows the wedding ceremony performed by a clergyman with a pointed hat. Rebecca is wearing a crown to make the analogy to Princess Joanna more evident. Fol. 38ᵛ comments as follows: like Rebecca, Joanna was married to her fiancé, Archduke Philip, in Lier and lovingly placed on the throne of the thirty estates left to him by his late mother Mary of Burgundy.

Fol. 40ʳ: Queen Esther's petition for her people (Esther 4.11; 5.2) is the subject of this two-partite stage. On the left, the Jewess Esther kneels death-defyingly – for it is forbidden on pain of death to approach the king without being asked – before her husband, King Ahasuerus. She asks for mercy for her people and her relative Mordecai. Next to him, dressed in a yellow cloak, appears the traitor Haman. On the right, Ahasuerus touches the queen's head with his sceptre and grants her requests. On fol. 39ᵛ, Joanna is called upon to protect her people from all who wish them ill. As Ahasuerus kindly restored Queen Esther, so Philip warmly embraces Joanna.

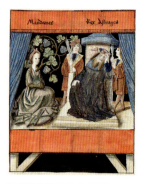

Fol. 41ʳ: The Median King Astyages dreams of a vine growing from the body of his daughter Mandane, symbolising the multiplicity of her offspring, and thus signifying a threat to his rule. Fol. 40ᵛ comments as follows: as King Astyages sees the vine growing from his daughter covering the whole earth, so Philip's fatherland hopes for many children from Joanna.

Fol. 42ʳ: Muhammad XII, also called Boabdil, capitulated after the siege of Granada by Spanish troops. On 2 January 1492, he surrendered the Emirate of Granada to the Catholic Kings. In this scene, Queen Isabella of Castile, the mother of Princess Joanna, is credited with the victory over the Muslims and is portrayed with her sword held upright. She is accompanied by two personifications; to her right the virtue of fortitude holding a column. Isabella eclipses the fame of all the nine following heroines, not only because of the weapons of her army but also by her unique spirit and the length of the siege. The inscription on the front of the stage underlines this message: all victorious women who have inspired poets are inferior to the sceptre-bearing (Queen Isabella) who conquered Granada.

Fol. 43ʳ: Deiphilis, the victress over the Thebans, is equipped with a helmet and armed with a lance.[1]

Fol. 44ʳ: Sinopis, the Queen of the Amazons, holds a sword in her right hand. Two female servants carry her helmet and a banner with her coat of arms.

Fol. 45ʳ: The amazon Hippolyta defeated both Hercules and Theseus. She wears a crown on her head and holds a sword in her left hand. She is surrounded by two women carrying her helmet and banner.

Fol. 46ʳ: The amazon Menelopa, Hippolyta's sister and comrade-in-arms, is wearing armour underneath her exotic dress.

Fol. 47ʳ: The Latin text describes Semiramis as the Empress of Babylon. She wears an elaborate crown and carries a sword. Her coat of arms consists of three thrones.

Fol. 48ʳ: Queen Lampeto, another famous amazon, carries a halberd and a sabre. She founded many great cities.

Fol. 49ʳ: Queen Tamaris, a ferocious fighter, captured and killed Croesus, King of the Persians, and Medians.

Fol. 50ʳ: Queen Theuca ruled the Illyrians and conquered several Roman legions.

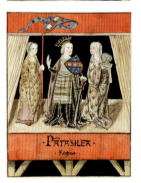

Fol. 51ʳ: Penthesilea, another amazon queen, fought alongside Hector and won many battles.

Fol. 52ʳ: The Queen of Sheba visits the wise King Solomon (1 Kings 10.2) and hands him a golden cup. A second gold vessel is offered to him by one of her court ladies. Eight men and a young woman surround Solomon's throne. Just as the Queen of Sheba paid tribute to King Solomon with gifts from her distant country, so Joanna came to the wise Philip with virginal shyness and gifts as an everlasting tribute (fol. 51ᵛ).

Fol. 53ʳ: The courtship and marriage of Florentius, Duke of Milan, with Meriana, Princess of Castile, is depicted in three separate stage compartments. On the left and right, the marriage candidates send a portrait of each other to their future partner. In the centre, the couple joins hands, and the wedding ceremony is performed. Fol. 52ᵛ states that just as Florentius and Meriana fell in love with each other at the sight of the portraits they received, so too did the portraits of Philip and Joanna ignite mutual love and marriage.

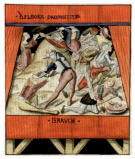

Fol. 54ʳ: On the left side of the stage, the prophetess Deborah prays for the salvation of Israel (Judges 5), her eyes fixed on the golden rays emanating from the sky. Thanks to Deborah's support, Baruch and his warriors succeed in destroying their enemies. On fol. 53ᵛ, the efficacy of Deborah's prayers is compared to the perseverance of Queen Isabella who helped King Ferdinand of Aragon to conquer Granada.

Fol. 55ʳ: Jahel kills the enemy commander Sisera whom she had given refuge in her tent (Judges 5.25-27). As Sisera rests on her bed, she drives a nail into his temple with a hammer. Jahel's female retinue recoils in horror. On fol. 54ᵛ, a parallel is drawn between Jahel and Joanna, in so far as the Spanish princess is expected to destroy the heads of her enemies with 'the nail of her exquisite power'.

Fol. 56ʳ: Three richly dressed maidens in blue, red-gold and pink robes sit on the stage. The one in the middle is holding a long rod that reaches far beyond the stage into the harbour-like area, filled with boats and barrels. Fixed to the end of the stick is a structure consisting of a crown, a dove and a small canopy of cloth. The Latin text of fol. 55ᵛ talks about a king marrying his daughter to the Duke of Brabant. The last sentence (fol. 56ᵛ) establishes a connection, by referring to King Ferdinand of Aragon who gave his daughter in marriage to Archduke Philip the Fair.

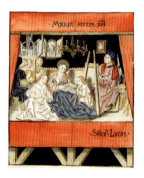

Fol. 57ʳ: The judgement of Paris is depicted on a stage that is clad in damask-like fabric. The scenery shows a stately building with two round-arched gates and a circular path running between them. Three naked goddesses, Pallas Athena, Juno, and Venus, are positioned on a mechanical device that moves around the fountain in the centre of the stage, so that the figures provide three perspectives on their bodies. On the far left, Paris has settled on the ground, while Mercury holds up a golden apple. The text on fol. 56ᵛ states that the three goddesses foretold the future to Paris and prophesied that Joanna, accompanied by good omens, would leave the ship carrying three gifts for Philip the Fair.

Fol. 58ʳ: This scene depicts the 'House of Pleasure and Merry-Making' where all sadness is set aside. Five couples are engaged in leisure time activities – dancing, eating, drinking, and embracing one another. On the left, a young man has fallen asleep in a lady's lap. The bed in the background suggests amorous encounters. A jester with a *marotte* in his hand points laughingly at the couple standing in front of the bed. A musician with a flute and drum is playing a melody for the couple on the right, who are served food and drink. In the foreground, a woman in red bends over a sheet of paper. Does she collect money for services rendered? Fol. 57ᵛ explains that on the occasion of Philip and Joanna's marriage, the hedonists are allowed to put aside all sadness and devote themselves to various pleasures.

Fol. 59ʳ: The Evangelist Luke, a doctor and painter by profession, sits at an easel with the colour palette in his left hand. Luke is painting a portrait of the Virgin Mary, sitting on the workshop floor. Four angels with flute, lute and organ play music for mother and child. The Evangelist is the patron saint of the Brussels's Guild of St Luke, whose members are all the artists and craftsmen involved in creating the festive entry. The text on page 58ᵛ makes the following connection: 'So the Creator, with some assistance of fate, sent Joanna of Spain to Brabant as an image to be embraced'.

---

1 In the fifteenth century *The Book of the City of Ladies* by Christine de Pizan is a widely used text in which these fierce women occupy a prominent position. Seven of the nine worthies are presented: Sinopis, ch.XVI; Hippolyta and Menelope, ch.XVIII; Semiramis ch. XV; Lampeto ch. XVI; Tamaris, ch. XVII; Penthesilea ch. XIX. The two heroines Sinopis and Theuca missing from Christine de Pizan`s Book can be found in the complete list of the nine worthies in the didactic poem *Le livre du Chevalier errant* by Tommaso III di Saluzzo. Christine de Pizan knew of this book and used it. Hers had a far greater circulation and impact than the *Chevalier errant*.

PART III: The heraldic Devices of Princess Joanna of Castile and Prince Philip the Fair

Fol. 60ʳ: This folio represents the coats of arms of the ten kingdoms Joanna brings into the marriage.

Fol. 61ʳ: This folio displays the coats of arms of the thirty estates that Philip the Fair brings into the marriage.

VERENA DEMOED

Manuscript 78 D5

The Latin Text: Transcription and Translation*

Part I (fols 1ʳ-31ʳ)

2ʳ

Quo Egregios animos novitatu[m]q[ue] cupidos q[uam] exertis brachiis pronis affectibus patulisque y[m]mo p[re]cordiis insignis Bruxellaru[m] ducatus Braba[n]tie opidi cives quinto ydus decembris anni nonagesimisexti in occursum serenissime Johanne gloriosissimi fernandi hyspanie Castillie, [etc.] regis Illustrissimi Philippi archiducis Austrie Romanoru[m] regis Maximiliani semper augusti filii co[n]iugis utpote eorum principis ac d[omi]ne desideratissime prodiere q[uamque] sinceriss[i]mis votis festivis applausibus profusis gaudiis Jocundu[m] eius suorumque adventu[m] excepere minime lateat hoc in libello su[m]mis quasi labris (sollicite depictas effigies intuenti) vide[ndum] erit ubi et pro subscriptis titulis seu argumentis qui ordine quo cuiusque officii dignitatisve prosilierint denique figuris (quas personagias vocam[us]) quid scenis operam dantes tropologes pretenderint quo et benignissima hera devotos sue excellentie cives foveat congratulansq[ue] inspector sine dente quid negligentie precipitior affectus admiserit suppleat liquide patebit.

> For it to be no longer concealed from the excellent minds who are keen on novelties, how the citizens of the prominent city of Brussels in the Duchy of Brabant on 9 December 1496 went to meet their most beloved princess and lady – the serene Joanna, daughter of the glorious Ferdinand, King of Spain, Castile, etc., married to the illustrious Philip, Archduke of Austria, son of Maximilian, King of the Romans, semper Augustus[1] – with outstretched

---

* Verena Demoed comments: 'Abbreviations in the Latin text have been resolved and placed in square brackets. In the English translation, words that do not appear in the Latin text have been written in italics and placed in square brackets'. In consultation with Tino Licht (Heidelberg, Department of Middle Latin and Neo-Latin), Claire Billen and Wim Blockmans a number of alterations were made to the first transcription and the translation of the Latin texts. The English text was revised by Annemarie Jordan Gschwend. We are grateful for having been able to consult the translations by Paul Vandenbroeck as a point of reference when working on this text, see: Vandenbroeck, 'A bride amidst Heroines, Fools and Savages', 2012.

1 'Semper Augustus' is an honorary title that was used by the emperors from the Middle Ages onwards. If translated literally, it means 'always augmentor'. I thank Dr Holger Kaiser for this information.

arms, loving feelings and widely opened hearts; and how they welcomed her and her retinue on their well-favoured arrival with sincere wishes of well-being, festive applauding and excessive joy, [*all this*] will be easy to see in this booklet (for anyone looking intently at the depicted images), where it will be readily accessible, especially with the help of the written captions or summaries, who, in which order and from which official duty or high office they came forward; and also what the tropologists[2], putting a lot of effort in the scenes, intended to depict through the figures (which we refer to as characters). So, the most benevolent mistress can think well of the citizens [*seeing how*] devoted [*they are*] to her excellence, and the approving, sympathetic spectator can get a complete picture of what he failed to notice in his over enthusiasm.

2ᵛ

Hoc scemate representatur Inclita Brusselaru[m] opidi scolaris indoles que quasi trecenti numero nitidis superpellitiis tecta binatim sub suis didascolis ecclesiasticas cruces vexillaq[ue] subsequens diversis facierum phisonomiis morumque presagiis egregios futuros cives sortemq[ue] varia[m] promittens p[ri]ma Illustrissime brabantino[rum] [etc.] d[omi]ne obviam facta processioni initium dedit.

This depiction displays the talented disciples of the city of Brussels, which – almost 300 in number, dressed in beautiful garments, following ecclesiastical crosses and banners, [*walking*] directly behind their school masters in pairs, with various facial features that expressed their morals well, promising hope of an illustrious future citizenry and a manifold fate – began the procession being the first to meet with the most illustrious Lady of Brabant.

3ᵛ

Hoc scemate rep[re]sentatur dicti opidi venerabilis De monte carmeli emulatio que viros doctos probosq[ue] complexa processione[m] suo ordine co[n]tinua[n]s In archiducalis conthoralis castos mentalesque amplexus fudit.

This depiction displays the venerable zeal of the Carmelites of the said city, which (consisting of learned and virtuous men, continuing the procession in its order) poured their chaste and spiritual embrace over the archducal spouse.

4ᵛ

Hoc scemate Rep[rese]ntatur dicti opidi spectabile fratrum minorum contuberniu[m] quod su[m]mo civiu[m] stipatum favore mixtos iuvenib[us] senes haud secus q[uam] gaudentes pronosq[ue] sub districtu processionis in occursum dedit.

---

2 After extensive discussions with historians and literary scholars, it was decided to keep the term 'tropologists' which leaves open who exactly is meant here, members of the crossbow guild, rhetoricians or else.

This depiction displays the admirable community of the Friars Minor, which (regarded with the greatest favour by the citizens, old men mixed with young ones, happy and kindly disposed) joined the procession in the jurisdiction [of Brussels].

5ᵛ

Hoc scemate Rep[re]sentatur capellanorum numerus qui variis scientiarum titulorum etatu[m]q[ue] distinctus insigniis spectaculo dignus regio spetimini cum urbana tum ecclesiastica gravitate no[n] min[us] t[ame]n devotione alacer sese obviam fecit.

This depiction displays a number of secular chaplains, who (decorated with various insignia of knowledge, glory and age, suitable for the spectacle, with a regal demeanour, with a worldly as well as a clerical solemnity and nevertheless devotedness) met with [Joanna], filled with joy.

6ᵛ

Hoc scemate Rep[rese]ntatur canonico[rum] regulariu[m] venerabilis ecclesia quo[rum] ante Bruxellas conditas predecessores diuturno t[em]p[or]e in silva carbonaria locum que[m] imp[re]sentiatu[m] colunt archiducali aule contiguu[m] possederunt que religiose se clare principi obtulit.

This depiction displays the venerable assembly of the Canons Regular (whose predecessors possessed for a long time before the foundation of Brussels a place in the Sonian Forrest[3] next to the archducal court that they still inhabit today) who presented themselves piously before the fair princess.

7ᵛ

Hoc scemate Rep[rese]ntatur venerabile dicti opidi ip[s]iusq[ue] patrone s[an]c[t]e Gudile canonico[rum] collegiu[m] q[uo]d ab baldrico comite bruxellen[se] anno quadragesimoseptimo sup[er] millesimu[m] magnifice fundatum tam venera[n]dissimis viris refertu[m] usque hodie extat ut non scientia non canicie non gravitate non fama alpes transcendente verum omni virtutis decore non heroas eoru[m] singulos s[ed] patriarchas estimaveris qui uti insignis opidi singulare specimen eo vultu sese in occursum sceptrigere dedere ut alacritate auctoritate gravitateq[ue] co[m]mixtis supra homine[m] aliquid intuentiu[m] oculis i[n]ge[re]re[n]t.

This depiction displays the venerable chapter of Canons of the said city and of its patron saint St. Gudula, which (magnificently founded in 1047 by

---

3 The Sonian Forrest (*Forêt de Soignes* or *Zoniënwoud*) is part of the scattered remains of the ancient *Silva Carbonaria* or *Charcoal Forest*. It was a favorite hunting ground of the Habsburg Imperial family.

Baldericus, Count of Brussels)[4] still exists today, consisting of such venerable men, that you would have thought every single one of them was not only a hero, but a patriarch, not only because of their wisdom, old age, earnestness and a renown that reached Italy, but also because of every graceful virtue possible. They (as an extraordinary example of this prominent city) came to meet the sceptre-bearing [*princess*] with such an expression on their faces that with a combination of alacrity, authority and earnestness they showed the spectators something more than human.

8ᵛ

Hoc scemate Representant[ur] <u>Centenarii</u> existentes numero quadraginta quatuor qui pro ordine politice publiceque rei instituti (sub se quilibet decem dece[n]narios viros habens) turbationes quasque sedant armamenta varia penes se pro ignibus inimicisve occurrendis habentes singuli cum suis in procubiis dum rumor ingruit correptis armis sese tenentes haud modicum p[re]sidiu[m] oppido afferunt hii flexo poplite decenti ordine p[ri]mi plebeie multitudinis occursum fecerunt.

This depiction displays the Hundredmen, being forty-four in number, who – established for the ordering of civic and public affairs (any one of them having ten Tenthmen under him) – suppress any disturbances, in the possession of different kinds of equipment for dealing with fires or enemies, every single one of them staying with their comrades at the watch house, when a report is brought in, holding the weapons they picked up in their hands, they helped defending the city in no small manner. They – with bent knees, in a well-formed row – were the first of the common people coming to meet [*the princess*].

9ᵛ

Hoc scemate Rep[re]sentantur <u>Jurati vel decani</u> qui ex singulis officiis mechanicisve artibus annue quatuor electi iura statutaq[ue] cuiusq[ue] officii seu artis custodiunt ac ne ars ulla corruptione in mercato[rum] fraudem ledat[ur] preservantes quasi plebeio[rum] capita a politice superintendentibus dum casus requirit vitande multitudinis ac co[n]fusionis gratia ad consultandu[m] assciscu[n]tur.

This depiction displays the Sworn or Deans, who (four in number yearly elected from every single trade or mechanical art) protect the laws and statutes of the arts, making sure that no mechanical art is damaged by corruption to the detriment of merchants. As the leaders of the common people they are consulted by the city government in required cases to avoid confusion among this great number of people.

---

4 This refers to Lambert II, count of Leuven (died 1054).

10ᵛ

Hoc scemate representatur diversorum genus mimo[rum] qui suapte se dissimulantes cum diversis musices instrumentis obviam sese ingessere.

> This depiction displays various sorts of mimes, who (concealing, as is their way, their true identity) went to meet [*Joanna*] playing various musical instruments.

11ᵛ

Hoc scemate Rep[rese]ntat[ur] hystrio quidam qui partim lunatico cerebro correptus populo frequentem risum extorq[ue]re suevit hic (q[uod] nec dii dedignant[ur]) suo modulo affectum pium kyrieleyson kyriel[eyson] alta voce ingemina[n]s Illustrissime d[omi]ne (an allusere prata vire[n]cia q[uo]q[ue]) prodidit.

> This depiction shows Hystrio, who – partly affected by his lunatic brain – often elicited laughter from the people. This one, which even the gods did not object to, gave testimony of his pious inclination by repeatedly singing in a high voice *Kyrie eleison Kyrie eleison* most illustrious Lord – or did [*the words*] allude to the green fields?[5]

12ᵛ

Hoc scemate Representant[ur] quidam qui se silvestres simulantes ac ethiopissam equo insidentem comitantes quod prefert scema exenium principi gloriose obtuleru[n]t.

> This depiction displays some men who (pretending to be wild men accompanying an Ethiopian woman who is sitting on a horse, as the depiction shows) giving the glorious princess a present.

13ᵛ

Hoc scemate Representat[ur] quida[m] qui spectaculi gr[ati]a grandiori equo vectus sede vice selle usus risum pluribus ministravit.

> This depiction displays someone who made many people laugh sitting on a big horse using a chair instead of a saddle on account of the spectacle.

---

5 The reference to the 'prata virencia' leaves room for interpretation. Does the author refer to the 'Elysian Fields' (Tino Licht), or does this point to a biblical place of green pastures and fresh water as described in Psalm 23,2 (Claire Billen).

14ᵛ

Hoc scemate Representant[ur] quidam qui co[m]posita satis arte sese provectioris etatis silvestres fi[n]xerant magnisque clavis quasi invicem decertantes gratum satis sup[er]cilium intuentib[us] extorseru[n]t.

> This depiction displays some people who dressed themselves quite artfully as young wild men and who (fighting among themselves as it were with big clubs) elicited an approving nod from the spectators.

15ᵛ

Hoc scemate Representant[ur] quidam qui traha vecti faciesq[ue] tecti diversis musis artis sue acceptissima[m] armonia[m] compegerunt.

> This depiction displays some people who – (riding in a sledge) and their faces covered – created with different musical compositions most acceptable harmony.

16ᵛ

Hoc scemate Rep[rese]ntat[ur] carnificu[m] opidi agilis iuvent[us] q[ue] trigi[n]ta sex novis tunicis utriusque principis (ut patet) colorib[us] distinctis tecti equis insidentes cereasq[ue] rutilantes faculas gestantes solitiq[ue] expediens et Juvenilis animi solitiq[ue] id genus tum affectus tu[m] emolumenti prestitere inditia.

> This depiction displays the quick youngsters of the Butchers' [guild] from the city, who (thirty-six [in number], dressed in new garments in the colours of both princes (as can be seen), sitting on horses and carrying torches of wax, glowing in reddish colour) eagerly and with their usual youthful spirit, demonstrate this kind of enthusiasm and effort.

17ᵛ

Hoc scemate Rep[rese]ntant[ur] clientes numero vigintisepte[m] qui iusticiario opidi iuramento ac salario obnoxii diem partib[us] dicere transgressores apprehendere vinculisq[ue] mancipare habent hii quasi politici corporis me[m]brum extremu[m] p[ri]mi suo ordine occursum fecere.

> This depiction displays the Sworn Sergeants, twenty-seven in number, who (bound by the city's judicial oath and payment) warrant parties to appear in court, apprehend law-breakers and can put them in irons. These men (the last link in the chain of public authority) were the first to come to meet [Joanna] in an orderly fashion.

18ᵛ

Hoc scemate Rep[rese]ntant[ur] <u>Octo famuli</u> d[omi]noru[m] opidi qui diversis linguis plurimaque industria prediti fide ac salario astricti aula[m] consulu[m] obvigilant p[re]conu[m] no[n]nu[m]q[uam] ecia[m] heraldo[rum] vices vel secreto vel palam missi apud diversos pro d[omi]no[rum] iussu occupant.

> This depiction displays the eight Messengers of the city's aldermen, who (speaking various languages and working very hard, bound by their loyalty and salary) keep an eye on the court of magistrates. Often taking the place of proclaimers and even heralds, and sent on secret or public missions, to various destinations, they busy themselves doing their masters' bidding.

19ᵛ

Hoc scemate Rep[rese]nta[n]tur <u>Octo pacificatores</u> opidi qui in egregio politices corpore laudabiliter adi[n]venti verboru[m] iniuriaru[m]q[ue] altricationes emulationesque quascumque citra legislato[rum] noticia[m] sua diffinitione sentenciaq[ue] sedare habent.

> This depiction displays the eight Peacemakers of the city, who in this illustrious political body, in a laudable way, can settle disputes about libel or injurious acts and rivalries, making decisions and pronouncements without the legislators' involvement.

20ᵛ

Hoc scemate Rep[rese]ntantur Octo qui sub nomine ghilde preside decano pro statutis Juribusque debite lanificium administrari excessus defectusque pa[n]no[rum] apprime corrigere hinccineq[ue] emergentes q[ue]relas co[n]troversiasq[ue] sua auctoritate ventilare suerunt.

> This depiction displays the Eight who (in name of the guild, presided by a dean, in accordance with the regulations and laws) were allowed to appropriately manage the wool-industry, especially to set right deviations and shortfalls of the wool-production and used to have the power to deal with complaints and quarrels that arise from these [*measures*].

21ᵛ

Hoc scemate Representa[n]t[ur] <u>sex secretarii</u> opidi qui camere co[n]sulat[us] vicissim inherentes uti lingua ac mens legislato[rum] eorumdem decreta partibus promunt eaq[ue] ip[s]a a[n]nalibus a[n]notantes secretorum quoru[m]que conscii nedu[m] secretando veru[m] co[n]sulendo consulub[us] su[m]mo adminiculo extant.

> This depiction displays the six City Secretaries, who (in turn, always present in the room of the city-council, so that the words and spirit of the legislators' decrees are related to the parties, and writing these things down in the records,

getting to know all their secrets) are of great help to the magistrates, recording as well as advising.

22ᵛ

Hoc scemate Rep[re]sentant[ur] sex qui sub nomine consulu[m] a[n]nue ex plebeia multitudine electi scabinis seu legislatorib[us] cum consilio tu[m] testimonio eoru[m] que aguntur in opem asciscunt[ur].

This depiction displays the Six [*craft guild members*], who are named counselors, elected on a yearly basis, from the plebeian lot are called upon for help by the aldermen and legislators to counsel [*them*] and to bear witness to their activities.

23ᵛ

Hoc scemate Representant[ur] hii qui vulgato nomine Receptores nominantur qui quidem rempublicam in materialibus administrantes erarii publici dispensatores noscuntur.

This depiction displays those who in the common tongue are called Receivers, who (administering the city in its material needs) are known as the treasurers of the public finances.

24ᵛ

Hoc scemate Representantur consules sive legislatores quorum septem scabini dicunt[ur] hii iura dicunt reliqui vero duo burges seu civiu[m] magistri nu[n]cupantur qui quasi eo[rum] auctoritate (cui proculdubio q[ui]vis incola obedit) Jus dicentium rigorem nunc mitigare nunc approbare creduntur hiique partibus quibusve civilium tum ad propositione[m] ammani (qui vice principis opido preest) criminalium actionum eque lancis pondus administrare iuraverunt.

This depiction displays the Magistrates or Legislators, of whom the seven who administer justice are called Aldermen. The other two, however, who – on their authority as it were (to which every inhabitant obeys without hesitation) – are believed to sometimes mitigate, sometimes approve of the rigor of the judges, are called burgomasters. And they have sworn to impartially give weight to criminal acts, on behalf of [*certain*] parties, [*individual*] citizens and at the suggestion of the Amman[6] (who as representative of the prince controls the city).

---

6 The Amman was the ducal officer, whose jurisdiction extended much beyond the aldermen's, encompassing a vast rural region around the city. The amman's role originated from the powers of the seigneurial mayor (see Claire Billen/ Chloé Deligne).

25ᵛ

Hoc scemate Rep[rese]ntat[ur] civiu[m] seu opidanoru[m] tum senum tum Juvenu[m] mixta congeries que pronis affectib[us] equos scandens (quod eorum cuilibet familiare hactenus extit) Burgismagistris comitivam dans illustrissime principi electorum (citra tamen electionem) civium et copiam et spectaculum fecit.

> This depiction displays a crowd of citizens or burghers, older and younger people mixed together, who – with high spirits mounting horses (which all of them seem to be very good at), escorting the Burgomasters – made [*apparent*] to the most illustrious princess the marvellous wealth of her elected citizens (without a choice having to be made).

26ᵛ

Hoc scemate Rep[rese]ntat[ur] spectabilis multitudo stipendario[rum] opidi puta presidum operaru[m] ac armamentoru[m] et ho[rum] qui artis sue exp[er]tissimi habentur ut sunt mathematici architecti antropoformite et id genus Ceteru[m] vigilu[m] turriu[m] ac portaru[m] opidi clamatoru[m] luminu[m] et igniu[m] qui singulis noctib[us] preconisantes hiis cautio adhibeatur opidu[m] circueunt luti villico[rum] qui mundandis plateis presunt [etc.] qui singuli vestib[us] coloris opidi insigniti si[n]gulas flambas deferentes pedes morose ex utroq[ue] platearu[m] late[re]) incedentes suis densitate ac faculis cu[m] tenebras tu[m] opprimentes profligantes usque in ducalem aulam i[n]iunctum famulatum exhibue[re].

> This depiction displays the respectable group of professionals, paid by the city, namely the controllers of public works, and those who are thought to be the best in their art, such as land surveyors, master-builders, sculptors and this kind of people. Furthermore, the watchmen of the towers and gates of the city, the extinguishers of lights and fires, who every night march around the city proclaiming that they should be cautious, the waste-masters, who preside over cleaning the streets, etc., who (all of them identifiable by clothing in the colour of the city, carrying a banner each, slowly walking from both sides of the roads, putting to flight the looming darkness with the density of their torches, all the way to the ducal court) showed [*their*] imposed servitude.

27ᵛ

Hoc scemate Rep[rese]ntatur <u>ghilda</u> sive electa societas Colvuriano[rum] seu bombardellio[rum] qui armis eoq[ue] genere bellici apparatus muniti cum tribus subsequentib[us] ghildis ad vel tenuissimu[m] rumore[m] domum opidi seu aulam co[n]sulu[m] occupantes Ibique iussa burgismagistro[rum] expectantes et principi et opido tum promptu[m] tum tutu[m] presidium exhibere soliti Itidem iuraverunt hii eque suis intersignitis vestibus tecti singulasque faces tenentes pedes ordine precedentiu[m] obsequiu[m] prebuerunt.

This depiction displays the excellent guild or society of the Culverin Bearers or the Shooters of Harquebuses, who protect themselves with weapons and this kind of military equipment, occupy the city hall or the court of the magistrates at the smallest sign of trouble together with the three following guilds, and wait there for the burgomaster's instructions, always providing the prince and the city with quick and safe protection, just like they have sworn to do. They (dressed in their uniforms that are all marked in the same way, each holding a torch, going on foot in the same well-ordered way as those that went before) showed their obedience [*to Joanna*].

28ᵛ

Hoc scemate Rep[rese]ntatur altera ghilda puta arcuum manualiu[m] tractores qui haud minus q[uam] precedentes suis tortisis lucem diei mentiti famulatui paruere.

This depiction represents the second guild, namely those wielding bows, who (not unlike the preceding [*guild*] emulating the daylight with their torches) obeyed in servitude.

29ᵛ

Hoc scemate Rep[rese]ntat[ur] tercia ghilda que Junior arbalista seu sancti Georgii dicitur hii ceteris paribus cereis luminib[us] propriisque intersigniis utentes iuxta co[m]missum ordinem p[re]dictu[m] observavere.

This depiction shows the third guild, that is called the Young Crossbow Bearers of Saint George. They (wielding the same torches of wax as the others, but their own coats of arms) adhered, as instructed, to the already mentioned good order.

30ᵛ

Hoc scemate Rep[rese]ntat[ur] ghilda q[ue] arbalistis utens magna cu[m] antiquitate t[em]p[or]is tum excellentia previlegioru[m] dicitur hec gravissimis viris fulta (q[uo]d ei ex usu est) serenissime d[omi]ne principu[m]q[ue] ac proceru[m] latera stipavit quorum singuli suis vestiu[m] intersigniis ge[m]mata[rum] phaleratha[rum]q[ue] manica[rum] fulgure choruscantes cum ardentibus facib[us] tumultuose populariu[m] multitudini tale silentium incusseru[n]t ut et vicissim visendi notandiq[ue] p[rese]ntibus adminiculo hiisq[ue] ac posteris miraculo fuisse potuerit.

This depiction displays the Great Guild of Crossbow Bearers. It is said to be very old and to have the greatest privileges. Made strong by eminent men (which is of use to it), it shields the side of the most serene Lady and the nobles. All of them (with their coats of arms on their clothing, glittering with bright jewels and shining ornaments that adorn the long sleeves of their tunics, with burning torches) caused such a silence among the mass of people, so that they in turn, notable and remarkable, could be an encouragement for the people present, and a source of amazement for them and posterity.

Part II (fols 31ᵛ-59ʳ)

31ᵛ

Sequu[n]tur effigies seu scemata figuraru[m] (quas personagias vocamus) in scenis seu elevatis et clausis esschaufaudis⁷ in conis vicorum locata[rum] q[ue] pretereu[n]tium cum oportunitate tu[m] requesta cortinis ad hoc aptatis nunc velabant[ur] nunc pateba[n]t obtutibus que nedu[m] gesto[rum] congrua fictione ac mirabili po[m]posoque apparatu q[uam] optime condecentis tropologie⁸ (ut patebit) applicatione cunctorum (l[itte]ratoru[m]que precipue) a[n]i[m]os oblectavere.
Primo hoc scemate Rep[rese]ntatur Q[ui] uti medio sonantium malleoru[m] dulcem musices melodia[m] Jubal seu tubal adinvenit Sic <u>Johanna hyspanie</u> gravi auctoritate qua[m] in triginta patrias accepit mille milium a[n]i[m]os in una[m] pacis accordantiam adunabit.

> What follows are the images or depictions of figures (which we refer to as characters) placed on stages or raised and closed-off platforms on the corners of streets, that were opened and closed at the convenience and request of the passers-by with curtains made for this purpose, which – with the appropriate simulation of gestures and wonderful and sensational props, applying the most fitting tropology (as will be clear) – pleased the hearts of all (but especially of the literati).
> This first depiction displays how – in the middle of clammering hammers – Jubal or Tubal invented the sweet melody of music. So Joanna of Spain will unite countless souls in one agreement of peace with the great power she received over thirty countries.

32ʳ

TUBAL I[N]VENTOR MUSICE
TUBAL CAIM

> Tubal the Inventor of Music
> Tubal Cain

32ᵛ

---

7 The term 'esschaufaudis' is derived from the French word *échaffaud* or scaffold.
8 The Latin expression 'tropologie' (*tropology*) relates to the multi-layered interpretation of literature by focusing either on the ethical lesson or the moral of the story. Tropology can also stand for a figurative mode of speech or writing.

Hoc scemate Rep[rese]ntatur Q[ui] uti Judith holofernem ad nichilum redigens proprio ense interfecit populu[m]q[ue] suu[m] israel redemit Sic illustrissima d[omi]na n[ost]ra Johanna quitq[ui]t adversi est perimens populum suuum liberabit.

> This depiction displays how Judith reduced Holofernes to nothing by killing him with his own sword, thereby liberating Israel, her people. So our most illustrious Lady Joanna will save her people by eliminating all that is unbeneficial to them.

33^r

IUDITH. HOLOFERNES

33^v

Hoc scemate Rep[rese]ntat[ur] Q[ui] uti Senior Thobias tobie filio suo sara[m] Raguelis filia[m] uxorem asscivit Sic Ro[ma]no[rum] rex Joha[n]na[m] hyspanie filiam / filio suo Philippo invictissimo conthorale[m] adoptavit.

> This depiction displays how Tobias the Elder took Raguel's daughter Sarah to wed his son Tobias. So the King of the Romans chose Joanna, Spain's daughter, to become the wife of his son, the invincible Philip.

34^r

Tobias pater Tobie.
TOBIAS. SARA.

> Tobias father of Tobias.
> Tobias. Sarah.

34^v

Hoc scemate Rep[rese]ntatur Q[ui] uti Raphael angelus sara[m] et tobiam casto amore orationibusq[ue] p[re]viis ab asmodeo salvavit Sic angelo ductore Johanna maris pericula sulcans philippo conjunge[n]da brabantie applicuit.

> This depiction displays how the angel Raphael safeguarded Sarah and Tobias against Asmodeus through chastity and prayer. So an angel guided Joanna across the perilous seas to Brabant to marry Philip.

35^r

Raphael Angelus
SARA TOBIAS

35ᵛ (Judges)

Hoc scemate Rep[rese]ntatur Q[ui] uti mulier Thecuites desup[er] fragmento mole abimelech excerebrans vita privavit Sic illustrissima d[omi]na n[ost]ra Johanna arxi austrie, Burgundie Braba[n]cie [etc] i[n]nixa letales inimicos conterere habebit.

> This depiction displays how a woman, Thecuites, took the life of Abimelech by crushing his skull with a stone from the citywall. So our most illustrious Lady Joanna, leaning on the bulwark of Austria, Burgundy, Brabant, etc. shall crush [our] deadly enemies.

36ʳ

MULIER TECUITES
ACHIMELECH

36ᵛ

Hoc scemate Rep[rese]ntatur Q[ui] uti Salomon sapientissimus filia[m] pharaonis regis egypti in uxorem suscepit Sic i[m]menso gaudio philippus austrie prudentissimus filia[m] hyspanie exertis brachiis excepit ac fovit.

> This depiction displays how Salomon the Wise once received the daughter of the Pharaoh, the King of Egypt, in marriage. So the clever Philip of Austria received the daughter of Spain with unmeasurable joy into his open arms and cherished [her].

37ʳ

filia pharaonis. Salomon

> Daughter of the Pharao. Solomon

37ᵛ

Hoc scemate Representat[ur] Q[ui] uti Abner marescall[us] exercitus quondam saul regis uxorem michol in ebron david regi reduxit Sic d[omi]n[u]s admiraldus hyspanie Joha[n]na[m] filia[m] castillie hyspanie [etc] Philippo coniugem in brabantia adduxit.

> This depiction displays how Abner, marshal in the army of the former King Saul, accompanied Michal to Hebron to marry King David. So a Spanish admiral brought Joanna, daughter of Castile, Spain, etc., to Brabant to marry Philip.

38ʳ

DAVID MICHOL ABNER

38ᵛ

Hiis tribus scematibus In una scena desuper [sexagint]a rutilantib[us] fla[m]bis p[ro]mine[n]tib[us] unacu[m] speculis decentissime co[m]positis rep[rese]ntat[ur] Q[ui] uti Rebecca per eleazarem servu[m] seniorem domus abrahe ex mesopotamia ysaac cu[m] nutrice et familia uxor accita Ip[s]iq[ue] vultu[m] pallio operiens in agro obviam facta demumq[ue] per eunde[m] in tabernaculu[m] matris sue introducta fuit Sic Illustrissima Johanna per claros ambatiatores ex hyspania cu[m] insigni classe profecta Inq[ue] lira brabantie opido mellifluo archiduci Philippo suo sponso letanter offenso solempni matrimonio gratisq[ue] himineis p[re]viis ab eodem in throno xxx patriaru[m] que[m] piissime memorie gloriosa eius mater maria liquerat amorosissime collocata extitit.

> These three depictions – on a single stage with sixty luminous torches burning from above, together with aptly placed mirrors – display how Rebecca is brought back from Mesopotamia with a wet-nurse and her family by Eliezer, an old servant in the house of Abraham, to marry Isaac. She approached him on a field while she covered her face with a veil. Finally she was led by him into his mother's tent. So the illustrious Joanna, accompanied by renowned ambassadors, departed from Spain with a fleet, and after she happily met the sweet archduke Philip, her spouse, in Lier, a town in Brabant, in a solemn marriage-ritual and with pleasing wedding-songs she was placed lovingly by him on the throne of the thirty countries that his glorious mother Mary, now deceased, left him.

39ʳ

Inveni quem diligit anima mea*
Canticorum [secundo]
Rebecca ysaack   Elyazar Abraham   ysaack Rebecca

39ᵛ

Hoc scemate Rep[rese]ntat[ur] Q[ui] uti Hester regina Judaica[m] plebem ab insidiis Aman mardochaeu[m]q[ue] eximens liberavit Sic Johanna hyspanie populu[m] suu[m] a malivolis tutabit. Et sicut assuerus rex persarum hester regina[m] judaici generis mitius a terra levavit. Sic archidux Austrie Philippus Joha[n]na[m] hyspanie cordialitus amplexus fuit.

> This depiction displays how Queen Esther guarded the Jewish people and Mordecai against Haman's treachery and saved them. So Joanna of Spain shall protect her people against those who wish them ill. And, as Assuerus, King of the Persians, gently raised Esther, Queen of the Jewish Tribe, so Philip, Archduke of Austria, very warmly embraced Joanna of Spain.

40ʳ

Rex Assuerus
Hester Regina

40ᵛ

Hoc scemate Rep[rese]ntat[ur] Q[ui] uti ex mandanes filia rex astrages vinea[m] florentem totam terra[m] tegentem vidit. Sic philippi patria prole[m] uberem ex johanna hyspanie speravit.

> This depiction displays how King Astyages saw a flowering vine that covered the whole earth growing from his daughter Mandane. So Philip's fatherland hoped for many children from Joanna of Spain.

41ʳ

Mandanes   Rex Astrages

41ᵛ

Hoc scemate Rep[rese]ntat[ur] Invictissima Castillie hyspanie [etc.] omni laude predicanda Elizabeth Regina Johanne n[ost]re mater Inclitissima que (ut scema prefert) garnapolitanu[m] regem pro genibus supplicem habens famosissima illa victoria quam non tam suo[rum] armis q[uam] suo animo cui par nu[m]q[uam] extitit et obsidionis diuturnitate eventuu[m] belli diversitate ac rei magnitudine nove[m] subsequentium ac o[mn]i[u]m illustriu[m] femina[rum] quas unq[uam] vel muse vel hystorie celebres cecinere gloria[m] fama[m]q[ue] obliterans i[m]mortales reportavit triumphos quos cu[m] verbis musisve minime vel silentio predicare indultum est.

> This image shows the invincible Queen of Castile, Spain, etc., Isabella, worthy of every praise, the renowned mother of our Joanna, who – having the King of Granada begging on his knees (as the depiction shows), belittling the glory and fame of all nine following illustrious women who have been praised in poems and famous stories with this well-known victory, not only because of the weapons of her army, but also because of her spirit, of which the like has never been found, and the length of the siege, the changes in successes during the war and the magnitude of the case – gained eternal triumphs that one may praise with words or poems, or in silence.

42ʳ

O[MN]ES QUAS MUSE POETARU[M] CANU[N]T VICTORIOSAS
SUPERAT SEPTRIGERA HISPANIE VINCE[N]S GRANATAS

> All victorious women who have been praised by inspired poets
> are inferior to the sceptre-bearing [queen] who conquered Granada.

42ᵛ

Hoc scemate Rep[rese]ntatur deiphilis que cum sorore eius argina famosissima[m] thebeo[rum] rempublicam cum civitate armo[rum] vi delevit.

> This depiction displays Deiphilis, who together with her sister Argina destroyed the famous state of the Thebans and its inhabitants with the force of weapons.

43ʳ

DEIPHILIS

43ᵛ

Hoc scemate Rep[rese]ntatur Sinopis feminiorum regina que ex circumjacentibus quibusq[ue] triumphos reportans cu[m]q[ue] hercule duros ictus conserens ex eo victrix evasisset nisi lis interempta feriendi copiam sustulisset.

> This depiction displays Sinopis, Queen of the Amazons, who – gaining triumphs over several surrounding [people] and exchanging severe blows with Hercules – would have come out of that [fight] victoriously [and] would have endured many more blows if the fight had not been interrupted.

44ʳ

SINOPIS

44ᵛ

Hoc scemate Rep[rese]ntatur Ypolita que cum menelope sorore herculem atque theseum pedestri certamine ac pugna alacri in terram supinos trusit.

> This depiction displays Hippolyta who with her sister Menelopa threw Hercules and Theseus backwards on the ground in a battle on foot and a spirited fistfight.

45ʳ

IPOLITA

45ᵛ

Hoc scemate Rep[rese]ntatur Menelopa que cum sorore ypolyta inge[n]tia arma conficiens totam grecia[m] triumphantissime subegit.

> This depiction displays Menelopa, who with her sister Hippolyta – making enormous weapons – submitted the whole of Greece triumphantly.

46ʳ

MENELOPA

46ᵛ

Hoc scemate Rep[rese]ntatur Semiramis babilono[rum] Imperatrix que armis instructissima hoc familiare habuit ut accepto ingrato nuntio haud prius comas capitis co[m]poneret q[uam] vel armis vel pace res decidisset.

> This depiction displays Semiramis, Empress of the Babylonians, who – being armed to the teeth – had this peculiar habit: whenever she received an unwelcome message, no sooner than she had brushed her hair, the case had already been decided with weapons or by peaceful means.

47ʳ

SEMIRAMIS
Imperatrix

47ᵛ

Hoc scemate Representatur Lampeto Regina feminio[rum] et macassinorum que ex europa et septe[n]trione victrix gloriosa evadens multaru[m] ac magnarum civitatu[m] conditrix extitit.

> This depiction displays Queen Lampeto of the Amazons and the Macassans, who coming gloriously and victoriously out of Europe and the North, has founded many great cities.

48ʳ

LAMPETO
Regina

48ᵛ

Hoc scemate Rep[rese]ntat[ur] Thamaris Clarissima que armis insignis crispantibus vexilloru[m] intersigniis (ut scematizat[ur]) cresum persarum atq[ue] medoru[m] Regem occisis ex suis triginta milib[us] cepit eique caput obtruncans ac in uterem sangui[n]e plenu[m] mergens (ut semper affecta[ve]rat) sanguine ebibito se saciaret Iussit.

> This depiction displays the renowned Tomyris, who – distinguished with weapons [and] heraldic arms emblazoned on waving flags (as is depicted) – captured Croesus, King of the Persians and Medians, after killing thirty thousand of his [soldiers], and severing his head from his body and putting it *in* a sack filled with blood, she punished him by letting him drink all that blood (for he had always been bloodthirsty).

49ʳ

TAMARIS
Regina

49ᵛ

Hoc scemate Rep[rese]ntatur <u>Theuca</u>,⁹ que Jullio[rum] sceptra gerens romanas legiones diversis cladibus attrivit semperque invicta et armis et virginitate nitida die[m] suu[m] obiens permansit.

> This depiction displays Teuta, who – wielding the sceptre over the Illyrians – destroyed the Roman legions in several encounters and she remained always unconquered on the battlefield and in bright chastity until the day of her death.

50ʳ

TEUCA
Regina

50ᵛ

Hoc scemate Rep[re]sentatur <u>Panthasilea</u> memoranda amasonu[m] regina que troyani Illius <u>hectoris</u> probitate affecta ultime troyanorum cladi summo presidio diversis armorum insigniis diu invicta extitit [con]tinuassetq[ue] glorie titulos nisi aut amati <u>hectoris</u> fun[us] aut infausta fa[c]ta (q[ue] plus equo <u>pirro</u> dexteras dederant) obstitissent.

> This depiction displays Penthesilea, the memorable Queen of the Amazons, who – touched by the Trojan Hector's goodness – was for a long time invincible during the final defeat of the Trojans with outstanding protection, marked by the different weapons [*she offered*]. And she would have continued to earn glorious titles, if not the death of her beloved Hector, or the unhappy destinies that stretched out their hand to Pyrrhus beyond the just.

51ʳ

PA[N]T[H]ASILEA
Regina

51ᵛ

Hoc scemate Rep[rese]ntatur Q[ui] uti regina <u>Saba</u> regem <u>salomonem</u> (sapientie eius gracia) a longinquis cum muneribus visitavit. Sic Johanna hyspanie <u>Philippum</u> sagacissimum cum virgineo pudore ac donis honorem perpetuu[m] impendere venit.

---

9 Teuta was queen regent of the Ardiaei, a tribe in Illyria.

This depiction displays how the Queen of Sheba honoured King Solomon (because of his wisdom) with exotic gifts from her far-off country. So Joanna came with virginal timidity and gifts to pay lasting tribute to the wise Philip.

52^r

Regina Saba Venit videre Regem Salomonem et audire Sapientiam eius.
REX SALOMON
REGINA SABA

The Queen of Sheba came to see King Solomon and to listen to his wisdom.

52^v

Hoc scemate Rep[rese]ntatur Q[ui] uti figure facieru[m] <u>florentii</u> ducis mediolanen[sis] et meriane filie regis Castillie mutuo p[rese]ntate amorem in alterutrum excandescere feceru[n]t exque hiis dicti matrimoniu[m] contraxerunt Sic vise <u>Philippi Johanneq[ue]</u> ymagines amorem vicissim reconciliantes celebres nuptias effeceru[n]t.

This depiction displays how Florentius, the Duke of Milan, and Meriana, the daughter of the King of Castile, fell heavily in love after seeing each other's portraits, and subsequently married. So, too, did the portraits of Philip and Joanna spark a mutual love, resulting in a memorable union.

53^r

FLORENCIUS
MERIANA

53^v

Hoc scemate Rep[rese]ntatur Q[ui] uti <u>baruch</u> ex inimicis oratione <u>delbore</u> prophetisse victoria[m] reportavit Sic <u>fernandus</u> hyspanoru[m] rex instantia Elizabeth eius regine ex garnato et adversariis victor evasit.

This depiction displays how Baruch once conquered his enemies thanks to the prayers of the prophetess Deborah. So Ferdinand, King of the Spaniards, conquered Granada and defeated his foes through the persistence of his Queen Isabella.

54^r

DELBORA PROPHE[T]ISSA
BARUCH

54ᵛ (Book of Judges)

Hoc scemate Rep[rese]ntatur Q[ui] uti Jahel mulier egregia Sizare Te[m]pora clavo perforavit. Sic Johanna hyspanie capita inimico[rum] n[ost]ro[rum] clavo discretissime auctoritatis sue dolabit.

> This depiction displays how Jael, an outstanding woman, pierced Sisera's temple with a nail. So Joanna of Spain shall batter the heads of our enemies with the nail of her exquisite power.

55ʳ

ZIZARUS IAHEL

55ᵛ

Hoc scemate Rep[rese]ntat[ur] Q[ui] uti imp[er]ator henricus semper augustus Godefrido barbato brabantie duci filia[m] suam Sophiam nuptui dedit Sic hyspanie rex d[omi]n[u]s Fernandus Philippo mellifluo austrie burgundie brabancie [etc.] duci Johanna[m] filia[m] suam in uxore[m] misit.

> This depiction displays how Emperor Henry, semper Augustus, gave his daughter Sophia in marriage to Godfrey the Bearded, Duke of Brabant. So the king and ruler of Spain, Ferdinand, sent his daughter Joanna as his wife to the sweet Philip, Duke of Austria, Burgundy, Brabant, etc.

56ʳ

TRES VIRGINES

56ᵛ

Hoc scemate Rep[rese]ntat[ur] Q[ui] uti tres dee paridi fata nuntiaverunt Sic Johanna[m] hypanie faustis comitatam tria dona Philippo afferentem applicuisse co[n]gratulantes avisarunt.

> This depiction displays how three goddesses foretold fate to Paris. So they predicted jubilantly that Joanna of Spain would disembark accompanied by good omens and carrying three gifts for Philip.

57ʳ

VENUS. IUNO. PALLAS.
PARIS MERCURIUS

57ᵛ

Hoc scemate rep[rese]ntat[ur] Q[ui] uti hii deliciosi cunctis se voluptatibus occupaveru[n]t sic occasione coniunctionis Philippi et Johanne ducum o[m]nibus tristiciis sese singuli exuentes cunctis iocis indulserunt.

This depiction displays how these hedonists have abandoned themselves in all kinds of pleasures. So have all – on the occasion of the marriage of their Duke and Duchess Philip and Joanna – laid aside all sadness and devoted themselves to all manners of merriment.

58ʳ

DOMUS DELICIE
ET IOCU[N]DITATIS

The House of Pleasure and Merrymaking

58ᵛ

Hoc scemate Rep[rese]ntat[ur], q[ui] uti congratulantib[us] <u>angelis</u> sanctus <u>lucas</u> ymaginem beatissime <u>marie</u> depinxit Sic parentib[us] fatis Rerum conditor <u>Johanna[m]</u> hyspanie amplectendam ymaginem brabantie advexit.

This depiction displays how Saint Luke painted the image of the Blessed Mary under angelic congratulations. So the Creator, with some assistance of fate, sent Joanna of Spain to Brabant as an image to be embraced.

59ʳ

MARIA MATER XPI
SANCTUS LUCAS

=============================

62

Notandum q[uod] Ignium Immensitas diversarum materiarum luminu[m]q[ue] eciam supra tecta mirabili ingenio instructorum qui ipsum opidum adinstar carbonis vivi accenderant (pro eo q[uod] nichil delicia[rum] eorum effigies visui afferunt) nulla scemata ponuntur eorum tamen eam fuisse copia[m] aspectu[m]q[ue] credatis que et si non troye carthaginisq[ue] incendia excessere nil tamen eis vicinius similiusve (eo dumtaxat q[uod] non tam diu arsere) unq[uam] visum fuerit.

It should be noted that the brightness of the fires and the torches of diverse materials, which were even placed on rooftops with great ingenuity and made the city glow like on fire, cannot be captured in the depictions (because images cannot convey their splendour to our eyes). You must believe, however, that these fires were so great in number and their effect so spectacular that, while the fires of Troy and Carthage may have been greater, nothing has ever resembled them more closely and similarly (even though they burned much shorter).

63-63^v

Hoc scemate quod sequetur Representatur Egregia ac incomparabilis domus consulum sive reipublice opidi <u>Bruxellensis</u> que pro facie seu anteriori parte ut patet (quantu[m] ars admisit) protracta est cuius situs commoditas ornatus amplitudo sumptuositas omnisque (supra qua[m] cogitari possit) architecture genus arsque sicut nec representari sic nec exprimi possunt quid nimirum cum nec visus perstringere sufficiat Ea siquidem (ut de decentissima penorum arcuationum aularum cameraru[m] tricliniorum tabernaculorum diversoriorum quibusve officiis exercitiis statibus apprime accomodorum mirabili proportionabilitate taceatur) est scaturientium in diversis locis fontium amenitas ut nec supra pinnacula locis accommodis desint quorum aliqui supra mirandum gratumque spectaculum susurriu[m]q[ue] consulibus quibusq[ue] refrigerium lavacrumq[ue] afferunt aliqui vero locis ubi vesice alleviate sunt fetorem tollunt Deniq[ue] picturarum ea dinoscitur excellentia ut vel unius camere exemplarioru[m] figurarum inexplicabilis ars aurea nomen (pro eo q[uod] nullo auro estimari possit) obtinuerit nec abs re cum non effigies quisq[ue] sed effectus intueri se credit Idq[ue] sit artis mendacium ut aliquando non nullos in amplexus attactusq[ue] compulerit Preterea bellici apparatus omne diversu[m]q[ue] genus (cuius speciebus singuli et conservandis et augme[n]tandis supplendisq[ue] presunt) decorem pariter et stuporem referre sicut nec facile sic nec tutum existit Turris que erea[m] ymaginem versatilem sancti michaelis opidi patroni sustinet nonaginta supra centum cubitos habet Domus vero in longitudine centum sexaginta et totidem quasi in quadro Verum in plaga occidentali habet turrim quamda[m] in qua privilegia secretissimaq[ue] q[ue]q[ue] continentur que sine aliquo ligno et structa et tecta tam mirabili opere existit ut in hoc solum ars (in ceteris pluribus dictum opidum incomparabile reddens) sese inferiorem reddiderit dictu[m]q[ue] edificium artem quamlibet excedere videatur Quibus o[m]nibus sed et civibus hiisq[ue] que eorum sunt sicsic illustrissima hera n[ost]ra Johanna archiducissa sese oblectet fruatur uberi herede ac pro voto de hiis iubeat ut et gratissimus locus (Isque inclitissime margarete Garnapolitanorum regine nativus) affectuosissimusq[ue] populus magnificentissime d[omi]nationi sue reco[m]mendati semper habeantur.

> The following depiction displays the wonderful and unrivalled town hall of Brussels. The facade has been rendered (insofar as the artwork allows). The pleasantness of the location, the decorations, size, opulence and architectural style and artistry (which far exceed one's expectations) cannot be captured in an illustration or in words. And no wonder, for the eye is incapable of taking it all in.
> Such is the beauty of the fountains that flow in various places, even from suitable places on the roofs (to say nothing of the exquisite and wonderful proportions of the storage rooms, the vaulting of the halls, the chambers, dining halls, canopies and meeting rooms, all of which are perfectly suited for the duties and activities of all the groups of the local community. Some

provide not only a wonderfully pleasant spectacle and charming clatter, but also refreshment and an opportunity for washing to all the magistrates, others remove the stench from places where bladders are emptied.

Finally, the building features a most exquisite set of paintings, which is of such a splendid nature that the indescribable artistry of the exemplary figures in one of the rooms has earned it the name of the Golden Room (for reason that its value cannot be expressed in gold). And for good reason, for to the beholder it would appear to be not a representation, but reality itself. And this has deceived people into touching or grabbing [*the paintings*].

Above all, it is not easy or without danger to relate the amazing beauty of all the different kinds of military equipment (whose splendour is not only preserved, but also increased and completed by one person each).

The tower that supports the revolving bronze statue of St. Michael, patron-saint of the city, is 190 cubits high.

The building is 160 [*cubits*] long, and the whole is almost a square. On the western side it has a tower, in which all the charters and secret documents are kept. This tower is built and roofed without any wood in a wonderful style that exists only in this work of art (that makes the said city incomparable in relation to all others) and seems to surpass all.

May all this, and the citizens and what is theirs, please our most illustrious heroine Joanna, Archduchess, in such a way, may she enjoy many heirs and may she rule over them as is her wish, so that her most magnificent rulership always favours this very pleasant place (the birthplace of the glorious Margaret, Queen consort of Granada) and its affectionate people.

Manuscript 78 D5

Reproduction of Text and Images

Berlin, ms 78 D5

Cover inside

Bound by C. Lewis 2.0.0

Ham. 353
Eriv. 148-1884

hr 37
IB No 218

57 without front: + 2pp of arms

Berlin, ms 78 D5

Duo Egregios animos nouitatisq; cupidos, in exercis machinis promis affectibus patulisq; vno effusis prodis, insignis Ruppellarie ducatus brabatie opidi ciues, quinto jdus decembris anni nonagesimi septi in occursum sereniss[im]e johanne gloriosissimi fernandi hyspanie Castille, et regis Illustrissimi Philippi archiducis Austrie Romanoru[m] regis Maximiliani semper augusti filij coniugis, vtpote eorum principis ac d[omi]ne desideratissime prodiere, quaq; smaerissime votis festiuis applausibus profusis gaudiis iuc[un]du[m] eius suoruq; aduentu[m] excepere, minime lateat, hoc in libello summi quasi labris solliciti depictas effigies intuenti videbit; Vbi et pro subscriptis titulis seu argumentis, qui ordine quo caiusq; officii dignitatisue prosiluerint, demq; figuris, quas personagias vocant, quid scene operam dantes, tropoloicos prenderint, quo et benignissima hera deuotos sue excellentie ciues foueat, congratulansq; inspector sine dente, quid negligentie precipitio[?] affectus admiserit, suppleat liquide patebit.

1496

Hinc De scemate representatur inclita Bruxellarum opidi scolaris Indoles, que quasi trecenti numero nitidis superpelliciis tecta, binatim sub suis didascolis, ecclesiasticas cruces bevillasque subsequens, diversis facierum phisonomiis, moribusque presagiis, egregios futuros cives sortemque variam promittens, ipsina Illustrissime brabantinorum etc. Jne obviam facta, processionj initium dedit.

Fols 2v-3

Hoc scemate repsentatur dicti opidi venerabilis de monte carmeli emulatio que viros doctos probosq3 ampleva processione suo ordine cotinuas In archiducali5 conthorali5 castos mentalisq3 amplevit sildit.

Hoc stemate Reputatur dicti opidi spectabile fratrum impiorum
contubernui quod summo ciuiu stipatum fauore, mixtos mulierib[us]
senes haud secus ip[s]i gaudentes pronosq[ue] sub districtu processionis
in oxursum dedit.

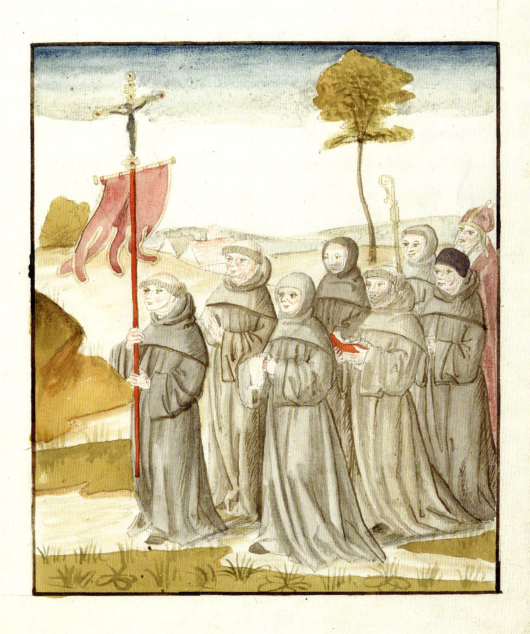

De fœcunditate Repsentatiuus capellanoru numerus qui variis scientiarum titulorum etatuq; distinctus insignime spectaculo dignus tertio specimine tum urbana tum ecclesiastica grauitate no minr in deuotione alacer sese obuiam fecit /;

De scismate Reputauit canonicor̄ regularui venerabilis ecclesia quor ante Bruxellas conditas, predecessores diuturno tp̄e in silua carbonaria locum q̄ impr̄sentiarū colunt arciducali aule contiguū possederunt, que resilitiose se clare principi obtulit.

De scemate Reputatur venerabile dicti opidi ipiusq̃ patrono sce Gudile canonicor collegiu̅ q̃d ab balduico comite bruxellen anno quadragesimoseptimo sup millesimu̅ magnifice funditum, tam venerandissimis viris refertu̅ vsq̃ hodie extat, vt non scientia, non canicie, non grauitate, non fama alyes transcendente, verum omni virtutis decore, non heroas coru̅ singulos, sz patriarchas estimaueris, qui du̅ insigne opidi singulare specimen, eo vultu sese in occursum septrigere dedere, vt alacritate, auctoritate, grauitateq̃ cornuu̅s supra hominem aliquid intuentui oculis ingeret.

                                    Centenarij
De scemate Representant centum viri existentes numero quadraginta quatuor qui pro ordine politico publiceq rei instituti Sub
se quilibet decem decenarios viros habent turbationes quasq sedant armamenta varia penes se pro ignibus minutis de occurrendis habentes singuli cum suis in proaulibus Dum rumor ingruit correptis armis sese tenentes Haud modici psidium oppido
afferunt j sin flevo poplice decenni ordine prius plebeie multitudini occursum fecerunt.

De fraternitate Repræsentantur Jurati vel Decani, qui ex singulis officijs mechanicis sive artibus, annue quatuor electi: iura statutaque cuiusque officij seu artis custodiunt, ac ne ars ulla corruptione in mercatorum fraudem lædat preservantes, quasi plebeiora capita a politice superintendentibus Dum casus requirit, vitande multitudinis ac confusionis gratia, ad consultandum assistuntur.

Hoc scemate representatur diversorum genus minor[um] qui suapte se dissimulantes cum diversis musices instrumentis obviam sese intessere.

De scemate Reputat[us] hystrio quidam, qui partim lunatico cerebro correptus populo frequentem risum extorquere suevit, hic sp[ir]itu s[an]c[t]o dedignant[e] suo modulo affectum pium kyrieleyson kyrieleyson alta voce ingeminans Illustrissime d[omi]ne (an alluser[it] p[re]fata viri cia s[upradicta?] q[ui]s) p[ro]didit.

Hoc scemate Representantur quidam qui se silvestres simulantes ac ethiopissam equo insidentem comitantes, qd prefert scema, eyceum principi gloriose obtulerūt.

De stemate Representat' quidam qui spectaculi gra grandiori equo vectus sede vice selle vsus risum pluribus ministrauit

Fols 13v-14

De scemate Representant quidam, qui coposita satis arte sese prouec tiore etatis siluestres fixerant manmsos clauis quasi inuicem de certantes gratum satis supatuum intuentib) cotospserit

Hoc scemate Representant quidam, qui trahia beatificiesq3 testi Diuersis musicis artis sue acceptissimam armoniam compererunt.

De sarmate Reputat' carnificu opidi aculeis iuuent? q̃ tristita seu nouis tunicas vtriusq̃ p̃ncipis vt patet coloribz distinctis recti equis insidentes cereasq̃ rutilantes faculas gestantes solst tig? expediens. et Iuuenilis animis ad genus tum affectus tu emolumenti prestitere subditia. ~ Asolutieʒ

Hoc scemate Reputant[ur] clientes numero viginti septem qui iusticiario opidi iuramento ac salario obnoxii diem partib[us] iteriter trans[-]gressores apprehendere vinculisq[ue] manupare habent, In quasi positia corporis membrum extremu[m] p[rim]i sui ordine octauis[?] fecere.

A descernate Repntant'. Octo famuli Jndoru opidi, qui diuersis linguis plurimaq; industria prediti fide ac salario astricti aula consulu obuigilant, proniu nonuq; eaa heraldoy vices vel secreto vel palam missi apud diuersos pro Jndoy jussu occupant;

De stemate Reputatur Octo pacificatores opidi, qui in egregio politices corpore, laudabiliter adiuuenti, verbo[rum] iniuriariu[m]q[ue] altricationes emulationesq[ue] quascu[m]q[ue] citra legislator[um] noticia[m] sua diffinitione sentenciaq[ue] sedare habent.

De scemate reputantur Octo, qui sub nomine Ghilde preside decano pro statutis iuribusque debite satisfaciunt administrari, excessus defectusque panor(um) apprime corrigere, huiusmodique emergentes querelas controuersiasque sua auctoritate ventilare suerunt.

De stemate Representat[ur] sex secretarij opidi, qui camere co[n]sulat[us] vicissim inherentes, vn[a] lingua ac mente legislator[um] eorundem decreta partibus promunt, eaq[ue] ipa a[n]nalibus a[n]notantes, secretorum quorumq[ue] consc[ii], nedu[m] secretando ver[um] co[n]sulendo, consulib[us] summo adminiculo extant.

Hoc stemate Repsentant scx̄ qui sub noīne consulū aīue ex plebeia multitudine electi scabinis seu legislatoribꝰ cuius consilio tū testimonio eorū que aguntur, in opem asasciunt.

De scismate Representant' hii qui vulgato nomine Receptores nominantur qui quidem rem publicam in materialibus administrantes erarii publici dispensatores notantur.

De scemate representantur consules siue legislatores quorum septem scabini dicuntur, hy iura dicunt, reliqui vero duo burses seu ciuiu(m) magistri nu(n)cupantur, qui quasi eor(um) auctoritate cui proculdubio om(n)is incola obedit ius dice(n)tium rigorem nu(n)c mitigare nu(n)c approbare creduntur, hisq(ue) partib(us) quibusue ciuiu(m) tum ad propositione(m) amani qui vice principis opido preest criminaliu(m) actionu(m) eq(ue) lance pondus administrare ut rauerunt.

De scemate Reputat' ciuiu[m] seu opidano[rum] tu[m] senu[m] tum iuuenu[m] mixta conseries, que promis affectib[us] equos scandens yd[eo] eo[rum] cuilibet familiare hactenus ext[i]tit Burgi[s]magistri[s] co[m]mitiua Dans illustrissime p[r]incipi electo[rum] (citra tamen electionem ciuium) et copiam et spectaculum ferit.

He de scemate Reputat(ur) spectabilis multitudo stipendiarior(um) opidi, puta presidium operarii ac armamentarii et hor(um) qui artis sue exp(er)tissimi habent(ur), (ut) sunt mathematici, architecti, antropoformite, et id genus; Ceteris vigilu(m) turriu(m) ac portaru(m) opidi, clamatoru(m) luminu(m) et ignium, qui singulis noctib(us) p(re)co(n)santes hu(m)c cautio adhibeat(ur) opidu(m) circuerunt, siu(e) villicor(um) qui mundan dis plateis p(re)sunt (etc). qui singula vestib(us) coloris opidi i(n)sig(n)iti si(n)gulas flambas deferentes pedes morose ex utroq(ue) platearu(m) late incedentes, suis densitate ac facul(a)e in tenebras i(n) oppriment(es) p(ro)fligantes usq(ue) in ducalem aulam iunctu(m) famulatu(m) exhibue(nt).

De scemate reputatur ghilda siue electa societas Coscincrianor[um] seu bombardellior[um] qui armis eor[um] tenere bellici apparatus mu[n]iti cum tribus subsequentib[us] ghildie ad hec tenuissim[us] rumore Domu[m] opidi seu aulam co[n]sulu[m] occupantes Ibiq[ue] iussa burgi[s] magistror[um] expectantes, et p[ri]ncipi et opido tu[m] promptu[m] tu[m] tutu[m] presidium exhibere soliti Itidem uiuarunt, In eque suis intersig[-]
nitis bestibus tecti Singulasq[ue] faces tenentes pedes ordine prece[-]
dentui obsequiu[m] prebuerunt.

De scæmate Repntatur altera tĥulda puta aratŭ manualiũ tractores qui haud minus q̃ precedentes suis tota sib lucem diei mentiti famulatui paruere.

Hasemate Repñtat tercia Mhilda, que humor arbalista seu sancti Georcii dicitur, hii ceteris paribus ceteris summibz proprijsqz interfignijs vtentes iuxta comissum ordinem pdictu observauere.

De scemate Reputat[ionis] cthuda q[ue] arbalistis vtens, magna di[citur] antiquitate tp[or]is, tum excellentia premi[ssorum?] dicitur hec gen-
uissimis viris fulta q[uo]d ex vsu est Serenissime d[omi]ne p[ri]ncip[i]b[us] ac
p[ro]cer[um] latera stipauit quorum singuli sius vestris intersignius
tesmatur phalerathar[um] maincar fulgur[um] choruscantes cum
ardentibus facib[us] tumultuose populariu[m] multitudini tale silentium imissu[er]unt vt et vicissim[?] visendi notandu[m] p[rese]ntib[us] ad-
miratio hui[us] ac posteris miraculo fuisse potuerit

Fols 30v-31

Sequitur effigies seu scemata figurarū quas personagias vocamus, in scenis seu eleuatis et clausis esschaufandis, in coīs vicorum socratas, q̄ preteritum cum oportunitate tū requesta, optime ad hoc aptans nunc volabant, nūc patebat obtinebus, que nedū gestoꝝ congrua fictione ac mirabili po posoqꝫ apparatu q̄ optime condecentis tropologie (vt patebit applicatione) cunctorum scatoriuꝙ precipue alios oblectauere.

Primo hoc scemate Reputatur. Q̄ vbi medio sonantium mal leorū dulcem musices melodia Jubal seu tubal adinuenit. Sic Johanna hyspanie graui auctoritate quā in triginta pa trias accepit, mille mutium alios in vna pace accordantiam aduinabit.

Fols 31v-32

H Defaemate Reputatur. Vti Iudith holofernem ad mensilium rediens proprio ense interfecit populusq; sui israel redemit Sic illustrissima Dna nra Johanna qui hys aduersi est primere populum suum liberabit

¶ De sama te bonitat. Qz vti Senior Thobias tobie filio suo sarā Raguelis filiā vxorem assciuit. Sic honor rex Johannā hyspanie filiam filio suo Philippo inuictissimo conthorale adoptauit.

De sacramente Reputatur. Vbi Raphael angelus sara et tobiam casto amore orationibusq́; puis ab asmodeo saluauit. Sic angelo auctore Johanna marie periculosa sulcans philippo coniunge da brabantie applicuit.

Hoc scemate reputatur. Ut bti mulier Theaute desup fragmento mole abimelech excerebrans vita priuauit. Sic illustrissima dna nra Johanna archi austrie Burgundie Brabacie etc. inipsa letales inimicos conterere habebit.

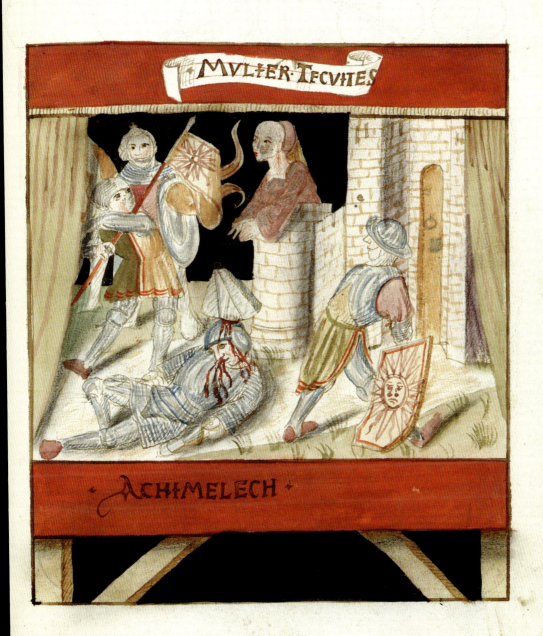

Hoc sermate Reputatur. Q̃ vt Salomon sapientissimus filiã pharaonis regis egypti in vxorem suscepit. Sic immenso gaudio philippus austrie prudentissimus filiã hyspanie evertis brachijs excepit ac fovit.

Hoc scemate representat. Qz vn Abner marescall9 exercitus quo dam Saul Regis hyorein(?) vnxit in Ebron Dauid vere reduxit Sic Dns admiraldus hyspanie Johana filia castillie hyspanie Philippo coniugem in brabantia adduxit.

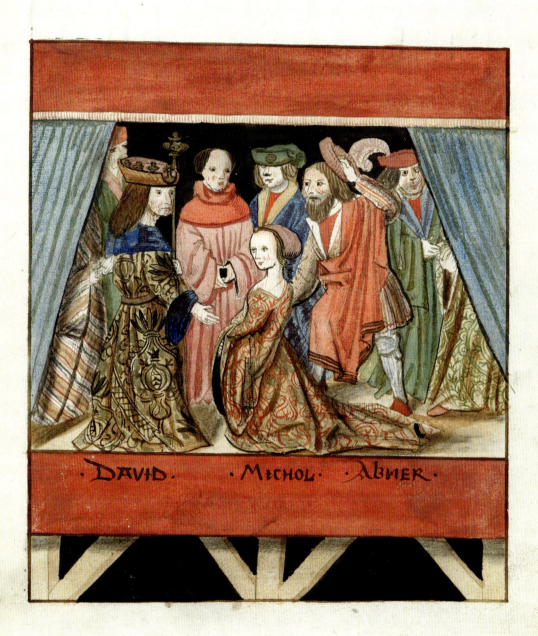

Ins tribus scematibus In vna scena desuper hyaº Rutilantibz flabis pumctibz vnacu specialis Scientissime compositis reputat. Et vti Rebecca per eleazarem seruu seniorem domus abrahe cp mesopotamia ysaac cu nutrice et familia hyor accita / spiqz vultu pallio operiens m actu obuiam facta / demuqz per eunde in tabernaculu matris sue introducta fuit. Sic Illustrissima Johanna p claros ambaciatores cp hyspania cu insigni classe profecta / frigz sua brabantie opido mellifluo archiducia Philippo suo sponso letanter offenso solempni matrimonio gratisqz himineis priusq ab eodem in throno yyv. patriaru que pijssime memorie ylosiosa ciuis mater maria siquerat amorosissime collocata extitit.

Hoc schemate reputat: Quod vti hester regina Judaicam plebem ab insidijs dnī Aman mardocheusq; eminens liberauit / Sic Johanna hyspanie populū suū a maliuolis tutabit / Et sicut assuerus rex persarum hester reginā Judaicā generis intuitus a terra leuauit / Sic archiduꝝ austrie Philippus Johāna hyspanie cordialiꝰ amplexus fuit.

De stemate Reputat̄. Q2 vt eo mandanes filia Rex astrages vineā florentem totam terra tegentem vidit. Sic philippi patria prole vberem ex Iohanna hyspanie sperauit.

De stemate reputat? Inuictissima Castilie hyspanie z̄ omni laude predicanda Elizabeth Regina, Johanne nec mater inclitissima, que vt fama prefert Jarnapolitanui regem pro gembus supplicem habent, famosissima illa victoria, qua non tam suor armis cp̄ suo animo, cui par nūcp extitit, et obsidionis diuturnitate euentuū belli diuersitate, ac rei magnitudine, noue subsequentium ac omn illustriū feminar, quas vncp vel muse vel hystorie celebres extuere, gloria famācp oblitterans, imortales reportauit triuin phos, quos cū verbis musisue minime vel silentio predicare insultum est.

De cemate Reputatur ꝺcipꝩlis q̃ue cum sorore eius arȝma famosissima thebeoꝰ rempublicam cum ciuitate armoꝰ vi ꝺeleuit

De stemate Reputatur Synopis femminor regina, que ex circumiacentibus quibusq; triumphos reportans, eius hercule duros ictus consecuta ex eo victrix euasisset, nisi lie intempta feriendi copiam sustulisset.

De scemate Repntatur. ypolita que cum menelope sorore Heraclem atq̇ theseum pedestri certamine ac pugna asacri in terram supinos trusit

De sarmate reputatur. Menelopaque cum sorore ypolita. mfcia
arma consiciens totam grecia triumphantissime subegit

Hoc scemate reputatur Semiramis babilonior Imperatrix q̄ armis instructissima hoc familiare habuit vt accepto ingrato nuntio haud prius comas capitis coponeret q̄ vel armis vel pace res redidisset.

Hoc sca[r]mate Representatur lampeto Reyna femina[rum] et marassi
no[rum] que ex europa et septe[n]trione victr[ix] gloriosa euade[n]s mul
taru[m] ac magnaru[m] ciuitatu[m] conditr[ix] extitit.

De sfcemate Repntat.° Thamaris clarissima, que armis insusme crispantibus hostio[ru]m intersicimus vt scematizat[ur] ceesu persarum atq[ue] medoru[m] Regem, occisis ex suis triginta m[ilibus] cepit, ei[us]q[ue] caput obtruncauit, ac in vterem sanguine plenu[m] mergens, vt semper af fectarat sanguine ebibito se saciaret iussit.

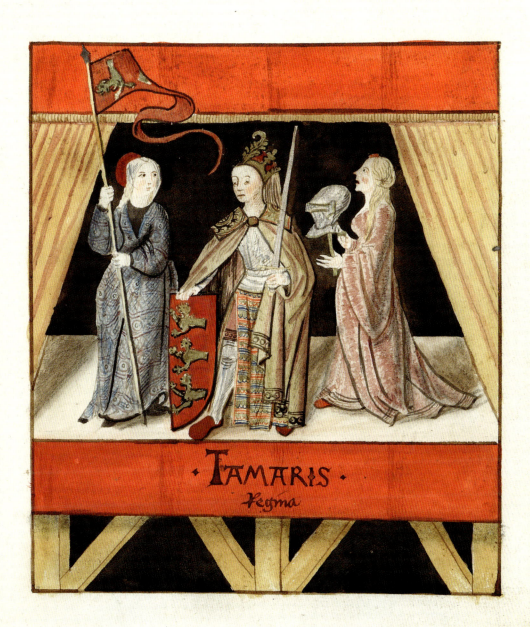

Hoc scemate reputatur Theuca que Iulior sceptra gerens romanas legiones diuersis cladibus attriuit, semperq; inuicta et armis et virginitate nitida obiens permansit.

dio libro

Hoc scemate Repsentatur Panthasilea memoranda amasonu[m] reyina, que troyanj Illius hectoris probitate affecta ultime troy anorum cladi summo presidio Diuersis armorum insigniis Inuincta extitit Ut nimia[s]setq[ue] ysto[r]ie titulos, nisi aut amati hecto ris fun[us] aut infausta fata q[ue] plus equo puero [ ]xprete[ ] dederant obstitissent.

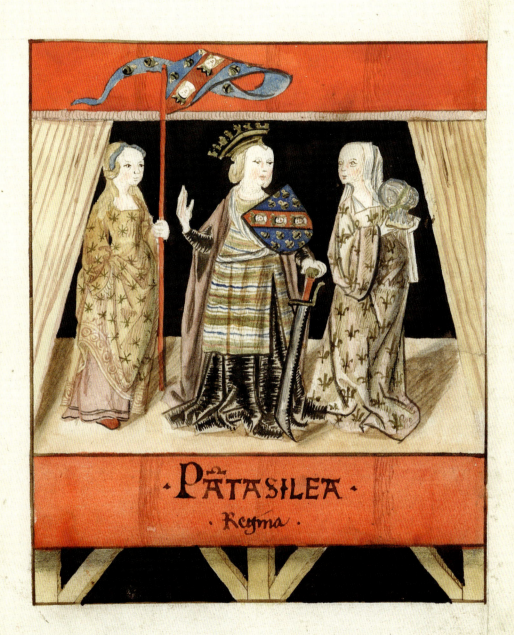

De stemate Reputatur Q³ vti regina Saba regem Salomonem sapientie eius gratia a longinquis cum muneribus visitauit. Sic Johanna hyspanie Philippum sapientissimum cum v[t]rinsecº pudore ac diuine honorem perpetuu impendere venit.

Regina Saba venit videre Regem Salomonem et audire Sapientiam eius.

· REX · SALOMON ·

· REGINA · SABA ·

Hoc scemate repsentatur. Q uti figure faceru florentiu ducis mediolanensis et meriane filie regis Castillie mutuo putate amorem in alterutrum excandescere fecerunt. Ergo hijs dicti matrimoniu contraxerunt. Sic vise philippi Johannes vmachines amorem viassim reconciliantes celebres nuptias effecerunt.

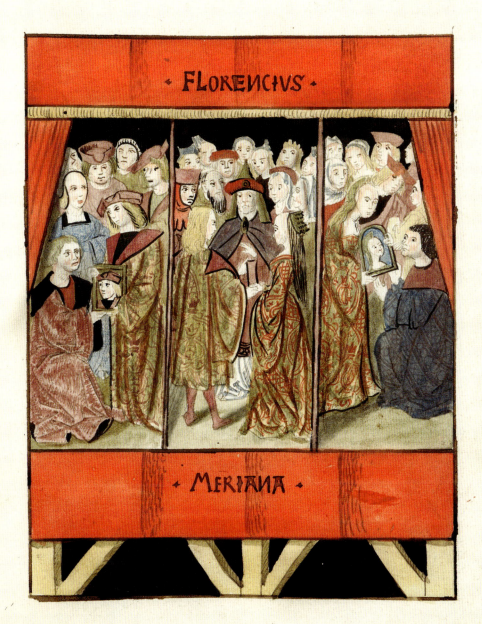

Hoc scemate Rep[rese]ntat[ur] Q[uod] v[t]i baruch ex munitis oratione delbore prophetisse victoria[m] reportauit Sic fernandus hyspano[rum] rex instantia Elizabeth eius regine ex granato et aduersarijs victor euasit.

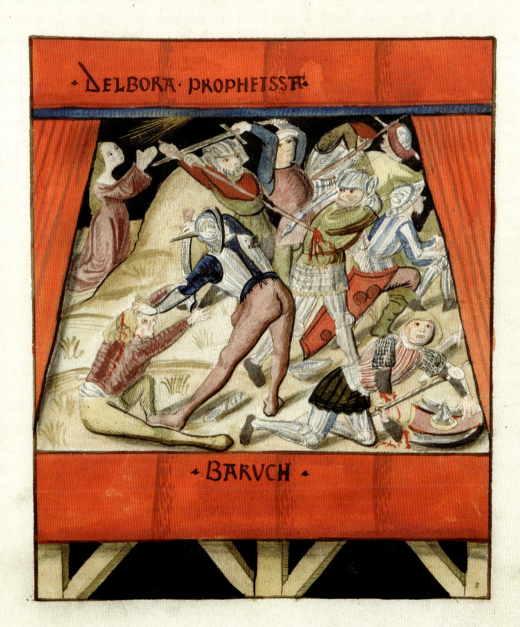

Hoc scemate reputatur Ut vti Jahel mulier egregia Sizare Tempora clauo perforauit Sic Johanna hyspanie capita inimicorum clauo discretissime auctoritatis sue dolabit

Fols 54v-55

De sarmate Reputat᷑. Et vñi inpator henricus semp augustus Godefrido barbato brabantie duci filiam suam Sophiam nuptui dedit. Sic hyspanie rex Iñs Fernandus philippo mellifluo aus᷑tric burgundie brabancie ꝛc. duci Johanna filiam suam in vxorem misit.

Hoc scemate repntat͛. De vti tres dee paridi fata nunciauerunt.
Sit Johanna hyspanie fausti͛ comitatam tria dona Philippo
afferentem applicuisse congratulantes auisarunt.

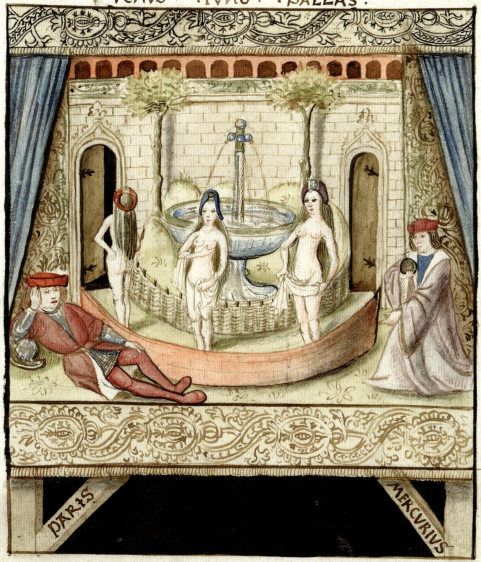

De feminate Reputat? Q? vti hu deliciosi cunctis se voluptatibus occupauerūt sic occasione coniunctionis Philippi et Johanne Juann omnibus tristiciis sese singuli eruentes cunctis iocis indulserunt.

De scemate Reputat*. Et vti congratulantib? angelis sanctus lucas ymaginem beatissime marie depinpit. Sic parentib? satis Rerum conditor Johanna hyspanie amplectendam ymaginem brabantie aduexit.

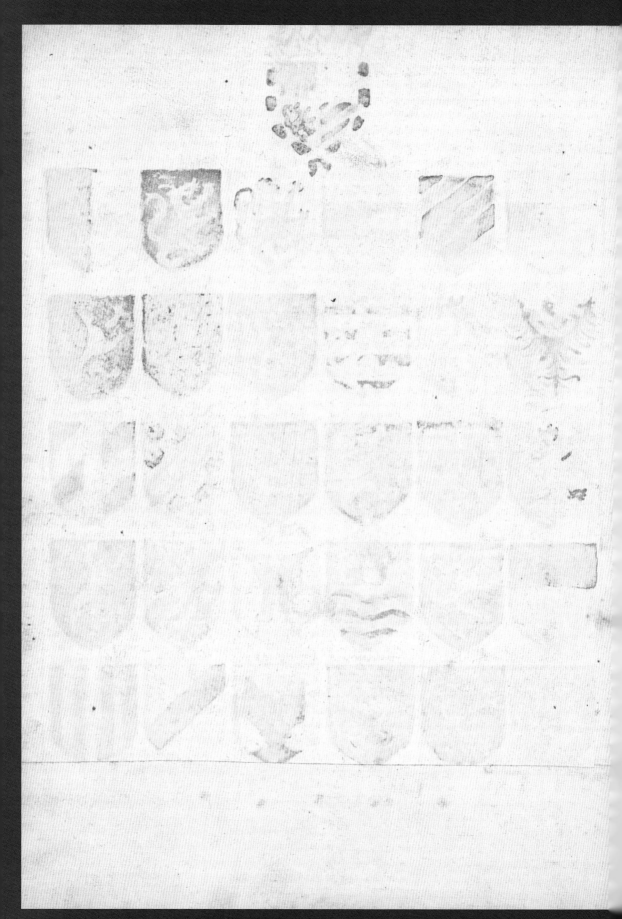

Notandum, qz Ignium immensitas diversarum materiarum summiq3 etiam supra tecta mirabili ingenio instructorum qui ipsum opidum ad instar carbonis viui accenderant (pro eo qz nichil deliciaru~ eorum effigies visum afferunt) nulla scemata ponuntur, eorum tamen tam fuisse copiam aspectusq3 credatis, que et si non trope cartha ginisq3 incendia excessere, nil tamen eis vicinius sum psisue eo du~taxat qz non tam diu arsere vnqz visum fuerit.

Berlin, ms 78 D5

De stemate quod sequetur Representatur Egregia ac
incomparabilis domus consilium siue reipublice
opidi Bruxellensis, que pro facie seu anteriori parte vt
patet (quam ars admisit) protracta est, cuius situs commoditas, ornatus, amplitudo, suptuositas, omnisque supra
quam cogitari possit architecture genus, artsque sicut nec representari, sic nec exprimi possunt, quid mirum cum nec
visus perstringere sufficiat. Ea siquidem (vt de decentissima penorum, arciuationum, aularum, camerarum, tricliniorum, tabernaculorum, diuersoriorum, quibusue officiis exercitiis, statibus apprime acommodorum, mirabili proportionabilitate taceatur) est scaturientium in diuersis locis fontium amenitas, vt nec supra vrinacula locis
acommodis desint, quorum aliqui supra mundum gratumque spectaculum susurrunt, consulibus quibusque refrigerium lauacrumque afferunt, aliqui vero locis vbi le-
sici alleuiate sunt fetorem tollunt. Demum picturarum ea
dimo satur excellentia, vt vel vnius camere exempsarioru
figuraturum inexplicabilis ars, aurea nomen (pro eo quod nullo auro estimari possit) obtinuerit, nec absque cum non ef-
fusie quisque sed effectus intueri se credit, Idque sit artis nec
natiuus, vt aliquando non nullos in amplexus attactusque
compulerit. Preterea bellici apparatus omne diuersusque
genus (suuis speciebus singuli et conseruandis et augmen-
tandis suspendesque presunt) decorem pariter et stuporem re-
fert, sicut nec facile sic nec titius existit. Turris que erea
ymaginem versatilem sancti michaelis opidi patroni sustinet nonaginta supra centum cubitos habet, Domus
vero in longitudine centum sexaginta et totidem quasi in
quadro. Verum in plaga occidentali habet turrim quamda
in qua priuilegia secretissimaque quoque continentur, que sine
aliquo signo et structa et tecta tam mirabili opere existit
vt in hoc solum ars (in ceteris pluribus dictum opidum

incomparabile reddens) sese inferiorem reddiderit, dictusq̃ edificium artem quamlibet excedere videatur. Quibus omnibus sed et omnibus hijsq̃ que eorum sunt sicsic illustrissima hera n̄ra Johanna archiducissa sese oblectet fruatur vberi herede, ac pro voto de hijs iubeat, vt et gratissimus focus (is) mellissime margarete Sarnapolitanorum regine natiuus) affectuosissimusq̃ populus magnificentissime Jnationi sue recomendati semper habeantur.

58 plate

Bibliography

Albrecht, Stephan, *Mittelalterliche Rathäuser in Deutschland. Architektur und Funktion* (Darmstadt: WBG, 2004)

——, 'Rathaus', in *Handbuch der politischen Ikonographie*, ed. by Uwe Fleckner, Martin Warnke, and Hendrik Ziegler, 2 vols (Munich: Beck, 2011), II, pp. 273-79

Alcalá, Ángel and Jacobo Sanz, *Vida y muerte del príncipe Don Juan. Historia y literatura* (Valladolid: Junta de Castilla y León. Consejería de Cultura y Turismo 1998)

Anderson, Ruth, *Hispanic Costume, 1480-1530* (New York: The Hispanic Society of America, 1979)

Anrooij, Wim van, *Helden van Weleer. De negen besten in de Nederlanden (1300-1700)* (Amsterdam: AUP, 1997)

Anagnostopoulos, Pierre, 'L'archange Michel et le démon de la flèche de l'Hôtel de Ville. Une girouette médiévale exceptionelle', *Studia Bruxellae* XII, 2018, pp. 206-34

——, 'Le saint Michel de la flèche de l'Hôtel de Ville (Grand-Place)', *Société royale d'archéologie de Bruxelles, Bulletin d'information*, n° 80, 2018, 7-12

Aram, Bethany, 'Juana "the Mad's" Signature: The Problem of Invoking Royal Authority, 1505-1507', *Sixteenth Century Journal* 29, (1998), 331-58

——, *Juana the Mad/ Juana, Queen of Castile'*, in *Renaissance and Reformation – Oxford Bibliographies online*, ed. by Margaret King (2023)

——, *Juana the Mad. Sovereignty & Dynasty in Renaissance Europe* (Baltimore: John Hopkins University Press, 2005)

——, *La reina Juana. Gobierno, piedad y dinastía* (Madrid: Marcial Pons, 2016)

——, 'Voyages from Burgundy to Castile: Cultural Conflict and Dynastic Transitions', in *Early Modern Dynastic Marriages and Cultural Transfer*, ed. by Joan-Lluís Palos, and Magdalena S. Sánchez (Farnham: Ashgate, 2016), pp. 91-114

Arnade, Peter J., *Realms of Ritual. Burgundian Ceremony and Civic Life in Late Medieval Ghent* (Ithaca, NY: Cornell Univ. Press, 1996)

Ars Habsburgica. New Perspectives on Sixteenth-Century Art, ed. by Fernando Checa, Miguel Ángel Zalama, Habsburg Worlds 6 (Turnhout, Brepols 2023)

Augustinus, Aurelius, *De civitate Dei / De la cité de Dieu*, French translation and gloss by Raoul de Praelles (between 1375 and 1420/1) Microfilm Edition, s. Sharon Smith Off Dunlap, Illustrations of Raoul de Praelles' translation of St. Augustine's *City of God* between 1375 and 1420, vol. I and II (unpublished doctoral thesis, University of New York, 1974)

Augustyn, Beatrijs, 'Staten van Brabant', in *De gewestelijke en lokale overheidsinstellingen in Brabant en Mechelen*, ed. by Raymond van Uytven and others, 2 vols (Brussels: Algemeen Rijksarchief, 2000), I, pp. 97-132

Avonds, Piet, *Brabant tijdens de regering van hertog Jan III (1312-1356). Land en instellingen*, Verhandelingen van de Koninklijke Academie voor Wetenschappen, Letteren en Schone Kunsten van België, Klasse der Letteren, 53, 136 (Brussels: Palais des académies, 1991)

Avril, François, and Nicole Reynaud, eds, *Les manuscrits à peinture en France (1440-1520)* (Paris: BnF, 1993)

Bartier, John, 'Un document sur les rivalités et les prévarications du patriciat bruxellois au XVe siècle', *Bulletin de la Commission royale d'Histoire*, 107 (1942), 337-79

Baumgärtel-Fleischmann, Renate, *Das Bamberger Heiltum von 1508/09 der British Library London (Add MS 15689)* (Bamberg: Historischer Verein, 1998)

Beatis, Antonio de, *Die Reise des Kardinals Luigi d'Aragona durch Deutschland, die Niederlande, Frankreich und Oberitalien, 1517-1518*, ed. by Ludwig von Pastor (Freiburg: Herder, 1905)

Beaufort, Christian, 'The Court Tournament', in *A la búsqueda del Toisón de Oro. La Europa de los Príncipes, la Europa de las ciudades*, ed. by Eduard Mira, and An Delva (Almudin: Generalitat Valenciana, 2007)

Belozerskaya, Marina, *Luxury Arts of the Renaissance* (Los Angeles: J. Paul Getty Museum, 2005)

Beneke, Sabine, ed., *Im Atelier der Geschichte. Gemälde bis 1918 aus der Sammlung des Deutschen Historischen Museums* (Dresden: Stiftung Deutsches Historisches Museum/ Sandstein, 2012)

Bernis, Carmen, *Trajes y modas en la España de los Reyes Católicos I. Las mujeres* (Madrid: CSIC, 1978)

Bevers, Holm, *Das Rathaus von Antwerpen (1561-1565). Architektur und Figurenprogramm* (Hildesheim: Olms, 1985)

Bianciotto, Gabriel, 'Passion du livre et des lettres à la cour du roi René', in *Splendeur de l'enluminure. Le roi René et ses livres*, ed. by Marc-Édouard Gautier, Angers and Paris (Paris: Actes Sud, 2010), pp. 85-104

Billen, Claire, 'Bruxelles première ville du Brabant, capitale de fait des Pays-Bas', in *Bruxelles*, ed. by Claire Billen, and Jean-Marie Duvosquel, (Antwerp: Mercatorfonds, 2000) pp. 58-69

———, 'La construction d'une centralité: Bruxelles dans le duché de Brabant au bas Moyen Âge', in *The Power of Space in Late Medieval and Early Modern Europe. The Cities of Italy, Northern France and the Low Countries*, ed. by Marc Boone, and Martha C. Howell, Studies in European Urban History 30, (Turnhout: Brepols, 2013), pp. 183-96

———, Chloé Deligne, and David Kusman, 'Les bouchers bruxellois au bas Moyen Âge. Profils d'entrepreneurs', in *Patrons, gens d'affaires et banquiers, hommage à Ginette Kurgan-Van Hentenryk*, ed. by Serge Jaumain, and Kenneth Bertrams (Brussels: Le livre Timpermann, 2004), pp. 69-92

———, and Chloé Deligne, 'Urban Space: Infrastructure, Technology and Power', in *City and Society in the Low Countries, 1100-1600*, ed. by Bruno Blondé, Marc Boone, Anne-Laure van Bruaene (Cambridge: Cambridge University Press, 2018), pp. 162-91

Bleyerveld, Yvonne, 'Chaste, Obedient and Devout: Biblical Women as Patterns of Virtue in Netherlandish and German Graphic Art, c. 1500-1750', *Simiolus* 28 (2000-2001), 219-50

———, *Hoe bedriechlijck dat die vrouwen zijn. Vrouwenlisten in de beeldende kunst in de Nederlanden circa 1350-1650* (Leiden: Primavera, 2000)

Blockmans, Wim P., 'Autocratie ou polyarchie? La lutte pour le pouvoir politique en Flandre de 1482 à 1492, d'après des documents inédits', *Bulletin de la Commission royale d'Histoire*, CXL, (1973), 257-368

——, 'Le dialogue imaginaire entre princes et sujets: les joyeuses entrées en Brabant entre 1494 et en 1496', in *À la Cour de Bourgogne. Le duc, son entourage, son train*, ed. by Jean-Marie Cauchies, Burgundica, 1 (Turnhout: Brepols, 1998), pp. 155-70

——, 'Diplomatie van vrouwen', in *Dames met klasse. Margareta van York, Margareta van Oostenrijk*, ed. by Dagmar Eichberger (Leuven: Davidsfonds, 2005), pp. 97-101

——, 'La Joyeuse Entrée de Jeanne de Castille à Bruxelles en 1496', in *España y Holanda*, ed. by Jan Lechner, and Harm den Boer (Amsterdam: Rodopi, 1995), pp. 27-42

——, ed., *1477. Le privilège général et les privilèges régionaux de Marie de Bourgogne pour les Pays-Bas* (Kortrijk-Heule: UGA, 1985)

——, *De volksvertegenwoordiging in Vlaanderen in de overgang van middeleeuwen naar nieuwe tijden (1384-1506)* (Brussels: Academy, 1978)

——, and Esther Donckers, 'Self-Representation of Court and City in Flanders and Brabant in the Fifteenth and Early Sixteenth Centuries', in *Showing Status. Representation of Social Positions in the Late Middle Ages*, ed. by Wim Blockmans, and Antheunis Jansen (Turnhout: Brepols, 1999), pp. 81-111

——, and Walter Prevenier, *The Promised Lands. The Low Countries under Burgundian Rule* (Philadelphia: Pennsylvania University Press, 1999)

Boese, Helmut, *Die lateinischen Handschriften der Sammlung Hamilton zu Berlin* (Wiesbaden: Harrassowitz, 1966)

Boffa, Serge, 'Réflexions sur la révolte des métiers bruxellois (22 juillet 1360)', in *Bruxelles et la vie urbaine. Archives-Art-Histoire. Recueil d'articles dédiés à la mémoire d'Arlette Smolar-Meynart (1938-2000)*, ed. by Frank Daelemans, and André Vanrie, 2 vols, (Archives et Bibliothèques de Belgique, numéro spécial 64, Brussels: KBR, 2001), I, pp. 163-85

Bonenfant, Pierre, and Madeleine Lebon, *Bruxella 1238: Sous les pavés l'histoire* (Brussels: LAP assurances, 1993)

Bonito Fanelli, Rosalia, 'The Pomegranate Pattern in Italian Renaissance Textiles: Origins and Influence', *Textile Society of America* (1994), 193-204

Born, Wolfgang, 'The Introduction of the Bulbous Dome into Gothic Architecture and its Subsequent Development', *Speculum*, 19/2 (1944), 208-21

Bouchet, Florence, 'Introduction au personnage de René d'Anjou: poète ou politique?', in *René d'Anjou, écrivain et mécène (1409-1480)*, ed. by Florence Bouchet (Turnhout: Brepols, 2011), pp. 13-21

Bousmar, Éric, 'Marguerite d'York et les putains de Mons, entre charité dévôte et offensive moralisatrice (1481-1485). Autour d'une fondation de repenties', in *Marguerite d'York et son temps*, ed. by Jean-Marie Cauchies, Publication du Centre européen d'études bourguignonnes XIVe-XVIe siècles, vol. 44 (Neuchâtel, 2004), pp. 81-102

Brachmann, Christoph, *Memoria Fama Historia* (Berlin: Mann, 2006)

———, 'Le Songe du Pastourel de Jean de Prier: Une chronique allégorisée au service de la mémoire lorraine de la bataille de Nancy (5 janvier 1477)', in *La culture de cour en France et en Europe à la fin du Moyen Âge*, ed. by Christian Freigang, and Jean-Claude Schmitt (Berlin: Akademie Verlag 2005), pp. 403-30

Brown, Andrew, and Graeme Small, *Court and Civic Society in the Burgundian Low Countries*, (Manchester: Manchester University Press, 2007)

Brown, Cynthia, 'Women Famous and Infamous: Court Controversies About Female Virtues', in *The Queen's Library. Image-Making at the Court of Anne of Brittany, 1477-1514* (Philadelphia: University of Pennsylvania Press, 2011)

Bruneel, Claude, 'Sus au monopole des bouchers bruxellois: le franc marché du vendredi (1771-1787)', *Bijdragen tot de Geschiedenis*, 81 (1998), 115-25

Brussels, Archief van de Stad Brussel, Historisch Achief, Register 3413 (*Liber Authenticus van de Broederschap van de Zeven Weeën / Liber Authenticus sacratissima utrisque christifidelium confraternitatis septem dolorem beatae mariae virginis nuncupatae*)

Bücken, Véronique, 'La peinture à Bruxelles à la fin du XVe siècle. Fortune critique et méthodologie', in *L'Héritage de Rogier van der Weyden. La peinture à Bruxelles 1450-1520*, ed. by Véronique Bücken, and Griet Steyaert (Thielt: Lannoo, 2013), pp. 13-36

Buitink, Saskia, ''Wt gelesen vrouwen om yn cameren te ordijneren'. Over de Neuf Preuses' (Verz. Leemans F.29V), in *Rapiarijs. Een afscheidsbundel voor Hans van Dijk*, ed. by Saskia Buitink, A. M. J. van Buuren, and I. Spijker, (Utrecht: Ruygh-bewerp, 1987), pp. 23-25

Bussels, Stijn, 'Powerful Performances. Tableaux Vivants in Early Modern Joyous Entries in the Netherlands', in *Le tableau vivant ou l'image performée*, ed. by Julie Ramos (Paris: Mare & Martin, 2014)

Calderón Acedo, Mónica, 'La construcción de la imagen de la reina Juana I de Castilla a través de su guardarropa', in *Las mujeres y el universo de las artes*, ed. by Concha Lomba Serrano, Carmen Morte García, and Mónica Vázquez Astorga (Zaragoza: Institución Fernando el Católico, 2020), pp. 225-35

Calvete de Estrella, Juan Cristóbal, *El felicissimo viaje d'el muy alto y muy Poderoso Principe Don Phelippe* (Antwerp: Nucio, 1552)

Calvi, Giulia, and Isabella Chabot, eds, *Moving Elites: Women and Cultural Transfers in the European Court System. Proceedings of an International Workshop, Florence, 12-13 December 2008* (Florence: European University Institute, 2010)

Campbell, Lorne, 'Rogier as a Designer of Works of Art in Media other than Oil on Panel', in *Rogier van der Weyden in Context*, ed. by Lorne Campbell, and others (Paris: Peeters, 2012), pp. 23-43

Carney, Jo Eldridge, *Fairy Tale Queens. Representations of Early Modern Queenship* (New York: Palgrave Macmillan, 2012)

Cassagnes-Brouquet, Sophie, 'Les Neuf Preuses, l'invention d'un nouveau thème iconographique dans le contexte de la Guerre de Cent ans', in *Le genre face aux mutations. Masculin et féminin, du Moyen Âge à nos jours*, ed. by Luc Capdevila, and others (Rennes: PUR, 2003), pp. 279-89

Cauchies, Jean-Marie, 'Baudouin de Bourgogne (v. 1446-1508), bâtard, militaire et diplomate. Une carrière exemplaire?', *Revue du Nord* 77 (1995), 257-81

———, 'Dans les allées et les coulisses du pouvoir: Philibert de Veyré, diplomate au service de Philippe le Beau (m. 1512)', in *Liber Amicorum Raphaël de Smedt*, ed. by Jacques Paviot, III (Leuven: Peeters, 2001), pp. 133-52

———, *Philippe le Beau, le dernier duc de Bourgogne* (Turnhout: Brepols, 2003)

———, 'La signification politique des entrées princières dans les Pays-Bas : Maximilien d'Autriche et Philippe le Beau', in *À la Cour de Bourgogne. Le duc, son entourage, son train*, ed. by Jean-Marie Cauchies, Burgundica 1 (Turnhout: Brepols, 1998), pp. 137-52

———, '¡No tyenen más voluntad de yr a España que de yr al infierno! Los consejeros flamencos de Felipe el Hermoso y del joven Carlos V frente a la herencia española', in *La monarquía de las naciones. Patria, nación y naturaleza en la monarquía de España*, ed. by Antonio Álvarez-Ossorio Alvariño, and Bernardo J. García García (Madrid: Fundación Carlos de Amberes, 2004), pp. 121-30

———, and Marie van Eeckenrode, '"Recevoir madame l'archiduchesse pour faire incontinent ses nopces…". Gouvernants et gouvernés autour du mariage de Philippe le Beau et de Jeanne de Castille dans les Pays-Bas (1496-1501)', in *L'héritière, le prince étranger et le pays. Le mariage de Jean l'Aveugle et d'Élisabeth*, ed. by Michel Pauly (Luxembourg: CLUDEM, 2013), pp. 263-77

Cetto, Anna Maria, *Der Berner Traian- und Herkinbald-Teppich* (Bern: Bernisches Historisches Museum, 1966)

Chmelarz, Eduard, 'Le Songe du Pastourel von Jean du Prier', *Jahrbuch der Kunsthistorischen Sammlungen des Allerhöchsten Kaiserhauses*, 13 (1892), 226-66

Christine de Pizan, *Das Buch von der Stadt der Frauen*, trans. and foreword by Margarete Zimmermann, rev. edn (Berlin: AvivA, 2023)

Coigneau, Dirk, '9 december 1448: Het Gentse stadsbestuur keurt de statuten van de rederijkerskamer De Fonteine goed. Literaire bedrijvigheid in stads- en gildeverband', in *Nederlandse literatuur, een geschiedenis*, ed. by Maria A. Schenkeveld-Van der Dussen (Groningen: Nijhoff, 1993), pp. 102-08

———, 'Roovere, Anthonis de', in *De Niederlandse en Vlaamse auteurs van middeleeuwen tot heden met inbegrip van de Friese auteurs*, ed. by Gerrit Jan van Bork, and Pieter Jozias Verkruijsse (Den Haan: Weesp, 1985)

Connochie-Bourgne, Chantal, and Valérie Gontero-Lauze, *Les Arts et les Lettres en Provence au temps du roi René* (Aix-en-Provence: Presses Univ. de Provence, 2013)

Conti, Santiago Fernández, 'Carlos V y la alta nobleza castellana: el almirante don Fadrique Enríquez', in *Carlos V y la quiebra del humanismo político en Europa (1530-1558)* (Madrid: Sociedad Estatal, 2001), II, pp. 29-51

Cools, Hans, *Mannen met macht. Edellieden en de moderne staat in de Bourgondisch-Habsburgse landen, 1475-1530* (Zutphen: Walburg, 2001)

Coomans, Janna, *Community, Urban Health and Environment in Late Medieval Low Countries*, (Cambridge: Cambridge University Press, 2021)

Coulet, Noël, Anne Planche, and Françoise Robin, *Le roi René. Le prince, le mécène, l'écrivain, le mythe* (Aix-en-Provence: Edisud, 1982)

Crombie, Laura, *Archery and Crossbow Guilds in Medieval Flanders 1300-1500* (Woodbridge: The Boydell Press, 2016)

———, 'From War to Peace: Archery and Crossbow Guilds in Flanders c. 1300-1500' (unpublished doctoral thesis, University of Glasgow, 2010)

Cuvelier, Joseph, *Les dénombrements de foyers en Brabant (XIVe-XVIe siècles)*, 2 vols (Brussels: Kiesseling and Imbreghts, 1912-1913)

Dacre, Jonathan, Boulton D'Arcy, and Jan R. Veenstra, eds, *The Ideology of Burgundy: The Promotion of National Consciousness, 1364-1565* (Leiden: Brill, 2006)

Damen, Mario, 'Prelaten, edelen en steden. De samenstelling van de Staten van Brabant in de vijftiende eeuw', *Bulletin de la Commission royale d'histoire. Académie royale de Belgique*, 182 (2016), 5-274

———, and Kim Overlaet, 'Weg van de staat. Blijde Intredes in de laatmiddeleeuwse nederlanden op het snijvlak van sociale, culturele en politieke geschiedenis', *Low Countries Historical Review*, 134 (2019), 3-44

Danckaert, Jacobus, *Het nieuw Brughsche herstelde stadhuys* (Brugge: Andries Wydts, 1711)

Davis, Natalie Zemon, 'The Reasons of Misrule', in *Society and Culture in Early Modern France* (Stanford: Stanford University Press, 1975)

De Boom, Ghislaine, *Eléonore, reine de France* (Brussels: Charles Dessart, 1943)

———, *Marguérite d'Autriche* (Brussels: Renaissance du Livre, 1946)

De Clerck, Lode, and Frans Dopéré, 'Apport de la chronologie de la taille des pierres', in *L'église Notre-Dame du Sablon*, ed. by Ministère de la Région de Bruxelles-Capitale, Direction des monuments et sites (Brussels, 2004), pp. 91-98

De Hemptinne, Thérèse, 'Jeanne de Castille, une reine entre folie et pouvoir, 1479-1555', in *Charles V in Context: the Making of a European Identity*, ed. by Marc Boone, and Marysa Demoor (Ghent: Ghent University, 2003), pp. 235-48

De Jandun, Jean, 'Tractatus de Laudibus Parisius', in *Paris et ses historiens aux XIVe et XVe siècles*, ed. by Antoine Le Roux de Lincy (Paris: Imprimerie impériale, 1867), pp. 32-79

De Jonge, Krista, 'La toiture pyramidale à bulbe, signe identitaire de l'architecture Habsbourg d'origine brabançonne au XVIe siècle', in *Toits d'Europe. Formes, structures, décors et usages du toit à l'époque moderne (XVe-XVIIe siècles)*, ed. by Monique Chatenet, and Alexandre Gady (Paris: Picard, 2016), pp. 25-46

———, Piet Geleyns, and Markus Hörsch, eds, *Gotiek in het hertogdom Brabant* (Leuven: Peeters, 2009)

De Keyser, Paul, 'Nieuwe gegevens omtrent Colijn Caillieu (coellin), Jan de Bartmaker (smcken), Jan Stecmacr (percheval) en Jan van den Dale', in *Tijdschrift voor Nederlandse Taal- en Letterkunde* 53 (1934), 269-79

De Keyzer, Piet, 'Het rhetoricaal "exemplum". Bijdrage tot de iconologie van onze Rederijkers', in *Vooys voor De Vooys. Huldenummer van de Nieuwe Taalgids* (Groningen, 1953), pp. 48-57

De Lalaing, Antoine, 'Relation du premier voyage de Philippe le Beau en Espagne, en 1501', in *Collection des voyages des souverains des Pays-Bas*, ed. Louis Prosper Gachard (Brussels: Hayez, 1876), pp. 121-385

De Lalaing, Jacques, *A Chivalric Life. The Book of the Deeds of Messire Jacques de Lalaing*, translation and comments by Rosalind Brown-Grant, and Mario Damen (Woodbridge: Boydell, 2022)

De la Torre, Antonio, and Francisco de la Torre, *Cuentas de Gonzalo de Baeza, tesorero de Isabel la Católica* (Madrid: CSIC, 2 vols, 1955)

De Leeuw, Rick, and Remco Sleiderink, *Ik Jan Smeken* (Bruges: Hannibal, 2017)

Deligne, Chloé, *Bruxelles et sa rivière. Genèse d'un territoire urbain (12e-18e siècle)*, Studies in European Urban History 1, (Turnhout: Brepols, 2003)

———, 'Édilité et politique. Les fontaines urbaines dans les Pays-Bas méridionaux au Moyen Âge', *Histoire urbaine*, 22 (2008), 77-96

———, 'Manneken-Pis dans l'espace bruxellois du Moyen Âge: distribution d'eau et centralité urbaine', in *Manneken Pis*, ed. by Manuel Couvreur, Historia Bruxellae (forthcoming)

De Mérindol, Christian, *Les Fêtes des chevalier à la cour du roi René* (Paris: Ed. du C.T.H.S., 1993)

———, *Le roi René et la seconde maison d'Anjou. Emblématique, art, histoire* (Paris: Léopard d'Or, 1987)

Demeter, Stéphane, and Cecilia Paredes, 'Le parcours de l'Ommegang, in *Ommegang!*, ed. by Jean-Paul Heerbrant (Brussels: Centre Albert Marinus, 2013), pp. 67-80

Demets, Lisa, *Onvoltooid verleden. De handschriften van de Excellente Chronike van Vlaenderen in de laatmiddeleeuwse Vlaamse steden* (Hilversum: Verloren, 2020)

De Padilla, Lorenzo, 'Crónica de Felipe I°, llamado el Hermoso', Colección de Documentos inéditos para la Historia de España, VIII (Madrid: La Viuda de Calero, 1846), pp. 5-267

De Praelles, Raoul, *Augustinus, Aurelius, De civitate dei / De la cité de dieu*, French translation and gloss by Raoul de Praelles (microfilm edition), s. Sharon, Smith Off Dunlap, *Illustrations of Raoul de Praelles' translation of St. Augustine's City of God between 1375 and 1420* vol. I and II (unpublished doctoral thesis, University of New York, 1974)

Depreter, Michael, *De Gavre à Nancy (1453-1477). L'artillerie bourguignonne sur la voie de la "modernité"*, Burgundica 18 (Turnhout: Brepols, 2011)

De Ridder, Juliaan, *Gerechtigheidstaferelen voor schepenhuizen in de zuidelijke Nederlanden in de 14de, 15de en 16de eeuw* (Brussels: Paleis der Academiën, 1989)

De Ridder, Paul, 'Une ville et sa cathédrale', in *La cathédrale des saints-Michel-et-Gudule*, ed. by Guido Jan Bral (Brussels: Racines, 2000), pp. 14-20

De Schrijver, Marc, and Christian Dothee, *Les concours de tir à l'arbalète des guildes médiévales* (Antwerp: Antwerps Museum en Archief den Crans, 1979)

Des Marez, Guillaume, *Guide Illustré de Bruxelles. Monuments Civils et Réligieux* (Brussels: Touring Club Royale de Belgique, 1979; first edn. 1918)

———, *L'organisation du travail à Bruxelles au XVe siècle*, Mémoires couronnés et autres mémoires publiés par l'Académie royale des Sciences, des Lettres et des Beaux-Arts de Belgique, 65, fasc. 1 (Brussels: Hayez, 1904)

Desprez-Masson, Marie-Claude, 'Jean Du Prier: intertextualité, théâtre et politique à la cour d'Anjou- Provence', in *Les Arts et les lettres en Provence au temps du roi René*, ed. by Chantal Connochie Bourgne, and Valérie Gontero Lauze (Aix en Provence: Presse Univ. de Provence, 2013)

———, *Le 'Songe du Pastourel' de Jean du Prier. Poésie et politique* (Montréal: CERES, 1989)

Devaux, Jean, Estelle Doudet, et Élodie Lecuppre-Desjardin, eds, *Jean Molinet et son temps. Actes des rencontres internationales de Dunkerque, Lille et Gand, 8-10 novembre 2007*, Burgundica 22 (Turnhout: Brepols, 2013)

De Vooys, *Vooys voor*, Huldenummer van de Nieuwe taalgids ter gelegenheid van de 80ste verjaardag van prof. dr. C. G. N. de Vooys op 26 mei 1953. (Groningen: Wolters, 1953)

D'Hulst, Henri, *Le mariage de Philippe le Beau avec Jeanne de Castille, à Lierre le 20 octobre, 1496* (Antwerp: Lloyd, 1958)

Dickstein-Bernard, Claire, 'Actes du tribunal de la gilde drapière de Bruxelles 1333-1435', *Bulletin de la Commission royale pour la publication des Anciennes Lois et Ordonnances de Belgique*, 35 (1995), 1-43

——, 'Bruxelles résidence princière (1375-1500)', in *Histoire de Bruxelles*, ed. by Mina Martens (Toulouse: Editions universitaires, 1976), pp. 139-65

——, 'La construction de *l'Aula magna* au palais du Coudenberg. Les préliminaires (1451-1452)', *Annales de la Société royale d'Archéologie de Bruxelles*, 67, 2006, 53-75

——, 'La construction de *l'Aula magna* au palais du Coudenberg, histoire du chantier (1452-1461?)', *Annales de la Société royale d'Archéologie de Bruxelles*, 68, 2007, 35-64

——, 'La gestion financière d'une capitale à ses débuts: Bruxelles, 1334-1467', *Annales de la Société royale d'Archéologie de Bruxelles*, 54, 1977

——, 'Une ville en expansion (1291-1374)', in *Histoire de Bruxelles*, ed. by Mina Martens (Toulouse: Editions universitaires, 1976), pp. 99-138

——, 'La voix de l'opposition au sein des institutions bruxelloises 1455-1467', in *Hommage au professeur Paul Bonenfant (1899-1965), Études d'histoire médiévale dédiées à sa mémoire par les anciens élèves de son séminaire à l'Université Libre de Bruxelles* (Brussels: Université Libre de Bruxelles, 1965), pp. 479-500

Domínguez Casas, Rafael, *Arte y etiqueta de los Reyes Católicos. Artistas, residencias, jardines y bosques* (Madrid: Alpuerto, 1993)

Doutrepont, Georges, and Omer Jodogne, *Chroniques de Jean Molinet (1474-1488)*, I, (Brussels: Académie royale de Belgique, classe des Lettres et des Sciences morales et politiques, 1935)

Dubois, Anne, and Bart Fransen, 'Master of the Joseph sequence, Zierikzee Triptych', in *The Flemish Primitives IV: masters with provisional names*, ed. by Pascale Syfer-d'Olne, Roel Slachmuylders, Anne Dubois, Bart Fransen, and Famke Peters (Brussels, 2006), pp. 68-97

Dürer, Albrecht, *Tagebuch der Reise in die Niederlande*, ed. by Fedja Anzelewsky (Zurich: Seefeld, 1988)

Duindam, Jeroen, *Dynasties. A Global History of Power, 1300-1800* (Cambridge: Cambridge University Press, 2016)

Dumolyn, Jan, and Anne-Laure van Bruaene, 'Urban Historiography in Late Medieval and Early Modern Europe', in *Urban History Writing in North-Western Europe (15th-16th Centuries)*, ed. by Bram Caers, Lisa Demets, and Tineke van Gassen (Studies in European Urban History 47) (Turnhout: Brepols, 2019), pp. 7-24

Dumont, Jonathan, and Élodie Lecuppre-Desjardin, 'Construire la légitimité d'un pouvoir féminin', in *Marie de Bourgogne. Figure, principat et postérité d'une duchesse tardo-médiévale / 'Persona', Reign, and Legacy of a Late Medieval Duchess*, ed. by Michael Depreter, Jonathan Dumont, Elizabeth L'Estrange, and Samuel Mareel (Turnhout: Brepols, 2021), pp. 41-60

——, Laure Fagnart, Pierre-Gilles Girault, and Nicolas Le Roux, eds, *La paix des Dames: 1529* (Tours: Presses universitaires François-Rabelais, 2021)

Du Puys, Remy, *La tryumphante et solemnelle entree faicte sur le nouuel et ioyeux aduenement de treshault trespuissant et tresexellent prince monsieur Charles prince de Hespaignes archiduc daustrice duc deBourgongne conte de Flandres.[etc] En sa ville de Bruges* (Paris: Gilles de Gourmont, 1515), see: London, British Library, C.44.g.11 – https://www.bl.uk/treasures/festivalbooks/BookDetails.aspx?strFest=0074

———, *La tryumphante entrée de Charles Prince des Espagnes en Bruges 1515*. A facsimile with an introduction by Sidney Anglo (Amsterdam: Theatrum Orbis Terrarum, [circa 1973])

Duverger, Jozef, *Brussel als kunstcentrum in de XIVe en XVe eeuw* (Antwerp: De Sikkel; Ghent: Vyncke, 1935)

Eichberger, Dagmar, '*Car il me semble que vous aimez bien les carboncles*. Die Schätze Margaretes von Österreich und Maximilians I', *Vom Umgang mit Schätzen*, ed. by Elisabeth Vavra, Kornelia Holzner-Tobisch, and Thomas Kühtreiber (Vienna: Österreichische Akademie der Wissenschaften, 2007), pp. 139-52

———, 'Esther – Susanna – Judith. Drei tugendhafte Frauen des Alten Testaments im dritten Teil der Hochzeitsmotette *Gratia sola Dei*', *Troja. Jahrbuch für Renaissancemusik* 15 (2016), 143-59

———, 'Illustrierte Festzüge für das Haus Habsburg-Burgund: Idee und Wirklichkeit', in *Hofkultur in Frankreich und Europa im Spätmittelalter. La culture de cour en France et en Europe à la fin du Moyen Âge*, ed. by Christian Freigang, and Jean-Claude Schmitt (Berlin: Akademie-Verlag, 2005), pp. 73-98

———, *Leben mit Kunst – Wirken durch Kunst. Sammelwesen und Hofkunst unter Margarete von Österreich, Regentin der Niederlande* (Turnhout: Brepols, 2002)

———, 'Oratio ad Proprium Angelum: The Guardian Angel in the Rothschild Hours', in *The Primacy of the Image in Northern European Art, 1400-1700: Essays in Honor of Larry Silver*, ed. by Debra Cashion, Ashley West, and Henry Luttikhuizen (Leiden: Brill, 2017), pp. 150-63

———, 'The Tableau Vivant, an Ephemeral Art Form in Burgundian Civic Festivities', *Parergon*, 6 (1988), 37-64, http://archiv.ub.uni-heidelberg.de/artdok/869/

———, 'Visualizing the Seven Sorrows of the Virgin: Early Woodcuts and Engravings in the Context of Netherlandish Confraternities', in *The Seven Sorrows Confraternity of Brussels: Drama, Ceremony, and Art Patronage (16th-17th Centuries)*, ed. by Emily S. Thelen, Studies in European Urban History 37 (Turnhout: Brepols, 2015), pp. 113-43

———, ed., *Women of Distinction, Margaret of York/Margaret of Austria* (Leuven: Davidsfonds, 2005)

Fagel, Raymond, 'Charles of Luxembourg The Future Emperor as a Young Burgundian Prince (1500-1516)', in *Carolus V imperator*, ed. by Pedro Navascués Palacio (Madrid: Lunwerg, 2007), pp. 8-16

———, 'Charles Quint comme "Roi Catholique": les nominations d'évêques originaires des Pays-Bas en Espagne, 1516-1555', *Publication du centre européen d'études bourguignonnes (XIVe-XVIe s.)* 38 (1998), 207-27

———, 'De Spaanse zomerkoning. Filips de schone als koning van Castilië', in *Filips de Schone, een vergeten vorst? 1478-1506*, ed. by Raymond Fagel, Jac Geurts, and Michael Limberger (Maastricht: Shaker, 2008), pp. 101-33

———, 'De wereld van Filips de Schone. De Europese politiek rond 1500', in *Filips de Schone, De schoonheid en de waanzin*, ed. by Paul Vandenbroeck, and Miguel Ángel Zalama (Bruges: Stad Brugge, 2006), pp. 51-68

———, 'Juana de Castilla y los Países Bajos. La historiografía neerlandesa sobre la reina', in *Juana I de Castilla, 1504-1555. De su reclusión en Tordesillas al olvido de la historia*, ed. by Miguel Ángel Zalama (Valladolid: Ayuntamiento de Tordesillas, 2006), pp. 87-106

Farkas-Kleisinger, 'Architekturrahmen in französischen und flämischen Stundenbüchern des 15./16. Jahrhunderts' (unpublished Master thesis, University of Vienna 2021)

Favresse, Félicien, *L'avènement du régime démocratique à Bruxelles pendant le moyen âge (1306-1423)*, Mémoires de l'Académie royale de Belgique, classe des Lettres et des Sciences morales et politiques 30 (Brussels: Hayez, 1932)

———, 'Comment on choisissait les jurés de métier à Bruxelles pendant le moyen âge', in *Études sur les métiers bruxellois au Moyen Âge*, Centre d'Histoire économique et sociale (Brussels: Université libre de Bruxelles, 1961), pp. 167-86

———, 'Documents relatifs à l'histoire politique intérieure de Bruxelles de 1477 à 1480', *Bulletin de la Commission royale d'Histoire*, 98 (1934), 29-125

———, 'Esquisse de l'évolution constitutionnelle de Bruxelles depuis le XIIIe siècle jusqu'en 1477', in *Études sur les métiers bruxellois au Moyen Âge*, Centre d'Histoire économique et sociale (Brussels: Université libre de Bruxelles, Institut de sociologie, 1961), pp. 213-52

Fernández de Pinedo, Nadia, and María Paz Moral, 'The Royal House of Isabel I of Castile (1492-1504): Use of Silk, Wool and Linen According to the Accounts of Gonzalo de Baeza', *Conservar Patrimonio*, 31 (2019), 53-66

Ferrandis, José, *Datos documentales inéditos para la historia del arte español. 3. Inventarios reales (Juan II a Juana la Loca)* (Madrid: CSIC, 1953)

Ferré, Rose-Marie, *René d'Anjou et les arts. Le jeu des mots et des images* (Turnhout: Brepols, 2012)

FitzStephen William, '*Descriptio Nobilissimae Civitatis Londoniae*', John Stowe, *A Survey of London*, ed. Charles Lethbridge Kingsford, (Oxford: Clarendon, 1908), II, pp. 218-29

Fleming, Gillian B., 'Juana I and the Struggle for Power in an Age of Transition, 1504-1521', unpublished doctoral thesis, London School of Economics, London, 2011 (http://etheses.lse.ac.uk/234/)

———, *Juana I. Legitimacy and Conflict in Sixteenth-Century Castile* (Cham, Switzerland: Palgrave, 2018)

For Pleasure and Profit: Six Dutch Rhetorician Plays, ed. and trans. by Elsa Strietman and Peter Happé, (Tempe: Arizona Center for Medieval and Renaissance Studies, 2013)

Franke, Birgit, *Assuerus und Esther am Burgunderhof. Zur Rezeption des Buches Esther in den Niederlanden (1450 bis 1530)* (Berlin: Mann, 1998)

Freigang, Christian, 'Zur Wahrnehmung regional spezifischer Architekturidiome in mittelalterlichen Diskursen', in *Kunst und Religion. Architektur und Kunst im Mittelalter. Beiträge einer Forschungsgruppe*, ed. by Uta Maria Bräuer, Emanuel S. Klinkenberg, and Jeroen Westerman (Utrecht: Clavis, 2005), pp. 14-33

———, and Jean-Claude Schmitt, eds, *La Culture de cour en France et en Europe à la fin du Moyen Âge* (Berlin: Akademieverlag, 2005)

Fritz, Johann Michael, *Goldschmiedekunst der Gotik in Mitteleuropa* (Munich: Beck, 1982)

Gachard, Louis Prosper, *Collection des voyages des souverains des Pays-Bas*, I, (Brussels: Hayez, 1876)

Gailliard, Jean, *Recherches historiques sur la chapelle du Saint-Sang* (Bruges: Gailliard, 1846)

Galesloot, Louis, 'Notes extraites des anciens comptes de la ville de Bruxelles', *Bulletin de la Commission royale d´Histoire*, second series, 9 (1867), 475-500

García Pérez, Noelia, ed., *Isabel la Católica y sus hijas. El patronazgo artístico de las últimas Trastámara* (Murcia: Universidad de Murcia, 2020)

Gautier, Marc-Édouard, ed., *Splendeur de l'enluminure. Le roi René et ses livres*, (Paris: Actes Sud, 2010)

Geleyns, Piet, and Pierre Smars, 'Het ontwerpproces en zijn context: de bouwmeester, de opdrachtgever en het ambacht', in *Gotiek in het hertogdom Brabant*, ed. Krista De Jong, Piet Geleyns, Markus Hösch (Leuven: Peeters, 2009), pp. 139-55

Godding, Philippe, 'L'adaptation de la justice échevinale aux besoins d'une ville en expansion: le cas de Bruxelles', in *Bruxelles et la vie urbaine. Archives-Art-Histoire. Recueil d'articles dédiés à la mémoire d'Arlette Smolar-Meynart (1938-2000)*, ed. by Frank Daelemans, and André Vanrie, 2 vols, (Archives et Bibliothèques de Belgique, numéro spécial 64, Brussels: KBR, 2001), I, pp. 29-72

Goedleven, Edgard, *La Grand-Place de Bruxelles. Au cœur de cinq siècles d'histoire* (Brussels: Racine, 1993)

Gómez de Fuensalida, Gutierre, *Correspondencia, embajador en Alemania, Flandes é Inglaterra (1496-1509)*, ed. by Duque de Berwick y Alba (Madrid: Legare, 1907)

Gómez-Chacón, Diana, 'Vestir a una Reina. Moda y lujo en la corte castellana del siglo XV', *Coleccionismo, mecenazgo y mercado artístico: orbis terrarum*, edited by Antonio Holguera Cabrera, Ester Prieto Ustio y María Uriondo Lozano (Seville: Universidad de Sevilla, 2020), pp. 178-96

Guardiola-Griffiths, Cristina, *Legitimizing the Queen: Propaganda and Ideology in the Reign of Isabel I of Castile* (Lewisburg: Bucknell University Press, 2011)

Guicciardini, Lodovico, *Descrittione di tutti i Paesi Bassi* (Antwerp: Silvius, 1567)

Guilardian, David, 'Les sépultures des comtes de Louvain et des ducs de Brabant (XIe-1430)', in *Sépulture, mort et représentation du pouvoir au Moyen Âge*, ed. by Michel Margue, 11e Journées lotharingiennes, *Publications de la section historique de l'Institut Grand-Ducal de Luxembourg*, 118, 491-539

Guillaume, Jean, 'Architectures imaginaires et "nouvelles inventions". L'apparition des toits cintrés en France au XVIe siècle', in *Toits d'Europe. Formes, structures, décors et usages du toit à l'époque moderne (XVe-XVIIe siècles)*, ed. by Monique Chatenet, and Alexandre Gady (Paris: Picard, 2016), pp. 9-24

Haemers, Jelle, 'Philippe de Clèves et la Flandre. La position d'un aristocrate au cœur d'une revolte urbaine (1477-1492)', in *Entre la ville, la noblesse et l'État: Philippe de Clèves (1456-1528), homme politique et bibliophile*, ed. by Jelle Haemers, Céline van Hoorebeeck & Hanno Wijsman, Burgundica 13, (Turnhout: Brepols, 2007), pp. 21-99

Ham, Laurens, Nina Geerdink, Johan Oosterman, Remco Sleiderink, and Sander Bax, 'Krijg je nog rente voor een lied? Stadsdichterschap als eer en verdienste door de eeuwen heen', in *Nederlandse letterkunde* 25.1 (2020), 99-131

Harris, Max, *Sacred Folly: A New History of the Feast of Fools* (Ithaca, NY: Cornell University Press, 2011)

Haufricht, Jocelyne, 'Les ducs de Bourgogne, comtes de Flandre, selon les enluminures de la Chronike van den lande van Vlaendre (fin XVᵉ siècle)', *Publications du Centre Européen d'Études Bourguignonnes* 37 (1997), 87-114

Hazebrouck-Souche, Véronique, *Spiritualité, sainteté et patriotisme. Glorification du Brabant dans l'œuvre hagiographique de Jean Gielemans (1427-1487)*, Hagiologia 6 (Turnhout: Brepols, 2007)

Hein, Jorgen, 'Isabella of Austria/ Isabel de Austria', in *The Inventories of Charles V and the Imperial Family/ Los inventarios de Carlos V y la familia imperial*, ed. by Fernando Checa Cremades (Madrid: Fernando Villaverde: 2010), vol. III, pp. 2601-23

Henne, Alexandre, and Alphonse Wauters, *Histoire de la ville de Bruxelles*, 3 vols (Brussels: Périchon, 1845)

———, and Alphonse Guillaume Ghislain Wauters, *Histoire de la ville de Bruxelles*, new ed. by Mina Martens, 4 vols (Brussels: Culture et civilisation, 1975)

Heymans, Vincent, ed., *L'hôtel de Ville de Bruxelles – Bilan de trois années d'études du bâti* (Studia Bruxellae, 12, 2018/1)

———, *Les sentinelles de l'histoire. Le décor sculpté des façades de l'hôtel de ville de Bruxelles* (Brussels: Ville de Bruxelles, 2000)

Hindriks, Sandra, *Der vlaemsche Apelles – Jan van Eycks früher Ruhm und die niederländische Renaissance* (Petersberg: Imhof, 2019)

Hoppe, Stephan, 'Translating the Past. Local Romanesque Architecture in Germany and its Fifteenth-Century Reinterpretation', in *The Quest for an Appropriate Past in Literature, Art and Architecture*, ed. by Karl A. E. Enenkel, and Konrad A. Ottenheym (Leiden: Brill, 2019), pp. 511-85

'How Mars and Venus dallied together', in *For Pleasure and Profit: Six Dutch Rhetorician Plays*, ed. and trans. in Dutch and English by Elsa Strietmann, and Peter Happé (Tempe: Arizona Center for Medieval and Renaissance Studies, 2013), pp. 1-73

Hüsken, Wim, 'Kunstwerk in de kijker (XII): Jan van Battel, Triptiek met Karel van Habsburg, koning van Spanje, Stedelijke Musea Mechelen, inv. Nr. S/0010', *Mededelingenblad Koninklijke Kring voor Oudheidkunde Letteren en Kunst van Mechelen* 45/4 (2014), 14-17

Hugo van der Goes, Zwischen Schmerz und Seligkeit, exh. cat. Berlin Gemäldegalerie, eds Stefan Kemperdick, Eric Eising, and Till-Holger Borchert (Munich: Hirmer, 2023)

Hummelen, Willem, M. H., 'Het tableau vivant, de "toog", in de toneelspelen van de rederijkers', *Tijdschrift voor Nederlandse Taal- en Letterkunde* 108 (1992), 193-222

———, M. H., 'Types and Methods of the Dutch Rhetoricians' Theatre', in *The Third Globe. Symposium for the Reconstruction of the Globe Playhouse*, Wayne State University, 1979, ed. by Cyril Walter Hodges, Samuel Schoenbaum & Leonard Leone (Detroit: 1981), pp. 164-89, 233-35, 252-53

Huygebaert, Stefan, Georges Martyn, Vanessa Paumen, and Tine Van Poucke, eds, *De kunst van het recht. Drie eeuwen gerechtigheid in beeld* (exh. cat. Bruges, Groeningemuseum / Tielt: Lannoo, 2016)

Isidor of Sevilla, *Chronica*, ed. by José Carlos Martín, CCSL, 112 (Turnhout: Brepols, 2003)

Jacobs, Thibaut, 'Des hôpitaux de métiers à Bruxelles? Nouvelles perspectives sur la charité et la bienfaisance en milieu urbain à la fin du Moyen Âge', *Revue belge de Philologie et d'Histoire*, 91 (2013), 215-55

Jacqmin, Yves, and Quentin Demeure, eds, *L'Hôtel de Ville de Bruxelles* (Brussels: Musée de la Ville de Bruxelles, 2011)

Janse, Herman, and , *Keldermans. Een architectonisch netwerk in de Nederlanden* (The Hague: Staatsuitgeverij, 1987)

Janssens de Bisthoven, Alin, 'Het beeldhouwwerk van het Brugsche stadhuis', *Gentsche bijdragen tot de kunstgeschiedenis*, 10 (1944), 7-81

Jean Molinet, Chroniques (1474-1506), ed. by Georges Doutrepont, and Omer Jodogne, 3 vols (Académie royale de Belgique, classe des Lettres et des Sciences morales et politiques. Collection des anciens auteurs belges), Brussels, vol. I (1474-1488), Bruxelles, 1935; vol. II (1488-1506), 1935; vol. III, 1937

Jean Molinet et son temps. Actes des rencontres internationales de Dunkerque, Lille et Gand, 8-10 novembre 2007, ed. by Jean Devaux, Estelle Doudet, and Élodie Lecuppre-Desjardin, Burgundica 22 (Turnhout: Brepols, 2013)

Jordan Gschwend, Annemarie, 'A Forgotten Infanta. Catherine of Austria, Queen of Portugal (1507-1578)', in *Women. The Art of Power. Three Women from the House of Habsburg*, ed. by Sabine Haag, Dagmar Eichberger and Annemarie Jordan Gschwend (Vienna: KHM-Museumsverband, 2018), pp. 51-63

———, 'Juana de Castilla y Catalina de Austria: la formación de la colección de la reina en Tordesillas y Lisboa', *Juana I de Castilla, 1504-1555. De su reclusión en Tordesillas al olvido de la Historia. I Symposio Internacional sobre la Reina Juana de Castilla. Tordesillas (Valladolid), 23 y 24 de Noviembre 2005*, ed. by Miguel Ángel Zalama (Valladolid: Ayuntamiento de Tordesillas, 2006), pp. 143-71

———, 'Ma Meilleur Soeur: Leonor de Austria, Reina de Portugal y de Francia/ Leonor of Austria, Queen of Portugal and France', in *The Inventories of Charles V and the Imperial Family/ Los inventarios de Carlos V y la familia imperial*, ed. by Fernando Checa Cremades (Madrid: Fernando Villaverde: 2010), vol. III, pp. 2545-2592

———, and Dagmar Eichberger, 'A Discerning Agent with a Vision. Queen Mary of Hungary (1505-1558)', in *Women. The Art of Power. Three Women from the House of Habsburg*, ed. by Sabine Haag, Dagmar Eichberger and Annemarie Jordan Gschwend (Vienna: KHM-Museumsverband, 2018), pp. 37-49

———, Fernando Pereira, and Maria Gamito, eds, *On Portraiture. Theory, practice and fiction. From Francisco de Holanda to Susan Sontag / O Retrato. Teoria, prática e ficção. De Francisco de Holanda a Susan Sonntag* (Lisabon: Universidade de Lisboa, 2022), online publication http://hdl.handle.net/10451/54999

Kaiser, Otto, *Einleitung in das Alte Testament – Eine Einführung in ihre Ergebnisse und Probleme*, sec. ed. (Gütersloh: Mohn, 1970)

Karaskova, Olga, 'Marie de Bourgogne et le Grand Héritage: L'iconographie princière face aux défis d'un pouvoir en transition (1477-1530)' (unpublished doctoral thesis, University of Lille, 2014)

———, '*Panthasilia virgo in civitatem Tryona amicabiliter recepta fuit*. La Joyeuse Entrée de Marie de Bourgogne à Bruges en 1477', in *Marie de Bourgogne. Figure, principat et postérité d'une duchesse tardo-médiévalee*, ed. by Michael Depreter, Jonathan Dumont, Elisabeth L'Estrange, and Samuel Mareel, Burgundica 31 (Turnhout: Brepols, 2021), pp. 103-14

———, 'Une princesse dans le miroir : Marie de Bourgogne est-elle la dédicatrice du *Miroir des Dames* de Philippe Bouton?', in *Women, Art and Culture in Medieval and Early Renaissance Europe*, ed. by Cynthia J. Brown, and Anne-Marie Legaré (Turnhout: Brepols, 2016), pp. 291-308

Kavaler, Matt, *Renaissance Gothic. Architecture and the Arts in Northern Europe. 1470-1540* (New Haven: Yale University Press, 2012)

Kayser, Christian, '"Brüsseler Spitze" – The Tower of Brussels town hall in the Context of Late Medieval Openwork Spires', in *L'hôtel de Ville de Bruxelles*, ed. by Yves Jacqmin, and Quentin Demeure (Brussels: Musée de la Ville de Bruxelles, 2011), pp. 149-78

Kelly, Henry Ansgar, ed., *Medieval Manuscripts, Their Makers and Users, a special issue of Viator in honor of Richard and Mary Rouse* (Turnhout: Brepols, 2011)

Kemp, Wolfgang, *Sermo Corporeus: Die Erzählung der mittelalterlichen Glasfenster*, (Munich: Schirmer-Mosel, 1987)

Kemperdick, Stephan, 'Die Geschichte des Genter Altars', in *Der Genter Altar der Brüder van Eyck. Geschichte und Würdigung*, ed. by Stephan Kemperdick, and Johannes Rößler (exh. cat. Berlin, Staatliche Museen / Petersberg: Imhof, 2014), pp. 8-69

Kerremans, Charles, *Étude sur les circonscriptions judiciaires et administratives du Brabant et les officiers placés à leur tête par les ducs antérieurement à l'avènemement de la Maison de Bourgogne (1406)*, Mémoires de l'Académie royale de Belgique, Classe des Lettres et des Sciences morales et politiques, 44, (Brussels: Palais des Académies, 1949)

Kipling, Gordon R., *From Art to Theatre. Form and Convention in the Renaissance* (Chicago: The University of Chicago Press, 1970)

———, 'Brussels, Juana of Castile and the Art of Theatrical Illustration (1496)', *Leeds Studies in English*, n.s., 32 (2001), 229-53

Köhl, Sascha, 'Brussels town hall in Context. Architectural Models, Historical Background, Political Strategies', in *L'hôtel de Ville de Bruxelles*, ed. by Yves Jacqmin, and Quentin Demeure (Brussels: Musée de la Ville de Bruxelles, 2011), pp. 236-54

———, *Das Brüsseler Rathaus. Repräsentationsbau für Rat, Stadt und Land* (Petersberg: Imhof, 2019)

———, 'Die Lücken füllen? Zur Repräsentation von „Geschichtsbildern" in und an Rathäusern niederländischer Residenzstädte', in *Geschichtsbilder in Residenzstädten des späten Mittelalters und der frühen Neuzeit. Präsentationen – Räume – Argumente – Praktiken*, ed. by Gerhard Fouquet, and others (Vienna: Böhlau, 2021), pp. 245-70

König, Eberhard, *Das Kalligraphiebuch der Maria von Burgund*. Brüssel, Bibliothèque royale de Belgique, ms II 845 (Luzern: Quaternio, 2015)

Koopmans, Jelle, and Darwin Smith, 'Un théâtre français du Moyen Âge?', *Médiévales*, 59 (2010), 5-16

Kramer, Femke, 'Staging practice in Brussel, 1559: Lawsuit reports concerning Het esbatement van de bervoete bruers', in *Formes teatrals de la tradició medieval*, ed. by Francesco Massip (Barcelona: Institut del Teatre), pp. 283-92

Krause, Stefan, *Freydal. Medieval Games. The Book of Tournaments of Emperor Maximilian I* (Cologne: Taschen, 2019)

———, Freydal: zu einem unvollendeten Gedächtniswerk Kaiser Maximilians I., ed. Stefan Krause, in *Jahrbuch des Kunsthistorischen Museums Wien*; Band 21 (2019), (Vienna: Böhlau, 2020)

Kruip, Marjolijn, 'Jan van Battel (1477-1557), heraldische schilder in Mechelen. Kunstenaar, werken en nieuwe vondsten', *Handelingen van de Koninklijke Kring voor Oudheidkunde, Letteren en Kunst van Mechelen* 119 (2015), 105-13

Kupper, Jean-Louis, 'Qui était saint Hubert?', in *Le culte de saint Hubert au Pays de Liège*, ed. by Alain Dierkens, and Jean-Marie Duvosquel, Saint-Hubert en Ardenne. Art-Histoire-Folklore, 1, 1990 (Brussels: Crédit communal de Belgique, 1991), pp. 13-17

Ladero Quadero, Miguel Ángel, *La armada de Flandes. Un episodio en la política naval de los Reyes Católicos (1496-1497)* (Madrid: Real Academia de la Historia, 2003)

———, 'Doña Juana, infanta y princesa', in *Doña Juana, reina de Castilla* (Madrid: Real Academia de la Historia, 2006), pp. 9-44

La Fons de Mélicocq, Alfonse, 'Les Archers, les arbalétriers et les arquebusiers du Nord de la France', *Archives historiques et littéraires du Nord de la France et du midi de la Belgique*, ser. III, vol. I (1850), 500-09

Lalou, Élisabeth, and Darwin Smith, 'Pour une typologie des manuscrits du théâtre médiéval, in *Le Théâtre de la cité dans L'Europe médiévale*, Proceedings of the SITM, (Perpignan, 1985), Fifteenth Century-Studies, 13 (1988), pp 569-79

Lane, Barbara G., *Hans Memling. Master Painter in Fifteenth-Century Bruges* (London: Harvey Miller, 2009)

Lavenus, Marielle, 'Lecture renouvelée des miniatures du Maître de Wavrin: *L' Histoire de Gérard de Nevers du manuscrit Bruxelles, KBR, ms 9631*' (unpublished doctoral thesis, University of Lille, 2021)

Lecuppre-Desjardin, Élodie, 'Les lumières de la ville: recherche sur l'utilisation de la lumière dans les cérémonies bourguignonnes (XIVe-XVe siècles)', *Revue Historique* 301 (1999), 23-43

———, *La ville des cérémonies. Essai sur la communication politique dans les anciens Pays-Bas bourguignons*, Studies in European Urban History (1100-1800) 4 (Turnhout: Brepols, 2004)

Lee, Sidney, ed., 'Lewis, Charles (1786-1836)', in *Dictionary of National Biography*, XXXIII (London: Smith, Elder & Co, 1883), see: https://en.wikisource.org/wiki/Dictionary_of_National_Biography,_1885

Leeuw, Rick de, & Remco Sleiderink, *Ik Jan Smeken* (Hannibal, 2017)

Lefèvre, Placide, Philippe Godding, and Françoise Godding-Ganshof, *Chartes du chapitre de Sainte-Gudule à Bruxelles*, Université de Louvain, Recueil de travaux d'Histoire et de Philologie, 6ᵉ série, 45 (Louvain-la-Neuve-Brussels: Nauwelaerts, 1993)

Legaré, Anne-Marie, 'Les cent quatorze manuscrits de Bourgogne choisis par le Comte d' Argenson pour le roi Louis XV', *Bulletin du bibliophile*, 2 (1998), 241-329

——, 'L'entrée de Jeanne de Castille à Bruxelles: un programme iconographique au féminin', in *Women at the Burgundian Court: Presence and Influence*, ed. by Dagmar Eichberger, Anne-Marie Legaré, and Wim Hüsken, Burgundica 17 (Turnhout: Brepols, 2010), pp. 43-55

——, 'Joanna of Castile's Entry into Brussels: Viragos, Wise and Virtuous Women', in *Virtue Ethics for Women, 1250-1500*, ed. by Karen Green, and Constant J. Mews (Dordrecht: Springer, 2011), pp. 177-86

Lehfeldt, Elizabeth A., 'Ruling Sexuality: The Political Legitimacy of Isabel of Castile', *Renaissance Quarterly* 53 (2000), 31-56

Le Livre des Tournois du Roi René de la Bibliothèque nationale (ms Français 2695), introduction by François Avril (Paris: Herscher, 1986)

Le privilège général et les privilèges régionaux de Marie de Bourgogne pour les Pays-Bas, ed. by Wim P. Blockmans (Kortrijk: UGA, 1985)

Les Chevaliers de l'Ordre de la Toison d'or au XVᵉ siècle, ed. by Raphael de Smedt (Frankfurt: Peter Lang, 2000)

Les maisons de la Grand-Place de Bruxelles, ed. by Vincent Heymans, 3ʳᵈ edition (Brussels: CFC, 2007)

Lestocquoy, Jean, *Deux siècles de l'histoire de la tapisserie, 1300-1500* (Arras: Commission départ. des Monuments hist. du Pas-de-Calais, 1978)

Ley, Judith, 'Das Rathaus der Freien Reichsstadt Aachen. Der Umbau der karolingischen Aula Regia zum gotischen Krönungspalast', in *Rathäuser und andere kommunale Bauten*, ed. by Michael Goer (Marburg: Jonas, 2010), pp. 159-74

Liber Authenticus sacratissima utrisque christifidelium confraternitatis septem dolorem beatae mariae virginis nuncupatae, Brussels, Archief van de Stad Brussel, Historisch Achief / Archives of the city of Brussels, Register 3413

Linke, Alexander, 'What is "Typology"?', in *Visual Typology in Early Modern Europe. Continuity and Expansion*, ed. by Dagmar Eichberger, and Shelley Perlove (Turnhout: Brepols, 2018), pp. 23-59

——, *Typologie in der Frühen Neuzeit. Genese und Semantik heilsgeschichtlicher Bildprogramme von der Cappella Sistina (1480) bis San Giovanni in Laterano (1650)* (Berlin: Reimer, 2014)

Lobelle-Caluwé, Hilde, 'Het Ursulaschrijn van Hans Memling. Ontwerp, constructie en oorspronkelijk uitzicht', in *Hans Memling*, ed. by Dirk de Vos, 2 vols (exh. cat. Bruges, Groeningemuseum / Brussels: Ludion, 1994), II: Essays, pp. 89-100

Lobo Cabrera, Manuel, *Isabel de Austria, una reina sin ventura* (Madrid: Catédra, 2019)

López Redondo, Amparo, 'Tejidos de la época de los Reyes Católicos en la Colección Lázaro Galdiano', in *Isabel I. Reina de Castilla*, ed. by Miguel Angel Ladero Quesado (Madrid: Dykinson, 2004), pp. 332-34.

Lüken, Sven, 'Kaiser Maximilian I. und seine Ehrenpforte', *Zeitschrift für Kunstgeschichte* 61 (1998), 456-57

Lugt, Trits, *Les Marques de Collections de Dessins & d'Estampes | Fondation Custodia* (The Hague: Nijhoff, 1956), no. L 1634; see http://www.marquesdecollections.fr/detail.cfm/marque/8036)

Macpherson, Ian, and Angus MacKay, *Love, Religion, and Politics in Fifteenth Century Spain* (Leiden: Brill, 1998)

Maesschalck, Alfonsine, and Jos Viaene, 'Het Stadhuis van Leuven', *Arca Lovaniensis*, 6 (1977), 7-255

―――, *Het stadhuis van Brussel* (Kessel-Lo: self-published, 1960)

Mareel, Samuel, 'Theatre and Politics in Brussels at the Time of Philip the Fair: The Leemans Collection', in *Books in Transition at the Time of Philip the Fair*, ed. by Hanno Wijsman, Ann Kelbers, and Susie Speakman Sutch, Burgundica 15 (Turnhout: Brepols, 2010), pp. 213-30

―――, *Voor vorst en stad: Rederijkerliteratuur en vorstenfeest in Vlaanderen en Brabant (1432-1561)*, (Amsterdam: Amsterdam University Press, 2010)

Marino, Nancy, 'La indumentaria de Isabel la Católica y la retórica visual del siglo XV', *Atalaya*, 13 (2013), online: https://doi.org/10.4000/atalaya.907

Mármol Marín, Dolores María del Mar, *Joyas en las Colecciones Reales de Isabel la Católica a Felipe II* (Madrid: Fundación Universitaria Española, 2001)

Martens, Mina, 'Initiation à une rencontre', in *La Grand-Place de Bruxelles* (Brussels: Vokaer/Liège: Desoer, 3rd ed., 1974), pp. 53-90

―――, 'Note sur l'époque de fixation du nom des sept lignages bruxellois', *Cahiers Bruxellois*, 4 (3-4), 1959, 173-93

―――, ed., *Histoire de Bruxelles* (Toulouse: Editions universitaires, 1976)

Mártir, Pedro [Pietro Martire d'Anghiera], *Epistolario*, ed. by José López de Toro, 4 vols (Madrid: Góngora, 1953-1957); Colección de Documentos Inéditos para la Historia de España, vols IX-XII

Martyn, Georges, 'Painted Exempla Iustitiae in the Southern Netherlands', in *Symbolische Kommunikation vor Gericht in der Frühen Neuzeit*, ed. by Reiner Schulze (Berlin: Duncker & Humblot, 2006), pp. 335-56

Matthews, Paul, 'Apparel, Status, Fashion. Woman's Clothing and Jewellery', in *Women of Distinction. Margaret of York / Margaret of Austria*, ed. by Dagmar Eichberger (Leuven: Davidsfonds, 2005), pp. 147-53

Matz, Jean-Michel, and Élisabeth Verry, eds, *Le roi René dans tous ses Ètats* (Paris: Ed. du Patrimoine, 2009)

Medieval Manuscripts, Their Makers and Users: a special issue of Viator in honor of Richard and Mary Rouse (Turnhout: Brepols, 2011)

Meijering, Stefan, and Bram Vannieuwenhuyze, 'Het Brusselse hof van Nassau. De oprichting van een laatmiddeleeuwse stadsresidentie', *Revue belge de philologie et d'histoire*, 88/2 (2010), 349-76

Meischke, Ruud, 'De stedelijke bouwopgaven tussen 1450 en 1500', in Herman Janse, and J. H. Van Mosselveld, *Keldermans. Een architectonisch netwerk in de Nederlanden* (The Hague: Staatsuitgeverij, 1987), pp. 87-103

———, *De gothische bouwtraditie. Studies over opdrachtgevers en bouwmeesters in de Nederlanden* (Bekking: Amersfoort 1988)

Meyer, Carla, *Die Stadt als Thema. Nürnbergs Entdeckung in Texten um 1500* (Ostfildern: Thorbecke, 2009)

Mezquita Mesa, Teresa, 'El Códice de Trajes de la Biblioteca Nacional de España', *Goya: Revista de Arte*, 346 (March 2014), 16-41

Monasticon Windesheimense, ed. by Willhelm Kohl, Ernest Perssons, and Anton G. Weiler, Teil 1: Belgïen (Archives et Bibliothèques de Belgique, 16, 1976)

Moore, Kathryn Blair, *The Architecture of the Christian Holy Land. Reception from Late Antiquity through the Renaissance* (Cambridge: University Press, 2017)

Morrison, Elizabeth and Anne D. Hedeman. *Imagining the Past. History in Manuscript Painting, 1250-1500*, exh. cat. (Los Angeles: J.P. Getty Museum, 2010)

Moser, Nelleke, *De strijd voor rhetorica: poëtica en positie van rederijkers in Vlaanderen, Brabant, Zeeland en Holland tussen 1450 en 1620* (Amsterdam: Amsterdam University Press, 2001)

Moss, Candida, and Liane Feldman, 'The New Jerusalem: Wealth, Ancient Building Projects and Revelation', *New Testament Studies* 66 (2020), 351-66

Müller, Hans-Dirk, 'Literatur und Kunst unter Maximilian I.', in *Kaiser Maximilian I. Bewahrer und Reformer*, ed. by Georg Schmidt-von Rhein (Ramstein: Paqué, 2002), pp. 141-51

Münzer, Jerónimo, *Viaje por España y Portugal* (Madrid: Polifemo, 1991)

Muller, Priscilla, *Jewels in Spain, 1500-1800* (New York: The Hispanic Society of America, 1972)

Murphy, Neil, 'Between Court and Town. Ceremonial Entries in the *Chroniques* of Jean Molinet', in *Jean Molinet et son temps. Actes des rencontres internationales de Dunkerque, Lille et Gand (8-10 novembre 2007)*, ed. by Jean Devaux, Estelle Doudet, and Élodie Lecuppre-Desjardin, Burgundica 22 (Turnhout: Brepols, 2013), pp. 155-61

Oosterman, Johan, 'Anthonis de Roovere. Het werk: overlevering toeschrijving en plaatsbepaling', *Jaarboek De Fonteine* (Ghent, 1995-1996), 29-104

———, 'De Excellente cronike van Vlaenderen en Anthonis de Roovere', *Tijdschrift voor Nederlandse Taal- en Letterkunde*, 118 (2002) 22-37

Pächt, Otto, and Dagmar Thoss, *Die Illuminierten Handschriften der Österreichischen Bibliothek. Französische Schule II Text- und Tafelband* (Vienna: Österreichische Akademie der Wissenschaften, 1977)

Page, Jamie, 'Masculinity and Prostitution in Medieval German Literature', *Speculum* 94 (2019) 739-73

———, *Prostitution and Subjectivity in Late Medieval Germany*, (Oxford: Oxford University Press, 2021)

Parker, Geoffrey, *Emperor: A New Life of Charles V* (New Haven: Yale University Press, 2019)

Pergameni, Charles, *Les archives historiques de la ville de Bruxelles. Notices et inventaires* (Brussels: Wauthoz-Legrand, 1943)

Pertcheval, Jan, *Den camp vander doot*, ed. by Gilbert Degroote, and A.J.J. Delen (Antwerp: De Seven Sinjoren; Amsterdam: Stichting 'Onze oude letteren', 1948)

Petitjean, O., *Historique de l'ancien grand serment royal et noble des arbalétriers de Notre-Dame du Sablon* (Brussels: Imprimerie et Publicité du Marais, 1963)

Piccard, Gerhard, *Wasserzeichen Buchstabe P* (Stuttgart: Kohlhammer, 1977), 3 vols; see also the database in the Hauptstaatsarchiv Stuttgart, https://www.piccard-online.de/start.php

Pleij, Herman, '7 maart 1500: De Brusselse stadsdichter Jan Smeken is uitgezonden naar Gent om te berichten over de doopfeesten van Karel V – De rederijkerij als beschavingsinstituut', in *Nederlandse literatuur, een geschiedenis*, ed. by Maria A. Schenkeveld-Van der Dussen (Groningen: Nijhoff, 1993), 121-25

Porras Gil, María Concepción, *De Bruselas a Toledo. El viaje de los Archiduques Felipe y Juana* (Valladolid: Ediciones Universidad de Valladolid, 2015)

———, Magnificentia y política. El banquete celebrado en Burgos (1502) en honor de los archiduques de Austria', *Potestas* 22 (2023), 47-66

Puteanus, Erycius, *Bruxella, incomparabili exemplo septenaria* (Brussels: Ioannis Mommarti, 1646)

Ramakers, Bart, 'Allegorisch toneel: Overlevering en benadering', in *Spel en spektakel: Middeleeuws toneel in de Lage Landen*, ed. by Hans van Dijk, and Bart Ramakers (Amsterdam: Prometheus, 2001), pp. 228-45

———, 'Walk, Talk, Sit, Quit? On What happens in Netherlandish Rhetoricians' Plays', in *Medieval Theatre Performance. Actors, Dancers, Automata and their Audiences*, ed. by Philip Butterworth, and Katie Normington (Cambridge: D.S. Brewer, 2017), pp. 35-51

———, *Spelen en figuren: toneelkunst en processiecultuur in Oudenaarde tussen Middeleeuwen en Moderne tijd* (Amsterdam: Amsterdam University Press, 1994)

Rapiarijs. Een afscheidsbundel voor Hans van Dijk, ed. by Saskia Buitink, Alphonsus Maria Joseph van Buuren, and I. Spijker, (Ruygh-bewerp 16, Utrecht: Instituut De Vooys voor Nederlandse Taal en Letterkunde, 1987)

Rapp Buri, Anna, and Monica Stücky-Schürer, *Burgundische Tapisserien* (Munich: Hirmer, 2001)

Renard, Étienne, 'La situation et l'étendue de la Forêt Charbonnière au premier millénaire: bilan historiographique et retour aux sources', in *La forêt en Lotharingie médiévale. Der Wald im mittelalterlichen Lotharingien, Actes des 18e Journées lotharingiennes, 30-31 octobre 2014*, ed. by Michel Pauly, and Hérold Pettiau, Publications de la Section Historique de l'Institut Grand-Ducal de Luxembourg 127, Publications du CLUDEM, 43 (2014), pp. 51-75

Reynebeau, Lieve, 'Een hofordonnantie en een état van Johanna van Castilië, 1500-1501', *Handelingen van de Koninklijke Commissie voor Geschiedenis* 165 (1999), 243-70

Reynolds, Catherine, 'Bruxelles et la peinture narrative', in: *L'héritage de Rogier van der Weyden. La peinture à Bruxelles 1450-1520*, exh. cat. Brussels, Musées royaux des Beaux-Arts, ed. by Véronique Bücken, and Griet Steyaert (Tielt: Lannoo, 2013), pp. 49-65

Robin, Françoise, *La cour d'Anjou-Provence. La vie artistique sous le règne du roi René* (Paris: Picard, 1985)

Rodríguez Villa, Antonio, *Doña Juana la Loca. Estudio histórico* (Madrid: Librería de M. Murillo, 1892)

Roobaert, Edmond, 'De Brusselse rederijkers in de 16de eeuw, hun plaats in het stadsgebeuren en hun beroepsactiviteiten', in *Eigen Schoon & De Brabander* 95 (2012), 541-94

———, 'Priesters en rederijkers te Brussel in de eerste helft van de zestiende eeuw', in *Spiegel der Letteren* 45.3 (2003), 267-94

Rossiaud, Jacques, *Medieval Prostitution*, trans. by Lydia Cochrane (New York: Blackwell, 1988)

Schandel, Pascal, 'Le maître de Wavrin et les miniaturistes lillois à l'époque de Philippe le Bon et de Charles le Téméraire' (unpublished doctoral thesis, University of Strasbourg, 1997)

Schnerb, Bertrand, 'Présence et influence des femmes à la cour de Bourgogne: Quelques réflexions historiographiques', in *Women at the Burgundian Court: Presence and Influence*, ed. by Dagmar Eichberger, Anne-Marie Legaré, and Wim Hüsken, Burgundica 17 (Turnhout: Brepols, 2010), pp. 3-9

Schroeder, Horst, *Der Topos der Nine Worthies in Literatur und bildender Kunst* (Göttingen: Vandenhoeck, 1971)

Schuster, Beate, *Die freien Frauen: Dirnen und Freudenhäuser im 15. und 16. Jahrhundert* (Frankfurt a. M.: Campus, 1995)

Sedlacek, Ingrid, *Die Neuf Preuses: Heldinnen des Spätmittelalters* (Marburg: Jonas, 1997)

Seipel, Wilfried, ed., *Kaiser Ferdinand I, 1503-1564. Das Werden der Habsburgermonarchie* (Vienna: KHM, 2003)

Serdon, Valérie, *Armes du diable. Arcs et arbalètes au Moyen Âge* (Rennes: Presses Universitaires de Rennes, 2005)

Silver, Larry, *Marketing Maximilian: The Visual Ideology of a Holy Roman Emperor* (Princeton: Princeton UP, 2008)

Sleiderink, Remco, 'The Brussels Plays of the Seven Sorrows', in *The Seven Sorrows Confraternity of Brussels: Drama, Ceremony, and Art Patronage (16th-17th Centuries)*, ed. by Emily S. Thelen, Studies in European Urban History 37 (Turnhout: Brepols, 2015), pp. 51-66

———, 'De dichters Jan Smeken en Johannes Pertcheval en de devotie tot Onze Lieve Vrouw van de Zeven Weeën. Nieuwe gegevens uit de rekeningen van de Brusselse broederschap (1499-1516)', in *Queeste* 19.1 (2012), 42-69

———, 'Grootse ambities. Culturele initiatieven van de stad Brussel ten tijde van Filips de Goede', in *De Macht van het schone woord. Literatuur in Brussel van de 14de tot de 18de eeuw*, ed. by Jozef Janssens, and Remco Sleiderink (Leuven: Davidsfonds, 2003), pp. 106-23

———, 'De schandaleuze spelen van 1559 en de leden van De Corenbloem: Het socioprofessionele, literaire en religieuze profiel van de Brusselse rederijkerskamer', in *Revue Belge de Philologie et d'Histoire* 92.3 (2014), 847-75

———, 'De kleine smid', in *Madoc. Tijdschrift over de Middeleeuwen* 31.2 (2017), 167-70

———, 'Johannes Steemaer alias Pertcheval. De naam en faam van een Brusselse rederijker', in *Want hi verkende dien name wale. Opstellen voor Willem Kuiper*, ed. by Marjolein Hogenbirk, and Roel Zemel (Amsterdam: Stichting Neerlandistiek VU, 2014), pp. 149-54

Smit, J. G., *Vorst en Onderdaan. Studies over Holland en Zeeland in de late Middeleeuwen* (Leuven: Peeters, 1995)

Smith, Elise Lawton, 'Women and the moral argument of Lucas van Leyden's Dance around the golden calf', *Art History* 15 (1992), 296-316

Smith, Sharon Off Dunlap, 'Illustrations of Raoul de Praelles' translation of St. Augustine's City of God between 1375 and 1420' (unpublished doctoral thesis, New York: New York University, 1974)

Smolar-Meynart, Arlette, 'Bruxelles: l'élaboration de son image de capitale en politique et en droit au moyen-âge', *Bijdragen tot de Geschiedenis*, 68 (1985), 25-45

——, 'Les guerres privées et la cour des apaiseurs à Bruxelles au Moyen Âge', in *Mélanges Mina Martens, Annales de la Société royale d'Archéologie de Bruxelles*, 58 (1981), 237-54

——, ed., *Rond het bombardement von Brussel van 1695. Verwoesting en wederopstanding* (= Het Tijdschrift van het Gemeentekrediet, 51, 1997/1)

Smuts, R. Malcolm, and Melinda Gough, 'Queens and the International Transmission of Political Culture', *The Court Historian. Queens and the Transmission of Political Culture: The Case of Early Modern France*, ed. by Melinda Gough, and R. Malcolm Smuts, 10, 1 (October 2005), pp. 1-13

Sölle, Dorothee, Joe H. Kircherger, Anne-Marie Schnieper, and Emil M. Bührer, *Große Frauen der Bibel in Bild und Text* (Osterfildern: Schwabenverlag, 2004)

Soler Moratón, Melania, 'Retratos de piedad, retratos de poder: las representaciones devocionales de Isabel I de Castilla y de su heredera, Juana I, y su simbología Pública', *Potestas* 20 (2022), 25-49; https://www.e-revistes.uji.es/index.php/potestas/article/view/5828/6864

Soly, Hugo, 'Plechtige intochten in de steden van de Zuidelijke Nederlanden tijdens de overgang van Middeleeuwen naar Nieuwe Tijd: communicatie, propaganda, spectakel', *Tijdschrift voor Geschiedenis* 97 (1984), 341-62

Sosnowska, Philippe, and , 'L'Hôtel de Ville de Bruxelles. Apport de l'archéologie à la compréhension d'un édifice majeur au travers d'une étude des maçonneries gothiques', in *L'hôtel de Ville de Bruxelles*, pp. 43-75

Spalatin, Georg, *Historischer Nachlaß und Briefe*, eds by Christoph G. Neudecker, and L. Preller (Jena: Mauke, 1851)

Speakman Sutch, Susie, 'Patronage, Foundation History, and Ordinary Believers. The Membership Registry of the Brussels Seven Sorrows Confraternity', in *The Seven Sorrows Confraternity of Brussels. Drama, Ceremony and Art Patronage (16th-17th Centuries)*, ed. by Emily S. Thelen, Studies in European Urban History 37 (Turnhout: Brepols, 2015), pp. 19-48

——, and Anne-Laure van Bruaene, 'The Seven Sorrows of the Virgin Mary: Devotional Communication and Politics in the Burgundian-Habsburg Low Countries, c. 1490-1520', in *The Journal of Ecclesiastical History* 61.2 (2010), 252-78

Spindler, Erik, 'Were Medieval Prostitutes Marginals? Evidenz from Sluis, 1387-1440', *Revue Belge de Philologie et d'Histoire / Belgisch Tijdschrift voor Filologie en Geschiedenis* 87 (2009), 239-72

Steenbergen, Gerard Jo, *Het landjuweel van de rederijkers*, (Leuven: Davidsfonds, 1950)

Stein, Robert, 'The Bliscapen van Maria and the Brussels policy of annexation', in *Publications du Centre Européen d'Études Bourguignonnes* 31 (1991), 139-51

——, 'Brussel: de Coudenberg. De groei van een regeringscentrum', in *Plaatsen van herinnering. Nederland van prehistorie tot Beeldenstorm*, ed. by Wim Blockmans, and Herman Pleij (Amsterdam: Bakker, 2007), pp. 326-37

——, 'Cultuur in context. Het spel van Menych Sympel (1466) als spiegel van de Brusselse politieke verhoudingen', *Bijdragen en mededelingen betreffende de geschiedenis der Nederlanden*, 113 (1998), 289-321

——, 'Cultuur en politiek in Brussel. Wat beoogde het Brusselse stadsbestuur bij de annexatie van de plaatselijke Ommegang?', in *Op belofte van Profijt. Stadsliteratuur en burgermoraal in de Nederlandse letterkunde van de middeleeuwen*, ed. by Herman Pleij, and others (Amsterdam: Prometheus, 1991), pp. 228-43

——, *Politiek en historiografie. Het ontstaansmilieu van Brabantse kronieken in de eerste helft van de vijftiende eeuw* (Leuven: Peeters, 1994)

——, 'Van publieke devotie naar besloten orde. De stichting van het klooster Scheut', *Millenium. Tijdschrift voor middeleeuwse studies*, 23 (2009), 12-37

——, 'Seventeen: The Multiplicity of a Unity in the Low Countries', in *The Ideology of Burgundy. The Promotion of National Consciousness (1364-1565)*, ed. by D'Arcy Jonathan Dacre Boulton, and Jan R. Veenstra (Leiden: Brill, 2006), pp. 223-85

Stoichita, Victor I., *L'instauration du tableau. Métapeinture à l'aube des temps modernes* (Paris: Méridiens Klincksieck, 1993)

Stolberg-Werningerode, Otto zu, *Neue deutsche Biographie*, Bd. 11, Kafka-Kleinfercher, (Berlin: Duncker& Humblot, 1977)

Strietmann, Elsa, and Peter Happé, 'How Mars and Venus dallied together', in *For Pleasure and Profit: Six Dutch Rhetorician Plays*, ed. and trans. in Dutch and English (Tempe: Arizona Center for Medieval and Renaissance Studies, 2013)

Sturgeon, Justin, *Text and Image in René d'Anjou's 'Livre des Tournois'. Constructing authority and identity in fifteenth- century court culture*, presented with a critical edition of BnF, ms français 2695, 3 vols (Woodbridge: The Boydell Press, 2022)

Suárez Fernández, Luis, *Política internacional de Isabel la Católica. Estudio y documentos*, V (Valladolid: Universidad de Valladolid, 1972)

Symes, Carol, *A Common Stage: Theater and Public Life in Medieval Arras*, (Ithaca, NY: Cornell University Press, 2007)

Tafur, Pero, *Andanças é viajes de Pero Tafur por diversas partes del mundo avidos* (Madrid: Ginesta, 1874)

Tammen, Björn, 'A Feast of the Arts: Joanna of Castile in Brussels, 1496', *Early Music History*, 30 (2011), 213-48

Tatarkiewicz Władysław, 'Theatrica, the Science of Entertainment: From the XIIth to the XVIIth Century'. *Journal of the History of Ideas* 26 (1965), 263-72

Thelen, Emily S., ed., *The Seven Sorrows Confraternity of Brussels: Drama, Ceremony, and Art Patronage (16th-17th Centuries)*, Studies in European Urban History 37 (Turnhout: Brepols, 2015)

Thieffrey, Sandrine, and Michiel Verwij, 'Cat. No 36: Livre de choeur de Philippe le Beau et Jeanne de Castille', in *Philippe le Beau (1478-1506). Les trésors du dernier duc de Bourgogne*, ed. by Bernard Bousemanne, and others (Brussels: Royal Library of Belgium, 2006) pp. 151-53

Thomas III. von Saluzzo, *Le livre du Chevalier errant*, ed. by Robert Fajen, Imagines Medii Aevi, 48 (Wiesbaden: Reichert 2019)

Torre, Antonio de la, and Francisco de la Torre, *Cuentas de Gonzalo de Baeza, tesorero de Isabel la Católica* (Madrid: CSIC, 2 vols, 1955)

Tremlett, Giles, *Isabella of Castile: Europe's First Great Queen* (London: Bloomsbury, 2017)

Trowbridge, Mark, 'Art and Ommegangen: Paintings, Processions, and Dramas in the Late-Medieval Low Countries' (unpublished doctoral thesis, New York Institute of Fine Arts, 2000)

Twomey, Lesley K., 'Juana of Castile's Book of Hours: An Archduchess at Prayer', *Religions* 11 (4) (2020), 201

Unger, Willem Sybrand, *Bronnen tot de geschiedenis van Middelburg in den landsheerlijken tijd*, 3 vols (The Hague: Unger, 1923-1931)

Unterholzner, Daniela, 'Bianca Maria Sforza (1472-1510): Herrschaftliche Handlungsspielräume einer Königin vor dem Hintergrund von Hof, Familie und Dynastie' (unpublished doctoral thesis, University of Innsbruck, 2015)

Uyttebrouck, André, 'Les résidences des ducs de Brabant, 1355-1430', in *Fürstliche Residenzen im spätmittelalterlichen Europa*, ed by Hans Patze, and Werner Paravicini, Vorträge und Forschungen 36 (Sigmaringen: Thorbecke, 1991), pp. 189-205

Van Bruaene, Anne-Laure, *Om beters wille: Rederijkerskamers en de stedelijke cultuur in de Zuidelijke Nederlanden (1400-1650)*, (Amsterdam: Amsterdam University Press, 2008)

———, 'Het Boek des Levens: Literaire corporaties, factiestrijd en de turbulente voorgeschiedenis van het Brusselse gezelschap Den Boeck (eerste helft van de 15de eeuw)', in *Revue belge de Philologie et d'Histoire* 86 (2008), 335-50

———, *Repertorium van Rederijkerskamers in de Zuidelijke Nederlanden (1400-1650)*, 2004. https://www.dbnl.org/tekst/brua002repe01_01_0061.php

———, '"A wonderfull tryumfe, for the wynnyng of a pryse": Guilds, Ritual, Theater, and the Urban Network in the Southern Low Countries, c. 1450-1650', *Renaissance Quarterly* 59 (2006), 374-405

Van de Kerckhof, Véronique, Helena Bussers, and Véronique Bücken, eds, Met passer en penseel. Brussel en het oude hertogdom Brabant in beeld, exh. cat. Brussels, Koninklijke Musea voor Schone Kunsten, (Brussels: Dexia, 2000)

Vandekerckhove, Simon, 'De Chronike van den lande van Vlaendre: Studie van het handschrift en uitgave van fol.148^v tot fol.415^v' (unpublished bachelor thesis, Ghent University, 2006-2007)

Vandenbroeck, Paul, 'A Bride Amidst Heroines, Fools and Savages. The Joyous Entry into Brussels by Johanna of Castile, 1496 (Berlin Kupferstichkabinett, ms 78 D5)', *Jaarboek Koninklijk Museum voor Schone Kunst Antwerpen* (2012), 153-94

——— 'Una novia entre heroínas, bufones y salvajes. La Solemne Entrada de Juana de Castilla en Bruselas, 1496', in *El legado de Borgoña. Fiesta y ceremonia cortesana en la Europa de los Austrias (1454-1648)*, ed. by Krista de Jonge, Bernardo José García, and Alicia Esteban Estríngana (Madrid: Marcial Pons, 2010)

Vandewalle, André, Guillaume Michiels, and Ant Michiels, *600 jaar Brugs stadhuis. 1376-1976* (Brussels: Bank Brussel Lambert, 1976)

Van Dijk, Hans, and Femke Kramer, '"Hue Mars en Venus tsaemen bueleerden": Het overspel van Mars en Venus', in *Europees toneel van Middeleeuwen naar Renaissance*, ed. by Martin Gosman (Groningen: Boekwerk, 2002), pp. 229-302

Van Dixhoorn, Arjan, *Lustige geesten: Rederijkers in de Noordelijke Nederlanden (1480-1650)*, (Amsterdam: Amsterdam University Press, 2009)

———, Samuel Mareel, and Bart Ramakers, 'The relevance of the Netherlandish rhetoricians', in *Renaissance Studies* 32.1 (2018), 8-22

Van Engen, John, *Sisters and Brothers of the Common Life. The Devotio Moderna and the World of the Later Middle Ages* (Philadelphia: University of Pennsylvania Press, 2008)

Van Herk, Anke, *Fabels van liefde: Het mythologisch-amoureuze toneel van de rederijkers (1475-1621)*, (Amsterdam: Amsterdam University Press, 2012)

Van Honacker, Karin, 'Bestuurinstellingen van de stad Brussel (12de eeuw-1795)', in *De gewestelijke en lokale overheidsinstellingen in Brabant en Mechelen tot 1795*, ed. by Raymond van Uytven, Claude Bruneel, Hilde Coppens, and Beatrijs Augustijn, 2 vols, Algemeen Rijksarchief in de provinciën, Studia 82 (Brussels: Algemeen Rijksarchief, 2000), II, pp. 393-461

Vannieuwenhuyze, Bram, '"allen dengenen die in der stad dienste sijn". Een overzicht van de stedelijke openbare ambten en diensten in het laatmiddeleeuwse Brussel 1229-1477' (unpublished master thesis, Ghent University, 2002)

Vanrie, André, 'L'église et son environnement', in *L'église Notre-Dame du Sablon*, ed. by Ministère de la Région de Bruxelles-Capitale, Direction des monuments et sites (Brussels: 2004), pp. 24-42

Van Sprang, Sabine, *Denijs van Alsloot (vers 1568-1625/26). Peintre paysagiste au service de la cour des archiducs Albert et Isabelle*, 2 vols (Turnhout: Brepols, 2014)

———, 'Van Loon et les tableaux de la chapelle ducale Saint-Hubert à Tervueren', in *Theodoor Van Loon, 'pictor ingenius' et contemporain de Rubens*, ed. by Sabine van Sprang, Cahiers des Musées royaux des Beaux-Arts de Belgique 10 (Brussels: Snoeck, 2011), 43-59

Van Tyghem, Frieda, 'Bestuursgebouwen van Keldermans in Brabant en Vlaanderen', in Herman Janse, and others, *Keldermans. Een architectonisch netwerk* (The Hague: Staatsuitgeverij, 1987), pp. 105-30

van Uytven, Raymond, '1477 in Brabant', in *Le privilège général et les privilèges régionaux de Marie de Bourgogne pour les Pays-Bas*, ed. by Wim Blockmans (Kortrijk-Heule: UGA, 1985), pp. 253-85

Van Uytven, Raymond, 'Le cœur des Pays-Bas bourguignons et habsbourgeois (1430-1531)', in *Histoire du Brabant du duché à nos jours*, ed. by Raymond van Uytven, Claude Bruneel, Jos A. M. Koldeweij, A.W.F.M. van de Sande, Jan A F. M. van Oudheusden (Zwolle: Waanders, 2004), pp. 213-52

———, 'Flämische Belfriede und südniederländische städtische Bauwerke im Mittelalter. Symbol und Mythos', in *Information, Kommunikation und Selbstdarstellung in mittelalterlichen Gemeinden*, ed. by Alfred Haverkamp (Munich: Oldenbourg, 1998), pp. 125-59

———, 'De opgang van een hoofdstad', in *Met passer en penseel. Brussel en het oude hertogdom Brabant in beeld*, ed. by Véronique Van de Kerckhof, Helena Bussers, and Véronique Bücken, exh. cat. Brussels, Koninklijke Musea voor Schone Kunsten, (Brussels: Dexia, 2000)

———, and , eds, *Histoire du Brabant du duché à nos jours* (Zwolle: Waanders, 2004), pp. 219-20

Van Wegens, Inge, 'Paper consumption and the foundation of the first paper mills in the Low Countries, 13th –15th century', in *Papier im mittelalterlichen Europa. Herstellung und Gebrauch*, ed. by Carla Meyer, Sandra Schultz und Bernd Schneidmüller (Berlin: De Gruyter, 2017)

Veldman, Ilja, 'The Old Testament as a Moral Code', *Simiolus* 23 (1995), pp. 215-39, republished in *Images for Eye and Soul: Function and Meaning in Netherlandish Prints (1450-1650)* (Leiden: Primavera, 2006), pp. 119-50

Vogelaar, Christiaan, ed., *Lucas van Leyden en de Renaissance* (Antwerp: Ludion, 2011)

Voltelini, Hans 'Urkunden und Regesten aus dem K. u. K. Haus-, Hof- und Staats-Archiv in Wien', *Jahrbuch der Kunsthistorischen Sammlungen des Allerhöchsten Kaiserhauses*, 11 (1890), I-LXXXIII

Vondel, Joost van den, *Inwydinge van 't stadthuis t' Amsterdam*, ed. by Marijke Spies, and others (Muiderberg: Dick Coutinho, 1982)

Vrancken, Valérie, 'Opstand en dialoog in laatmiddeleeuws Brabant. Vier documenten uit de Brusselse opstand tegen Maximiliaan van Oostenrijk (1488-1489)', *Bulletin de la Commission Royale*, vol. 181 (2015), 209-66

Vrancken, Valerie, *De Blijde Inkomsten van de Brabantse hertogen* (Brussels: ASP, 2019)

Vrancken, Valérie, 'Een papierstrijd in laatmiddeleeuws Brabant. De Brusselse opstand tegen Maximiliaan van Oostenrijk (1488-1489)' (unpublished master thesis, Katholiek Universiteit Leuven, 2012)

Walter, Barbara, 'Fons Vitae und Zeichen städtischen Rechts. Mittelalterliche Stadtbrunnen im Heiligen Römischen Reich' (unpublished doctoral thesis, Albrecht-Ludwigs-Universität Freiburg i. Br., 2015; https://nbn-resolving.org/urn:nbn:de:bsz:25-freidok-1514243

Walter, Gibson, 'Lucas van Leyden and the Old Testament', *Print Collector's Newsletter* XIV (1983), 127-30

Warnaar, Geert, *Ruusbroec. Literature and Mysticism in the Fourteenth Century* (Leiden: Brill, 2011)

Waterschoot, Werner, 'Jan van den Dale, "eenen vermaerden Retoricien"', in *Tijdschrift voor Nederlandse Taal- en Letterkunde* 119.1 (2003), 265-78

Wauters, Alphonse, *Notice Historique sur les anciens serments ou guildes d'arbalétriers, d'archers, d'arquebusiers et d'escrimeurs de Bruxelles* (Brussels: Briard, 1848)

———, *À propos de l'exposition nationale d'architecture: études et anecdotes relatives à nos anciens architectes* (Brussels: Alliance typographique, 1885)

———, *Ville de Bruxelles. Inventaire des cartulaires et autres registres faisant partie des archives anciennes de la ville* (Brussels: Bartsoen, 1888)

Weigert, Laura, *French Visual Culture and the Making of Medieval Theatre* (Cambridge: University Press, 2015)

———, '"Vocamus Personagias": The Enlivened Figures of Ephemeral Stagings', in *French Visual Culture and the Making of Medieval Theatre* (New York: University Press, 2015), pp. 27-73

Weissberger, Barbara F., *Isabel Rules: Constructing Queenship, Wielding Power* (Minneapolis: University of Minnesota Press, 2004)

Wellens, Robert, 'La domination espagnole (1506-1700)', in *Histoire de Bruxelles*, ed. by Mina Martens (Toulouse: Editions universitaires, 1976), pp. 193-232

———, *Les Etats Généraux des Pays-Bas des origines à la fin du règne de Philippe le Beau (1464-1506)* (Heule: UGA, 1974)

Wescher, Paul, *Beschreibendes Verzeichnis der Miniaturen – Handschriften und Einzelblätter – des Kupferstichkabinetts der Staatlichen Museen Berlin* (Leipzig: Weber, 1931), pp. 179-80

Wiesflecker, Hermann, *Kaiser Maximilian I.*, I, *Jugend, burgundisches Erbe und Römisches Königtum bis zur Alleinherrschaft 1459-1493* (Munich: Oldenbourg, 1971)

Wils, Lode, 'De werking van de Staten van Brabant omstreeks 1550-1650 volgens Leuvense Archiefbronnen', *Standen en Landen*, 5 (1953), 3-19

Wilson, Christopher, *The Gothic Cathedral. The Architecture of the Great Church, 1130-1530* (London: Thames & Hudson, 1990)

Zalama, Miguel Ángel, 'En torno a la formación del gusto artístico de la reina Juana I', Atalaya, 20 (2020) https://journals.openedition.org/atalaya/5136

———, 'Las hijas de los Reyes Católicos. Magnificencia y patronazgo de cuarto reinas', *Las mujeres y el universo de las artes*, ed. by Concha Lomba Serrano, Carmen Morte García, and Mónica Vázquez Astorga (Zaragoza: Diputación de Zaragoza| Institución 'Fernando el Católico', 2020), pp. 31-54

———, 'Lujo, magnificencia y arte en la formación de los tesoros de las hijas de los reyes católicos. Un ensayo sobre la valoración de las artes', in *Entre la política y las artes. Señores del poder*, ed. by Miguel Ángel Zalama, and María Concepción Porras Gil (Madrid: Iberoamericana and Vervuert, 2022) pp. 11-43

———, *Vida cotidiana y arte en el palacio de la reina Juana I en Tordesillas* (Valladolid: Universidad de Valladolid, 2003)

Zemon Davis, Natalie, 'The Reasons of Misrule', in *Society and Culture in Early Modern France*, ed. by Natalie Zemon Davis (Stanford: Stanford University Press, 1975)

Zurita, Jerónimo, *Historia del Rey don Fernando el Católico. De las empresas y liga de Italia*, ed. by José Javier Iso, 4 vols (Zaragoza: Fundación Fernando el Católico, 2005)

Zylbergeld, Léon, 'L'artillerie de la ville de Bruxelles au milieu du XVe siècle d'après un inventaire de 1451-1452', *Revue belge d'Histoire militaire*, 23, 7, (1980), 609-46

Index

architecture   181-82, 197, 200

Boterpot   94, 194-95, 197-200
Brabant   32-33, 41, 43, 73, 77-78, 84, 87, 96, 112, 117, 127-32, 136, 138-41, 147. 154-55, 157, 162, 170, 174, 185-86, 198, 201-205, 235, 246-47, 251-52, 267, 274
Butchers   78, 81, 90-91, 95, 106, 131, 241, 260
Brussels government   22, 28, 78, 80, 86, 88-89, 93-98, 110, 132, 223
Bulbous spire   182, 197-200
Burgundy   31, 41, 57, 60, 71, 125, 127, 138, 147, 154, 162, 204, 217, 223, 267, 274

Catholic Kings   41, 45, 49, 50, 51, 55, 62, 65, 67, 69, 138, 248
chamber(s) of rhetoric   22, 30, 78, 90, 104, 107-109, 111-13, 115-16, 118, 139, 146, 166, 169, 173
chastity   144, 153, 266, 272
city poet   28, 107-108, 114, 116-20, 146, 176
civic archive(s)   181, 186, 194, 201, 226, 233
civic bodies   77-78, 80, 84, 87, 104-105, 189, 261
competition(s)   109, 113, 115-16, 123, 130, 132, 166, 168, 170, 174, 176, 186, 202
confraternity   69, 109, 114-21, 130
courage   32, 124, 131, 134, 143
courtier(s)   30, 43, 45, 47, 49, 56, 66, 69, 104, 125, 131, 202
craft guild(s)   77-78, 88, 90-91, 93, 95, 97, 165, 262

dowry   53, 55, 67, 162

encomium   181, 187, 189
entertainment   29, 90, 165-66, 169, 170, 173-76, 178-79, 217, 219, 221
entries (festive, joyous, royal)   26, 28, 39, 43, 53, 62, 78-79, 83, 87, 90, 104-105, 107-108, 110, 112-13, 117, 120-21, 126-30, 144, 146, 166, 203, 210, 211

Female Worthies   123-26, 132-136
Ferdinand II of Aragon   21, 30, 42, 67, 69, 134, 136-37, 139, 159-60, 163, 251, 255, 273-74
fool(s)   81, 90, 166, 170-73, 177, 239, 240
fountain(s)   21, 32, 59, 81, 98, 100, 106, 175, 182, 187-89, 240, 252, 276
Flanders   71, 124, 126-32, 147, 170, 204, 208, 210, 220
Frederick III   107-108, 110-11, 113, 127, 178

Habsburg   23, 32, 35, 50, 53-55, 57, 59, 60, 62, 65-66, 70-71, 73, 75, 123, 125, 138-41, 147, 162, 211, 225-26
Hendrik De Lichte   114-16, 118, 120-21
Heroine(s)   24, 32, 123-25, 132-33, 158, 161, 248, 277

Isabella I of Castile   21, 30, 33-34, 37, 40, 42, 47, 49, 53-58, 57-59, 60-65, 67-68, 71-73, 75, 130, 133-135, 137-38, 143, 158-60, 163, 248, 251, 269, 273

Jan Smeken   26, 28, 32, 107-108, 111-21, 132, 146, 176
jewels   34, 53, 55, 62-63, 67-68, 71-73, 158, 167, 232, 264

Johannes Pertcheval   86, 197, 109, 114-16, 118, 120, 121
Judgement of Paris   27, 111, 115, 165, 175, 252

marriage   39-40, 43-45, 50, 53-54, 57, 60-62, 129, 134, 136-41, 143, 147, 151-57, 161-2, 174, 177, 210, 246, 251-53, 267-68, 274-75
Mary of Burgundy   35, 37, 54, 57, 70, 105, 120, 125-27, 143, 146-47, 157, 210, 212, 221, 247
Maximilian I   19, 26, 30, 41, 48, 54-55, 67, 69, 78, 91, 93, 101, 107-108, 110, 113-15, 126-32, 138-40, 143-44, 148-49, 152-54, 162-63, 169-70, 210, 221-22, 228, 135, 246, 255
military guilds (culverin-bearers, arquebus-bearers, crossbowmen, master gunners)   28, 77, 82, 89-90, 100-105, 107, 109-12, 116, 120, 130, 169-72, 174-75, 211, 239, 244

Ommegang   28, 84, 101-104, 106-107, 110, 112, 118, 168, 175, 197, 203

patrician families   28, 66, 77, 86, 92-96
peace/peacemakers   78, 81, 84, 91-93, 114, 126-27, 139, 141, 143, 145-46, 149, 151, 162, 176, 141, 261, 265
Philip the Fair   21-22, 30, 35, 37, 39, 41, 44, 53-54, 56, 58-59, 61, 66-67, 69-71, 73, 78-79, 84, 90, 108, 114, 116, 120, 125, 143-44, 147, 149, 151, 154-55, 159, 162, 210, 235, 246-67, 251-53
pyrotechnic(s)   34, 109-10, 165, 168, 170

queenship   40, 73

religious institutions (monasteries, chapters, canons)   40, 77, 80, 83-86, 120, 171, 238-39, 257
Rogier van der Weyden   38, 98, 181, 190, 192-93

spectacle(s)   71, 73, 97, 109, 165-66, 171, 179, 197, 217, 257, 259, 277
strength   32, 143, 154, 159, 163

tableu(x) vivant(s)   25, 31, 107, 108-11, 115-17, 120, 123, 138, 143, 146, 149, 152, 155-56, 158, 169, 181, 210, 245
textile(s)   27, 34, 53, 55, 62, 65-66, 75, 155, 177, 226, 242
town hall(s)   21-23, 35, 111, 128,, 140-41, 179, 181-95, 197, 200-201, 203-206, 211, 229, 276
trousseau   34, 53-56, 58, 62, 65, 67, 71, 75, 153

wild men   81, 165, 171-73, 240, 259-60
wisdom   32, 124, 136, 141, 143, 158, 163, 258, 273